Prentice Hall

The Reader's Journey

Grade Eight

Teacher's Resources

PEARSON

Boston, Massachusetts
Chandler, Arizona
Glenview, Illinois
Shoreview, Minnesota
Upper Saddle River, New Jersey

ISBN 978-0-13-363628-4

PEARSON

ISBN 0-13-363628-3

2 3 4 5 6 7 8 9 10 12 11 10 09 08

Contents

Unit 3

Unit 6

Teaching Aids

Name ______________________________ Date ______________

Screening Test

Read the passage. Then, answer the questions.

Webster Industries hopes to eradicate the personal use of company property on company time. Telephones, faxes, and computers are company property and should be used for business purposes only. This includes voice mail, electronic mail, and computer files. Employees may need to use these communication tools for personal reasons from time to time. If and when that time comes, employees should keep their personal use to a minimum and should do so only during nonwork hours such as lunchtime.

1 Based on its use in the selection, what is the meaning of *eradicate*?

A explain

B put an end to

C make a decision about

D enforce

2 Which statement best paraphrases the last sentence in the selection?

F Employees should make phone calls or send e-mails only during their lunch breaks.

G Employees should use company equipment for personal reasons only in case of emergency.

H Employees may use company property but only if they do so quickly and when their supervisor is absent.

J If necessary, employees may use company equipment for personal reasons briefly and during breaks.

3 Which word best describes the overall tone of this selection?

A frustrated

B cautionary

C sarcastic

D apologetic

4 What is the purpose of this selection?

F to show employees how to use computers for personal reasons

G to describe how to fix a fax machine

H to explain the rules for taking a lunchtime break

J to inform employees of the rules for using office equipment

5 Based on the information in this selection, you can conclude that—

A Webster Industries is a large and successful business

B Webster Industries uses expensive business equipment

C too many employees at Webster Industries are using company property for personal reasons

D many employees at Webster Industries fail to take their jobs seriously and are about to lose their jobs

6 Which statement is a fact in this passage?

F Telephones, faxes, and computers are company property.

G Telephones, faxes, and computers should be used for business purposes only.

H Employees are encouraged to keep their personal use to a minimum.

J Employees should use company property for personal reasons during nonwork hours.

Name ______________________________ Date ______________

Read the passage. Then, answer the questions.

What could chocolate and commercial cola drinks possibly have in common? Both contain caffeine and are popular around the world. The main ingredient in chocolate comes from the beans of the cacao tree, and the flavoring for many cola drinks originally came from the nuts of the kola tree. Although they grow in different parts of the world, the cacao tree and the kola tree are part of the same plant family.

7 Which sentence best helps you set a purpose for reading this passage?

A What could chocolate and commercial cola drinks possibly have in common?

B Both contain caffeine and are popular around the world.

C The main ingredient in chocolate comes from the beans of the cacao tree, and the flavoring for many cola drinks originally came from the nuts of the kola tree.

D Although they grow in different parts of the world, the cacao tree and the kola tree are part of the same plant family.

8 Chocolate and cola drinks are alike because both contain—

F kola nuts

G caffeine

H cacao beans

J cocoa

9 What is the author's purpose?

A to entertain

B to persuade

C to inform

D to reflect

Read the passage. Then, answer the questions.

(1) One of the most breathtaking places in the world, the Grand Canyon, lies in northwestern Arizona. (2) It is about 277 miles long, 1 mile deep, and anywhere from 1 to 18 miles wide. (3) In 1869, an American geologist named John Wesley Powell led a river expedition through the canyons of the Green and Colorado Rivers. (4) Powell named the area the Grand Canyon, and his exploration of the area was one of the greatest adventures in American history. (5) Few people remember Powell today, but he and his fellow explorers accomplished an extraordinary feat that would be difficult even with today's technology.

10 Based on the information in the selection, which sentence best states the thesis?

F sentence 1

G sentence 2

H sentence 4

J sentence 5

11 Suppose that you are using this selection as a source for a research paper. This source is probably an example of—

A a speech

B an interview

C a journal entry

D a magazine article

Name ______________________________ Date ______________

Read the passage. Then, answer the questions.

My Story
by Carla Perez

I was born in Boston, Massachusetts on October 21, 1995. I spent the first eight years of my life there with my parents, Isabel and Xavier Perez. I loved living in Boston, and though I knew that my parents had hoped to relocate to a smaller town with a slower pace, I never could have imagined living anyplace else. I was happy at my school, I had many friends who lived in my neighborhood, and my entire family lived within walking distance of our apartment. In addition, Boston is a great place to live. It has so much culture. If you're interested in history, you'll find many historic attractions in Boston. Its population is also diverse, so you're exposed to many cultures by living in Boston. Best of all, the food there is great!

Naturally, I was very upset when my parents told me that we were moving to Keene, New Hampshire, a small town about two hours from Boston. My dad had been offered a job at a college there, and my parents had been thrilled by the opportunity. They promised me that I would love Keene once I gave it a chance, but I had my doubts. After all, I was a city girl.

It's been six years since we moved and I must admit that my parents were right. I love Keene, and living in a small town does have its perks. It's a lovely old town near the mountains, and without the city lights, the stars appear clear and bright. Out here, we're surrounded by nature. On the weekends, we hike, canoe, ride horses, ski, or bike. My mom and I often ride our bikes down the country roads and take photos of the covered bridges throughout the county. We always find something to do here.

I was also able to make friends quickly. In fact, my best friend Zoe lives next door. She and I walk to school together and are both part of the drama team. Right now, we are preparing for a production that is part of the big Keene Pumpkin Festival this fall. The festival is a special event in town that no one is sure to miss!

12 On the basis of this story, you can conclude that Carla is—

F lazy

G imaginative

H adaptable

J bored

13 Which sentence best states the theme of the passage?

A People can learn from their mistakes.

B Cities are exciting yet dangerous places.

C Making friends in a new place can be difficult.

D Giving things a chance may change your attitude.

Name ______________________________ Date ______________

14 What does the author's attitude reveal about Keene, New Hampshire?

F It is boring and lacks cultural diversity.

G It is a town steeped in history and tradition.

H It is a small town that offers many activities.

J It is an isolated community cut off from other towns by mountains.

15 Which phrase from the selection foreshadows a future event?

A my parents had hoped to relocate to a smaller town with a slower pace

B my entire family lived within walking distance of our apartment

C my parents told me that we were moving to Keene, New Hampshire

D my parents were right

Read the passage. Then, answer the questions.

Daniel Parsons lives just four blocks from the hospital in Bolton, New Jersey. Neighbors still call him "Doc" and often stop to visit the doctor who retired several years ago. Doc was a great doctor, not only because he was highly skilled in the field of medicine but because he truly cared about people. He never turned a patient away and would even leave his home in the middle of the night to tend to a child sick with fever or to help deliver a baby. Although he never married or had children of his own, he was never lonely while he was working; his patients were his family.

However, Doc grew old and his own health began to suffer, and the day came when he had to retire. The hardest thing about retirement for him was missing his patients. He thought about moving to a retirement community but decided against it. So he moved a big comfortable chair to his front porch, and to this day, he sits there when the weather permits. Doc visits with the people who pass by. Many of them are his former patients.

16 What is the setting of this passage?

F a hospital

G Bolton, New Jersey

H Dr. Parsons's front porch

J a retirement community

17 Based on information in the passage, you can infer that Dr. Parsons—

A is lonely

B likes people

C prefers cold weather

D gossips with neighbors

18 Why does Daniel Parsons visit with former patients?

F He misses them.

G He feels obligated.

H He has nothing better to do.

J He lives close to the hospital.

19 How is Daniel Parsons's conflict resolved in the story?

A He adopts his patients as his family.

B He retires from his career as a doctor.

C He moves closer to the hospital in which he works.

D He sets a chair on the porch where he can see people.

Name ______________________________ Date ______________

Read the passage. Then, answer the questions.

Jingle, jangle go the keys,
I'm at the door, so eager to please.
You're home! You're home!
I've been alone all day;
Now can we go out to play?
I didn't mean to chew the rug,
Chase the cat, or break your mug.
Please don't be mad; I'm just a dog.
But I'd be a good girl, you'd see,
If you'd spend more time with me.

20 To which of the five senses does line 1 appeal?

F sight

G hearing

H touch

J smell

21 Who is the speaker in this poem?

A a cat

B a dog

C a poet

D a child

Read the passage. Then, answer the questions.

"Who's that?" asked Geeta.

Karyn looked at the tall, athletic woman with gray hair tied back in a short ponytail. "Oh, that's my grandmother. She's training for the City Run next week."

The two girls finished their run and sat under the shade of some large oak trees at the side of the track. The older woman joined them shortly.

"How's it going, Nanna?" Karyn asked.

"Pretty good," her grandmother replied. "I cut three seconds off my best time."

Geeta looked at the older woman. "How long have you been running?" she asked.

"Most of my life," Nanna replied. "But not on a team. You girls are lucky."

"What do you mean?" Geeta asked, confused.

Nanna told the girls about the old days when women had few opportunities to race. She explained how things changed when Kathryn Switzer entered the Boston Marathon in 1967. "She registered as K. Switzer so no one would know that she was a woman," Nanna said. "She finished in four hours and 20 minutes, better than some men."

Nanna rose to her feet and said good-bye to the girls. The girls watched Nanna as she jogged through the grass to the parking lot.

"Your grandma is pretty cool," Geeta said.

Name ______________________________ Date ______________

22 **What causes Karyn to look over at the woman who is running?**

F She sees that the woman is running fast.

G Geeta asks who the woman is.

H She is looking for another friend.

J She recognizes that the woman is Kathryn Switzer.

23 **What effect do you predict that meeting Nanna will have on Geeta?**

A She will like Karyn more as a friend.

B She will want to enter the Boston Marathon.

C She will appreciate being able to participate in sports.

D She will come back to the track more often.

Read the passage. Then, answer the questions.

Rebecca moved around in her seat nervously. Her teacher had asked the students to give oral reports on family history. All the students had wonderful stories. Pedro said that his great-grandfather had been a cowboy. Angelica's ancestors had come from Ireland on a ship.

When her turn came, Rebecca rose slowly and walked to the front of the class. She took a deep breath and began. "My family is from Germany," she started. "They were Jewish, and in the 1930s, Adolf Hitler and the Nazis were rounding up Jews and putting them in work camps. My family knew that they were not safe where they were, so they packed what few things they could carry and left home with some other families from their neighborhood."

She told how her great-grandparents had decided to flee to America. "They had to walk to Germany's border," Rebecca said. "It was more than a hundred miles. They traveled at night and slept during the day. It was very dangerous and very hard."

Rebecca held up a tiny doll. "My grandmother carried this in her pocket for weeks. It's still dirty from the trip because my grandmother never washed it. She said that it reminded her of what she and her family endured for freedom."

The class was silent for a moment, and then the students asked many questions about Rebecca's story and her family. At that moment, the butterflies in Rebecca's stomach were replaced with a glow of pride. The teacher's encouraging smile told her that she had helped her classmates learn about courage.

24 **What inference can you make about Rebecca's nervousness about giving her report?**

F She gets poor grades in school.

G She is unpopular at school.

H She thinks that her classmates have better stories to tell.

J She thinks that her classmates will laugh at the doll.

25 **What is the main idea of the last paragraph?**

A The teacher decides that Rebecca needs help.

B The class misunderstands Rebecca's story.

C Students often ask too many questions about families.

D Rebecca changes from being nervous to feeling proud.

Name ______________________________ Date ______________

Read the passage. Then, answer the questions.

Scene 2. An autumn night outside a dilapidated stone house. The house yields no signs of life. A tall wrought-iron fence surrounds the property, and the gate stands open to an overgrown garden in the front yard. Ivy grows up the walls of the house and nearly covers the front door. The wind is blowing, rustling the leaves of the trees. The front gate swings slightly on its rusted hinges, making a screeching sound. Branches from a knotty old oak tree are tapping a second-floor window of the house.

Keira: Are you sure that this is the right place?

Malcolm: This is the address I was given.

Keira: I don't see any lights on in the house. It doesn't look like anyone's at home. In fact, it doesn't seem as though anyone's lived here for years.

Malcolm: *[He reaches into his pocket and takes out a slip of paper.]* Yes. This is the place. 423 Abbott Lane.

Keira: I don't know, Malcolm. Maybe we should go back to the office to check the address.

Malcolm: *[To the audience]* She never listens to me. *[To Keira]* There's nothing to check. See? *[He shows her the slip of paper.]*

Keira: Well, maybe the address is wrong. *[The sound of a snapping tree branch comes from a darkened corner of the garden.* KEIRA *and* MALCOLM *jolt.]* Did you hear that?

Malcolm: It was probably just a cat. Come on, let's try the door.

Keira: I don't think that we should tempt fate. Let's just go back to the office.

Malcolm: Don't be a wimp. We'll just knock on the door. If nobody's home, we'll leave. If someone answers the door, then we have a job to do. Mysteries don't solve themselves. We promised Davis we'd check into this. We owe it to him to at least investigate this matter. Davis said that the person who sent the mummy to the museum left this return address.

26 How do the stage directions add suspense to Scene 2?

F They create a dark, eerie setting.

G They reveal Keira and Malcolm's feelings.

H They explain why Keira and Malcolm are at the house.

J They give background information about the mummy.

27 Which of the following terms best describes Malcolm's private comment to the audience?

A aside

B dialogue

C monologue

D soliloquy

Name ______________________ Date ____________

Grammar

Read the following questions. Then, choose the best answer.

28 Which sentence contains correct capitalization?

F Taylor goes to Lincoln middle school.

G Sacramento is the capital of california

H Mexico lies to the South of the United states.

J This Friday, Aisha's class is going on a field trip.

29 Which sentence contains a correctly used semicolon?

A However; your ideas are significant.

B Jared is allergic to cats; but not to dogs.

C After the game; Mark and Antonio went swimming.

D For breakfast we had pancakes; for lunch we had salad.

30 Choose the sentence in which the reflexive pronoun is used correctly.

F Sheila grabbed the doll that belonged to herself.

G Father and myself took a walk in the park.

H Jack owes it to himself to study hard for the test.

J They went to the pool with Mom, Dad, and myself.

31 Which of the following is a complete sentence?

A When Janet turned in her paper.

B And took the bus to school yesterday.

C Whenever the dog chewed her shoes.

D I watched the entire movie.

32 Choose the sentence in which a subordinating conjunction is used correctly.

The car broke down. We waited for the tow truck.

F After the car broke down, we waited for the tow truck.

G The car broke down on the way to Charleston, South Carolina.

H The car broke down, and we waited for the tow truck.

J Our car often breaks down, so we bought a new car.

33 Complete this sentence with a proper noun.

_______ wants to win the race.

A My brother

B Theodore

C She

D That girl

Vocabulary

Read the following questions. Then, choose the best answer.

34 What does the Greek root *logos*, used in the word *logical*, mean?

F reason

G loud

H see

J read

35 The correct way to combine *response* with the suffix *-ible* is to—

A add the suffix to the end of the base word (responseible)

B drop the *i* and add the suffix (responseble)

D drop the *e* and add the suffix (responsible)

D drop the *e* and the *i* and add the suffix (responsble)

Name ____ Date ______________

Diagnostic Test 1

Unit 1

Read the passage. Then, answer the questions.

Dragons in World Cultures

Dragon myths have been told for thousands of years in various cultures throughout the world. Most people are familiar with the fire-breathing dragon of European folklore. This huge, snakelike monster is almost invariably portrayed as a menace to society. Eventually, outraged citizens raise a clamor, and some valiant individual must step forward to battle the dreadful beast.

European Cultures

In medieval tales, it is usually a brave knight who volunteers to slay the dragon and free the maiden it holds captive. Of course, the dragon has no intention of giving up without a fight. In the end, however, the knight's endeavor to vanquish his opponent is always successful. Despite its cunning and great physical strength, the wicked dragon is eventually slain, and its killer walks away with wealth and great honor.

1 On the basis of the title and the subheading, what do you predict the next paragraph will be about?

A three- and four-toed dragons

B dragons in Asian cultures

C the deeds of famous knights

D medieval weapons and armor

2 Which detail from the selection supports your prediction?

F Dragon myths have been told for thousands of years in various cultures throughout the world.

G This huge, snakelike monster is portrayed as a menace to society.

H Usually, a brave knight volunteers to slay the dragon.

J The dragon has no intention of giving up without a fight.

3 What kind of information might lead you to modify a prediction about a fire-breathing dragon in a European folktale?

A The dragon protects the children in a village.

B The dragon has the head of a snake.

C The dragon kills six villagers.

D The dragon lives in a forest near a castle.

4 Which detail supports the prediction that the knight who slays the dragon will win the heart of the maiden?

F The brave knight volunteers to slay the dragon.

G The brave knight frees the dragon's prisoner.

H The dragon has no intention of giving up without a fight.

J The dragon is cunning and has great physical strength.

Name ______________________________ Date ______________

(1) Alex picked up the bat and tapped his foot with it. (2) He pulled the bat through the air several times, practicing his swing. (3) He adjusted his helmet and tugged on his glove. (4) He was hitting below .500 for the first time in his career, and he knew that the managers were talking about sending him down to the minors. (5) Alex had doubled his practice time this week and felt good about the changes he had made. (6) He stepped up to the plate, swung the bat over his shoulder, and looked the pitcher squarely in the eye. (7) "Give me your best shot," Alex mumbled under his breath.

(8) The fans in the bleachers scrambled for the ball.

5 Which part of the story is the exposition?

A sentence 1

B sentence 2

C sentence 3

D sentence 4

6 The main type of conflict is —

F character against nature

G character against self

H character against society

J character against character

Read the following questions. Then, choose the best answer.

7 Based on your understanding of the prefix *inter-*, what do you conclude that the italic word in this sentence means?

An *international* delegation discussed ways to end global warming.

A between nations

B around nations

C within a nation

D outside a nation

8 The suffix *-yze* changes the word *analysis* from —

F a noun to a verb

G a verb to a noun

H an adjective to a noun

J an adverb to a verb

9 Which word in this sentence is an abstract noun?

When Sam hit the ball, the players shouted with joy.

A Sam

B ball

C players

D joy

10 How many proper nouns are in this sentence?

Tim and his brother Brad went to the Giants game on Saturday.

F two

G three

H four

J five

11 Which of these sentences contains a correctly punctuated possessive noun?

A Anns bicycle is parked next to the cafeteria.

B The womens' guild will meet this Friday.

C The teenagers' backpacks are stored in their lockers.

D At the meeting, they discussed their countrie's futures.

12 The correct spelling of the plural of *wolf* is —

F wolf

G wolfs

H wolve

J wolves

Name ________________________________ Date ________________

Reading Skills: Making Predictions

Reinforcement 1-2

When you **make predictions** as you read, you make logical guesses about what will happen next in a story. You can make predictions based on prior knowledge, things you already know. You can revise predictions based on new information that is presented in the story. You can support predictions with details from the story.

Answer the questions about making predictions.

1. The title of a story is "Surf Dog." What do you predict this story will be about?

____

2. On what did you base your prediction in question 1?

A. story details
B. new information
C. prior knowledge
D. song lyrics

3. Read the beginning of the story, and then answer the question that follows.

Milo is a little white mutt weighing only nine pounds. He lives in Hawaii and he loves to surf. It all began accidentally, when Milo fell off a fishing boat and went splashing into the sea.

With this new information, will you revise your prediction? Explain.

____

____

____

4. Read the next passage from the story, and then underline some of the story details that support your prediction.

He paddled until a chunk of driftwood floated past. He climbed onto it, panting. He stood on it as it drifted closer to shore, where surfers were waiting for the waves to come in. Milo's driftwood caught a wave! He held on and rode it in to shore. All the surfers cheered. They adopted the little surfing dog as their mascot.

5. Look at your predictions. Were you correct? Explain.

____

____

6. Continue this passage, writing a couple of lines predicting what will happen next to Milo.

____

____

Name ______________________________ Date ______________

Reading Skills: Making Predictions

Extension 1-2

Different nonfiction texts require different reading strategies. **Making predictions** about a text before you read can help you choose the best reading strategy. An informational text that includes diagrams, illustrations, tables, and captions must be read slowly and carefully. You should stop and make sure you understand how the text relates to the other elements. An article or autobiography that is mostly text can be read more quickly, but not as quickly as fiction. You still need to look for information. Before reading any text, it helps to list questions you have so you can look for the answers as you read.

Use the table below to help you make predictions about "The Greenhouse Effect" in Lesson 5 and "Occupation: Conductorette" by Maya Angelou in Lesson 6.

Text Feature	"The Greenhouse Effect"	"Occupation: Conductorette"
What can you predict by looking at the title, heads, and other boldface text?		
What can you predict by looking at illustrations, captions, legends, pull-boxes or sidebars?		
What reading strategy should you use to approach this text?		
What questions do you have about the text that you can look for the answers to while reading?		

Name ______________________ Date ______________

Vocabulary: Prefixes and Suffixes

Reinforcement 1-3

A **prefix** is one or more syllables added to the beginning of a word. A prefix changes the meaning of a word or makes a new word. Every prefix has a meaning.

Prefix	Meaning	Examples
pre-	before, in advance	predict, preheat, preview
re-	again, back	revise, recall, review

Add *pre-* or *re-* to each underlined word to form a new word that fits the meaning of the sentence. Write each new word on the line.

1. ____________ After you read the chapter, view all its main ideas.

2. ____________ Before we left home, we took the caution of locking up.

3. ____________ Don't judge him before you really get to know him.

4. ____________ We had to program the VCR after the power failure.

5. ____________ Before the movie began, we saw views of coming films.

A **suffix** is added to the end of a word to change its meaning or part of speech. The suffixes *-ize* and *-yze* change words to verbs. The suffixes *-tion* and *-sion* change verbs to nouns.

analysis → analyze — When you make an analysis, you analyze something.
final → finalize — When you make your decision final, you finalize it.
educate → education — When you educate people, they receive an education.
persuade → persuasion — When you persuade someone, you use persuasion.

Choose the correct word to complete each sentence. Write the word on the line.

6. intend intention
I ____________ to study computers.
That is my ____________.

7. modern modernize
They plan to ____________ the old building.
They want to make the building more ____________.

8. revise revision
I had to ____________ my essay.
My ____________ was much better than my first draft.

Name ______________________ Date ______________

Vocabulary: Prefixes and Suffixes

Extension 1-3

Think of **prefixes** and **suffixes** as building blocks. You can build words by combining these building blocks in different ways. Consider the word *undecided.* It uses the prefix *un-* and the suffix *-ed.* If you remove the prefix, you have the word *decided.* If you replace the suffix with *-sion,* you can make the word *decision.* Remember that you will sometimes have to make small spelling changes in order to add a suffix, such as taking away the final *-de* in *decide* in order to add the suffix *-sion.*

un- + **decide** + **-ed** = **undecided**

undecided – **un-** = **decided**

decided – **-ed** = **decide**

decide + **-sion** = **decision**

Use the word parts provided to build new words. You may have to take away word parts before adding new ones. Write your new words as word equations to match the sample above. Make spelling changes as needed when adding suffixes. Then, write what you think each new word means.

1. misinterpret (-ed, re-, -tion)

2. exclude (in-, -sion)

3. review (pre-, inter-)

4. international (-ize, -tion)

Name ____________________ Date ____________

Analyzing an Informational Text: Reading a Diagram

Reinforcement 1-5

Diagrams full of arrows can be confusing, but a legend can help the reader make sense of them.

Look at the diagram of photosynthesis below. Then, read the statements that follow. Match each statement to one of the arrows to complete the legend.

1. _____ a plant takes in water from the ground through its roots
2. _____ a plant releases oxygen into the air
3. _____ a plant takes in energy from sunlight
4. _____ a plant takes in carbon dioxide from the air through its leaves
5. _____ high-energy sugar molecules produced are used to carry out the plant's functions.

Name ______________________ Date ____________

Analyzing an Informational Text: Reading a Diagram

Extension 1-5

A process diagram uses images and words to show how to do something or how a process works. "The Greenhouse Effect: Differences Between Natural and Amplified Warming" explains the process of the greenhouse effect. Whether in your science book or in directions for how to put together a desk, process diagrams share the features of a drawing that shows the parts and a legend that explains how those parts work together.

Complete the following activities.

1. Think of a process you know from science, such as the water cycle or how to grow a plant. Talk to your science teacher or look in your science book for ideas. Create a diagram to show that process. Write a legend that uses 4–8 steps to explain the process. If you need more space, use a separate sheet of paper.

Read the questions below, then write a question of your own about the diagram and legend. Share your diagram and legend. Have classmates answer the questions on a separate sheet of paper. Correct the responses and share the results with the class.

2. What is the purpose of this diagram?

3. What information does the legend add to the diagram?

4. What main idea does the author use the diagram to show?

5. ____

____

____

Name ______________________ Date ____________

Literary Analysis: Narrative Texts

Reinforcement 1-6

When an author writes a narrative about his or her life, the main **character** is the narrator and writer. He or she will be referred to as "I" in the text. Readers learn about the other characters through the eyes of the narrator.

- **Conflicts** are problems or obstacles. Sometimes the conflicts are inside a character, like when someone has a difficult time making an important decision. In other situations, the conflict is outside a character, like when a character has a disagreement with another character, or when a character faces an angry dog. In a narrative about a writer's life, the writer presents conflict as he or she sees it.
- In a narrative about the author's life, readers hear about the plot and setting through the narrator's eyes. This means readers learn not just what happens and where it happens but how the narrator feels about these events and settings.

Read this selection from *The Day It Rained Cockroaches.* In it, author Paul Zindel remembers arriving at a new home with his sister. Then, respond to each item.

Mom opened the front door and we went inside. We were so excited, we ran through the echoing empty rooms, pulling up old, soiled shades to let the sunlight crash in. We ran upstairs and downstairs, all over the place like wild ponies. The only unpleasant thing, from my point of view, was that we weren't the only ones running around. There were a lot of cockroaches scurrying from our invading footfalls and the shafts of light.

"Yes, the house has a few roaches," Mother confessed. "We'll get rid of them in no time!"

1. Who are the characters in this narrative? Who is "I"?

____

____

2. What is the main conflict in this narrative? How does the narrator feel about the conflict?

____

____

3. Where does this narrative take place? How does the narrator feel about this place?

____

____

____

Name ____________________ Date ____________

Literary Analysis: Narrative Texts

Extension 1-6

The main character of a nonfiction narrative is usually the author. This gives readers a chance to get to know the author. Some authors tell you about themselves directly. Other authors use plot, conflict, setting, and dialogue to give readers clues about themselves. Most authors will use a combination of both techniques.

Read the excerpt from *Narrative of the Life of Frederick Douglass* in Unit 3, Lesson 11. Think about how it compares to "Occupation: Conductorette" by Maya Angelou as you answer the questions below.

1. Who was Frederick Douglass?

2. How would you describe Frederick Douglass, based on what you read?

3. What do you think Frederick Douglass believes?

4. How does the reader discover what kind of person Frederick Douglass is and what he believes?

5. How are Frederick Douglass and Maya Angelou alike? How are they different?

6. How does the way Maya Angelou reveal her personality and beliefs compare to the way Frederick Douglass reveals his personality and beliefs? Explain.

Name ______________________ Date ______________

Literary Analysis: Conflict

Reinforcement 1-7 A

Plot is the arrangement of events in a story. A story's plot includes five main parts. The **Exposition** is the introduction of the characters, setting, and basic situation. **Rising action** refers to events that increase tension about the conflict. **Climax** is the point of greatest tension in the story. **Falling action** refers to the events that follow the climax and reduce tension. The **Resolution** is the final outcome of the story.

Conflict is a struggle between two forces. Conflict drives the action of the plot and appears in the form of **external conflict** or **internal conflict.**

For each question, choose the letter of the best answer.

1. At the beginning of a story, you learn that Mary and Lisa are friends who always walk home from school together. What is this part of the story called?

   A. climax B. exposition C. rising action D. falling action

2. A little later in the story, Mary steals a tube of lip gloss from a drug store. Lisa tells her to go back and pay for it, but Mary just shrugs. What is this part of the story called?

   A. climax B. exposition C. rising action D. falling action

3. One day Mary dares Lisa to take something from the store. Lisa is torn between doing the right thing and proving herself to her friend. Finally, she takes a bottle of nail polish, but she is caught by the store manager. While the manager threatens to call the police, Mary sneaks away. What is this part of the story called?

   A. climax B. rising action C. falling action D. resolution

4. The next day, Mary apologizes to Lisa for getting her into trouble. What is this part of the story called?

   A. climax B. rising action C. falling action D. resolution

5. Mary and Lisa decide they have learned their lesson and will walk straight home without any stops from that day on. What is this story part called?

   A. climax B. rising action C. falling action D. resolution

6. Does this story include external conflict, internal conflict, or both? Explain your answer using text from the story to support your ideas.

   ____

   ____

   ____

   ____

Name ______________________________ Date ______________

Literary Analysis: Understanding Plot

Reinforcement 1-7 B

Plot is the arrangement of events in a story (beginning, middle, end). In addition to a story's conflict, the plot usually includes these parts: **exposition, rising action, climax, falling action,** and **resolution.**

Complete the definitions below by writing the correct literary term on the line provided.

1. The ____________ introduces and increases the central conflict.
2. The ____________ is the beginning of the story. It introduces the characters, the settings, and the basic situation.
3. The ____________ is the point in the plot when the conflict reaches its greatest intensity. This is also called a turning point.
4. The ____________ resolves the conflict and ties up all the plot's loose ends.
5. The ____________ consists of everything that happens after the climax, as the conflict starts to wind down and move toward a resolution.

Label the story diagram below using the literary terms mentioned above.

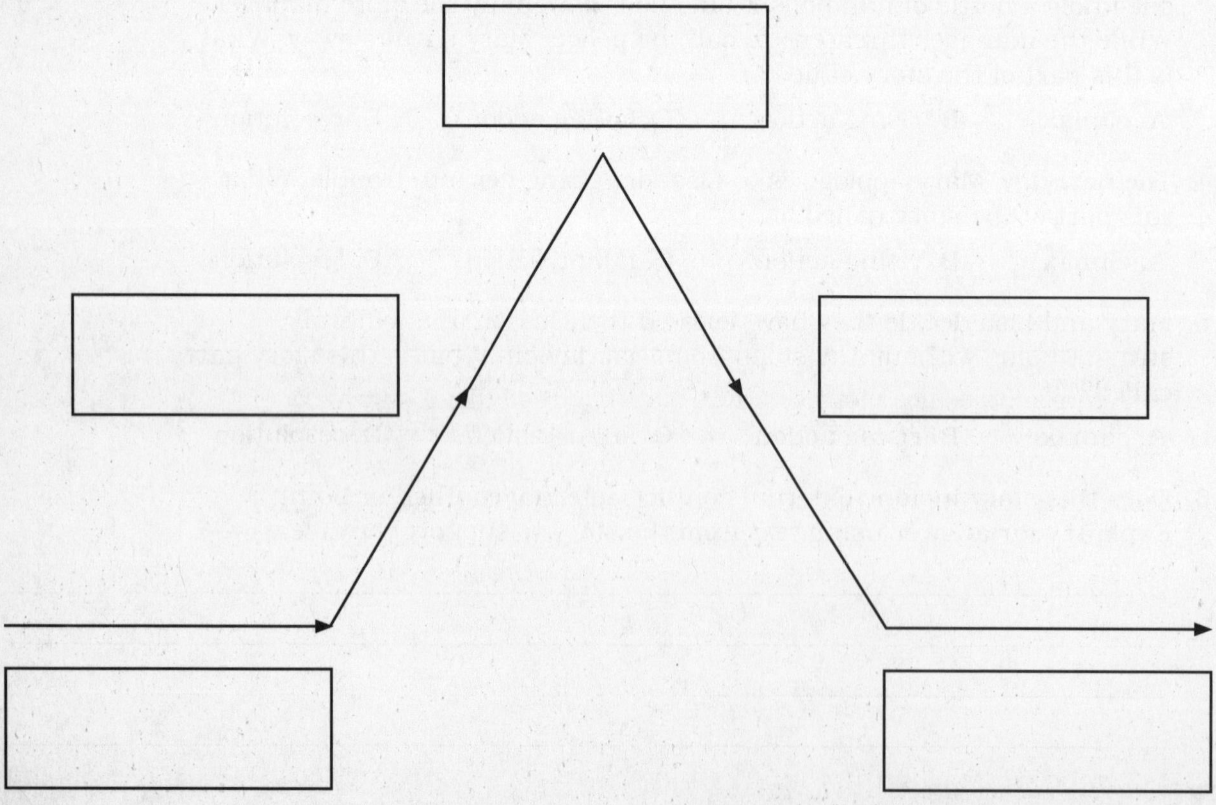

Name ______________________________ Date ______________

Literary Analysis: Conflict

Extension 1-7

A fable is a simple story that gives a moral lesson about life. Usually fables are very short and contain few characters. The plot in a fable is often reduced to a few short events.

Read this passage from the Aesop's fable "The Ant and the Dove."

An Ant went to the bank of a river to quench its thirst, and being carried away by the rush of the stream, was on the point of drowning. A Dove sitting on a tree overhanging the water plucked a leaf and let it fall into the stream close to her. The Ant climbed onto it and floated safely into the bank. Shortly afterwards a birdcatcher came and stood underneath the tree, and laid his lime-twigs for the Dove, which sat on the branches. The Ant, perceiving his design, stung him in the foot. In pain the birdcatcher threw down the twigs, and the noise made the Dove take wing.

Answer these questions about the passage.

1. What are the conflicts in the story? Are they internal or external?

____

____

2. How are the conflicts related?

____

____

____

3. Does the fable follow the five-part pattern described on the third page of Lesson 7 in your work text? Explain why or why not.

____

____

____

Write Aesop's fables are often so short that they read like a summary of a story. On a separate sheet of paper, rewrite the fable. Use vivid details to describe the action in each scene, and use dialogue to enrich the story. Think about what motivates the characters and try to describe or demonstrate it. Be sure to show the different phases of the story, including exposition, rising action, climax, falling action, and resolution. Include some internal conflicts. Be creative.

Name ______________________________ Date ______________

Language Coach: The Writing Rules

Reinforcement 1-8 A

In order for writers to make their writing clear and easy to understand, writers follow writing rules.

Rule #1: Parenthetical remarks are usually unnecessary.

Incorrect: I (really) didn't study enough for the test.

Correct: I really didn't study enough for the test.

Rule #2: Eliminate commas that are not necessary.

Incorrect: I think, I have a baseball game, today.

Correct: I think I have a baseball game today.

Rule #3: Never split infinitive verbs (verbs after the word *to*)

Incorrect: The soloist hoped to sweetly sing.

Correct: The soloist hoped *to sing sweetly.*

Rule #4: Use hyphens to join compound adjectives before a noun.

Incorrect: Many cold blooded reptiles eat mice.

Correct: Many cold-blooded reptiles eat mice.

Rule #5: Use apostrophes in their proper place and omit them if they are unnecessary.

Incorrect: My friends' pen exploded in his' pocket.

Correct: My friend's pen exploded in his pocket.

Write the letter of the writing rule needed to correct each sentence on the line provided. Then, use the rule to edit the sentence.

A. Split Infinitive

B. Unnecessary Parentheses

C. Hyphenate a Compound Adjective

D. Misplaced Apostrophe(s)

E. Misplaced Comma(s)

1. _____ *The Grapes of Wrath* is (considered to be) one of the best works of American literature.

2. _____ Ms. Sullivans' class read several different Irish poet's poems.

3. _____ The student wanted to carefully listen to the teacher's lecture since it would be on the exam.

4. _____ Romance novels' main characters are often broken hearted heroines.

5. _____ Herman Melville's, novel, *Moby Dick* opens with one of the most, famous lines in literature.

Name ______________________________ Date ____________

Language Coach: Common and Proper Nouns

Reinforcement 1-8 B

A **common noun** is the general name of a person, place, or thing (*student, park, toy*) whereas a **proper noun** is the specific name of person, place, or thing (*Roger, Central Park, Super Blocks*).

Underline all the common nouns in the passage below. Then, proofread the passage and capitalize all the proper nouns.

On july, 4, 1776, all fifty-six members of the second continental congress gathered together in anticipation, eager to sign a document that would forever change the future of the thirteen colonies. Written by thomas jefferson, the document declared the separation of the thirteen colonies from great britain and its ruler, king george III. This document is known as the declaration of independence. Among those to sign the declaration were john hancock, ben franklin, and future president of the united states of america, john adams. After the declaration was signed, a large bell outside independence hall echoed throughout the streets of philadelphia, indicating the birth of a new nation. This bell would later be known as the liberty bell.

Circle the proper noun in each pair of words. Then, write another proper noun that could be used for the common noun on the line.

1. country	France	____________
2. sports team	Toronto Maple Leafs	____________
3. February	month	____________
4. day	Wednesday	____________
5. Robot Dreams	book	____________
6. musician	Bono	____________
7. Valentine's Day	holiday	____________
8. National Geographic	magazine	____________
9. author	J.K. Rowling	____________
10. movie	The Sandbox	____________
11. Boston	city	____________
12. building	White House	____________
13. Nobel Prize	award	____________

Name ______________________ Date ____________

Language Coach: Concrete, Abstract, and Possessive Nouns

Reinforcement 1-8 C

Concrete nouns name people, places, or things that can be perceived by the five senses (sight, hearing, taste, touch, smell). **Abstract nouns** name ideas, beliefs, qualities, or concepts that cannot be perceived by the senses.

Concrete Nouns: car, book, moon, Mariella, ocean, music, cookie

Abstract Nouns: happiness, excitement, anger, understanding, disbelief

A **possessive noun** shows ownership. It always has an apostrophe. Use a possessive noun to show that something belongs to someone.

Singular Possessive (singular noun)	Add an apostrophe and an *s* ('s)	the cat → the cat's bed John → John's baseball
Plural Possessive (plural noun that ends in *s*)	Add only an apostrophe (')	cats → cats' bed boys → boys' baseball
Plural Possessive (plural noun that does not end in *s*)	Add an apostrophe and an *s* ('s)	children → children's toy women → women's shoes

Underline each concrete noun once and each abstract noun twice.

1. Italy is known for its rich cultural heritage.
2. Visitors are drawn by the beauty of its beaches, vineyards, and mountains.
3. Cities such as Florence, Rome, and Venice also attract tourists.
4. People find inspiration in the great artworks displayed at the museums.
5. They seek relaxation in the Italian countryside.

Write the possessive form of each noun in parentheses.

6. (Teresa) friend ______________________
7. the (Joneses) front yard ______________________
8. the (bloodhound) search ______________________
9. the (children) toys ______________________
10. the (artist) style ______________________
11. her (parents) careers ______________________
12. he (men) tennis team ______________________
13. the (teachers) lounge ______________________

Name ______________________ Date ____________

Language Coach: Spelling Plural Nouns

Reinforcement 1-8 D

Although most plural nouns end in *–s* or *–es,* such as *dogs* or *turtles,* many plural nouns have slightly different or irregular endings. The following spelling rules will help you write plural nouns.

A. For nouns that end in *–s, -x, -ch,* or *–sh,* add *–es.*
toss—toss*es,* couch—couch*es*
ax—ax*es,* bush—bush*es*

B. For nouns that end in a consonant plus *y,* change the *y* to an *i* and add *–es.*
party—part*ies,* century—centur*ies*

C. For some nouns that end in *–f* or *–fe,* use *–ves.* (Some just add *–s.*)
thief—thie*ves,* life—li*ves*

D. Some nouns change their spelling to from the plural.
mouse—mice, foot—feet, ox—oxen

Complete the chart below by writing the singular or plural form of each noun shown. Then, write the letter of the spelling rule used.

	Singular	Plural	Rule
1.	box		
2.	family		
3.		leaves	
4.	wish		
5.		glasses	
6.	cliff		
7.	foot		
8.	beach		
9.		mice	
10.		spies	

Name ______________________________ Date ______________

Language Coach: Nouns

Extension 1-8

Noun Poems

You can use your understanding of the relationships between the different types of nouns to write poems using only nouns. All the nouns should be connected to the proper noun in the first line.

Line 1: proper noun
Line 2: common noun
Line 3: concrete noun, concrete noun, concrete noun
Line 4: abstract noun, abstract noun, abstract noun
Line 5: common noun, common noun
Line 5: (same as line 1)

Here is a sample poem:

Jackie Robinson
baseball player
bat, ball, glove
skill, speed, courage
man, hero
Jackie Robinson

Try to write two original noun poems using the formula above. Write your poems on a separate sheet of paper if you need more space.

________ ________ ________, ________, ________ ________, ________, ________ ________, ________ ________	________ ________ ________, ________, ________ ________, ________, ________ ________, ________ ________

Create Now write another original poem using only nouns. You can invent your own formula, or you can write without a formula.

____

____

____

____

____

Name ______________________________ Date ______________

Writer's Workshop: Descriptive Essay

Reinforcement 1-9

A **descriptive essay** creates a picture in words to share a vivid experience. It forms an image of a person, thing, or place by painting pictures with words. In a good description, the reader will be able to do more than see the scene. He or she will be able to hear, taste, smell, and feel it as well. That is why it is important to make the best word choices and to classify your details so they can be presented in an organized way. Good descriptive essays create very coherent and detailed impressions.

Read each example from a descriptive essay. Then, answer each question.

1. He had once been a strong man, but the years of working outside had taken their toll on him. Grandpa used to be able to pick me up and twirl me around for hours. Now, he walked slowly, leaning on his old hand-carved walking stick.

What is the main impression you get about the writer's grandfather?

____

____

____

2. When Lila walked into a room, everyone turned around. It wasn't that she was beautiful, or even especially brilliant. But when she smiled at you, you felt as though there was no one else around. She made you feel special.

How would you describe Lila, based on this example?

____

____

____

Complete the following exercise on a separate sheet of paper.

Create Choose one of the following subjects or think of another place that is special to you. List six or seven details that describe that place. Include details that appeal to at least three senses. Some of the details should also reflect your feelings about the place.

a. a room in a house

b. a landscape through which you have traveled by plane, car, train, or boat

c. a place associated with a holiday

d. an imaginary place you would like to visit

e. the inside of a closet

Name ____________________ Date ____________

Writer's Workshop: Descriptive Essay

Extension 1-9

Writers use sensory details to bring a description to life. Think of sensory details as a tool to paint a mental picture. You can use sensory details to tell about a person's actions, character traits, appearance, or behavior. In each case, choose words that appeal to the senses of sight, sound, smell, taste, and touch. These words will often be adjectives, but don't forget about verbs. For example, use colorful verbs such as *vault* or *leap* instead of *jump*.

Identify sensory details—adjectives and verbs—about each aspect of the person you are describing. Record your details in the chart below.

Text Feature	Sight	Smell	Taste	Sound	Touch
Appearance					
Character Traits					
Behavior					
Actions					

Now look at your essay draft. Find at least three places to add sensory details. Write your original sentence and your revised sentence on the lines below.

1. ____________________

____

2. ____________________

____

3. ____________________

____

Name ______________________ Date ____________

Mid-Unit Benchmark Test — Unit 1

Reading Skill: Making Predictions

Read the following questions. Then, choose the best answer.

1 What are the two main things that you should consider in order to make accurate predictions in a story?

A the author and the personalities of the characters

B the title and the names of the characters

C the plot and the cultural context of the work

D story details and your own experience

2 Read these sentences from a story. Then, choose the best prediction of what will happen next.

In the early morning, Cara stood at the bus stop on Round Lake Road. She clutched her textbooks to her side and stamped her feet to keep warm.

F Cara will greet her brother when he comes home from school on the bus.

G Cara will get on the bus when it comes and go to school.

H Cara will read her textbooks as she takes the bus to the movies.

J Cara and her family will move to a warmer climate.

Read the passage. Then, answer the questions.

(1) In the ballroom, the orchestra began to play. (2) Jorge listened, tapping a foot to the rhythm. (3) Across the table Anna smiled, tapping a foot as well. (4) Jorge rose from his chair at the table and smiled back at Anna. (5) "Shall we?" he said, motioning toward the dance floor. (6) The tablecloth hung low between them, and as Jorge moved forward, he stepped on it. (7) Then, his legs in a tangle, he fell flat on his face.

3 From the details in sentences 1–5, which of these predictions seems most likely to happen?

A Jorge will refuse to ask Anna to dance with him.

B Anna will refuse to dance with Jorge when he asks.

C Jorge and Anna are going to get up and dance.

D Jorge is going to trip and fall on his face.

4 Which detail in the selection should make you reconsider your first prediction and expect a different outcome?

F Jorge taps his foot to the music.

G Anna taps her foot to the music.

H Jorge motions toward the dance floor.

J Jorge steps on the tablecloth.

Name ______________________________ Date ______________

Literary Analysis

Read the following questions. Then, choose the best answer.

5 Which type of writing is a nonfiction narrative?

A a novel

B a biography

C a stage drama

D a poem that tells a story

6 What is the term for the part of a story that provides background information about main characters and their situation?

F exposition

G climax

H falling action

J resolution

7 Which of these is a good example of an internal conflict?

A A knight struggles to defeat a fire-breathing dragon.

B A lawyer struggles to prove the innocence of her client.

C A farmer struggles to bring his crops through a bad drought.

D A student struggles to come to the right decision.

8 In what part of a story are problems worked out so that the conflict is eliminated?

F exposition

G rising action

H foreshadowing

J resolution

Read the passage. Then, answer the questions.

Aaron and I had hiked quite a distance and were tired when we made camp. By the time dinner was over, we were more than ready for bed. Because of our exhaustion, we did not clean up properly. I should have known better than to leave food around in Yellowstone Park at night. At any rate, some time during the night, I was awakened by a loud clamor. Glancing over, I saw a big, dark shape in the dim light. Blinking my eyes, I realized that it was a grizzly bear. The leftovers we had foolishly left near camp had attracted the menacing beast! Deeply afraid, I remained very still and hoped that Aaron would do the same. I breathed a sigh of relief when the bear went lumbering off into the night.

9 The student underlined the words *camp, Yellowstone Park,* and *night* when marking this text because they reveal —

A how the conflict is resolved

B important details about the setting

C exactly what happens in the passage

D important details about the characters

10 Why might a student draw a box around the word *clamor* when marking this text?

F This word relays the meaning of the passage.

G The student uses this word often when writing.

H This word describes how the characters felt.

J The student is unfamiliar with this word.

Name ______________________________ Date ______________

Read the passage. Then, answer the questions.

(1) Jean, a high school student, was such a good swimmer that she was able to get a summer job as a lifeguard at the local pool. (2) She had no idea that the experience would test her skill and quick thinking more than ever before. (3) One Thursday afternoon, Dean and Frank Rinaldo showed up at the pool. (4) Noisy and reckless, the two teenaged brothers quickly drove the other swimmers away. (5) They paid no attention when Jean told them to behave. (6) Jean was just about to phone her supervisor when she saw the brothers crash into each other and begin to sink. (7) No one was there to help as Jean dove into the pool and struggled to pull them out. (8) They were very heavy, but she finally managed to drag out first Dean and then Frank. (9) Dean was conscious but in pain. (10) Frank was unconscious, and Jean had to give him mouth-to-mouth resuscitation. (11) When he finally began breathing, Jean raced to her cell phone and called an ambulance. (12) After the brothers recovered, they apologized to Jean and never behaved badly at the pool again.

11 Around what conflict do the events in the story center?

A Jean and the doctor's struggle to save the lives of the injured Rinaldo brothers

B Jean's struggle to control the crowds at the swimming pool

C Jean's struggle to get the Rinaldo brothers to behave at the swimming pool

D Jean's struggle to be the best swimmer she can be

12 Which part of the story is the exposition?

F sentence 1

G sentence 2

H sentence 3

J sentence 12

13 Where does the climax of the story take place?

A sentence 3

B sentences 4–5

C sentences 6–11

D sentence 12

Vocabulary

Read the following questions. Then, choose the best answer.

14 Which statement is true about the prefixes *pre-* and *re-*?

F *Pre-* and *re-* usually have similar meanings.

G *Pre-* and *re-* often have opposite meanings.

H *Pre-* and *re-* are never used with the same roots.

J *Pre-* is much more frequently used than *re-*.

15 Based on your understanding of the prefix *pre-*, where in a textbook chapter would you probably find a *preview*?

A before the chapter starts

B in the middle of the chapter

C at the end of every section

D at the end of the entire chapter

Name ______________________ Date ____________

16 Based on your understanding of the prefix *re-*, when are you likely to *regain* something?

F when you have never had it

G when you have had it at least once before

H when you do not want it

J when you understand it fully

17 Which choice explains how the prefix *pre-* is part of the meaning of the word *prefix*?

A A *prefix* is something you fix, or attach, before a word or a root.

B A *prefix* is something you fix in your mind beforehand.

C A *prefix* is something that happens before something else.

D A *prefix* is something that you determine over and over until it is fixed in your mind.

18 Based on your understanding of the prefix *re-*, what do you conclude the italic word in this sentence means?

As she sang the song, the singer kept having trouble with the high notes of the *refrain.*

F the opening notes of a song

G an introductory part of a song that has a different tune from the rest

H the highest notes in a song

J a line or stanza that is sung over and over in a song

19 How does the suffix *-ize* or *-yze* affect the word or root to which it is attached?

A It turns the word or root into a verb.

B It turns the word or root into an adjective.

C It turns the word or root into a noun.

D It gives the word or root an opposite meaning.

20 In this sentence, what does the word in italics mean?

The potters will *individualize* each mug by putting a different design on the handle.

F people who show unique qualities

G to make special or appropriate to each person

H to turn something into something else

J special; unique

21 Based on your understanding of the prefix *re-*, what is the meaning of *rebound*?

A move closer

B leap over

C go between

D spring back

22 Based on your understanding of the prefix *pre-*, what does the word in italics mean in this sentence?

Early in the 1980s, the house building industry saw a significant increase in the production of *prefabricated* housing.

F made with bricks

G assembled beforehand

H built on concrete foundations

J constructed quickly

23 Based on your understanding of the suffix *-ize*, what does the word *characterize* mean?

A to describe a person's individual qualities

B to create a fictional setting

C to watch how someone behaves

D to choose actors for roles in a play

24 Which of these words is generally used as a noun?

F invent

G inventive

H reinvent

J invention

Name ______________________ Date ____________

Grammar

Read the following questions. Then, choose the best answer.

25 **Which statement is true about common and proper nouns?**

A A proper noun is more specific than a common noun.

B A proper noun is more polite than a common noun.

C A common noun usually begins with a capital letter.

D A proper noun usually begins with a lowercase letter.

26 **How many proper nouns are in this sentence?**

Sally Harding and her brother visited the D-Day Museum in New Orleans.

F two

G three

H four

J six

27 **Which sentence below uses correct capitalization?**

A Carmine saw the united Nations and a museum when he visited New York city.

B Carmine saw the United Nations and a Museum when he visited New York City.

C Carmine saw the United Nations and a museum when he visited New York City.

D Carmine saw the United Nations and a museum when he visited new york city.

28 **Which of these sentences uses plural nouns correctly?**

F The wifes used the knifes to cut bunchies of berrys from the leafs.

G The wives used the knives to cut bunches of berries from the leaves.

H The wives used the knives to cut bunchies of berries from the leavs.

J The wifes used the knifes to cut bunches of berryes from the leaves.

29 **Which of these spelling rules is accurate?**

A To form the plural of any noun that ends in *y*, change the *y* to an *i* and add *es*.

B To form the plural of any noun that ends in *y*, just add *s*.

C To form the plural of a noun that ends in a vowel + *y*, change the *y* to an *i* and add *es*.

D To form the plural of a noun that ends in a consonant + *y*, change the *y* to an *i* and add *es*.

30 **What type of noun names something that can be perceived by one or more of the five senses?**

F a common noun

G a proper noun

H a concrete noun

J an abstract noun

31 **Which word in this sentence is an abstract noun?**

The child showed great kindness to the stray puppy that she found on the street.

A child

B kindness

C puppy

D street

32 **Which of these sentences uses possessive nouns correctly?**

F The Miller brothers' invention was a children's game in which each player's marker was a different zoo animal.

G The Miller brother's invention was a childrens' game in which each player's marker was a different zoo animal.

H The Miller brother's invention was a children's game in which each players' marker was a different zoo animal.

J The Miller brothers' invention was a childrens' game in which each players' marker was a different zoo animal.

Name ______________________ Date ____________

Short Answer

Reading Skill: Making Predictions

33 What is the best procedure for making predictions as you read a story?

34 What is a diagram?

Literary Analysis

35 What is the climax of a story?

36 Name four elements that a narrative contains.

Essay

Write on a separate sheet of paper.

37 Think of a children's story that you read or heard when you were younger. Then, on a separate sheet of paper, write a short version of the story with a new ending. You may include details that help point to the new ending, or you may make the ending a complete surprise.

38 Think of a place that you enjoy visiting. Perhaps you enjoy visiting a friend's house or a neighborhood restaurant. Write a descriptive essay in which you provide many details about this place and explain why you enjoy going there.

39 Recall an incident in your life that you think others would find entertaining or interesting to read about. Then, on a separate sheet of paper, write a brief essay about the incident. Tell what happened, how you felt at the time, and why the experience made an impression on you.

Name ______________________________ Date ______________

Diagnostic Test 2 | Unit 1

Read the passage. Then, answer the questions.

Chapter One
The Life of Coretta Scott King

Coretta Scott grew up on a farm in a small hamlet near Marion, Alabama. She was an excellent student and graduated at the top of her high school class in 1945. She enrolled at Antioch College as a music and education major. Unfortunately, the local public schools refused to accept any African American student teachers.

Working for Civil Rights

Denied the right to be a classroom teacher, Scott decided to pursue her education in music. She wanted to become a professional singer. While studying at the New England Conservatory of Music in Boston, she met a theology student named Martin Luther King, Jr. They married in 1953 and moved to Montgomery, Alabama, where Dr. King began his work as a minister. Because of their strong belief in equal rights for everyone, the Kings soon became influential leaders in the civil rights movement. They gave many speeches and led many marches. Just days after her husband's death in 1968, Coretta Scott King led 50,000 people in a civil rights march. She then traveled to other countries to speak out for equal rights. She opened the King Center in 1981 to educate people about Dr. King's work and beliefs.

1 The author's purpose for writing this selection is to —

A reflect on growing up in Alabama

B persuade people to learn more about the civil rights movement

C inform the reader about the life of Coretta Scott King

D entertain the reader with details about life in the 1950s

2 Which details most clearly point to the author's purpose for writing the selection?

F technical language

G historical facts

H humorous stories

J emotional language

3 What is the author's attitude toward Coretta Scott King?

A pity

B admiration

C indifference

D amusement

4 Which detail is least important to the purpose of this selection?

F Local public schools refused to accept African American student teachers.

G Scott wanted to become a professional singer.

H The Kings gave many speeches and led many marches.

J The King Center opened to educate people about Dr. King's work and beliefs.

Name ______________________ Date ______________

Read the passage. Then, answer the questions.

The first rays of sun illuminated the frost on the inside of the window. Jack knew then that the temperature had dipped below zero overnight. The tiny cabin on Mount Rainier was little more than a shack. It had smelled musty when he and Armando first entered it last night, but the strong odor of smoke from the fire filled his nostrils now.

Jack was glad to see that Armando was sleeping on the tattered cot. His friend had fallen more than 30 feet onto a rocky ledge. Jack was certain that Armando's leg was shattered.

Jack began to think of the treacherous route back to the nearest town. He would have to cross rugged terrain and frozen streams. But Jack knew that he would have to make it there today to find a doctor. Jack drew in a deep breath and began to pack. As his resolve grew, his shaking hands began to steady. He would not let his friend down.

5 Which detail best describes the setting of this selection?

A The tiny cabin on Mount Rainier was little more than a shack.

B Jack was glad to see that Armando was sleeping on the tattered cot.

C But Jack knew that they would have to make it there today to find a doctor.

D As his resolve grew, his shaking hands began to steady.

6 Which word describes the overall mood of the selection?

F angry

G impatient

H hopeless

J suspenseful

7 What is the theme of this selection?

A Be careful when building campfires.

B Tough times call for courageous actions.

C Spending time outdoors is important.

D Always pack enough supplies when hiking.

8 Which details of the setting are most important in conveying the mood?

F "musty," "the inside of the window," "smoke from the fire"

G "last night," "nearest town"

H "below zero," "rugged terrain," "frozen streams"

J "rays of sun," "tattered cot"

Read the following questions. Then, choose the best answer.

9 Choose the personal pronoun that best completes the sentence.

Tamika and ______ walked to the mall.

A me

B I

C mine

D my

10 Which word is spelled correctly?

F choclate

G asprin

H bevrage

J decathlon

Name ______________________________ Date ______________

Reading Skills: Author's Purpose

Reinforcement 1-11

An **author's purpose** is his or her main reason for writing. The most common purposes for writing are to inform, to persuade, and to entertain. To determine an author's purpose, notice the types of details included in the work. Writers may use facts and statistics to inform or persuade. They may use stories about personal experiences to inform or entertain. Often, authors will have more than one purpose—to inform while entertaining, for example.

Read each paragraph. Then, respond to each item.

When you buy a bicycle helmet, make sure it fits you well. The foam pads should touch your head all around, and the helmet should sit level. Tighten the straps so that they are snug but comfortable. You must not be able to pull off the helmet, no matter how hard you try.

1. Is the author's main purpose to entertain, to inform, or to persuade?

____

2. List two details from the paragraph to support your answer to question **1**.

____

____

It was a beautiful day. Ramona put on her helmet, hopped on her bike, and headed to a desert bike path near her house. She was peddling merrily along when suddenly she heard a loud, hissing sound. "Oh, no," she thought, "not a snake!" She peddled faster but noticed that her bike was bouncing badly. When she looked back, she saw that her rear tire was flat. "So that was the hissing!" No snake, after all—just a flat tire and a ruined bike ride.

3. Is the author's main purpose to entertain, to inform, or to persuade?

____

4. List two details from the paragraph to support your answer to question **3**.

____

____

5. On the blanks below, create your own paragraph involving bicycles. Your purpose should be clearly stated and supported with details.

____

____

____

____

____

____

Name ______________________________ Date ______________

Reading Skills: Author's Purpose

Extension 1-11

An anecdote is a short personal account of an interesting or humorous situation or event. Good anecdotes are always entertaining, but people often have another purpose for telling them. You might tell an anecdote to inform someone of what happened or how you felt. You might tell an anecdote to reflect on a situation or on the people involved. Or you might tell an anecdote to persuade someone to agree with you. Whatever your other purpose is, your anecdote will have to be entertaining to be successful.

Read the following anecdotes and answer the questions that follow.

a. When I was learning to ride a bike, I fell and skinned both my knees. I kept falling, just like you do. It was hard. My brother said maybe I should try again another day, but I wouldn't give up. I kept trying until it got dark, and finally I learned to ride. I felt like I was flying! Soon you will too! Come try again!

b. I always thought I looked bad in hats. Last summer I was on a crowded street and someone behind me dropped a hat on my head. I was so surprised, I stopped where I was, but when I turned around, whoever did it had gone. I went into a store to look in a mirror, and the hat actually looked good on me!

c. Every time I see my cousins, they tease me just for wearing glasses. If I want to get away from them, the only other choice is to sit with the adults and listen to them talk about boring politics and complain about their health problems. I guess that's why I never get excited before Thanksgiving, like all my friends do.

1. What purpose does each anecdote have, other than to entertain?

   a. ______________________________

   b. ______________________________

   c. ______________________________

2. Choose one anecdote and tell how the writer uses entertainment to accomplish another purpose.

   ____

   ____

Apply Think of an anecdote that you told recently, and what your purpose was in telling it. Write it on a separate sheet of paper. Make sure that your writing is entertaining and has at least one clear purpose.

Name ______________________ Date ______________

Literary Analysis: Setting and Mood

Reinforcement 1-12

The **setting** of a story is the time and place of a story's action. The time may be the past, present, or future. The place can be a person's home, the ocean, a circus tent—anywhere. The setting helps create the **mood** of the story. The following details help contribute to the setting.

- the characters' customs, values, and beliefs
- what the land looks like
- what the weather is like or what the season is
- the historical time period of the action

Read the following selection, looking for clues about the time and place. Then, answer the questions.

We landed our Jetstar on the first pod we could locate. Traffic was heavy on Andaron at this time of the morning—8027 onstar time—and we needed to hurry. It was another gloomy morning. The sky was filled with huge blue and white drops that threatened to splatter all over the windshield.

Laura and I were the first people to arrive at work. Commander Voss took one look at us and said, "What happened to you two? You look like you were caught in a meteor avalanche!"

"No, boss," said Laura calmly. "Just a blue-and-white shower; a little heavier than usual, I guess. We forgot to wear our auto-protective devices."

Voss wasn't impressed. "Well, what do I train you for? Never mind, let's get to work. We have a lot to talk about today. Our planet is in grave jeopardy of disintegrating from this disturbing weather pattern."

That was Voss—always exaggerating. The fact is that Andaron has not had any bad weather in hundreds of years, so people tend to overreact if the sun doesn't shine.

1. When are the events in the story probably taking place?

____

2. Underline the clues you used to figure out your answer to question 1.

3. Where does the selection take place?

____

4. Circle the clues you used to figure out your answer to question 3.

5. What is the mood of the story? Explain.

____

____

____

____

Name ______________________________ Date ____________

Literary Analysis: Setting and Mood

Extension 1-12

Authors use **setting** to show the reader a character's traits, actions, thoughts and emotions. For example, a gloomy character may be described as living in a dark, stuffy house, or the sun may come out just when character feels happy about something. Sometimes a setting can serve as a detailed metaphor for something that is happening in a character's life, or for the theme of a work of literature.

Read this passage from *Tears of Autumn* and answer the questions that follow.

Hana Omiya stood at the railing of the small ship that shuddered toward America in a turbulent November sea. She shivered as she pulled the folds of her silk kimono close to her chest and tightened the wool shawl about her shoulders. . .

. . . She clung to the moist rail and breathed the damp salt air deep into her lungs. Her body seemed laden and lifeless, as though it were simply the vehicle transporting her soul to a strange new life, and she longed with childlike intensity to be home again in Oka Village.

She longed to see the bright persimmon dotting the barren trees beside the thatched roofs, to see the fields of golden rice stretching to the mountains where only last fall she had gathered plum white mushrooms, and to see once more the maple trees lacing their flaming colors through the green pine . . .

Why did I ever leave Japan? she wondered bitterly. Why did I ever listen to my uncle? And yet she knew it was she herself who had begun the chain of events that placed her on this heaving ship. It was she who had first planted in her uncle's mind the thought that she would make a good wife for Taro Takeda, the lonely man who had gone to America to make his fortune . . .

1. What is the setting established in the first two paragraphs?

____

____

2. What other setting is described in the third paragraph? How does it contrast with the setting on the ship? ______________________________

____

3. What situation is the main character in, and how does she feel about it?

____

____

4. How do the settings in this passage parallel the character's situation and express her feelings? Explain.

____

____

Name ______________________________ Date ______________

Comparing Literary Works: Theme

Reinforcement 1-13

The **theme** of a literary work is its central idea, insight, or message. It is usually a generalization about life or people. Some themes are stated directly. For example, in most fables the story teaches one or more animal characters a lesson. This lesson is directly stated at the end of the fable as a moral, such as "Always tell the truth." An implied theme is not directly stated. Instead, the writer presents it through the actions and experiences of the characters. For example, picture a story about a tiny man who must defeat a wicked dragon. Physically, he is no match for a huge dragon, so he uses cleverness to win. The story events and outcome suggest the theme of "Brains are mightier than brawn." Readers can often find more than one theme in a story.

Read the passages. Then, respond to each item.

A. A dog named Harry found a meaty bone and wanted to save it for later. But he was too lazy to bury the bone. He decided to trick another dog into doing it for him. "Hey, Fuzzy! If you bury this bone for me, I'll share it with you," he said. Fuzzy agreed and trotted off to bury the bone. Later that day, Harry was hungry. He dug up an entire field, but he couldn't find his bone. He learned that laziness does not lead to success. Meanwhile, Fuzzy enjoyed his tasty, meaty bone.

B. Two birds, Marge and Helen, saw a birdhouse in an apple tree. Both thought it was a perfect place for a nest, but it was only big enough for one of them. "Let's rest a bit, Helen," Marge said. When Helen fell asleep, Marge started building a nest. By the time Helen woke up, Marge was almost finished. Helen flew over to the birdhouse. "I'll bet your nest is lovely," she said. "May I go inside and see it?" "Well, all right," agreed Marge. Once inside, Helen pushed straw up against the opening. "Thanks, Marge," she said. "It's really cozy in here."

1. Does Passage A or B have a directly stated theme? ____________
   Underline its theme.

2. In your own words, state the implied theme of the other passage.

   ____

   ____

   ____

   ____

3. A story can have more than one theme. In Passage A, what theme might Fuzzy's actions and the story outcome suggest?

   ____

   ____

   ____

   ____

Name ______________________________ Date ______________

Comparing Literary Works: Theme

Extension 1-13

The writers of *The Grass Harp* and *Child of the Owl* both explore themes related to family. Because family is a universal experience, there are many themes related to family. Learning to recognize universal experiences can help you narrow down theme possibilities and compare individual writers' specific approaches to a particular theme.

Complete the following activities.

1. With a partner or small group, brainstorm as many themes as you can that relate to family. Think about both negative and positive themes. Record your themes in the cluster diagram below.

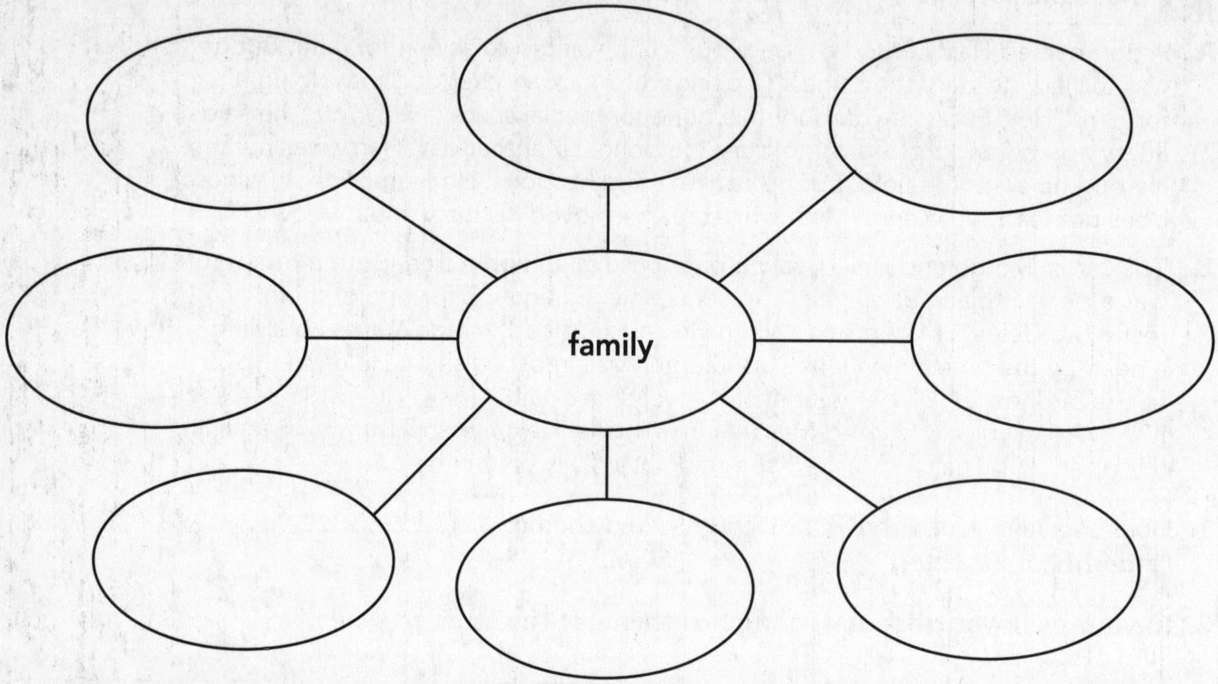

2. Now read *Water Man Comics* by Dav Pilkey from lesson 6 in your work text. Discuss this autobiographical essay with your partner or group. Then, write a short paragraph explaining the essay's theme and comparing it to the themes of *The Grass Harp* and *Child of the Owl.*

____

____

____

____

____

____

Name ______________________ Date ______________

Language Coach: Personal Pronouns

Reinforcement 1-14 A

Personal pronouns take the place of nouns and other pronouns. Depending on how they are used in a sentence, their case changes.

	Nominative Case	Objective Case	Possessive Case
Use	the pronoun is the subject of the verb	the pronoun is used as a direct or indirect object	is used to show ownership
Examples	I, you, she, it, we, they	me, you, him, her, it us, them	my, mine, your, yours, his, her, hers, its, our, ours, their, theirs

Underline the personal pronouns in each sentence. Then, identify the case of each personal pronoun and write its case (**N** for Nominative, **O** for Objective, or **P** for Possessive) underneath each pronoun.

Example: I lost the pocket calculator that Julio let me borrow.
O

1. I asked my friends, "Have you found the calculator today?"
2. "Oh, so the strange object we found is yours?" Vince kidded me.
3. "Why isn't your name on the back?" his brother Jack said.
4. I said it was not mine; my brother Julio owned the calculator.
5. "You should feel lucky it was found by us," Mara said.
6. "Its case is ripped, but I bet your father could repair it."
7. Later, she and we boys discussed our summer plans.
8. "Are you going to try out for our community play?" Vince asked.
9. "No. Why? Are you two trying out?" I asked him and his brother.
10. They said they would rather try their luck as villains.

Name ______________________ Date ____________

Language Coach: Reflexive Pronouns

Reinforcement 1-14 B

A **reflexive pronoun** indicates that someone or something performs an action to, for, or upon itself. A reflexive pronoun always ends with *-self* or *-selves*, agrees in number with a noun or pronoun that appears earlier in the sentence, and appears with another noun or pronoun. It should never take the place of a noun or pronoun.

INCORRECT → Mike, Roberta, or myself will volunteer to present first.
CORRECT → Mike, Roberta, or I will volunteer to present first.

The chart below lists reflexive pronouns and their uses.

Reflexive Pronouns	Singular	Plural	Example
First Person	myself	ourselves	I took **myself.**
Second Person	yourself	yourselves	**You** are proud of **yourself.**
Third Person	himself, herself, itself	themselves	**They** asked **themselves.**

Reflexive pronouns are often used in the following situations:

When to use Reflexive Pronouns	Example
When the subject and object are the same	I hurt myself. He brought it on himself.
As the object of a preposition, referring to the subject	I bought a present for myself. That man is talking to himself.
When you want to emphasize the subject	I'll do it myself. They ate all the food themselves.

Circle the letter of the sentence that uses reflexive pronouns correctly.

1. A. Everyone except myself seemed to understand the math problem.
   B. Everyone except me seemed to understand the math problem.

2. A. The group consisted of two guides, a family of six, and us.
   B. The group consisted of two guides, a family of six, and ourselves.

Underline the reflexive pronouns and circle the nouns or pronouns they refer to. Label sentences as correct or incorrect and explain why.

3. I thought we could solve it myself. ______________________

4. Yvette sent herself a postcard from Paris. ______________________

5. They know how to enjoy yourselves. ______________________

6. You should not be too hard on yourself. ______________________

Name ______________________ Date ____________

Pronoun Agreement

Reinforcement 1-14 C

An **antecedent** is the noun (or group of words acting as a noun) for which a pronoun stands.

Antecedent **Pronoun**
Mr. Jacobs asked **his** students to write reports on marine animals.

Sometimes the antecedent of a pronoun is an indefinite pronoun. **Indefinite pronouns** refer to people, places, or things, often without specifying the antecedent. Notice that a few indefinite pronouns can be either singular or plural, depending upon their use in the sentence.

Indefinite Pronouns			
Singular		Plural	Singular or Plural
another	much	both	all
anybody	neither	few	any
anyone	nobody	many	more
anything	no one	others	most
each	nothing	several	none
either	one		some
everybody	other		
everyone	somebody		
everything	someone		
little	something		

On the line provided in each sentence, write a pronoun that agrees with its antecedent. Then, underline the antecedent.

1. As the moon rose, ____________ cast a soft glow on the mountains.
2. I bought a used bike, but it broke down and left ____________ stranded.
3. Neither of the kittens is ready to leave ____________ mother yet.
4. The children took their baths, and then ____________ went to bed.
5. Everyone in the room seemed to be holding ____________ breath.

Rewrite each sentence, correcting any errors in pronoun-antecedent agreement.

6. Ask someone on the girls' swim team to show you their technique.

____

7. Nobody on the boys' soccer team ever forgets their cleats.

____

8. The drawer had two pencils and a notepad inside them.

____

Name ______________________ Date ____________

Spelling Tricky and Difficult Words

Reinforcement 1-14 D

If you mispronounce a word, then you are likely to misspell the word as well.

Let's take the example of adding an extra syllable that should not be there.

If you say pen-tath-a-lon,	→	you might spell "pentathalon" (incorrect)
If you say pen-tath-lon,	→	you might spell "pentathlon" (correct)

Say each word aloud. Write the number of syllables it contains. (You may consult a dictionary if you wish.)

1. mischievous ____________
2. chocolate ____________
3. wintry ____________
4. aspirin ____________
5. gardener ____________

Underline the five misspelled words in the paragraph. Give the correct spelling for each on the lines that follow.

In a mischievious move, my parents told us that we were going someplace special. We ended up going to see an opra! So we traveled twenty miles in blustery, wintery weather to see four hours of loud, old-fashioned singing. Luckily, the theater sold choclate candy between acts, so all was not lost.

6. ____________
7. ____________
8. ____________
9. ____________
10. ____________

Name ______________________________ Date ______________

Language Coach: Personal and Reflexive Pronouns

Extension 1-14

Sometimes a sentence uses personal and reflexive pronouns incorrectly.

Example *Sandy and me are going to the store.*

"Me" is an objective case pronoun, and should not be used as the subject.

Sometimes the correct case is used, but the pronoun and its antecedent don't agree in number or gender.

Example *The African elephant is threatened by hunters, and their habitat is shrinking.*

"The African elephant" is singular, and "their" is plural.

Sometimes a sentence uses personal and reflexive pronouns in such a way that the exact meaning of the sentence isn't clear. For example:

UNCLEAR: *Lucille told Linda that no one would give her an answer.*

The reader is left to wonder if "her" refers to Lucille or Linda.

CLEAR: *"No one would give me an answer," Lucille told Linda.*

You are an editor for a teen adventure magazine. Correct any grammar mistakes in the following article. Ask your teacher for a list of proofreading marks to use. If any sentence is unclear, highlight it and write your questions in the margin.

Enrico, Yolanda and myself are traveling deep into the Congo. Every traveler should do their research and find a skilled guide before setting out. Our guide told Enrico that there were monkeys watching him. They threw sticks down at us. Monkeys love throwing sticks, even when they are big. Me and Yolanda spotted a baby monkey clinging to his mother's back. There were parrots everywhere. The tropical parrot was gorgeous, but their noisy chatter made it impossible to talk. At dusk, we hung our mosquito nets around ourselves, and listened to their frustrated buzzing. I had promised myself I would see the Congo, and I love it.

Name ______________________________ Date ____________

Writer's Workshop: Personal Narrative

Reinforcement 1-15

When you write a **personal narrative,** you tell the story of one of your own experiences. That experience might have led to an insight, a solution to a problem, or a change in thinking. For example, you might write about going skiing for the first time. In your narrative, you would do the following.

- Tell events in order. You might begin by telling about putting on the ski equipment. Then, you might tell about going up a bunny hill on a rope tow.
- Use descriptive details. You might tell how steep the hill was, how cold the day was, how sunny it was, how windy it was, and so on.
- Give your reactions and thoughts. You might have felt a little nervous. You might have wondered if you would fall and hurt yourself. You might have realized just how difficult skiing is, and how challenging it is to try something new. These details are important to your personal narrative.

Read the passage, and then complete the activities that follow.

My family and I drove to the Grand Canyon this summer. At first I didn't want to go. Slowly, though, I changed my mind. We drove through the incredible scenery of the desert. The sunsets were astonishing, coloring the faraway mountains with shades of gold and orange. Even before we got to the Grand Canyon, I realized that I would not have wanted to miss this for the world.

1. Underline three words or phrases in this passage that indicate time order.
2. Draw a double-underline under one descriptive detail in the paragraph.
3. Circle the narrator's initial feeling about the trip, as well as the narrator's final feeling about the trip.

Complete these activities for a personal narrative of your own.

4. List a personal experience that made you realize something new. You might choose a trip, a sporting event, or a play.

____

____

5. Give a descriptive detail from this experience.

____

____

6. Describe one of your reactions to the experience.

____

____

____

Name ______________________________ Date ______________

Writer's Workshop: Personal Narrative

Extension 1-15

Writers use first-person perspective to make a narrative more personal by sharing their thoughts, feelings, and observations. However, using first-person perspective limits how much a writer can reveal about other people. Readers learn a lot about the narrator, but they only learn as much as the narrator can know about the other people. The narrator has to report dialogue or actions that show what other characters think and feel.

For example, a first-person narrator might write:

As we approached the door, I felt paralyzed by fear.

A first-person narrator describing another character opening the door might write:

As we approached the door, Harry's hand trembled and his eyes grew wide.

A first-person narrator might also use dialogue:

"I'm scared," I said to Harry.

"Well, I'm absolutely petrified!" he replied.

Complete the following activities to improve your personal narrative.

1. Identify several actions you described yourself doing in your personal narrative. Write a sentence for each action that describes what you were thinking or feeling at the time.

____

____

____

____

____

____

____

____

____

____

____

2. On another sheet of paper, identify actions done by other characters in you narrative. For each action, write 1–2 sentences that show what they might have been thinking or feeling. Use physical description or dialogue.

3. Revise your personal narrative to incorporate some or all of the new sentences.

Name ______________________________ Date ______________

End-of-Unit Benchmark Test | Unit 1

Reading Skill: Author's Purpose

Read the following questions. Then, choose the best answer.

1 In a detective story or mystery, what is usually the author's main purpose?

A to entertain readers with an interesting puzzle

B to inform readers about police procedures

C to describe the appearance of a crime scene

D to convince readers that crime does not pay

2 For which type of writing is the author's main purpose usually to persuade readers to think or act in a certain way?

F biography and autobiography

G nonfiction travel writing

H newspaper editorial

J magazine article

3 Which of these items most often signals writing meant to inform the reader?

A highly emotional language

B images and figurative language

C interesting characters and situations

D facts and technical language

4 For which type of writing is it most important to question and evaluate the author's statements and check the author's facts?

F persuasion

G description

H explanation

J narration

Better Morning

Waking up to a fresh cup of coffee has never been so easy. Percolite Plus offers an auto timer feature that allows you to prepare your coffee the night before. Just pour in the water, fill the filter with coffee, and set the timer. The next morning, the aroma of fresh coffee will awaken you. Percolite Plus is your answer to waking up happy.

5 What is the purpose of this selection?

A sell a product

B state a fact

C explain a process

D make an agreement

6 From the information in the selection, what can you conclude about its author?

F The author drinks coffee every morning.

G The author is someone who knows a lot about coffee.

H The author knows how you can have a happier morning.

J The author wants the details to persuade you to use the coffee maker.

Name ______________________________ Date ______________

Literary Analysis

Read the passage. Then, answer the questions.

When I was a young man, I worked as an extra in Hollywood. I appeared in the crowd scenes in several films. Because it was easier to get jobs if you supplied your own costumes, I had a closet stuffed with costumes, including a cowboy outfit, a Roman toga, and a suit of armor. I wore the toga when I worked on a film called *Spartacus* about a slave revolt in ancient Rome. I had to arrive at the Hollywood sound stage at five o'clock each morning. It was so early that I wore my watch to make sure I got there on time. During shooting one day, I forgot to take off my watch. No one on the set noticed, and no one noticed it later when they were making the final cut of the film. So if you ever see *Spartacus*, look for the Roman slave wearing a modern wristwatch. That fellow would be me.

7 What is the specific purpose of this selection?

- **A** to inform the reader about the difficulties of making a film that is set in the past
- **B** to persuade the reader to see the film *Spartacus*
- **C** to share the writer's interesting and amusing experiences as an extra in films
- **D** to explain the process by which a person can become an extra in films

8 The author achieves his purpose by—

- **F** using technical language to describe how films are made
- **G** giving factual information about working in Hollywood
- **H** sharing reasons for the author's earlier behavior
- **J** telling about a humorous event at the end

Read the passage. Then, answer the questions.

Snoring: Comical Ailment or Serious Symptom?

Snoring is often the subject of comedy, but it can be more serious than most people realize. Sometimes it is a sign of obstructive sleep apnea, a medical condition in which the upper air passages narrow during sleep because of the combined effect of a blockage, relaxing muscles, and gravity. As the air passages narrow, breathing lessens, the oxygen level in the blood drops, and the patient snores to try to get more air. When the throat tissues collapse further, the patient stops breathing altogether, at which point he or she awakens, regains control of the throat muscles, and begins breathing normally. The patient then falls back asleep, but the cycle repeats throughout the night. In fact, a patient suffering from severe sleep apnea may awaken more than a hundred times a night. In most cases, because the patient awakens only partially, he or she is unaware of what is happening.

Name ______________________ Date ______________

9 **What is the main purpose of this magazine article?**
- A to entertain
- B to inform
- C to narrate
- D to persuade

10 **Which phrase best describes the attitude of the magazine article's author?**
- F humorous and witty
- G technical and informative
- H serious and sad
- J tense and frightening

Literary Analysis

Read the following questions. Then, choose the best answer.

11 **In a discussion of literature, to what does the term *mood* refer?**
- A the author's attitude toward his or her subject or audience
- B the attitude or feelings that each character expresses
- C the time and place in which the work happens
- D the feeling or atmosphere that the work creates for the reader

12 **Which statement about the theme of a work is true?**
- F There is usually just one correct interpretation of a work's theme.
- G The theme of a work is usually directly stated at the end.
- H The theme of a work is never directly stated but is always implied.
- J The theme of a work is often a generalization about life or people.

Read the passage. Then, answer the questions.

> The road was a dead end into the heart of the country. Where the woodland broke into a field, the sun poured down like honey from the vivid blue sky. Usually this was a quiet spot, but today—the first really warm day of spring—was a little different. The warm sun had melted the snows to create temporary pools of water, and in those pools thousands of frogs were hatching. They made a joyful symphony, higher pitched than the calls of birds but more tuneful than any insects'. It would last for only a day or two, and then it would be over.

13 **Which aspect of the setting is most important to the description in this selection?**
- A the customs and beliefs of the characters and the physical features of the land
- B the physical features of the land and the weather or season of the year
- C the weather or season of the year and the historical era in which the action takes place
- D the physical features of the land and the customs of the characters

14 **What mood do the details in this setting description help create?**
- F an eerie, somewhat frightening mood
- G a quiet and thoughtful mood
- H a strange but cheerful mood
- J a tense and hectic mood

Name ______________________________ Date ______________

Read the passages. Then, answer the questions.

A cold wind raked across the barren moor and night was beginning to set in when we reached our final destination. The horses' hooves beat a steady drum as the carriage proceeded up the sweeping length of the driveway. At last we came to a stop in front of a crumbling mansion. One light shone brightly near an upper window, but the rest of the house was in inky darkness.

15 Which phrase best describes the mood of the selection?

A sad and mournful

B bleak and eerie

C angry and resentful

D charming and whimsical

16 Which of these images from the selection most clearly contributes to the mood?

F the cold wind raking across the moor

G the steady drum of the horses' hooves

H the sweeping length of the driveway

J the light shining in an upper window

17 What is the main purpose of this selection?

A to inform

B to explain

C to reflect

D to entertain

18 Which words from the selection most clearly contribute to the mood?

F "cold," "final," "steady"

G "sweeping," "brightly," "inky"

H "final, "crumbling," "brightly"

J "barren, "crumbling," "inky"

Once a lion captured a mouse and was about to eat it. "Spare me!" cried the mouse. "I am but a small mouthful to you, yet my family needs and loves me. If you let me go, I will help you in return." The lion did not think that anything so small could ever help him, but he was touched by the tiny creature's plight and amused by the bold claim of future aid, so he decided to let the mouse go. Years later, the lion was captured by some men. He was all tied up in a cage when the mouse came by and saw him. When the men went to sleep, the mouse slipped into the cage and gnawed through the ropes. Later, when the men opened the cage to feed him, the lion was able to escape. The mouse had saved the creature who had spared him, thereby proving that kindness will be rewarded.

19 What is the stated theme of this selection?

A My family needs and loves me.

B I will help you in return.

C He decided to show compassion.

D Kindness will be rewarded.

20 Which of these is an additional theme of the selection?

F Do not judge capability by appearances.

G Those who love their families will show compassion to others.

H Do not let great changes catch you sleeping.

J Human beings are stronger and more clever than the strongest beast.

Name ____ Date ______________

Grammar

Read the following questions. Then, choose the best answer.

21 What do personal pronouns do?

A replace nouns in sentences

B describe or modify nouns

C connect nouns to sentences

D indicate people only

22 How many personal pronouns does this sentence contain?

Jane and I asked the boys to find the book for us, but they could not find it in time.

F one

G two

H three

J four

23 What is the case of the personal pronoun in this sentence?

The tune is borrowed, but the words are mine.

A nominative

B objective

C possessive

D reflexive

24 What is the antecedent of the pronoun *ourselves* in this sentence?

Because the train was nearly empty, Yvonne and I had a whole car to ourselves.

F Yvonne

G I

H Yvonne and I

J train and car

25 Which of these sentences uses pronouns correctly?

A The boys tried to take care of the problem themselves.

B Alyson and myself went to the computer store.

C You students should do yourself a favor and study more.

D No one but myself understood the situation.

26 Which of these sentences uses pronouns correctly?

F Each of the girls had their own bicycle.

G All of the girls had her own bicycle.

H Both of the girls had their own bicycle.

J One of the girls had their own bicycle.

Spelling

27 Which word is spelled correctly?

A clarfy

B emrald

C economical

D delcatessen

28 In which sentence is the italic word spelled correctly?

F Jacob's family bought a TV with a *plasima* screen.

G The nurse told Sara to put *ointement* on her wound.

H All cars need regular *maintenance* to perform well.

J The dog was the *culperit* in the case of the missing shoe.

Name ______________________ Date ____________

Short Answer

Reading Skill: Author's Purpose

29 What is the general purpose of an opinion essay?

____

____

30 What type of details are often found in writing that is meant to entertain?

____

____

Literary Analysis

31 What makes up the setting of a story?

____

____

32 What common theme about overcoming challenges is often found in literature?

____

____

Essay

Write on a separate sheet of paper.

33 A story can convey a certain mood. On a separate sheet of paper, write a one-paragraph introduction to a story that conveys a confused, hectic mood.

34 Recall a fictional film or TV drama that taught a life lesson that you think applied to your own experiences in the real world. On a separate sheet of paper, write a brief personal essay explaining how the theme or lesson of that work applied to your own experience.

35 Think of a value that is important to you or an observation you have made about life or human behavior. How could you convey that value or observation by telling a story? On a separate sheet of paper, jot down ideas for a short story that conveys your value or observation as its main theme.

Name ______________________ Date ____________

Diagnostic Test 1 — Unit 2

Read the passages. Then, answer the questions.

No one knows for sure when the game of chess was invented. An early version of the game was popular at the end of the tenth century. The modern game was developed in southern Europe a few centuries later.

Players in the sixteenth century wanted others to study their games in order to become better players. The best players were proclaimed "masters" and were highly honored. Books on chess were soon being read all over the world and the game grew in popularity.

After the Russian Revolution, the Russian government deliberately set out to dominate world chess. It set up a program of chess education for children. It offered financial support to the country's best players. Russian players dominated the game throughout the twentieth century.

Computer programs that play chess first appeared in the 1960s, but these programs were no match for the top human players. It was not until 1997 that a chess computer called Deep Blue was able to narrowly defeat world champion Garry Kasparov in a series of games. Kasparov concealed his disappointment as best he could, but he could not hide the embarrassment he felt over losing to a machine.

1 Why doesn't anyone know when chess was invented?

A It is a secret.

B No one recorded the date.

C It was during the Russian Revolution.

D Players in the sixteenth century were better players.

2 Why did the Russian government set up chess instruction for young children?

F Children were the masters of the game.

G The schools needed to teach more classes in games.

H Computers were new to most adults, but children knew them.

J Children are easier than adults to train to play games such as chess.

3 From the information in the fourth paragraph, readers can infer that computer programs that play chess

A are popular in Russia.

B can beat all players.

C have improved over time.

D are used in schools.

4 What can you infer about Garry Kasparov?

F He is a very clever man.

G He knows little about computers.

H He is sensitive and his feelings are easily hurt.

J He learned to play during the Russian Revolution.

Name ______________________________ Date ______________

> Dark clouds were gathering in the northern sky. The air was heavy and everything felt sticky. Tamira recalled hearing the weather forecast on the radio while she was dressing for school. "Severe thunderstorms are forecast for this afternoon, sometime after 3," the announcer had said. She should have remembered her umbrella.
>
> Somewhere in the distance, Tamira could hear the rumble of thunder. She ran for the bus, anxious to get home before the storm. She had to walk three blocks from the bus stop to her grandmother's house. "I can't get this new shirt wet," she thought. "Mom doesn't know I wore it to school."
>
> The bus traveled slower than normal. The traffic seemed heavier, and Tamira grew more anxious at each red light. Through the front window of the bus, she could see flashes of lightning against the ever-darkening sky.
>
> "This is going to be close," she thought.

5 Which of the following story events is a flashback?

A Dark clouds were gathering in the northern sky.

B "Severe thunderstorms are forecast for this afternoon, sometime after 3," the announcer had said.

C Somewhere in the distance, Tamira could hear the rumble of thunder.

D The traffic seemed heavier, and Tamira grew more anxious at each red light.

6 Which of the following story details is an example of foreshadowing?

F Dark clouds gathered in the nothern sky.

G She should have remembered her umbrella.

H She had to walk three blocks from the bus stop to her grandmother's house.

J "I can't get this new shirt wet," she thought.

Read the following questions. Then, choose the best answer.

7 What is the origin of a word?

A its history

B its spelling

C its definition

D its pronunciation

8 Which sentence uses the verb *try* in the past tense?

F I am trying to run five miles every day.

G Sasha tried to jump rope, but she failed.

H Hector tries to complete his homework before dinner.

J Senator Jackson will try to visit our school next week.

9 Choose the correct form of the irregular verb in the sentence.

Our class has ________ Todd Stephens to represent us at the state science fair.

A chose

B choose

C chosen

D choosing

10 In which sentence do the subject and verb agree?

F Molly and Jason have given their report.

G A box of geraniums are on the back porch.

H One of the flowers have pink blossoms.

J A few of us is going to the mall this afternoon.

Name ______________________ Date ______________

Reading Skills: Making Inferences

Reinforcement 2-2

Readers often have to make **inferences,** or logical guesses, about characters, setting, and events by recognizing and using details in the story. For example, the detail that a girl is smiling added to the detail that she is looking at a photograph helps you infer that looking at the photograph makes her happy.

Read the paragraph. Then, respond to each item.

Lana paced back and forth across the living room carpet. She stopped and picked up a magazine from a table. After flipping through the pages impatiently, she let it drop. She tugged at a strand of hair and continued her pacing, back and forth, back and forth. She sighed, then stopped and slumped down on the sofa.

1. How do you think Lana feels?

____

____

2. Underline two details that helped you infer Lana's feelings.

Read each passage. Then, respond to each item.

You ask your brother how his first day at his new job went. He frowns and says, "I don't even want to talk about it."

3. What would you guess happened?

____

Your friend promises you that you can borrow her roller skates, but when she comes over, she forgets to bring them. When you remind her, she says, "Oh, right. Maybe some other day." The next time you get together, she never mentions the skates. You ask her one last time. She looks away from you as she says, "I think they are probably the wrong size for you."

4. What can you infer about your friend and her skates?

____

____

5. Underline two details that support your inference.

Smita jumped to her feet after reading the letter from the university and cried, "Yes!"

6. What would you guess happened?

____

____

Name ______________________________ Date ______________

Reading Skills: Making Inferences

Extension 2-2

Studying Body Language

A good writer does not always state the conflict in a story. Instead, the writer conveys tension through dialogue and by describing the behavior of the characters. The description of certain behaviors can lead the reader to make inferences about the characters' actions or feelings. These behaviors may be running, crying, hugging, or even the characters' physical distance from each other. Consider the method Naomi Shihab Nye uses to show conflict in this passage from "Hamadi."

> Two thin streams of tears rolled down Tracy's face. Eddie had drifted to the other side of the group and was clowning with Cameron, doing a tap dance shuffle.

Though there are only two sentences in this passage, the reader can make several inferences based on the characters' body language and distance from each other. Because Tracy is crying, she must be unhappy. Because Eddie is no longer near her and having fun without her, Tracy must feel rejected or abandoned. The fact that Tracy feels these emotions must mean she likes Eddie.

Read the following passage and then answer the question that follows.

> A huge smile filled Annabelle's face as she walked past the window of the toy store. She broke free from her mother's grasp and ran towards the door. Her mother chased after her, but it was too late, she had already made it through the door, and had the toy in her hand. Annabelle's smile grew larger. Her mother put her hands on her hips and tapped her foot, shaking her head from left to right.

1. What can you inferences can you make about what is happening and how Annabelle and her mother feel about the situation? Support your inferences with body language clues. Write your answer on a separate sheet of paper.

Complete the activity below.

2. Body language and physical distance from others can reveal a lot about a character's disposition and relationship to other characters. Work in groups of three. Two group members discuss how they can use body language and physical distance from each other to show a situation in which particular emotions and a relationship are involved. Then these two group members act out the situation without speaking. The third group member observes the body language and physical distance to infer the emotions expressed, in addition to the relationship demonstrated. Then, group members switch roles, using body language and physical distance to convey different situations.

Name ________________________________ Date ______________

Vocabulary: Word Origins

Reinforcement 2-3

-similis-, -differre-, and -spec-

The origin of a word is the word's history. Many English words have origins in the Latin and Greek languages. Knowing the origins of different words can help you understand the meanings of related words.

Origin	Meaning	Example
-similis- (Latin)	same	similar
-differre- (Latin)	carry apart	difference
-spec- or -spect- (Latin)	see	aspect

Read the paragraph. Underline every word with an origin that is listed above.

The two teams are very similar. For example, there is a similitude in the way they play defense. However, if you inspect them carefully and look beyond their similarities, you will see some important differences. One aspect in which they differ is in their quarterbacks. I'm sure most spectators can easily differentiate between one quarterback's spectacular skills and the other's fumbling efforts. Similarly, it is easy to see that the way the coaches manage their teams is quite different.

Now, write each underlined word in the correct column to show its origin.

-similis-	-differre-	-spec-

Apply On a separate sheet of paper, write three sentences using three of the words from above.

Name ______________________________ Date ______________

Vocabulary: Word Origins

Extension 2-3

All English words are built on roots. Knowing the root and understanding the origin of a difficult word can help you figure out its meaning.

Look at the words in the box. What is the word root of each? Write the root below each word as well as the origin of the root. Use a dictionary for help.

facsimile	trilogy	spectators
__________	__________	__________
logo	conclusive	dialogue
__________	__________	__________

Identify the word from the box that completes each sentence. Not all words from the box will be used.

1. Finally we have found __________ evidence that will help us solve this case.
2. The coffee company's __________ showed a steaming mug that matched their motto "Always hot, always fresh!"
3. Dora could not wait for the second movie of the __________ to be released in theaters.
4. Yasmin wanted copies of the memo for the meeting at noon, so she asked Chase to make a __________ for everyone.

Think of a word for each of the following roots provided. Write the words and their definitions in the chart provided. If necessary, use a dictionary to help find the definition for each word.

Root	Origin	Meaning	Words
-fin-	Latin	end, limit	5. Word: __________ Definition: __________
-graph-	Greek	write	6. Word: __________ Definition: __________
-mon-	Greek	one, single	7. Word: __________ Definition: __________

Apply On a separate sheet of paper, write a paragraph that uses all of the words you came up with. For additional challenge, come up with more words that use the given roots and include those in your paragraph.

Name ______________________________ Date ____________

Literary Analysis: Flashback

Reinforcement 2-5 A

Flashbacks are scenes that show events happening in the past. Usually, flashbacks interrupt the chronological order of a story to show past events. The following is an example of a flashback:

> The sky blackened and the wind grew strong. Captain Tom Dell remembered his first big storm at sea. "Wake up, young Tom, and get yourself on deck. There's a whopper of a storm comin', and we have to secure the ship!"

Read the passages below. Then, explain what information helps you identify each flashback.

Grandma wrung her wrinkled hands in her rocker as she recalled the day my Grandpa left for Germany with the rest of his troop. Her eyes became dark clouds and her brow furrowed as she stared out the window, pensive. It was nearly sixty years ago when the proud, fit Navy officer tipped his cap and squeezed the slim, young woman fighting back tears in the kitchen before hopping in the Jeep waiting out front.

____

____

____

____

____

____

____

____

Shana stepped off the platform onto the packed subway car. Last time she rode the A line was with Larisse over a year ago. She smiled to herself as she remembered sprinting down the long, cement corridors and jumping through the closing doors, spilling orange juice on Lar and nearly losing her backpack. She snorted, recalling the look on her friend's fuming face. The car jerked around the bend and the screeching wheels snapped her back to the present.

____

____

____

____

____

____

____

____

Today is my fortieth birthday. As I stare at the candles blazing on the cake, images of my childhood fill my head. I am sitting on the stoop of the cabin we call home. Seven of us live here, including Gramps.

____

____

____

____

____

____

Name ____________________ Date ____________

Literary Analysis: Foreshadowing

Reinforcement 2–5 B

Foreshadowing is a technique that uses clues to hint at events that will happen later in the story. Setting, dialogue, action, and comments by the narrator can all foreshadow events in a story. The following is an example of foreshadowing:

> The wind was gentle, and the sky was mostly clear. We saw a few wisps of dark clouds, but the captain assured us we had nothing to worry about.

The text hints that the crew will need to worry about an approaching storm.

Circle the event that each statement foreshadows. Then, explain why the event you chose is an example of foreshadowing.

1. A couple holds hands walking in the park. The man lets go of the woman's hand.

   A. the man will have hand surgery
   B. the couple will break up
   C. the man will be late for work

   ____

   ____

2. Jason and Louise sit in a dugout rolling their eyes as Adam goes up to bat. "Great," Jason said. "He hasn't hit a ball all season. Now we'll never win the game."

   A. Louise will bat next, winning the game
   B. Jason will strike out
   C. Adam will hit the ball, winning the game

   ____

   ____

3. Anika and Munna had been hiking for a couple of hours. Suddenly, Anika says, "Isn't that a bear track?" "Are you kidding?" Munna laughed. "There aren't any bears in these woods!"

   A. they will find more bear tracks
   B. they will run into a bear
   C. they will run into a moose

   ____

   ____

Name ______________________ Date ______________

Literary Analysis: Foreshadowing

Extension 2-5

Foreshadowing Through the Senses

In "The Scarlet Ibis," James Hurst describes in rich detail the setting of the story—particularly the lush landscape and climate. Hurst chronicles the story through the changing seasons and weather, noting how those changes affect the flora, fauna, and characters. Because setting is so significant to the events of the story, it is not surprising that Hurst uses the landscape and weather to foreshadow events.

Complete the activities below.

1. Setting is one element of a story through which events can be foreshadowed. What other aspects of a story might a writer use to foreshadow events?

____

____

____

Because a story depends on the reader to picture mentally the people, events, and actions, there are limitations to how a story might use foreshadowing. Consider how a movie might use foreshadowing in ways that a written story could not use. A movie stimulates more of the viewer's senses than a story; a movie depends on involving the senses, for the way in which a movie uses images and sounds determines how suspenseful, funny, or emotionally provoking the movie can be.

2. Think of two movies you have seen recently that use foreshadowing. Describe how each movie provides clues that hint of something to come. Keep in mind that movies use more than images to tell a story.

Movie	Example of Foreshadowing	Sense(s) Involved

Name ______________________ Date ____________

Language Coach: Action and Linking Verbs

Reinforcement 2-6 A

An **action verb** tells what action someone or something is performing.

Examples: the snail *crawls*, the dog *barks*, the ants *march*

A **linking verb** is a verb that connects a subject with a word that describes or identifies it. Forms of the verb *be* are the most common linking verbs. Other linking verbs are *seem*, *feel*, *taste*, *smell*, and *look*.

Examples: I *am* sure; she *is* certain; it *tastes* delicious

Underline the action verb in each sentence.

1. My cousins visit our house often.
2. My brother chases them out of his room.
3. We laugh at their silly riddles.
4. Sometimes I read them a story.
5. Other times, we play games in the basement.
6. Occasionally, my mom drives us to the movies.

Write the linking verb from each sentence in the blank. Then, circle the two words that the verb connects.

Example: Everything seems great at the fair. seems

7. After the bell, the hallways looked crowded. ____________
8. My backpack feels heavier than yesterday. ____________
9. The school bus sounds like a lion. ____________
10. The pigeons look fatter than ever! ____________
11. The basketball courts seem busier than last time. ____________
12. I was our team captain. ____________
13. The other team is much faster. ____________
14. The roasted peanuts smell delicious! ____________
15. Sadly, the peanuts taste burnt. ____________
16. They were absolutely terrible. ____________

Name ______________________________ Date ______________

Language Coach: Principal Parts of Regular Verbs

Reinforcement 2-6 B

A **verb** has four principal parts: *present, present participle, past, and past participle.* The past and past participle of a regular verb are formed by adding *–ed* or *–d* to the present form. Sometimes you will have to double a final consonant or change y to i before adding *–ed* or *–ing.*

Present	Present Participle	Past	Past Participle
Basic form	Add *–ing* after am, is, or are	Add *–ed* or *–d*	Add *–ed* or *–d* after has, have, had
they listen she looks	they (are) listening she (is) looking	they listened she looked	they (have) listened she (has) looked

Write the principal parts for each regular verb below. The first one is done for you.

Present	**Past**	**Past Participle**	**Present Participle**
1. he fixes	he fixed	he has fixed	he is fixing
2. I step	________	________	________
3. you explain	________	________	________
4. we deny	________	________	________
5. she combines	________	________	________
6. they hurry	________	________	________

Underline the verb in each sentence. Write *present, past, past participle,* or *present participle* to identify the principal part used on the line provided.

Example: The cheering section yells after each play. present

7. For centuries, the house cat has lived with humans. ________
8. An Egyptian tomb painting showed a house cat. ________
9. The great cats roam wild on the African plains. ________
10. The lions and tigers are hunting their prey. ________
11. The cat has hunted alone since prehistoric times. ________
12. People sometimes capture small wild cats for pets. ________
13. Some governments have stopped this practice. ________

Name ______________________________ Date ______________

Language Coach: Irregular Verbs

Reinforcement 2-6 C

Irregular verbs are verbs whose past and past participle forms do not follow a predictable pattern. For regular verbs, the past tense is formed by adding -ed or -d to the tense form, as in follow, followed. With an irregular verb, the past and past participle are not formed according to this rule.

Present Tense: School begins at 8:00.

Past Tense: School began at 8:00.

Past Participle: School has begun at 8:00.

Some Irregular Verbs

Present	Present Participle	Past	Past Participle
bring	(is) bringing	brought	(have) brought
rise	(is) rising	rose	(have) risen
go	(is) going	went	(have) gone
choose	(is) choosing	chose	(have) chosen
do	(is) doing	did	(have) done
see	(is) seeing	saw	(have) seen

Underline the correct form of the verb.

1. The dough should (raise, rise) for about twenty more minutes.
2. You mean I (did, done) the wrong page of math homework?
3. Now I wish that I had (went, gone) with you.
4. Marco Polo (saw, seen) many strange sights in his travels.
5. Amelia Earhart (did, done) what few other people dared to do.
6. The patriot said, "I (done, did) my best for my country."
7. They (went, gone) away without saying goodbye.
8. Kerry, have you (brung, brought) your tennis racket?
9. Our little kitten has (drank, drunk) all its milk.
10. Have you (chose, chosen) your partner yet?

Name ______________________________ Date ______________

Language Coach: Subject/Verb Agreement

Reinforcement 2-6 D

A **verb** must agree with its subject in number. The number of a word can be either *singular* or *plural*. A singular word indicates one. A plural word indicates more than one.

Singular Subject	Singular Verb	Plural Subject	Plural Verb
baby	crawls	babies	crawl
monkey	swings	monkeys	swing

Complete the chart using the correct form of subject and verb. The first one is done for you.

	Singular Subject	Singular Verb	Plural Subject	Plural Verb
1.	dog	*barks*	*dogs*	bark
2.		listens	teachers	
3.	student			write
4.	basketball player	jumps		
5.			girls	step
6.		plays	children	
7.	librarian			whisper
8.		grows	trees	

Fill in the chart. Write the correct present-tense form of each verb. The first one is done for you.

	Singular	Plural
9.	The swan glides gracefully.	The swans glide gracefully.
10.	The building ______________.	The buildings collapse.
11.	I ______________ in marathons.	They run in marathons.
12.	Mr. Wilson works in the garden.	The Wilsons ______________ in the garden.
13.	He ______________ lettuce.	They plant lettuce.
14.	Then, he sows the seeds.	They ______________ the seeds.
15.	The dog ______________ over there.	The dogs live over there.
16.	He wants to join the band.	They ______________ to join the band.
17.	Jerry plays the trumpet.	Jerry and I ______________ the trumpet.
18.	The blackboard ______________ scratched.	The blackboards were scratched.

Name ______________________ Date ______________

Language Coach: Irregular Verbs

Extension 2-6

It can be difficult to remember the definitions of similarly spelled words. Take the words lay and lie, for example. One definition of lay is "to place or set down." One definition of lie is "to be or to stay at rest in a horizontal position."

The following sentences use verbs lay and lie in the present tense:

I need to lay the fabric on the floor so I can measure and cut it.

Mom told me to go lie down after she noticed me yawning and nodding off in the chair.

Lay and *lie* are irregular verbs, so remembering their present and past participles can be challenging.

Present	Meaning	Present Participle	Past	Past Participle
lay	"to put or set down"	(is) laying	laid	(had) laid
lie	"to be or to stay at rest in a horizontal position"	(is) lying	lay	(had) lain

Underline the correct form of the verb.

1. I thought I had (laid, lain) my glasses on the dresser, not the TV stand.
2. To help us remember the difference between lay and lie, our teacher told us to think of this fact: chickens (lie, lay) eggs.
3. Yesterday, Jordan (laid, lay) on his bed reading for hours.
4. The fallen tree had (laid, lain) across the road until the fire department came to clear the debris.

Pretend you are a magazine editor. You have been given an assignment to write the weekly opinion piece in which you may write about any topic of your choosing. There are only two requirements that must be met in your article:

1) It must be creative and entertaining to read.
2) It must contain eight irregular verbs in the correct principle tense.

Create Write your article on a separate sheet of paper. Underline all irregular verbs. Then, make a chart that shows the four principal parts of five of the irregular verbs that you used. Use a dictionary as needed.

Name ______________________ Date ______________

Writer's Workshop: Short Story

Reinforcement 2-7

A **short story** is a brief piece of fiction. Short stories include the following elements:

- one or more characters
- a clear setting, or time and place in which the action occurs
- a conflict or problem that is faced by the main character
- a plot that develops the conflict, leads to a climax (or turning point), and a resolution of the conflict
- a theme that reflects an idea about life or human nature
- dialogue that reveals the characters' thoughts and feelings

Read the following passage. Then, answer the questions.

All day, the snow kept falling. The weatherman reported on television that the Northeast could expect at least ten inches by the end of the day. Newscasters were telling people not to drive unless it was an emergency. The Sampsons weren't worried, though. They had plenty of food. They invited their next-door neighbors, the Thomas family, to come over and play some board games with them. Everything was fine until a few hours later, when Mrs. Sampson started to feel cold. Something was wrong with the heat.

1. Who are the main characters in this passage?

____

2. What conflict do the main characters face?

____

Create Reread the passage above and prepare to add to it. Using the lines provided, or a separate sheet of paper if needed, add one or more characters, and create a brief dialogue between the characters. Make sure the dialogue is related to the story and helps build the action.

____

____

____

____

____

____

____

____

Name ____________________ Date ____________

Writer's Workshop: Short Story

Extension 2-7

Flashback and Foreshadowing in Your Short Story

You can use different literary techniques when you write a short story. You have learned two of these techniques: flashback and foreshadowing. Choose one technique to use in your short story.

Complete the following activities.

Prewriting

First, gather details about your story. Answer the questions below to clarify the conflict you want to develop in your story. Decide which technique you want to use.

What is the problem or conflict in your story?	
How will the problem reveal itself?	
How will the problem intensify?	
How will each of the characters react to the problem?	
How will the problem reach resolution or be solved?	

Drafting

Think about how the conflict will reveal itself. How can you use flashback or foreshadowing to introduce the conflict? How can you use flashback or foreshadowing to intensify the conflict?

Use the chart to help you plan where in your story the technique you chose will be most effective. Write in the spaces provided examples of your technique. For instance, if you chose flashback, you might use a character's memory to add to the rising action.

	Rising Action	Climax	Falling Action
Flashback			
Foreshadowing			

Name ______________________ Date ____________

Mid-Unit Benchmark Test — Unit 2

Reading Skill: Making Inferences

Read the passage. Then, answer the questions.

> The sun peeked through the tent window, warming Jeremiah as he woke. A large smile broke across his face as he scurried out of his sleeping bag. He threw on the outfit that he had chosen the night before and hustled out the tent's gaping door. He stepped onto the dew-soaked grass and embraced the brisk air. Other early risers milled about their campsites. Birds chirped as they fluttered through the majestic cluster of trees. *What a day for a hike*, Jeremiah thought.
>
> A few embers glistened from last night's campfire. His father would use these embers to cook his famous vegetable omelettes. His mother would use the berries that they gathered yesterday to make a refreshing fruit salad. Jeremiah's stomach growled with thoughts of the upcoming meal.
>
> Jeremiah hurried over to his backpack and heaved it onto a large tree stump. He opened it and surveyed everything that he had packed the night before: compass, change of clothes, bug spray, apples, granola, and bottled water. It was all in order. All he had to do now was wait for everyone else to wake up.

1 From the details in the selection, what inference can you make about Jeremiah's location?

A He is in the woods.
B He is in his backyard.
C He is on a beach.
D He is at a playground.

2 Which details in the selection help you infer that the events take place in the early morning?

F "A large smile broke across his face" and "hustled out the tent's gaping door"
G "embraced the brisk air" and "It was all in order"
H "warming Jeremiah as he woke" and "dew-soaked grass"
J "Jeremiah hurried over to his backpack" and "onto a large tree stump"

3 From the details in the selection, what inference can you draw about Jeremiah's feelings?

A He is worried that it will rain.
B He is hoping to go home soon.
C He is not very hungry.
D He is excited about going on a hike.

4 What do the selection details suggest about Jeremiah and his family's eating habits?

F They eat healthy food.
G They love sweets.
H They often eat red meat.
J They often skip breakfast.

5 Which of these steps is basic to making inferences?

A focusing on the main ideas
B examining clues in the text
C separating fact from opinion
D restating in simpler words

Name ______________________ Date ______________

Literary Analysis

Read the following questions. Then, choose the best answer.

6 What does flashback mean?

F The narrator gives a vivid physical description of a main character.

G A story shows an event that happened earlier.

H Main characters must overcome a problem or struggle.

J The author uses dialogue to reveal a character's personality.

7 What is foreshadowing?

A where and when the story takes place

B the way the story makes you feel

C clues about events that will happen later

D the sequence of events in the story

Read the passage. Then, answer the questions.

Monique stared down the endless track, squinting toward the finish line. A few girls chattered; most stretched or stood in idle concentration. The rain from the night before still lingered in scattered shallow puddles on the track. *I'll have to watch out for those,* Monique thought.

Monique glanced over at Carla. Carla glared back at her. Monique looked away and tightened her jaw. She would NOT let Carla get to her.

At breakfast, she had tried to talk to her mother about Carla, but once again, her mother refused to take her side. "Now, Monique, are you sure that Carla intentionally pushed you?" she asked, piling steaming pancakes onto a plate.

"Mama, how many times do I need to tell you? She never runs a fair race. She's always pushing and shoving." Monique took a deep breath. "I'm tired of it."

"Be sure that you play fair, no matter how Carla acts. Focus on your own behavior," Monique's mother preached. Monique nodded her head. As much as she hated to admit it, her mother was right.

"Runners set!" the official bellowed. Monique crouched down. BANG! She shoved off, bursting in front of the other runners.

As they rounded the track, Carla closed in on her. Monique felt Carla's elbow graze her arm. *Here she goes,* she thought. Monique ignored Carla, focusing on the upcoming puddle instead. Monique swerved to avoid the puddle and managed to avoid Carla's intentional shove. Carla wobbled a bit and splashed into the puddle. Her feet began to skid, but Monique reached over and steadied her. Carla looked over at Monique in surprise. Monique shrugged her shoulders and smiled. Carla smiled back and retreated into her own lane.

8 Which of the following story events is a flashback?

F Monique notices the puddles on the track.

G Monique talks with her mother about Carla.

H Monique swerves to avoid the puddle.

J Monique helps Carla regain her balance.

9 Which of the following story details is an example of foreshadowing?

A "*I'll have to watch out for those,* Monique thought."

B "'Runners set!' the official bellowed."

C "Carla looked over at Monique in surprise."

D "Carla smiled back and retreated into her own lane."

Name ______________________________ Date ______________

10 **Which detail in the selection helps you identify the flashback?**

F "Monique stared down the endless track, squinting toward the finish line."

G "At breakfast, she had tried to talk to her mother about Carla."

H "She shoved off, bursting in front of the other runners."

J "Her feet began to skid, but Monique reached over and steadied her."

11 **Which of the following story details foreshadows that Monique will run a fair race?**

A "Monique looked away and tightened her jaw."

B "'Mama, how many times do I need to tell you?'"

C "As much as she hated to admit it, her mother was right."

D "She shoved off, bursting in front of the other runners."

Vocabulary

Read the following questions. Then, choose the best answer.

12 **What is the origin of the word *evidence*?**

F It comes from a Greek word meaning "reason."

G It comes from a Greek word meaning "truth."

H It comes from a Latin word meaning "see."

J It comes from a Latin word meaning "clue."

13 **How is the origin of the word *monologue* reflected in its meaning?**

A A *monologue* is the words spoken by one person.

B A *monologue* is the study of communication.

C A *monologue* is something an actor must memorize.

D A *monologue* is a speech that you see, rather than hear.

14 **In what language does the word *indicate* have its origin?**

F Greek

G Latin

H French

J German

15 **The prefix *pro-* can mean "before." Based on your understanding of word origins, what do you conclude the italic word in this sentence means?**

I read the prologue and went on to read Chapter 1.

A a final chapter

B a logical summary

C an argument in favor of an issue

D words that come before the main part

16 **What is the meaning of the root shared by the words *different* and *differentiate*?**

F to show

G to end

H to carry apart

J to see easily

17 **In what language does the word *conclusion* have its origin?**

A Latin

B Greek

C German

D French

Name ______________________ Date ______________

Grammar

Read the following questions. Then, choose the best answer.

18 Identify the action verb in this sentence:

The twins usually arrive on time for the gym class, but today they are late.

F arrive
G time
H gym
J are

19 What are the principal parts of regular verbs?

A present, past, present participle, past participle
B present, past, future, participle
C present, base, present participle, past participle
D present, past, future, perfect

20 Which is true of regular verbs?

F Their present and present participle have the same form.
G Their past participle ends in *-ing.*
H Their past and past participle have the same form.
J Their present participle ends in *-ed.*

21 Which form of the verb correctly completes this sentence?

Cindy was _______ at the clown.

A smile
B smiles
C smiling
D smiled

22 Which form of the verb correctly completes this sentence?

Yesterday the dress still _______ fifty dollars.

F costs
G cost
H costed
J costing

23 Identify the sentence in which the verb in italics is a linking verb.

A As he walked through the garden, he *smelled* the roses.
B The roses *smelled* like a fragrant, sweet perfume.
C He *saw* several new bushes in the corner by the trellis.
D Some of the bushes *had grown* very tall.

24 In which sentence is the verb in italics used correctly?

F The auctioneer *has spoke* into the microphone.
G She *has put* the chair up for bidding.
H Jamal *bringed* an auction guide with him.
J He *bidded* twice on the chair.

25 Which sentence uses correct subject-verb agreement?

A Among the items were a box of eggs.
B There was only eleven eggs in the box.
C Some of the eggs was broken.
D Gregory and Stuart eat a lot of eggs.

26 Which sentence uses correct subject-verb agreement?

F A nest of robins sits in the tree.
G There is two birds in the next.
H Sandy and Joanne sits near the nest.
J One of the girls scare the birds.

27 Identify the sentence in which the verb in italics is an action verb.

A My mother *is* excited about cooking for my friends.
B Maria *seems* to enjoy the salad.
C Tina *tasted* my mother's pineapple cake.
D Ben *was* late for lunch.

Name ______________________ Date ____________

28 **Which form of the verb correctly completes this sentence?**

Jonathan has ______ an essay about his summer job.

F write
G writed
H wrote
J written

29 **Identify the linking verb in this sentence:**

That movie is enjoyable, but I want to play outside.

A That
B is
C but
D want

Short Answer

Reading Skill: Making Inferences

30 **If you read this sentence in a selection, what inference could you make about how Hope feels?**

Hope's hands began to shake as she approached the edge of the diving board.

____

____

____

31 **If you read this sentence in a selection, what inference could you make about Noah's swimming abilities?**

Noah glided through the water like a duck across a pond.

____

____

____

Literary Analysis

32 **What words or phrases might a character in a book or movie use to indicate that the story is jumping to a scene from the past?**

____

____

____

33 **Imagine that you are reading a story about a football team that loses all of the time. What event might the following story detail foreshadow?**

Our hard work finally paid off. Our coach's usual scowl was replaced with a wide smile. "It's about time you made a play like that. Now you're starting to look like a real team."

____

____

____

Name ______________________________ Date ______________

Essay

Write on a separate sheet of paper.

34 Write a short story in which a detective uses inferences to solve a mystery. Be sure to have the detective use clues along with his or her background knowledge to solve the mystery.

35 Think about a time in your life when you were surprised. Now think about the clues that foreshadowed this surprise event. Write several paragraphs describing these clues and how they foreshadowed the event.

36 Think of a movie or book that contains a flashback. Write several paragraphs describing this flashback and what the flashback tells you about the character that it focuses on.

Name ______________________ Date ______________

Diagnostic Test 2 — Unit 2

Read the passages. Then, answer the questions.

Like modern scientists, ancient astronomers learned a great deal from observing the stars. However, because they did not have the sophisticated instruments of modern astronomers, the ancients made a very important, but incorrect, assumption. For thousands of years, these astronomers believed that the Earth was at the center of the universe.

It was not until 1543 that Nicolaus Copernicus of Poland proposed a strange and intriguing theory: the Earth revolved around the sun. Many found it impossible to accept this sudden, abrupt turnabout from a long-held belief. Earth, as the center of the universe, placed humans in the central role. Copernicus's theories were rejected as false.

In the early 1600s, a crude telescope was invented. In Italy, Galileo Galilei refined the design to make it twenty times stronger than the human eye. Upon first using it, he immediately found undiscovered stars. He also located four moons revolving around Jupiter. He made other discoveries that similarly supported Copernicus's idea that the Earth, infact, does revolve around the sun. However, it wasn't until the late 1600s that the English scientist Sir Isaac Newton had new evidence that finally convinced people that Galileo and Copernicus were correct. "If I have seen further it is by standing upon the shoulders of giants," Newton wrote. Modern astronauts would surely agree.

1 How are ancient and modern astronomy alike?

A Both study the stars.

B Both place humans in the center of the universe.

C Both think the sun revolves around Earth.

D Both reject Newton's theories.

2 How was Galileo's discovery of Jupiter's moons similar to Copernicus's theory?

F Galileo's discovery proved Copernicus's theory impossible.

G Both were rejected as false by scientists of their time.

H Galileo's discovery proved that he misunderstood Copernicus's data.

J Both confirmed that Earth was the center of the universe.

3 How were Copernicus, Galileo, and Newton alike?

A They believed that Earth was at the center of the universe.

B They stood up for their beliefs and changed astronomy.

C They located four moons revolving around Jupiter and Earth.

D They had little evidence to support their theories.

4 How do modern methods of astronomy differ from ancient methods?

F Today's astronomers keep their findings to themselves.

G Today's astronomers know that Earth is the center of the universe.

H Today's astronomers use sophisticated equipment and space travel.

J Today's astronomers rely on what they can see with their eyes.

Name ______________________________ Date ______________

Kayla picked herself up and brushed the dirt from her knees. It was the third time she had fallen from her new racing bike. She was close to tears.

"I know I can do this," she said to herself. "Dinah and Jessica can ride their bikes. My bike isn't that much different from theirs."

She remembered her father's advice. "Focus on the road. Look straight ahead. That will help your balance."

She adjusted the helmet over her black hair and hopped on the bike again. She started slowly, the bike's wheels wobbling down the bike path. Then she gained speed. She had done it!

5 Which of these character traits best describes Kayla in this passage?

A responsible

B determined

C indifferent

D selfish

6 In this passage Kayla is ______.

F an antagonist

G a minor character

H a round character

J a dynamic character

Read the following questions. Then, choose the best answer.

7 Which is an example of verbal irony?

A Nicki, the worst player on the team, scores the winning goal in the state hockey tournament.

B "Nice dress," said the bully to the small girl, whose dress was dirty and stained.

C Shawn stumbles, then falls during his dance routine. His teacher likes his determination and gives Shawn the lead in the recital.

D The villain in the play tries to help the police detectives, but the audience knows she stole the jewels.

8 Which sentence uses a verb in the future tense?

F Doug plays baseball every day after school.

G Doug's sister Darlene goes to all of his games.

H His team will play Concordia High next Friday.

J Doug's team lost the state championship last year.

9 Which sentence describes the action in a past perfect tense verb?

A The action started in the past and ended in the past.

B The action started in the past and continues to the present.

C The action starts at a time in the future and ended at a time in the past.

D The action started in the past or the present and ends at a time to come.

10 Which sentence uses a verb in the past tense?

F Jason lives near the public library.

G Hector will work at the city pool this summer.

H Tamika works at the library during the school year.

J Carla worked at a fast-food restaurant last summer.

11 Which word is spelled correctly?

A pleasent

B boyant

C anonymous

D epologue

Name ______________________________ Date ______________

Reading Skills: Compare and Contrast

Reinforcement 2-9

When you **compare** two people or things, you explain how they are alike. When you **contrast** two people or things, you tell about how they are different. A good tool for comparing and contrasting literature is to ask questions, so you can notice similarities and differences in characters, settings, moods, and ideas. Here are some questions you might ask:

- How is one character different from another?
- How is this story like another that I have read?
- How is this character's experience different from my own experience?

As you read literature, pay attention to dialogue and descriptions of how the characters speak and act. Pay attention to words that compare and contrast characters or events. Examples of words that compare are both, alike, and like. Examples of words that contrast are although, but, while, both, and however.

Example Comparison: Juliet in Romeo and Juliet and Maria in West Side Story are both young women in love.

Example Contrast: Juliet is a girl of noble birth, while Maria is an immigrant.

Read each item. Then, answer the questions.

1. Both Olympic athletes had the patience to work hard to achieve their dreams. They had trained on the race track for years, in all kinds of weather.

   a. What or whom is being compared or contrasted? ______________
   b. Is comparison or contrast being used? ______________
   c. What clues helped you decide whether it was a comparison or a contrast?

   ____
   ____
   ____

2. San Francisco was enjoying weather in the 50s in late January. However, New York City was in the midst of a frosty chill. Mark was glad to be on a plane headed toward a milder climate.

   a. What or whom is being compared or contrasted? ______________
   b. Is comparison or contrast being used? ______________
   c. What clues helped you decide whether it was a comparison or a contrast?

   ____
   ____
   ____

Name ______________________ Date ______________

Reading Skills: Compare and Contrast

Extension 2-9

Comparing City Dwellers

When you read the selection "Animals Among Us," you inferred the effects certain wild animals have on cities and their inhabitants. Some of these effects may be harmless, while others may prove troublesome.

Choose three animals discussed in this selection. Copy the Venn diagram on a separate sheet of paper to compare and contrast the effects of their presence in the city. Write what is true of each kind of animal in the appropriate places in the diagram. Write things that are true of all three animals in the middle. Then, answer the questions.

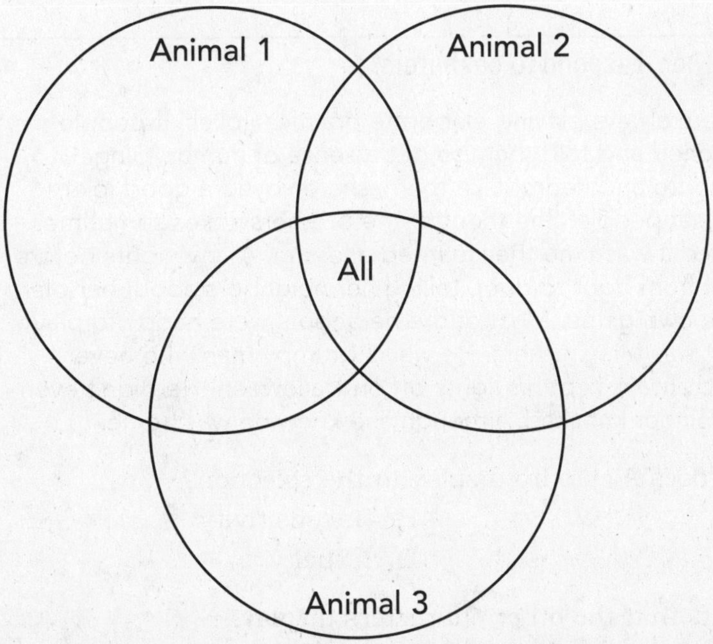

1. Of the animals you chose to compare and contrast, which is the least likely to be a nuisance to the city? Why?

____

____

2. Compared to the other animals you chose, which animal is the most dangerous?

____

____

3. Have any of the animals you chose had a similar effect on the city? Explain.

____

____

____

Name ______________________________ Date ______________

Literary Analysis: Character

Reinforcement 2-10 A

A **character** is a person, or an animal with human traits, who contributes to the action of a story. Character traits are the personal qualities, attitudes, and values that make a character unique. For example, one character may be lazy and untrustworthy, while another is hardworking and dependable.

- **Round characters** are complex, showing many different character traits. For example, a character's actions and dialogue might reveal that, although she is tough and demanding, she can also be sensitive, considerate, and humble.
- **Flat characters** are one-sided, showing just a single trait. For example, the villains in many TV and movie comedies are flat characters. They are portrayed only as "bad guys."

Read the selection. Then, respond to each item.

Alejandro and Pedro were always playing elaborate practical jokes. If people got upset, the boys laughed and told them to get a sense of humor. Ginger lived next door to Alejandro and Pedro. Like them, she enjoyed a good joke, but she didn't like to upset people. She thought the brothers' jokes sometimes went too far. She decided it was time they learned a lesson. A few nights before Halloween, Ginger went from door to door, telling her neighbors about her plan to beat the boys at their own game. Most of the neighbors were happy to play along. The only holdout was Mr. Cruthers. He was a grumpy man who never said hello to anyone and always kept his lights off on Halloween. He didn't even answer the door when Ginger knocked, although she knew he was home.

1. Which character trait does Alejandro display in the selection?

   A. thoughtfulness B. insensitivity
   C. unfriendliness D. cruelty

2. List the character traits that the other characters display.

   Pedro: ______________________________

   Ginger: ______________________________

   Mr. Cruthers: ______________________________

3. Which character(s) would you describe as flat? Explain.

   ____

   ____

   ____

4. Which character(s) would you describe as round? Explain.

   ____

   ____

   ____

Name ____________________ Date __________

Literary Analysis: Characterization

Reinforcement 2-10 B

Character traits are the qualities, attitudes, and values that a character possesses (*forgetful, artistic, honest*). The ways in which an author reveals what a character's traits are is called **characterization.**

Direct Characterization is when the author makes a direct statement about a character's personality or appearance.

Indirect Characterization reveals character's traits by:

- Showing the character's actions
- Presenting the character's words and thoughts
- Describing the character's appearance
- Revealing other characters' words, thoughts, and actions in regards to him or her

Identify each character's trait. Then, explain why it is an example of direct or indirect characterization.

1. Kara's long, brown hair whipped in the wind, her knobby knees green with grass stains from the day's soccer game.

   ____

   ____

2. Meghan's little sister hid under the dining room table when her parents' company came over for dinner.

   ____

   ____

3. Neha thought she was a shoe-in for winning the election for class president. She knew there was no way she could lose.

   ____

   ____

4. Li Qiang has been terrified of roller coasters ever since she went on Kunda-Ka last summer.

   ____

   ____

5. "Ask Chris about your science homework. He always knows the answer!" Jasmine suggested.

   ____

   ____

Name ______________________________ Date ______________

Literary Analysis: Character

Extension 2-10

Character Profile

A doctor might conclude that the cause of Doodle's death in "The Scarlet Ibis" is a congenital heart defect, a heart problem Doodle is born with. Though Doodle's health is certainly fragile, there are other factors that lead to his death. The narrator's behavior toward his brother could be considered a cause of Doodle's death. If the narrator had not run in the rain, forcing Doodle to exert himself to keep up, would Doodle have died?

The narrator's treatment of his brother Doodle is at times harsh and cruel. What motivates the narrator to behave this way? How do the narrator's character traits contribute to Doodle's death? Complete the activities that follow.

1. You can write a character profile of the narrator that provides details for and explains his behavior toward Doodle. Use the chart to gather these specific details about his personality.

Character Trait of the Narrator	How the Trait Influences Doodle's Death

2. Write a character profile that discusses how the narrator's character traits affect his behavior toward Doodle, and ultimately, Doodle's death.

____

____

____

____

____

____

Name ______________________________ Date ______________

Literary Analysis: Point of View

Reinforcement 2-11 A

Point of view is the perspective from which a story is told.

- In **first-person point of view**, the story is told by a character who is in the story and is part of the action. The first-person narrator uses the pronouns *I*, *me*, and *we* when speaking about himself or herself. The reader sees and knows only what the narrator sees and knows.
- In **third-person point of view**, the storyteller is not a character in the story but tells events from the "outside." This narrator can describe the thoughts and actions of any or all of the characters in the story and uses pronouns such as *he*, *she*, and *they* to describe the characters.

Read the story excerpts. Write F-P if the excerpt is told from the first-person point of view. Write T-P if the excerpt is told from third-person point of view.

1. _____ Ted says that being a good magician isn't easy. He and Gina practice their tricks for hours a day. Sometimes they watch themselves in the mirror as they do the tricks. Sometimes they might invite an audience to watch. "The hand is quicker than the eye!" Ted always says.

2. _____ Laura and I were completely silent. We crouched down behind the bushes, afraid to even breathe. Was that really a bear in our woods? What should we do?

3. _____ I watched Mario as he took his time putting on the skates. Why had he told Lola that he could play hockey? I noticed that she hadn't been that impressed. Why did he always have to make up stories? I could tell that Mario was feeling nervous. He was stalling for time, trying to stay off the ice as long as possible.

4. _____ Identical twins Max and Bart used to dress the same way, speak the same way, and go everywhere together. However, ever since they started high school, the boys look quite different. Max dresses in khakis and button-down shirts. Bart wears all black, all the time.

5. _____ "A storm is coming," said Marla. "We'd better get off the beach." Dark clouds were forming, and the wind was getting stronger. Marla, Kara and Grace quickly folded the towels while D. J. called her dad on her cell phone. When Mr. Martin got the call, he was already about to leave to pick up the kids at the lake.

Write On a separate sheet of paper, write a brief paragraph in either first-person or third-person point of view. Exchange papers with a partner and guess which point of view the paragraph is written in.

Name ______________________________ Date ______________

Literary Analysis: Irony

Reinforcement 2-11 B

Irony is the result of a contrast between appearance and reality, meaning and intention, and expectation and outcome.

Verbal Irony	Situational Irony	Dramatic Irony
Words are used to suggest the opposite of what is meant.	What appears to be true to a character is not what the reader or audience knows to be true.	An event occurs that directly contradicts expectations.
↓	↓	↓
A mom comments on her daughter's devil costume and says, "You look like an angel!"	A boy spends hours washing his dog. The dog then rolls in mud.	In Shakespeare's play, *Romeo and Juliet*, Romeo kills himself because he thinks Juliet is dead even though the audience knows she is alive.

Circle the letter that best completes the sentence to form an example of irony. Then, write an alternate ironic ending on the lines provided.

1. **Verbal Irony** Roger just bought a beat-up, rusty car from a used car lot. Eager to show it to his friends, he says . . . ______________________ ______________________	**A.** "The salesman was practically giving it away!" **B.** "Anyone want a ride?" **C.** "It sure is a fixer-upper." **D.** "Isn't it a beauty?"
2. **Situational Irony** A group of friends decides to take a road trip. After hours of packing, they finally leave the driveway and . . . ______________________ ______________________	**A.** argue about the music. **B.** notice they have half a tank of gas. **C.** get a flat tire. **D.** stop for something to eat.
3. **Dramatic Irony** In a movie, a boy spends the whole film working up the courage to ask a certain girl to a dance even though the audience knows . . . ______________________ ______________________	**A.** she already has a date **B.** his best friend is not going to the dance **C.** his mom is a chaperone **D.** he has never been to a dance.

Name ______________________ Date ____________

Literary Analysis: Point of View

Extension 2-11

Writers have at their fingertips a literary device that controls a reader's access to their characters' thoughts, emotions, and motives. While the reader might often know what one character is thinking and feeling, the reader might never be allowed to glimpse at the thoughts of another character. In this way, point of view is a powerful tool that manipulates the reader's connections to the characters in a story.

Read this passage from "Hamadi" by Naomi Shihab Nye.

Susan loved to see how her mother knew every word of every verse without looking at the paper, and her father kept his hands in his pockets and seemed more interested in examining peoples' mailboxes or yard displays than in trying to sing. And Saleh Hamadi—what language was he singing in? He didn't even seem to be pronouncing the words, but humming deeply from his throat. Was he saying, "Om?" Speaking Arabic? Once he caught her looking and whispered, "That was an Aramaic word that just drifted into my mouth—the true language of the Bible, you know, the language Jesus Christ himself spoke."

1. From which point of view is this passage told? Explain.

____

____

2. Hamadi is different from the others. How does the story's point of view add character to Hamadi?

____

____

____

3. Why do you think Naomi Shihab Nye chose to write "Hamadi" using this point of view?

____

____

____

4. Rewrite the passage from "Hamadi" using the first-person point of view.

____

____

____

____

____

Name ______________________________ Date ______________

Listening and Speaking: Oral Interpretation of Literature

Reinforcement 2-12

The best way to present a literary term is to give clear examples of how they are used in a text. You and your group members need to teach the class about how conflict affects a literary work. Remember, the conflict in a literary work is a struggle between two forces. Conflict drives the action of the plot. There are different kinds of conflict.

- In an external conflict, a character is struggling against an outside force, such as another character, nature, or society.
- In an internal conflict, a character is struggling within himself or herself. The struggle is based on desires, beliefs, feelings, or needs.

The resolution, or outcome, of the conflict takes place when the problems have been worked out or when one force in the conflict wins over the other.

Discuss with your group each of the following situations and decide whether each example of conflict is internal or external. Write your decision for each example along with an explanation. For item 4, come up with your own situation as a group that demonstrates conflict. Write that situation and then identify which type of conflict your example represents and why.

1. Two Iditarod racers are sledding through the Alaskan wilderness. Both racers hope to win this year's trophy.

____

2. A hurricane hits a coastal area of the United States. Major floods spread throughout the area. A woman tries to drive her car to higher ground.

____

3. Angela tells a secret to her friend Adam about another friend, Steven. Adam thinks he should tell Steven what Angela said, but he doesn't want to lose Angela's friendship. Adam thinks about the problem for several hours.

____

____

____

____

____

____

Present As a group, choose two of the situations from above and write a possible resolution for each situation on a separate sheet of paper. Then, present the selected conflicts to your classmates, stating whether they are internal or external conflicts, and sharing the two different resolutions that you have written. Discuss how the resolutions serve to resolve the conflicts. Open up the discussion to questions from the audience and be prepared to offer more examples to better their overall understanding of conflict as a key literary term.

Name ______________________ Date ____________

Listening and Speaking: Oral Interpretation of Literature

Extension 2-12

How Does Point of View Affect a Story?

In his short story "The Tell-Tale Heart," Edgar Allen Poe uses the first-person point of view to give the reader complete access to the narrator's thoughts, fears, and actions. As a result, the reader is an intimate witness to the narrator's conflict, which gradually intensifies as the story progresses, building suspense and adding to the eerie mood.

Suppose you retold Poe's short story from a different perspective. Could you make the story just as suspenseful as Poe did? Without using the pronouns I, me, or my, how could you reveal the narrator's thoughts, fears, and actions?

You will work with a group of three to determine how a different perspective alters or enhances a story. You will share your ideas with the class.

1. Choose a scene from "The Tell-Tale Heart." With your group members, rewrite the scene using one of these perspectives: omniscient third-person point of view or limited third-person point of view.

2. After you have rewritten the scene from this different point of view, read it to the class. While you read, ask your audience to think about how this rewritten scene is different from the one in Poe's story. Have your audience decide whether your scene is written in omniscient or limited third-person point of view.

3. Discuss the effects of your group's point of view on character and suspense. Ask your audience the following questions.
   - How did this point of view reveal the narrator's character? Was it more effective or less effective than using the first-person point of view?
   - What did using this point of view achieve that Poe's first-person point of view did not? Explain.
   - Did this scene seem more or less exciting and suspenseful in this point of view or in Poe's first-person point of view? Why?

4. Analyze your own rewritten scene after discussing the effects of your group's point of view on character and suspense. On a separate sheet of paper, write your answers to the above questions from item 3. Each group member should work independently.

5. Review the assessment rubrics for both speaking and listening in your work text. Use these rubrics as a guide to evaluate your group's reading as well as the audience's participation. Write a brief evaluation.

____

____

____

Name ______________________________ Date ______________

Language Coach: Verbs—Simple Tenses

Reinforcement 2-13 A

A **tense** is a form of a verb that shows time of action or state of being. The **present tense** (what is taking place now) is written using the base form of the verb. To change a verb to its past tense, add *–d* or *–ed* to the verb's base form. Sometimes, you will have to double the final consonant or change *y* to *i* before adding *–ed.* To change a verb to its ***future tense,*** use *will* before the base form.

Present Tense	Past Tense	Future Tense
Base Form	Add *–d* or *–ed;* or change *–y* to *i* and add *–ed;* or double the final consonant and add *-ed*	Use will before the base form
I listen you carry he, she, it jogs	I listened you carried he, she, it jogged	I will listen you will carry he, she, it will jog

Write the present, past, and future tense of each verb on the lines provided.

	Present	**Past**	**Future**
1. play	________	________	________
2. pretend	________	________	________
3. live	________	________	________
4. try	________	________	________
5. plan	________	________	________
6. learn	________	________	________

Read the following passage and underline and change each incorrect verb tense. Then label each verb tense change P (present), PT (past tense), or F (future tense).

Space fascinated the human race. The idea of space travel starts long ago. In 1687, Sir Isaac Newton describes the laws of motion. In 1865, Jules Verne creates *From the Earth to the Moon,* the first science-fiction story about space travel. In 1919, Robert Goddard explains the value of rockets. In 1957, the Soviet Union launches *Sputnik I* into orbit. Today, space shuttles will make interplanetary travel possible. Shuttle crews around the world continue the launching of satellites and space telescopes for years to come. Perhaps someday shuttle crews build a space station on another planet.

Name ________________________________ Date ______________

Language Coach: Verbs—Perfect Tenses

Reinforcement 2-13 B

The **tense** of a verb shows the time of an action. The **perfect tense** describes an action that was or will be completed at a certain time. In perfect tenses, the helping verb changes tense. The chart lists the perfect tenses.

Verb Tense	invite (invited)
Present Perfect: action begun in the past that continues up to the present have + past participle	I have invited my friends to the party.
Past Perfect: action begun in the past that ended had + past participle	I had invited my friends to the party, but some couldn't make it.
Future Perfect: action begun in the past or present, completed in the future will have + past participle	By tonight, I will have invited everyone.

Underline the perfect tense verbs in the sentences, and write what tense forms they are.

Example: past perfect Suzie had hoped to win last week's race.

1. ____________ Have you heard of the lost city of Atlantis?
2. ____________ I had not thought about it for years.
3. ____________ Soon I will have read almost everything on the subject.
4. ____________ They say that Atlantis had been a rival of Athens.
5. ____________ There have been many references to this strange place in myths.
6. ____________ Perhaps Atlantis had sunk during an earthquake.
7. ____________ Since then, many adventurers and scholars have looked for it.
8. ____________ By now, they will have searched both seas and oceans.
9. ____________ They will have discovered many lost cities in the process.
10. ____________ No one has ever found evidence of Atlantis's existence.

Name ______________________________ Date ______________

Language Coach: Vowel Sounds in Unstressed Syllables

Reinforcement 2-13 C

In many words, the vowel sounds in one or more certain syllables is not clear. Because these unclear vowel sounds occur in syllables that are not stressed or accented, they can lead to spelling mistakes.

The *i* in *episode,* for example, sounds the same as the *e* for competent. The "uh" sound may be spelled by any vowel, and it may occur in more than one syllable, as in *accompany.*

Study the word list, and note the spelling of vowels in unstressed syllables.

pleasant	bargain	desperate	buoyant	hesitate
syllable	anonymous	benefit	adjourn	epilogue

Circle the letter of the correctly spelled word to fill in the blank.

1. The speech was so fascinating that I took in every ____________.
   A. syllible B. syllable C. sylluble D. sylleble

2. There is a new prescription-drug ____________ for senior citizens.
   A. benafit B. benifit C. benefit D. benufit

3. The plot centered on who had written the ____________ note.
   A. anonamous B. anonmous C. anonimous D. anonymous

4. One should never ____________ to greet a new student in class.
   A. hesatate B. hesitate C. hesutate D. hesetate

5. The holiday shoppers were ____________ to find the hot new toy.
   A. desprate B. desprit C. desparate D. desperate

6. The ____________ was longer than the rest of the book.
   A. epulouge B. epilogue C. epalogue D. epelogue

7. Free public education is our country's greatest ____________.
   A. bargain B. bargin C. bargun D. baragen

8. The ball was ____________ and thus easy to recover from the pond.
   A. bouyent B. bouyunt C. bouyant D. boyint

9. There is nothing more ____________ than a long walk on the beach.
   A. pleasunt B. plesant C. pleasant D. pleasent

Name ______________________________ Date ______________

Language Coach: Choosing the Right Word

Reinforcement 2-13 D

An author's **word choice** refers to his or her selection of particular words to convey meaning and to express specific ideas and attitudes. Writers choose vivid adjectives and verbs to help readers visualize descriptions and actions exactly.

Dull Phrase	**Vivid Phrase**
tall building	eighty-story glass skyscraper in downtown Chicago
tasty chicken	succulent barbecued chicken

Complete each sentence by writing specific and vivid words and phrases in the blanks.

1. The __________ dog __________ down the street.
2. The house with a __________ and __________ is believed to be haunted by a __________.
3. Mrs. Dunderman's __________ always eats __________ for dinner.
4. Troy's __________ was __________ by his little brother, Tyrese.
5. Last week, just after __________, the fire alarm __________.

Replace each phrase below with a more vivid description without using the words provided.

Example: sad movie: the heart-wrenching romantic drama

6. scary ride: ______________________________
7. smart teacher: ______________________________
8. loud child: ______________________________
9. old car: ______________________________
10. tiring game: ______________________________
11. interesting book: ______________________________
12. hard test: ______________________________
13. dirty shoes: ______________________________

Name ______________________ Date ______________

Language Coach: Verbs—Perfect Tenses

Extension 2-13

Authors often use present, past, or future perfect tense to give the reader a better idea of when an action occured or will occur. For example, the use of past perfect tense helps the author organize events or ideas to show that a past action happened before another past action.

Complete the following activities.

Use each verb in the chart to write a sentence in the present, past, or future perfect tenses. Underline the perfect tense verbs in each sentence. One sentence for each tense has been written already.

Verb Tense	Verbs		
	Bring	See	Search
Present Perfect		Chloe has seen volcanoes and geysers erupt on her travels around the world.	
Past Perfect			Before Robin went to the music store, he had searched his entire house for extra guitar strings.
Future Perfect	Once I have completed the move, I will have brought my computer, chair, and file cabinet to my new office.		

Apply In the story "The Scarlet Ibis" from Lesson 2, the author James Hurst frequently uses the past perfect tense when describing the actions of the characters. Underline the sentences you find that use the past perfect tense and write those examples on a separate sheet of paper.

Name ______________________________ Date ______________

Writer's Workshop: Compare-and-Contrast Essay

Reinforcement 2-14

In a **compare-and-contrast** essay, a writer tells about similarities and differences between two or more things. To show these similarities and differences, the writer gives facts and details about each thing. A well-written compare-and-contrast essay includes these elements:

- a topic involving two or more subjects
- subjects that have some important similarities and some important differences
- facts and descriptions that show how the subjects are alike and different
- organizational patterns that helps readers understand the comparison. In block organization, or subject-by-subject organization, the writer presents all the features of one subject and then all the features of the second subject. In point-by-point organization, the writer discusses one point about both subjects and then moves on to a second point.

Read the passage. Then, respond to each item below.

Cats do not mind being left alone during the day. They are so independent, they may not even come when you call them. Dogs, on the other hand, need companionship. They like to play with their owners and can be trained to come, fetch, and beg.

1. Circle the type of organization used in this example.

   block   point-by-point

2. What are the two points of comparison in the example?

   ____

   ____

   ____

3. What could be a third point of comparison between cats and dogs?

   ____

   ____

4. What language is used to signal that two things are being contrasted?

   ____

Create On a separate sheet of paper, write a paragraph in which you compare two animals. Use at least two points of comparison. You may use either block organization or point-by-point organization.

Name ______________________ Date ______________

Writer's Workshop: Compare-and-Contrast Essay

Extension 2-14

Comparing Three or More Related Subjects

So far you have written an essay analyzing the similarities and differences between two related subjects. You can, however, write a compare-and-contrast essay using three, four, or even five related subjects.

Remember that when you wrote a compare-and-contrast essay using two subjects, you organized your points in a clear and concise way. When you compare three or more subjects, you must pay extra attention to the organization of your points because there are more elements involved. You do not want to present your points in a way that would confuse your reader.

Think of a topic in which you can compare three things, such as three sports or activities, three places you have visited, or three items of your choice.

1. Before you write your essay, list facts and details about each subject.

Subject 1: ______	Subject 2: ______	Subject 3: ______
______	______	______
______	______	______
______	______	______
______	______	______

2. Once you know which similarities and/or differences you will write about, choose the block method or the point-by-point method of organization. Which method might be more useful for comparing three or more subjects? Explain.

____

____

____

____

____

3. On a separate sheet of paper, first organize your details using the method you chose. Then, create a Venn diagram for these three subjects. Finally, write your essay. You may wish to volunteer to share your essay with your classmates.

Name ______________________________ Date ______________

End-of-Unit Benchmark Test — Unit 2

Reading Skill: Compare and Contrast

Read the following questions. Then, choose the best answer.

1 **Which of these sentences contains a comparison?**

A Many tourists visit Brazil during the festival known as Carnival.

B Rio de Janeiro is a large city in Brazil, which is in South America.

C Like Rio de Janeiro, São Paulo is a large city on the coast of Brazil.

D People in Brazil speak Portuguese, for Brazil was once a colony of Portugal.

2 **Which of these statements expresses a contrast?**

F The Nile, like the Amazon, is a very long river.

G The Nile is in Africa, while the Amazon is in South America.

H Only some portions of the Nile and the Amazon are easily navigated.

J Both the Nile and the Amazon are important to the people along their banks.

Read the passage. Then, answer the questions.

Most people have heard of Sherlock Holmes, the fictional London detective created by Sir Arthur Conan Doyle. Fewer people know, however, that Doyle borrowed the idea for the brilliant Holmes from American author Edgar Allan Poe. Several decades before Doyle wrote, Poe created Inspector Dupin of Paris, France, a detective who used his amazing intellect to solve puzzling crimes. The very first Sherlock Holmes story, "A Scandal in Bohemia," involves a stolen document in a plot quite similar to the plot of Poe's earlier tale "The Purloined Letter."

3 **What basic comparison does the selection make between Sir Arthur Conan Doyle and Edgar Allan Poe?**

A Both authors wrote detective stories.

B Both were American authors.

C Both authors are little known today.

D Both authors borrowed ideas from other authors.

4 **Which words in the second sentence of the selection express a contrast?**

F *fewer* and *however*

G *however* and *idea*

H *borrow* and *idea*

J *fewer* and *people*

5 **According to the selection, how is the character of Inspector Dupin like the character of Sherlock Holmes?**

A He is French.

B He is very clever.

C He lives in London.

D He is based on a real person.

6 **What similarity or difference between Doyle's and Poe's works does the selection point out?**

F Both works are set in Paris.

G Both works have similar plots.

H "A Scandal in Bohemia" was written before "The Purloined Letter."

J "A Scandal in Bohemia" is fiction, but "The Purloined Letter" is nonfiction.

Name ______________________________ Date ______________

Read the passage. Then, answer the questions.

> Olivia was a hard worker who put in long hours at the plant. Yet she always had a kind word for her fellow workers, from the plant manager to the cleaning staff. Her sunny disposition cheered people up, and coworkers often came to her for advice and assistance. Her brother Franz, on the other hand, would never win any popularity contests. "You ought to stop doing favors for the whole world," he often told his sister, "and start looking out for Number One." Still, Franz worked as hard as Olivia did at the plant. Eager to be promoted, he often agreed to come in on weekends.

7 Which contrast most clearly applies to the characters in the selection?

A Franz is kinder than his sister.

B Franz is smarter than his sister.

C Franz is more trusting than his sister.

D Franz is more selfish than his sister.

8 What is similar about the perspectives of the two characters in the selection?

F Both believe in working hard.

G Both believe in stepping on toes to get ahead.

H Both believe in helping others.

J Both believe in being popular at and away from work.

Literary Analysis

Read the following questions. Then, choose the best answer.

9 Why do writers often create antagonists?

A to serve as the main character

B to create conflict for the main character

C to add suspense to the story

D to develop the strengths and weaknesses of the characters

10 What purpose do the minor characters serve in a story?

F They create the main conflict.

G They are the focus of attention.

H They enrich the narrative and take part in the action.

J They demonstrate the importance of the theme.

11 Which character is most likely to have the fewest personality traits?

A a flat character

B a major character

C a round character

D a dynamic character

12 Who is the narrator in a story with omniscient third-person point of view?

F an all-knowing character who is part of the action

G a character who is part of the action and uses the pronouns *I, me,* and *my*

H an all-knowing observer who can describe everything that happens and can reveal every character's thoughts and feelings

J an observer who views the world through a single character's eyes and reveals only what that character is experiencing

Name ______________________________ Date ______________

Read the passage. Then, answer the questions.

> Leona was a goodhearted, outgoing person, but she did like to gossip. She did not realize that her gossiping could cause problems for others. After all, her gossip was never unkind; she liked to spread the news, not make snide comments about it. One day at the mall, she saw Elise Mondego. Then, at the other end of the mall, she saw Elise's boyfriend, Charley Parks. Smiling broadly, she asked Charley whether he was there to meet Elise. Angrily, Charley stated that Elise had told him that she was visiting her grandmother. The next day, a furious Elise told everyone about Leona's big mouth. Leona learned the dangers of gossip, and from then on she was much more careful about the news she spread.

13 Which of these character traits does Leona display in this selection?

A friendliness

B shyness

C nastiness

D cleverness

14 What sort of character is Charley Parks in this selection?

F flat and static

G flat and dynamic

H round and static

J round and dynamic

15 Which of these character traits does Elise display in this selection?

A honesty

B loyalty

C forgetfulness

D vengefulness

16 What makes Leona a dynamic character in the selection?

F She is a basically good person with one flaw.

G She has a lively personality.

H She learns a lesson and changes as a result.

J She speaks to more than one character.

Read the passage. Then, answer the questions.

The New House

Arlen was impressed by the new house. He especially liked the high gables on the second floor and the large porch that ran along the front of the house. "I'd love to live in a house like that," he thought to himself.

From the start, Eva considered the house an awful monstrosity, way too big for the small plot of land on which it stood. "It's like an elephant on a postage stamp," she told herself, though she did not share her thoughts with Arlen. She hated large, gabled houses and always would, recalling the dreary summers that she spent at Old Pines.

17 What is the point of view of the selection "The New House"?

A first-person, narrated by Arlen

B third-person, limited to the thoughts and impressions of a single character

C first-person, narrated by Eva

D third-person, providing the thoughts and impressions of each character

18 What sort of character is Eva in this selection?

F flat and static

G flat and dynamic

H round and static

J round and dynamic

Name ______________________ Date ____________

Read the passage. Then, answer the questions.

Our Farm

Our farm was on Stone Church Road near the parkway. I was very upset when my parents sold it, but Dad said the buyers made him an offer he couldn't refuse. Mom agreed with the decision. "We're not getting any younger, Johnny," she told me. "And the price they offered was a good one."

19 What is the point of view of the selection "Our Farm"?

A third person, providing the thoughts and impressions of every character

B first person, narrated by Johnny

C third person, limited to the thoughts and impressions of only one character

D first person, narrated by Dad

20 Which pronouns in the selection "Our Farm" help indicate the point of view?

F *my, him,* and *he*

G *our, we,* and *they*

H *our, I,* and *me*

J *him, he,* and *we*

Read the passage. Then, answer the questions.

The sneer is gone from Casey's lip, his teeth are clenched in hate;
He pounds with cruel violence his bat upon the plate;
And now the pitcher holds the ball, and now he lets it go,
And now the air is shattered by the force of Casey's blow.

Oh, somewhere in this favored land the sun is shining bright,
The band is playing somewhere, and somewhere hearts are light:
And somewhere men are laughing, and somewhere children shout,
But there is no joy in Mudville—mighty Casey has struck out.

—from "Casey at the Bat" by Ernest L. Thayer

21 Which technique best contributes to the poem's humorous effect?

A using irony so that readers are surprised to learn what happens at the end

B combining two points of view in an unusual way

C including a character with silly personality traits

D describing a common situation from an unusual perspective

22 What is the point of view in the poem "Casey at the Bat"?

F first-person, narrated by Casey

G first-person, narrated by a sportswriter

H third-person, narrated by an all-knowing observer

J third-person, narrated by a person who views events through Casey's eyes

Name ______________________________ Date ______________

Grammar

Read the following questions. Then, choose the best answer.

23 How do you form the future tense of regular verbs?

A Leave the base form as it is.

B Use *will* before the base form.

C Use *have* before the base form.

D Add *-d* or *-ed* to the base form.

24 Which sentence uses a verb in the future tense?

F Angela usually goes to the mall every Saturday.

G Angela will probably go to the mall next Saturday.

H Since October, Angela has gone to the mall every Saturday.

J By tomorrow, Angela will have gone to the mall every Saturday in October.

25 How do you form perfect tenses of verbs?

A Use the helping verb *will* and the base form of the verb.

B Use a form of the helping verb *be* and the past participle of the verb.

C Use a form of the helping verb *have* and the present participle of the verb.

D Use a form of the helping verb *have* and the past participle of the verb.

26 Which verb correctly completes this sentence by using the future perfect tense?

By the end of the week, you ______ the entire book.

F had read

G have read

H will be reading

J will have read

27 What tense is the italic verb in this sentence?

Kristin has *boiled* the water for tea.

A present

B past

C present perfect

D past perfect

28 Which sentence uses a verb in the past tense?

F My dog ate all of his food.

G My dog has eaten all of his food.

H My dog always eats all of his food.

J By this afternoon, my dog will have eaten all of his food.

Spelling

Read the following questions. Then, choose the best answer.

29 In which sentence is the italic word spelled correctly?

A Sally is a *mischievious* child.

B The bright red banner was very *noticible.*

C My sister is applying to *college.*

D I will meet you at the new *resteraunt.*

30 Which word correctly completes the following sentence?

My brother is very good at ______.

F geometry

G geomitry

H geomotry

J geomatry

Name ______________________________ Date ______________

Short Answer

Reading Skill: Compare and Contrast

31 Write a sentence that makes a comparison.

32 Write a sentence that states a contrast.

Literary Analysis

33 In terms of flat, round, static, and dynamic, which combination makes for the most complex character?

34 What is the point of view of a story?

Essay

Write on a separate sheet of paper.

35 You are planning a summer trip to a state that is far from your home state. Should you travel by car or by plane? Write a comparison-and-contrast essay in which you examine the similarities and differences between the two methods of travel.

36 Think of a character who made a strong impression on you. It could be a character you encountered in a TV show or film, or it could be someone in a book or story. On a separate sheet of paper, write a one-paragraph profile of this character.

37 Sometimes events do not turn out the way we expected them to. On a separate sheet of paper, write a short story that ends in situational irony. Include details at the beginning of the story that will lead to an ironic ending.

Name ______________________ Date ____________

Diagnostic Test 1

Unit 3

Read the passage. Then, answer the questions.

Over the centuries, wigs have been popular accessories in various cultures. In ancient Egypt, both men and women of the nobility wore wigs on special occasions. These wigs were made of human hair and were usually adorned with flowers and gold ornaments. There are even paintings of dead Egyptians wearing wigs. Egyptians believed that everything needed in the afterlife must be buried with the dead.

In ancient Rome, blond hair was preferred to dark hair. Therefore, many women wore wigs made from the hair of blond captives.

Through the years, wigs went in and out of style, often on the whims of a king or queen. For example, King Louis XIII of France went bald at an early age, so he wore a wig of long, curly locks.

In the 1700s, wigs for women were designed with support wires and powder that raised the hair three feet into the air. Some wigs included cages of live birds or models of sailing ships. Only a very agile woman could move easily in such a headpiece without tipping over!

1 What is the main idea of this selection?

A Ancient Egyptians and Romans wore wigs.

B Women who wore very tall wigs had to be agile.

C Wigs have been a popular accessory throughout history.

D Wig styles were sometimes determined by kings and queens.

2 Which of the following details best supports the main idea?

F "Over the centuries, wigs have been popular accessories for various cultures."

G "In ancient Egypt, both men and women of the nobility wore wigs on special occasions."

H "Egyptians believed that everything needed in the afterlife must be buried with the dead."

J "Only a very agile woman could move easily in such a headpiece without tipping over!"

3 Which of the following statements could be added to help support the main idea?

A Archeaologists have found many Egyptian artifacts.

B Kings and queens had much influence over popular opinion.

C Many people are willing to sacrifice comfort for the sake of fashion.

D In colonial America, wealthy men often wore wigs.

4 If the main idea of a selection is not directly stated, it is—

F implied

G nonexistent

H meaningless

J unreasonable

5 Supporting details—

A add information about the main idea

B identify the most important idea

C suggest what a selection is about

D restate the main idea

Name ______________________________ Date ______________

Read the passage. Then, answer the questions.

> Depending on the railway car you were riding in, traveling by train in the late 1800s could be a grand experience or an awful one. If you were in a Pullman train car, you could expect considerable luxury and a great deal of service. A Pullman car boasted leather seats, lamps with silk shades, chandeliers, and gourmet food. However, only the wealthy could afford such a ride. For most passengers, trains provided a different experience. A long train ride was often a cheerless journey, due to hard seats, terrible food, and bad smells.

6 What kind of organization did the author use for this passage?

F problem and solution

G compare and contrast

H chronological

J cause and effect

7 Why does the writer include a description of a regular train car?

A to show how Pullman and his train cars became successful

B to criticize a passenger for riding in it rather than a Pullman car

C to demonstrate how Pullman cars were similar to regular cars

D to contrast its poor conditions with the comfort of a Pullman car

Read the passage. Then, answer the questions.

> Last night I attended the varsity baseball game. As usual, the players stomped the other team, pushing their winning streak up to ten games. However, our stands were only half full.
>
> When football season comes around, everyone makes it to the games. The basketball team also plays to a packed gymnasium. But for some reason, the baseball team never receives this support.
>
> We owe it to these baseball players to go to their games. They practice hard, and their hard work shines through. Kyle Rodder's pitching has been amazing. Some of the plays that Marcus Garrett makes at shortstop do not seem humanly possible. And Rod Folley regularly sends the ball out to the parking lot.
>
> So gather some of your friends, and come out to the ballpark. The only downside is that your throat may hurt from all of the cheering that you will do!

8 This passage is an example of ______ writing.

F expository

G chronological

H persuasive

J humorous

9 Which word best describes the tone of this passage?

A amused

B vengeful

C supportive

D depressed

Name ________________________ Date ____________

Reading Skills: Identifying Main Ideas and Supporting Details

Reinforcement 3-2

The major topic of each selection that you read or write is the main idea. Most writers convey their main idea in an introduction and use related details to support it in paragraphs that follow.

Main ideas aren't always stated directly. Sometimes they are **suggested** or **implied.** To find main ideas that are not stated, you have to read the supporting details carefully.

Read the following article. Then, answer the questions that follow.

The zoo got a new member on Friday when a baby penguin hatched. Zookeepers had been expecting the hatching for several weeks.

"I'm just glad that the parents can stop worrying about an egg," said head zookeeper Willa Lewis.

The male chick hatched at 7:45 A.M. on a plastic iceberg in the penguin tank. He wobbled up to his parents, and after a brief greeting, zookeepers took him to be examined. Zookeepers decided to name him Zeki, which is a Turkish name meaning "clever." He weighed 4 ounces and was given a clean bill of health.

"Everyone at the zoo is very happy that he has arrived," said Lewis. "Penguins are one of our favorite attractions and hopefully lots of people will come to see our newest addition."

1. What is the main idea?

____

____

2. Is the main idea implied, suggested, or stated directly? Explain.

____

____

3. What are the supporting details?

____

____

____

4. Which detail is interesting but doesn't support the main idea?

____

____

5. What would be a good title for this article? Explain why you chose this title.

____

____

Name ______________________________ Date ______________

Reading Skills: Identifying the Main Idea and Supporting Details

Extension 3-2

The main idea of a text is usually stated in the first paragraph and supported by details in later paragraphs. When the main idea is not stated, you have to work backwards. First identify details that all seem to be related. Then make an inference based on the details to identify the main idea.

Read the following details.

Paulo rides his bicycle almost every day.
When sent on an errand, Paulo takes his bicycle.
Paulo will turn down a game of catch with his friends in order to ride his bicycle.

What main idea would these details suggest?

Example answer: Paulo greatly enjoys riding his bicycle.

Write the main idea based on the details.

1. Details:
   - Grizzly bears can grow about 10 feet long and weigh over 1,000 lbs.
   - Polar bears range from about 6 to 10 feet long and can weigh about 1,700 pounds.
   - Black bears are approximately 5 to 6 feet long.

   Main Idea: ______________________________

2. Details:
   - My friend, Clarissa, helped my family when our house burned down.
   - When other kids criticized me, Clarissa defended me.
   - Many nights Clarissa and I stay up late discussing our feelings.

   Main Idea: ______________________________

3. Details:
   - Tsunamis are rare events that follow an underwater earthquake.
   - A Tsunami can travel about 500 miles per hour in deep water.
   - Due to the dangers of Tsunamis, the Pacific Tsunami Warning Center was established in 1949.

   Main Idea: ______________________________

4. Details:
   - Our school took a vote, and decided on a dance.
   - An End of the Year Dance Committee was created.
   - The school announced the date and location of the dance.

   Main Idea: ______________________________

Name ______________________________ Date ______________

Vocabulary: Synonyms and Antonyms

Reinforcement 3-3

Synonyms and **antonyms** are terms that describe how the meanings of two words are related. A word that is a synonym of another word has nearly the same meaning as that word. A dictionary definition of a word might give its synonyms.

mean: adj., nasty, unkind, cruel, callous

A word that is an antonym of another word has a meaning that is the opposite of that word. Not every word has an antonym. Some words add prefixes like *un-* or *in-* to reverse the meaning of a root word.

capable (able to do) + in- *means* (not able to do) **incapable**

Circle the words that are synonyms in each sentence.

1. Some days my sensible friend Gloria isn't always level-headed.
2. It's hot and humid today, but not as muggy as yesterday.
3. She was accused of prevaricating, but she was not lying.
4. Amber was furious about her broken project, but didn't want to show her anger.

Underline the words that are antonyms.

5. Those two have remained friends, even though they were once bitter enemies.
6. The kitchen was spacious, while the den was cramped.
7. Some of the songs are traditional and others are modern.
8. Try to focus on your goal and not be distracted by unimportant details.

Supply either the synonym for the underlined word or the antonym for the initial word, in the spaces provided below.

9. *Consistent* means "same," so *inconsistent* means ______________.
10. *Correct* means "right," so ______________ means wrong.
11. *Connected* means "linked," so *unconnected* means ______________.
12. *Earned* means "gained by work," so ______________ means *not deserved*.
13. *Relevant* means "pertinent," so ______________ means not *pertinent*.
14. *Replaceable* means "returnable," so *irreplaceable* means ______________.

Name ______________________ Date __________

Vocabulary: Synonyms and Antonyms

Extension 3-3

Knowing the synonyms and antonyms of words can provide thoughtful writers with powerful vocabulary tools. Instead of using simple, vague words your writing, you can employ colorful words with more precise meanings. For example, instead of using the word *good*, you could use words such as *beneficial*, *superb*, or *tasty*, depending on the context. Instead of *bad*, you could say *detrimental*, *abysmal*, and *disgusting*. Remember, there are slight variations in meaning to all these synonyms and antonyms.

Look at the following sentence as an example.

Roberto was a nice man, but his brother was mean.

By adding synonyms and an antonym, the sentence conveys far more meaning.

Roberto was an affable man, but his brother was malicious.

Read the following sentences. Add synonyms and antonyms to improve the sentences. Note that it is easier to compare and contrast using synonyms and antonyms.

1. Climbing the mountain should have been easy, but the weather made it hard.

____

____

2. At first the news was sad, but after other reports came in, everyone grew happy.

____

____

3. The horse proved that he was strong despite the cold conditions.

____

____

4. The car was dirty, but after much scrubbing, it came out clean.

____

____

5. The landscape in front of them seemed pretty, although the road ahead would soon be ugly.

____

____

Name ________________________________ Date ______________

Literary Analysis: Expository Writing

Reinforcement 3–4

Expository writers use four main organizational methods in their writing. Signal words can help you identify and follow these different methods.

Organizational Method	Signal Words
Cause and effect	because, since, as a result of, cause, effect, so, affected, factor
Chronological	first, next, last, finally, step 1 (2, 3, etc.), next week, yesterday, before, after
Compare and Contrast	also, like, similarly, unlike, on the other hand, in contrast
Problem and Solution	problem, difficulty, issue, challenge, solution, in response, as an alternative, method

Read this excerpt from "Sleep, It's Healthy."

Since the beginning of time, sleep has been an important factor in maintaining good health. While people sleep, they refuel their bodies and minds to help them through the next day. Many people do not get the proper amount of sleep, however, and this has a negative effect on their health.

During the day our bodies and minds consume a great deal of energy. Sleep recharges our bodies and minds, giving our bodies and minds a chance to recover the energy that we have lost. We wake up feeling refreshed because, while we sleep, our brains do not need to focus and our muscles can relax.

1. Circle signal words that identify the organizational method. Name that method.

Method: ________________________________

Write an example sentence for each method of organization. Use at least one signal word for each example. Underline the signal words.

2. Cause and Effect ________________________________

____

3. Chronological ________________________________

____

4. Compare and Contrast ________________________________

____

5. Problem and Solution ________________________________

____

Name ______________________________ Date ____________

Literary Analysis: Expository Writing

Extension 3-4

Graphic Organization

In expository writing, information can be organized to show cause-and-effect relationships. The following graphic organizers can be used to visualize these relationships.

- Two-column Chart: This chart helps you see which events are causes and then link those events to the effects they create.

Cause	Effect

- Flow Chart: This series of connected boxes helps you track multiple causes and effects.

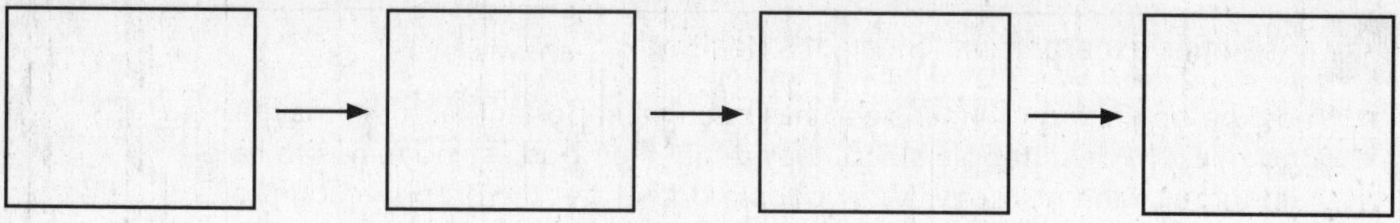

Complete the activities below on organizing expository writing.

1. Read the following excerpt, *How the Power Is Sent to the Wheels*, from "What Makes a Car Run." Then, choose the graphic organizer above that best displays the cause-and-effect relationships in the passage. Complete the graphic organizer on a separate sheet of paper and explain your choice.

   The up-and-down motion of the pistons produces power. However, to move a car forward, the up-and-down motion has to be changed to a turning or spinning motion. Piston rods connect the pistons to the backbone of the engine, the crankshaft (KRANK shaft). As the pistons move up and down, they move the piston rods. The piston rods then turn the crankshaft. The crankshaft changes the up-and-down motion to a spinning motion. As the crankshaft turns, it spins the flywheel. In most cars, the spinning power is carried to the rear wheels that move the car.

2. The flow chart structure can also organize problems-and-solutions and inferences, simply by changing the symbols in-between the boxes. In the space below, demonstrate how the flow chart can be used to organize problem-and-solutions or inferences.

Name ______________________________ Date ______________

Literary Analysis: Persuasive Writing

Reinforcement 3-5 A

Persuasive writing attempts to convince audiences to share the writer's opinion. It uses several techniques, including the three below.

- **Opinions:** Writers share their own opinions. This invites audiences to decide if they feel the same way or if they can imagine themselves feeling that way.
- **Emotional Appeal:** Writers use language that invites readers to feel angry, scared, excited, proud, hopeful, and so on.
- **Facts:** Writers provide factual information to support and make opinions more credible.

Read the following excerpt from "America the Not-So-Beautiful" by Andrew A. Rooney and respond to the items that follow.

Next to saving stuff I don't need, the thing I like to do best is throw it away. My idea of a good time is to load up the back of the car with junk on a Saturday morning and take it to the dump. There's something satisfying about discarding almost anything. Throwing things out is the American way. We don't know how to fix anything and anyone who does know how is too busy to come so we throw it away and buy a new one. Our economy depends on us doing that. The trouble with throwing things away is, there is no "away" left.

1. What personal opinion does the writer share about throwing things away?

____

____

____

2. What emotion does the writer appeal to with the following sentence? "Throwing things out is the American way." How does this help to advance the writer's position?

____

____

____

____

3. Does the word *junk* carry a positive or a negative connotation? ______________
What word could the writer use to create a positive or neutral connotation?
Positive: ______________ Neutral: ______________

4. Does the writer support his opinions with any facts? If not, what facts could the writer add to make his opinion believable?

____

____

____

Name ________________________________ Date ______________

Literary Analysis: Propaganda

Reinforcement 3-5 B

Propaganda is a form of persuasion that can be positive or negative. Three popular forms of propaganda include the *bandwagon technique, glittering generalities,* and *testimonials.*

Bandwagon technique

- tries to convince you that everyone else is doing it
- *"Don't be the last on your block to try it!"*

Glittering generalities

- uses statements that have no real meaning, but sound positive.
- *"Buy the best for less!"*

Testimonials

- stories, quotations, or personal experiences of individuals used to make a product or idea sound worthwhile.
- *"My hair has never looked better thanks to Shampoozle!" says Chantelle, international supermodel*

Circle the type of propaganda each advertisement uses. Then write your own slogan using the same form of propaganda on the lines provided.

1. A cereal box's slogan is "So Good, You'll Feel Great!

   a. bandwagon technique
   b. glittering generalities
   c. testimonials

   ____

   ____

2. Marge Renfro says, "she'll never have to clean again," now that she uses XYZ cleaning product.

   a. bandwagon technique
   b. glittering generalities
   c. testimonials

   ____

   ____

3. *Headache Be Gone* is doctor recommended and endorsed by the Horrible Headache Association.

   a. bandwagon technique
   b. glittering generalities
   c. testimonials

   ____

   ____

4. A group of hip teens jamming to music in a convertible pull up next to a guy on an old bicycle. "How do you ride?"

   a. bandwagon technique
   b. glittering generalities
   c. testimonials

   ____

   ____

Name ______________________________ Date ______________

Literary Analysis: Understanding Tone

Reinforcement 3-5 C

The **tone** of a literary work reflects the author's attitude toward the subject and the characters. It can often be described in a single word (*informal, friendly, or serious*). An author establishes tone through descriptive details, sentence structure, and creating specific feelings using word choice. Word choice is also known as **diction.**

A **denotation** is a word's definition. A **connotation** is a shaded meaning of a word that affects different people in different ways.

(positive connotation)
thrifty

frugal → *careful in the management of money* (denotation)

miserly
(negative connotation)

Underline the words and details in each passage that suggest the author's tone. Then circle the letter that best describes the overall tone of each passage and explain if the author establishes tone using denotations or connotations, or both.

1. "Downtown San Francisco became alien and cold, and the streets I had loved in a personal familiarity were unknown lanes that twisted with malicious intent."
   —*I Know Why the Caged Birds Sing* by Maya Angelou

   a. indifferent **b.** energetic **c.** angry **d.** lonely

   ____

   ____

   ____

2. "It is difficult to escape the influence of television. If you fit the statistical average by the age of 20 you will have been exposed to at least 20,000 hours of television. You can add 10,000 hours for each decade you have lived after the age of 20. The only things Americans do more than watch television are work and sleep."
   —*The Trouble with Television* by Robert MacNeil

   a. passionate **b.** critical **c.** humorous **d.** informative

   ____

   ____

   ____

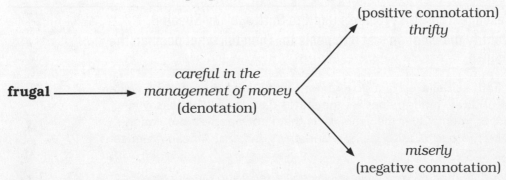

Name ______________________________ Date ______________

Literary Analysis: Persuasive Writing

Extension 3-5

In persuasive writing, writers use **emotional appeals** to appeal to both positive emotions, such as pride, and to negative emotions, such as fear.

Tone is the author's attitude toward his or her audience and subject. It can change throughout a piece of writing. In persuasive writing, the tone at the end of a piece is often the most urgent, because the writer often asks the audience to decide or to take action.

Read this passage from "On Women's Right to Suffrage" by Susan B. Anthony. Identify the emotion that it appeals to. Then tell what position the author is arguing.

The Founding Fathers believed in a government that would promote the welfare of its people. Curiously, though, they let the states decide who had a say in running that government. Over the years, laws that kept people from voting were endured by the poor, Catholics, non-Christians, Indians, African Americans, and women.

Wyoming allowed women to vote while it was still a territory. Other territories and states let women vote in local elections. Finally, one by one, states started to let women take part in elections. Women even began to hold elected office. Still, it was not until 1920 that they could vote everywhere in the United States.

It took many years and various changes in our laws to give all adult citizens the right to vote. We should all have a downright feeling of pride that we can vote. That right gives us the ability to direct the course of our own lives and that of our country's history.

1. Emotional Appeal:

____

2. Position:

____

3. What does the author want readers to think or do about voting rights? How does her tone reflect this? Identify language in the final paragraph that creates the tone.

____

____

____

Apply On a separate sheet of paper, write a persuasive paragraph on your views about women's right to suffrage. Identify the emotional appeal and tone you used in your paragraph using support from your paragraph.

Name ______________________ Date ____________

Listening and Speaking: Delivering a Persuasive Speech

Reinforcement 3-6

A persuasive speech requires special preparation and delivery. Proper planning can simplify the task of convincing the audience of your ideas.

The first step is selecting a topic that is not too broad or unfocused for a short speech. Decide the key points you want to make. Find facts, visual elements, and details that support your ideas. Above all, practice delivering your speech. Judge it as if you were in the audience.

List five possible topics for your persuasive speech below. Use the questions on the right to help you pick one of the five topics. Then, circle the topic you choose to speak about.

Possible Topics:
1. ______________
2. ______________
3. ______________
4. ______________
5. ______________

- Which topic will be most interesting to the majority of students?
- Can I support my opinions on this topic with facts?

Use the graphic organizer below to help prepare supporting details for your persuasive speech. Balance the number of opinions and facts so that your speech is more believable. Then, answer the questions that follow.

Opinions	Facts

6. What tone will your speech have? Explain. ______________________

____

7. What kind of visual aids can you use to support your speech? Explain.

____

____

____

Name ______________________ Date ______________

Listening and Speaking: Delivering a Persuasive Speech

Extension 3-6

A persuasive speech is designed to cause an audience to respond. As the speaker, you want your audience to be convinced to take action or agree with your opinion. You need to consider who your audience is, choose a clear position, and support that position with convincing information and facts. Use the chart below to successfully create your persuasive speech.

Read the following chart headings and suggestions. Provide the information called for in each element of the persuasive speech.

Topic • Choose one of the given topics or create your own.	• Should people on skateboards, roller-blades, and bicycles, use the sidewalks on school grounds? • How late should eighth graders be allowed to stay up on a Saturday night?
Possible Audience • Who will hear your speech? • Who is likely to agree or disagree?	
Position • What opinion will you be presenting? • Will you present more than one position?	
Key Points • Cite at least three reasons for your opinion.	
Information and Facts • Supporting evidence • Facts, quotes, anecdotes	
Possible Visual Elements • Pictures, illustrations, charts, or artwork	
Possible Form of Organization • Opening, supporting statements, and summary	

Name ______________________________ Date ______________

Language Coach: Adjectives, Articles, and Adverbs

Reinforcement 3-7 A

Several parts of speech allow writers to modify, or tell more about, the main parts of their sentences.

- **Adjectives,** including the **articles** *a, an,* and *the,* tell about or describe nouns. Adjectives can answer the questions *What kind, Which One, How Many, How Much,* and *Whose.*
- **Adverbs** add meaning to verbs, adjectives, or other adverbs. They often end with the suffix *-ly.* Adverbs can answer the questions *When, Where, In What Manner,* and *To What Extent.*

Underline the adjectives in each sentence, including the articles *a, an,* and *the.* Circle the words they modify.

1. The young girl dropped her ice cream cone.
2. There are five jars on the shelf.
3. Did you speak to the newspaper reporter?
4. I watched a tiny fly get eaten by a spotted bullfrog.
5. The hungry boy ate four hamburgers.

Underline the adverbs in each sentence below. Then, on each line, write the question the adverb answers—*Where, When, In What Manner,* and *To What Extent.*

6. Today I am going to the fair with my friends. ______________________________
7. The plate went crashing to the floor. ______________________________
8. The long column of soldiers marched rapidly through the pass. ______________
9. Jed's experiment went horribly wrong. ______________________________
10. Lights flashed outside. ______________________________

Apply Complete the paragraph below by adding adjectives and adverbs.

A ____________ tree came down in the recent storm. The tree ____________ crushed a power line. The houses on Henry's block were left without electricity. Henry quickly called the ____________ company. The repair crews were ____________ busy. It took them a ____________ time to come and fix the power lines. The power was ____________ restored.

Name ______________________________ Date ______________

Language Coach: Comparative and Superlative Forms

Reinforcement 3-7 B

Adjectives and adverbs are used to make comparisons. The **comparative form** is used to compare *two* people or things. The **superlative form** is used to compare *more than two* people or things.

Positive	Comparative	Superlative	Rule
sweet near	sweeter nearer	sweetest nearest	Add *–er* and *–est* to most one-or-two syllable words.
artistic easily	more artistic more easily	most artistic most easily	Use more or most (and less or least) with most adverbs ending in *–ly* and modifiers with three or more syllables.
good, well bad, badly many, much little	better worse more less	best worst most least	Memorize the irregular forms for some adjectives and adverbs.

Underline the form of the adjective or adverb that correctly completes each sentence. Write (C) for comparative or (S) for superlative in the space provided.

1. Lisa is (taller, tallest) than her brother. ____________
2. Do you know the (later, latest) score of the game? ____________
3. My grade was (worse, worst) than my last one. ____________
4. I like pizza (better, best) than tacos. ____________
5. Which part of the test did you complete (more, most) quickly? ____________
6. Ryan throws a baseball (harder, hardest) than Nick. ____________
7. Nate is the (fast, fastest) runner I've ever seen! ____________
8. This is the (happier, happiest) day of my life! ____________
9. I just gave the (worse, worst) speech of my life! ____________
10. Marvin earned his (good, best) score in today's meet. ____________
11. This bracelet is (less, least) costly than the one in the other store. ____________
12. The Drama Club has (more, most) members than the Science Club. ____________

Name ______________________________ Date ______________

Language Coach: Modifiers

Reinforcement 3-7 C

A **modifier** is an adjective or adverb word, phrase, or clause that changes a noun, verb, or entire sentence by adding information.

When a modifier is placed too far away from the word it modifies, it is called a **misplaced modifier.**

Incorrect: Lucy studied for her biology test diligently.
Correct: Lucy *studied diligently* for her biology test.

When a modifier has no subject or the doer of the phrase is not stated, it is called a **dangling modifier.**

Incorrect: Although nearly finished, we left the play early
Correct: After eating her breakfast, *Nell* missed the bus.

Without changing the meaning, rewrite each sentence so that there are no misplaced modifiers. Write the new sentence on the line provided.

1. Taz and Linus sang along to Travis's guitar loudly.

____

2. Sizzling on the grill, Taz smelled the chicken.

____

3. He barely threw that ball thirty feet.

____

4. A dog appeared in my dreams that sang like an angel.

____

5. I was told that I won the scholarship by my professor.

____

Rewrite the following sentences to eliminate the dangling modifiers.

6. To raise a good dog, patience is useful.

____

7. After eating the dinner, the kitchen was left.

____

Name ______________________________ Date ______________

Language Coach: Prepositions and Prepositional Phrases

Reinforcement 3-7 D

A **preposition** is a word that relates the noun or pronoun following it to another word in the sentence (see chart below). A **prepositional phrase** begins with a preposition and ends with a noun or pronoun (*in the gymnasium, during the assembly*).

Location				Time	Other Relationships
above	below	inside	past	after	about
across	beside	into near	through	as	despite
against	between	off	to toward	before	except for
along	beyond	on	under	during	like
among	by	out	up	since	of
around	down	outside	within	until	per
at	from	over			than
behind	in				with, without

Underline the prepositional phrases in each sentence. Some sentences contain more than one phrase. Then, rewrite the sentence using at least one different prepositional phrase.

Example: My brother walked near the park.
My brother walked *into the movie theatre.*

1. From the meeting we strolled into the restaurant.

____

2. We listened intently throughout the manager's presentation.

____

3. A group of students demonstrated in front of the building.

____

4. The sound of falling rain can be very soothing.

____

5. At dawn we attempted to cross the river.

____

6. The investigators from the police station found evidence under the bridge.

____

Name ______________________ Date ____________

Language Coach: Modifiers

Extension 3-7

Adjectives and **adverbs** allow writers to create more vivid pictures of people, places, ideas, objects, and actions. **Prepositions** and **prepositional phrases** allow them to be more specific in telling what happens where and when. **Comparative** and **superlative forms** allow writers to insert their preferences or priorities in the text. Writing that effectively uses these parts of speech becomes more interesting and informative to readers.

Read this passage. Circle the adjectives, underline the articles, double underline the prepositional phrases and draw a box around the prepositions.

But, what is the real reason for eyebrows? Most scientists believe the primary purpose is to keep moisture out of the eyes. The arched shape of our eyebrows and the direction of the hair growth help to divert rain and sweat to the sides of the face. In addition, our brows catch snow, dust, and other small debris. This may have given early humans a slight edge in the fight for survival. Someone looking for shelter or trying to outrun a predator would have had a distinct advantage if salty, irritating sweat were diverted from the eyes. Today, humans don't depend on eyebrows for survival, but our brows still perform the useful function of helping to keep our vision clear.

Use the above paragraph to complete the following activities.

1. Choose a sentence and rewrite it, adding two adverbs.

____

____

2. Choose a sentence and rewrite it, adding a comparative form.

____

____

3. Choose a sentence and rewrite it, adding a superlative form.

____

____

4. Tell how each of the words you added changed the meaning of the sentence.

____

____

____

____

Name ______________________________ Date ______________

Writer's Workshop: Cause-and-Effect Essay

Reinforcement 3-8

As you shape your writing, you'll need an organizer that fits the information. In addition to a two-column cause-and-effect chart, you can use the following alternative organizers.

Cause/ Effect	Organizer Layout
For **many causes/single effect,** use a web with several cells on a top row and one cell below.	Cause → Effect; Cause → Effect; Cause → Effect
For **single cause/many effects,** use a web with a single cell on the top row and several cells below.	Effect → Cause; Effect → Cause; Effect → Cause
For a **chain of causes and effects,** use a sequence organizer that links several cells with arrows in chronological order.	Cause → Effect → Cause → Effect

Read each situation. Identify the best kind of organizer on the lines provided. Then, create and complete the organizer on a separate sheet of paper.

1. Jorge recorded the results of his experiment on sleep deprivation on the campus bulletin board. The same week, a reporter from the school newspaper wrote an editorial calling for a later start to school. Concerned parents had also recently met with the Board of Education to push for less homework. As a result of these many factors, a committee was created to consider ways to increase sleep for the community's teenagers. ______________

2. The actress that plays the lead role was ill and couldn't perform. Because Maddie couldn't perform, several changes resulted. Ilana took over the role. The programs were changed to reflect the new cast. The band changed the music to fit Ilana's voice. ______________

3. In a series of accidents, first Erin dropped the eggs. As a result, she had to go out to the store for more eggs. At the store, she left her purse behind. This meant that she had to go back to the store to get it. On her second trip out, Erin locked the door without taking her house key. When she returned from the store, she couldn't get into the house. Finally, Erin's father came home and let her in. ______________

Analyze Identify the key words used in each situation that leads readers through the organization. Record your work on a separate sheet of paper.

Name ________________________________ Date ______________

Writer's Workshop: Cause-and-Effect Essay

Extension 3-8

Essay Outline

As with all expository writing, you can write a cause-and-effect essay from an outline. Outlines identify your main points and list the ways that you will support them. You can use a K-W-L Chart to focus your research goals and findings, but when it comes time to draft, a traditional outline is usually most helpful.

Review the following example of an outline. The capital letters stand for each section of the paper, the numbers stand for individual paragraphs, and lowercase letters represent supporting evidence.

A. Introduction: Background sound helps people get to sleep and sleep more soundly.
B. Body of the Paper: Background and discussion.
- **1.** Information on number of people with sleep problems.
  - **a.** personal example
  - **b.** published study
  - **c.** expert quotation
- **2.** Problems people develop due to lack of sleep.
  - **a.** example from observation
  - **b.** statistics on sleep-deprived driving
  - **c.** personal example
- **3.** Types of music or white noise technologies available.
  - **a.** recordings of ocean or other soothing sounds
  - **b.** radio or I-pod with automatic shut off
  - **c.** white noise generator

C. Conclusion

1. What is the main idea of the essay represented in the outline? How does the outline organize the supporting information? ______________________________
____
____

2. On a separate sheet of paper, create a paragraph based on one of the subheads in section B. Research information to help support your paragraph's main idea.

3. Take the information from your research and K-W-L chart and create a multi-section outline for your cause-and-effect essay, with entries for each body paragraph and piece of supporting evidence. Use as many body paragraph entries as you need, but keep entries brief. Write your outline on a separate piece of paper.

4. Exchange outlines with a partner. Read your partner's suggested outline and identify areas that are unclear or where you think additional explanation may be necessary. With your own outline, consider conducting additional research to explain areas your partner found confusing.

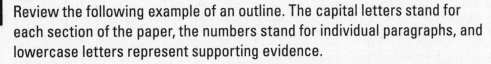

Name ______________________________ Date ______________

Mid-Unit Benchmark Test — Unit 3

Reading Skill: Identifying Main Idea and Supporting Details

Read the passages. Then, answer the questions.

The argument over whether slavery should be legal in the United States became heated when, in 1817, Missouri applied to become a state. At the time, there were an equal number of states that did not support slavery as there were states that did. Slavery was legal in Missouri, so if it joined the Union, there would no longer be a balance. The Missouri Compromise was reached, which stated that Maine would be accepted as a free state, and Missouri would be a slave state. From then on, slavery was banned from the territories north of Missouri's border. This compromise seemed to settle the issue. However, the conflict between the North and South over slavery continued to worsen.

1 Which sentence best states the main idea of the passage?

A The Missouri Compromise settled the argument between free states and slave states.

B The Missouri Compromise allowed Missouri and Maine to become states in the Union.

C The Missouri Compromise settled the issue of slavery by banning slavery in territory north of the Missouri border.

D The Missouri Compromise kept the balance between free and slave states, but the argument over slavery continued.

2 Which detail best supports the main idea?

F Slavery was legal in Missouri.

G The conflict between the North and the South over slavery worsened.

H Missouri wanted to become a state.

J Slavery was banned from the territories when Missouri applied to become a state.

3 Which of the following is the best choice for the title of this passage?

A "Events Leading to the Civil War"

B "Compromises Work"

C "The Argument over Slavery"

D "Should Slavery Be Banned?"

A book that was popular in 1744 described how to play a game called baseball. A pitcher threw a ball underhand to a batter, who tried to hit the ball with a bat. The bat had a flat end. A catcher stood behind the batter. If the batter hit the ball, the batter ran to a base and back again to score a point. The bases were marked with posts, rather than with bags.

In 1828, another book described a game called rounders. It was very much like modern baseball, with a diamond-shaped infield and a base on each corner. A batter was out after three strikes. If the batter hit a ball pitched to him, he could run. A fielder who caught the ball could make an out by throwing the ball and hitting the runner with it.

Name ______________________ Date ____________

4 **Which sentences best state the main idea of these two paragraphs?**

F Early baseball was played with a flat bat and was unlike baseball today. The game of rounders was similar to modern baseball.

G The game of baseball has been played since 1744. Rounders was a game similar to baseball.

H A game called baseball was played in 1744. A game called rounders, similar to modern baseball, was played in 1828.

J Baseball was first played in 1744 with flat bats. Rounders was played with bats and bases.

5 **Which detail supports the main idea of the first paragraph?**

A A popular book described a game called baseball.

B Bases were marked with posts rather than bags.

C A batter tried to hit the ball thrown to him.

D Batters can score a point if they hit the ball.

Vocabulary

Read the following questions. Then, choose the best answer.

6 **Which of these words is a synonym for *obstacles* as it is used in the sentence?**

She had to work hard to overcome many obstacles before she finished her education.

F passages

G difficulties

H drawbacks

J enemies

7 **The word *ingenious* can mean "clever." Which of these words is the best synonym for *ingenious* as it is used in the sentence?**

His plan for winning the game was ingenious.

A smart

B witty

C unusual

D simplistic

8 **Which sentence contains a synonym of *elated*?**

F The coach was overjoyed that the team won its first game of the season.

G The birth of the new baby was a happy occasion.

H No one received an A, but most students were pleased with their grades.

J Everyone at the party was in a cheerful mood.

9 **The word *approach* can be used as a verb or a noun. Which word is a synonym of *approach* as it is used in this sentence?**

What approach do you want to use to beat the other team?

A act

B method

C close

D join

Name ______________________________ Date ______________

10 Which sentence contains an antonym of the word *biased*?

F He is known for his straight talk and level-headed thinking.

G The judge is noted for making fair-minded decisions.

H Many people think that his decisions are unfair.

J The letters to the editor often contain incredible statements.

11 Which of these pairs of words are antonyms?

A accurate, factual

B credible, unbelievable

C their, there

D support, uphold

Literary Analysis

Read the passage. Then, answer the questions.

In 1960, President Kennedy challenged young people to join the Peace Corps. Why might someone want to join the Peace Corps? Peace Corps volunteers help people in developing nations. Peace Corps volunteers might counsel teens in Belize, launch a computer center in Armenia, or teach chemistry in a high school in Ghana. Since the 1960s, more than 178,000 Peace Corps volunteers have had the satisfaction of living and helping others in 138 countries around the world. Individuals who join the Peace Corps know that they have served their country, served humanity, and made a difference in the world.

12 In the second sentence of this selection, the author uses—

F a persuasive word

G an ethical appeal

H a rhetorical question

J an emotional appeal

13 What persuasive technique does the author use in the last sentence of this selection?

A facts

B opinions

C rhetorical question

D emotional appeal

14 The organizational method that arranges events in the order in which they happen is—

F cause and effect

G problem and solution

H chronological

J compare and contrast

15 Which sentence has a formal tone?

A I beg your forgiveness in this matter.

B Tara is all thumbs in the kitchen.

C Jake could hardly believe he won the contest!

D It's useless trying to motivate Dan.

Name ______________________________ Date ______________

16 The tone of a literary work reflects the author's—

F education

G background

H attitude

J family life

17 Which word carries a negative connotation?

A stubborn

B lean

C fragrant

D strong-willed

Grammar

Read the following questions. Then, choose the best answer.

18 In this sentence, identify the adjective that is not an article. What word does the adjective modify?

The hungry man quickly looked around the park for a place where he could eat lunch.

F man

G looked

H park

J he

19 What question does the adjective in this sentence answer?

Jerry quickly grabbed two pieces of pizza.

A Which one?

B Whose?

C How many?

D How much?

20 Which sentence contains an article?

F Tall trees sway in high winds.

G Those girls were very late to class.

H Dr. James prescribed some medicine.

J Andrew was the last to arrive.

21 Which word in this sentence is an adverb?

Wild animals are very cautious when they sense the presence of human beings.

A wild

B very

C cautious

D presence

22 The word *joyfully* answers which of the following questions?

F To what extent?

G In what manner?

H Where?

J When?

23 How many adverbs does this sentence contain?

Yesterday the main dish was so spicy that Maria barely tasted the rest of the meal.

A one

B two

C three

D four

24 Which sentence contains a prepositional phrase that is used correctly?

F Ten teams attempted to win the tournament.

G Bad weather forced the tournament to be postponed.

H When the tournament resumed, most spectators had left.

J The judge presented flowers to the winner.

25 Which sentence uses a comparative or superlative form correctly?

A I can walk farther in those shoes than in these.

B The original version is more good than the remake.

C Of the two top runners, who is fastest?

D That is the worstest song I ever heard.

26 **Which word in this sentence is the superlative form of an adjective?**

Even though the flashlight helped us see the path more clearly, it did little good in the darkest part of the forest.

F more

G clearly

H good

J darkest

27 **Which sentence is true of the comparative form?**

A It is always an adjective.

B It usually ends in *-ly.*

C It uses *most* with two-syllable adverbs.

D It compares two items.

28 **What is the best way to rewrite this sentence?**

Hanging in the hallway, Tamika saw her painting.

F Tamika, hanging in the hallway, saw her painting.

G Tamika saw her painting hanging in the hallway.

H Hanging, Tamika saw her painting in the hallway.

J In the hallway, hanging, Tamika saw her painting.

Short Answer

Reading Skill: Identifying Main Ideas and Supporting Details

29 **Explain how to find the main idea of a selection.**

____

____

30 **Where in their writing do writers usually convey the main idea?**

____

Literary Analysis

31 **Which method of organizing information would you use in writing an essay that explains how to play a video game? Explain your reasons for choosing that method.**

____

____

____

32 **Write a one-sentence emotional appeal meant to persuade a reader to wear a seat belt.**

____

____

Name ______________________________ Date ______________

Essay

Write on a separate sheet of paper.

33 **Think of an activity that you enjoy, such as playing a particular sport, planting a garden, cooking your favorite meal, or some other activity. Then, write a brief essay explaining each step in the process. Assume that the audience is unfamiliar with this activity.**

34 **Think about your favorite television commercial. What techniques are used to persuade you to buy the product? Write a brief evaluation of the commercial. Describe the persuasive techniques used in it, and rate their effectiveness.**

35 **Suppose that you have been asked to write a cause-and-effect essay on the effects of eating healthful food. Develop a K-W-L chart to plan your essay. Then write a multiparagraph essay.**

Name ______________________________ Date ______________

Diagnostic Test 2 — Unit 3

Read the passage. Then, answer the questions.

The most entertaining carnival in the United States is the annual Mardi Gras celebration in New Orleans. Each year, tourists flock from all over the country to be a part of the celebration. Costumed men and women balance on the highest tier of multilevel floats and shower the crowd below with colorful beads and trinkets. It is one of the most amazing sights you will ever see!

Those who prefer quiet celebrations, however, should stay away. The noise level at Mardi Gras can be excessive, and the crowds that line the parade route tend to get rowdy. Dealing with these crowds can be frustrating. The local police are kept very busy trying to keep the public safe during Mardi Gras season.

After the parade, the party continues at costume balls decorated in the official colors of the carnival: purple, which stands for justice; green, which stands for faith; and gold, which stands for power. Although most tourists think of Mardi Gras as just an excuse to enjoy a party, some local people continue to honor the customs and traditions that reflect the carnival's ancient origins as a religious festival. Either way, everyone has a good time at Mardi Gras. Anyone there will tell you that it is the best celebration of its kind.

1 Which statement is a fact?

A "The most entertaining carnival in the United States is the annual Mardi Gras celebration in New Orleans."

B "It is one of the most amazing sights you will ever see!"

C "Some local people continue to honor the customs and traditions that reflect the carnival's ancient origins as a religious festival."

D "Dealing with these crowds can be frustrating."

2 A reader can determine that a statement is a fact by—

F checking encyclopedias, almanacs, or reliable websites

G making a logical guess

H looking for signal words

J rereading the statement carefully

3 Which statement is an opinion?

A "Each year, tourists flock from all over the country to be a part of the celebration."

B "Costumed men and women balance on the highest tier of multilevel floats and shower the crowd below with colorful beads and trinkets."

C "After the parade, the party continues at costume balls."

D "Either way, everyone has a good time at Mardi Gras."

4 Which word helps you recognize that the following statement is an opinion?

"Anyone there will tell you that it is the best celebration of its kind."

F Anyone

G best

H celebration

J kind

Name ______________________________ Date ______________

Read the passage. Then, answer the questions.

from *The Autobiography of Benjamin Franklin*

This excerpt from Benjamin Franklin's autobiography describes how Franklin became an apprentice to his brother James, a Boston printer.

In 1717 my brother James returned from England with a press and letters to set up his business in Boston. I liked it much better than that of my father, but still had a hankering for the sea. To prevent the apprehended effect of such an inclination, my father was impatient to have me bound to my brother. I stood out some time, but at last was persuaded, and signed the indenture when I was yet but twelve years old. I was to serve as an apprentice till I was twenty-one years of age, only I was to be allowed journeyman's wages during the last year.

5 You can tell that this excerpt comes from an autobiography because it —

- **A** is told from first-person point of view
- **B** has lengthy sentences
- **C** contains formal language
- **D** addresses personal matters in someone's life

6 Which word best describes the author's style?

- **F** critical
- **G** playful
- **H** formal
- **J** poetic

Read the following questions. Then, choose the best answer.

7 Which sentence contains a correctly used coordinating conjunction?

- **A** Carla was upset because she received a low grade.
- **B** Theo and Jerome scored highest on the test.
- **C** I always eat breakfast before I leave in the morning.
- **D** Although Bernice is an excellent swimmer, she will not go in the lake.

8 Which sentence contains a correctly used subordinating conjunction?

- **F** I want to leave early, but we have to wait for my brother.
- **G** Carla has to clean her room and water the plants.
- **H** Owen must take his medication, or he will not feel well.
- **J** My dog tries to jump over the fence when he sees a squirrel.

9 Which of the following is a definition of a homonym?

- **A** words that sound alike and have the same meaning
- **B** words that sound alike but have different meanings and spellings
- **C** two or more words that have the same meaning
- **D** words that are spelled alike but have different sounds

10 Which words are homophones?

- **F** fair, fare
- **G** nice, kind
- **H** and, but
- **J** dark, bark

Name ______________________ Date ____________

Reading Skills: Differentiating Between Fact and Opinion

Reinforcement 3-10

A **fact** is something that happened or that can be proven. To find out if something is a fact, look for it in reference books or online reference sources. An **opinion** cannot be proven. It is what someone thinks or believes. Look for clue phrases such as *I think, I believe, in my opinion,* or words such as *best* or *worst.*

Nonfiction often contains a mix of fact and opinion. A selection that contains facts in support of its opinions offers the reader more reliable information than one with lots of opinions without much backing.

Read the following passage. Underline the facts. Circle opinions or words that show you an opinion. Then, answer the questions.

But, what is the real reason for eyebrows? Most scientists believe the primary purpose is to keep moisture out of the eyes. The arched shape of our eyebrows and the direction of the hair growth help to divert rain and sweat to the sides of the face. In addition, our brows catch snow, dust, and other small debris. This may have given early humans a slight edge in the fight for survival. Someone looking for shelter or trying to outrun a predator would have had a distinct advantage if salty, irritating sweat were diverted from the eyes.

1. One statement reads, "The arched shape of our eyebrows and the direction of the hair growth help to divert rain and sweat to the sides of the face." Could this be proven? How?

____

____

2. What facts in the passage support the idea that eyebrows may have given early humans a slight edge in the fight for survival?

____

____

3. Find an opinion in the passage. How do you know it is an opinion?

____

____

4. Do you feel that the opinions in this passage are firmly grounded in facts? Explain your answer.

____

____

____

Name ______________________ Date ______________

Reading Skills: Differentiating Between Fact and Opinion

Extension 3-10

Whether reading a persuasive piece of writing or listening to someone pose an argument, it is important to distinguish between the facts and opinions presented before formulating your own opinion. Likewise, it is important to back up an opinion with solid facts when trying to convince others of that opinion.

Complete the following activities.

1. In the table below, write three opinions about exercise.

Opinions

2. On a separate sheet of paper, write a paragraph about exercise using the opinions you wrote.

3. Research and write three facts about exercise that support the opinions you listed above.

Facts

4. Use your facts and opinions to write a paragraph about exercise on a separate sheet of paper.

5. Compare the two essays on exercise. Which essay is more convincing? Why?

____

____

____

____

____

____

Name ________________________________ Date ______________

Literary Analysis: Biography and Autobiography

Reinforcement 3-11 A

A **biography** tells about a person's life. It is written by someone other than the subject of the biography. Biographies are written using the third-person point of view, and they include pronouns like *he* and *she.* An **autobiography** also tells about someone's life, but the author is writing his or her own story. It is written in the first-person point of view.

Write *B* if the statement describes a biographical essay or *A* if it describes an autobiographical essay. Write *B* and *A* if the statement describes both forms or *NA* if it does not apply to either form.

1. ____ The writer uses the pronoun *I* to express the writer's feelings.
2. ____ The writer may need to do research about someone's life.
3. ____ This essay is a type of fiction.
4. ____ The writer presents a true account of a person's experience.
5. ____ The writer uses the pronoun *he* or *she* to tell a person's story.
6. ____ The writer might describe a person's achievements.

Write either *biographical* or *autobiographical* to describe each passage. Then, explain your answer.

7. I was young—only about four years old—when I first experienced the joy of sledding down the snow-covered hill in the park down the block from our house.

____

____

8. Mr. Barns was a handsome man, and he had always been athletic. His skill with a golf club was well known in Ridgeville.

____

____

Write a brief biographical or autobiographical passage. Exchange papers with a partner and have them identify the form you chose.

____

____

____

____

____

____

Name ______________________ Date ______________

Literary Analysis: Author's Perspective

Reinforcement 3-11 B

Understanding an **author's perspective** helps a reader interpret events and characters in light of their context. In order to understand an author's perspective, examine the criteria below.

Time Period
When did the author live?

Social Position
What role did the author have in society?

Age
How old was the author?

Surroundings
Where did the author live?

Attitude
How did the author feel?

Read the passage below then answer the following questions.

Prior to the 1950s in the United States, a typical teenager was expected to take on adult responsibilities, such as leaving school and getting a job to help pay family bills. They had little free time. However, after WWII, American parents had greater wealth. Aware of the sacrifices they had made during the Depression and war, they used their wealth to send teenagers to college and give them spending money. These teenagers had plenty of free time to develop their own hobbies and interests. The increase of spending power that offered ways for them to keep entertained in this free time, such as the hula hoop, resulted in teenagers becoming a focus of advertisements. They became identified as a unique group with their own interests.

1. How might an author writing before the 1950s describe a teenager?

____

____

____

____

____

____

____

2. How would an author writing after the 1950s describe a teenager differently?

____

____

____

____

____

____

____

Name ______________________ Date ______________

Literary Analysis: Biography and Autobiography

Extension 3-11

Maya Angelou's Autobiography

An **autobiography** can give the reader a vivid taste of life in a more compelling way than a dry historical account might. Combine that with an inside look at someone's thoughts, feelings, and actions, and you get a story that is hard to resist. Reading an individual's story can also highlight the time and place in which he or she lived. Maya Angelou's "Occupation: Conductorette" from *I Know Why the Caged Bird Sings*, gives the reader a glimpse into the reality of life in San Francisco during the 1940s.

Reread "Occupation: Conductorette" from Unit 1, Lesson 6 and answer the questions below.

1. What key event does this autobiography describe? ______________________

____

____

2. Analyze the effect of Maya's mother's support on Maya's actions.

____

____

____

Write four additional questions about Maya Angelou that can be answered by reading the excerpt. Then, exchange papers with a partner and answer each other's questions using the text. Write your answers on a separate sheet of paper.

3. ______________________

____

____

4. ______________________

____

____

5. ______________________

____

____

6. ______________________

____

____

Name ______________________ Date ____________

Comparing Literary Works: Author's Style

Reinforcement 3-12

Style refers to an author's usual manner of writing. An **author's style** may be lighthearted or dramatic, casual or structured, expressive or instructive, compassionate or unfavorable. Style is revealed by elements such as word choice, tone, and length of sentences. It shows you how the author feels or thinks. The style of a piece of writing should match its objective.

Read the following paragraphs about Smithfield, North Carolina. Pay attention to the author's style in each piece.

Sally loved the town of Smithfield. She thought small towns were like people—the more you got to know them, the better you liked them. Sally invited Juan, her best friend, to Smithfield. Juan loved the movies at the Ava Gardner Museum. They were a snapshot in time.

Come to Smithfield, North Carolina! You'll find a lot to see and do! For example, you can visit the museum of film star Ava Gardner. There you can view her old movies and costumes. In Smithfield, you can also shop in a variety of fine outlet stores where you'll save a lot of money!

1. How are the two paragraphs alike? ______________________

2. In which piece has the author presented information about Smithfield in a straightforward, formal style? ______________________

3. Which selection uses figurative language? ______________________

4. Does the author's style fit the purpose of each piece? Explain.

5. Which piece of writing do you prefer? Why? ______________________

Name ______________________________ Date ______________

Comparing Literary Works: Author's Style

Extension 3-12

Authors of nonfiction often employ a specific style. Their writing may be formal or informal. It may utilize vocabulary that is playful or serious, and it may be friendly or persuasive in tone. For example, in the two paragraphs about Bermuda from your work text, the authors use different styles. The first style is informal and presents figurative language to express enthusiasm, while the second style is more formal and the language is less emotional. An author's style suits his or her purpose for writing.

Imagine that you have taken a trip to a famous place in your county or state. Complete the following chart to record elements of style for each of the following purposes: to tell a friend or to create a travel advertisement about the place.

	To Tell a Friend	To Create an Advertisement
tone		
sentence length		
vocabulary		
purpose		

Create Use the details you have gathered in your chart to guide you as you write a brief letter to a friend or create a travel advertisement. Remember to make the style suit your purpose and audience.

____

____

____

____

____

____

____

____

____

____

____

____

____

____

Name ______________________ Date ____________

Language Coach: Combining Sentences with Conjunctions

Reinforcement 3-13 A

A **conjunction** is a word that connects two or more parts of a sentence.

Coordinating conjunction
- Joins words of the same kind, such as two nouns or two verbs.
- Creates compound sentences.

Lara loves ice hockey. +
Sam loves ice hockey. =
Lara and Sam love ice hockey.

Subordinating conjunction
- Connects two complete ideas and shows that one is dependent on the other.
- Creates complex sentences.

Maven lost his homework. +
Maven earned a zero. =
Since Maven lost his homework, he earned a zero.

Conjunction Word Bank					
Coordinating			**Subordinating**		
and	not	yet	after	before	until
but	or		although	if	when
for	so		as	since	while
			because	unless	whenever

Using the conjunction word bank above, write the appropriate coordinating or subordinating conjunction on the line to complete each sentence.

1. Aunt Jennifer came with us, ____________ Uncle Steve stayed home.
2. ____________ she has the time, Mom volunteers at the hospital.
3. ____________ you need help, please call me.
4. Napolean was a brilliant general, ____________ he made several costly mistakes.
5. ____________ I sent the letter off, I remembered the stamp.
6. I bought ____________ wrapped a gift for Petra.
7. Carla has not called, ____________ has she written.
8. Do you want a hamburger ____________ a hot dog?
9. ____________ the rain stops, the firewood will be too wet to burn.
10. ____________ it is Saturday, I slept until noon.
11. My vacation was brief ____________ restful.
12. ____________ waiting for the doctor, Rick read a magazine.

Name ______________________________ Date ______________

Language Coach: Spelling Homophones

Reinforcement 3-13 B

Homophones are words that sound the same but have different spellings and different meanings. Choosing the wrong homophone will give your sentence a different meaning and confuse readers, so it's important to be sure you've got the right one. The word homophone comes from Greek words meaning "same sound."

Underline the correct homophone in each sentence.

1. We decided we wanted to see a movie, (to/too).
2. The center fielder (cot/caught) the ball to end the inning.
3. I tried not to (peek/peak) when my brother told me to close my eyes.
4. There was a stain on the (sealing/ceiling) from the time water leaked in from the rainstorm.
5. I had to (hall/haul) my suitcase up two flights of stairs when I went to visit my grandparents.
6. I made sure the line was (taut/taught) before I hammered in the tent (steak/stake).
7. He saved me a (piece/peace) of cake from the party.
8. The flowers she arranged for the centerpiece were (reel/real).

Apply Choose the correct word to fill in each blank. Write your answers on the lines.

heel, heal	not, knot	road, rode
they're, their	real, reel	war, wore

My first marathon was a race I'll remember for a long time. To start with, I ____________ new running shoes, which was a big mistake. They gave me a terrible blister on my ____________. Even though I took it easy, partway through the race, I got a ____________ in my calf. It tensed right up! The ____________ was pretty good, though, since it didn't have too many potholes. The fans lining the road were great! The sound of ____________ cheers really kept me going. When I was done, my coach gave me a big hug and said, "Now you're a ____________ runner!

Name ______________________ Date ____________

Language Coach: Spelling Homophones

Extension 3-13

English is full of words that sound alike but are spelled differently and have different meanings. For example, *right* and *write* are pronounced the same, but are spelled and defined differently. The prevalence of homophones is partly because English has incorporated words from many languages.

Write a homophone for each of the words below.

1. meat ______________________
2. bear ______________________
3. flower ______________________
4. hay ______________________
5. poll ______________________
6. fare ______________________

Write On the lines provided below, write a brief story about a school fair. Use all twelve words from the homophones activity above.

Name ______________________________ Date ______________

Writer's Workshop: Persuasive Essay

Reinforcement 3-14

When authors use words to change people's thinking or influence their actions, they are using persuasion. A **persuasive essay** states and defends a belief on a current issue with facts and expert opinions. An effective persuasive essay considers counterarguments.

Complete the following activities.

1. Which of the following would be good topics for a persuasive essay? Check three.

- ☐ We should wear uniforms to school.
- ☐ Students should be allowed to bring cell phones to school.
- ☐ Students and their families have magazines at home.
- ☐ We all like to read about global warming.
- ☐ We need to develop new sources of energy.

2. Choose one of the checked topics and complete the two-column chart. List three possible oppositions to your idea and match them with three counterarguments.

Arguments	Counterarguments

Read this excerpt from a persuasive essay and then answer the questions.

I believe that people cause global warming. Our cars and fossil fuel plants emit greenhouse gases and cause climate patterns to change. Some scientists state that global warming is the result of natural factors. However, scientists at NOOA and at the Pew Center agree with my opinion. These scientists tell people to stop cutting down trees and to stop air pollution.

3. What is the writer's opinion about global warming? ______________________

____

4. What facts does the writer include? ______________________

____

____

5. Underline the sentence in which the writer presents a counterargument.

Name ______________________________ Date ______________

Writer's Workshop: Persuasive Essay

Extension 3-14

Writers create **persuasive essays** to convince an audience. They may want readers to believe as they do, or to take action. Therefore, the author may use facts and opinions to show readers why they should adopt a particular belief or action.

Read the following paragraph from a persuasive essay.

Baseball has provided a home to players from a variety of races. In 1947, Jackie Robinson was in his rookie year as modern baseball's first black player. Over the years, he helped the Brooklyn Dodgers win six pennants. Robinson himself won many awards, including Rookie of the Year, and he was inducted into the Baseball Hall of Fame. Spectators had rejected and booed him, but his hits and stolen bases later forced fans to admit that he was an accomplished player. Robinson showed that a team could be greatly improved with the skills that players from all races bring to the game.

1. What is the author trying to persuade you to think?

____

____

____

2. Underline three facts the author presents to persuade you that baseball should adopt players from a variety of races. Write the fact that you find most convincing and explain why.

____

____

____

____

Write In the space below, brainstorm people you consider to be role models. Then, on a separate sheet of paper, write a brief essay convincing a committee to award your role model with an award. Your role model can be a relative, famous person, and so on. Support your opinions with facts about the individual.

____

____

____

____

____

____

____

Name ______________________________ Date ______________

End-of-Unit Benchmark Test — Unit 3

Reading Skill: Differentiating Between Fact and Opinion

Read the following questions. Then, choose the best answer.

1 Which of the following statements is a fact?

A Paris is a beautiful city.

B Paris is the capital of France.

C Paris is a better place to visit than Rome.

D Paris has the best museums in the world.

2 Which of the following statements is an opinion?

F Spring always begins in March.

G Summer is the hottest time of year.

H Winter is long and boring.

J Autumn is a time of harvest and cooling temperatures.

3 How do you determine whether a statement is an opinion?

A by citing sources

B by doing research

C by looking for words that reveal a writer's feelings

D by referring to an event that has already happened

4 Which statement supports the opinion that dogs make better pets than cats?

F Dogs need daily walks.

G Dogs do not sharpen their claws on furniture.

H Dogs require regular visits to the veterinarian.

J Dogs come in a variety of colors.

Read the passage. Then, answer the questions.

Until the twentieth century, women were unfairly denied the right to vote in Great Britain. The movement for women's rights began in England in 1792. Many women, known as suffragists, were sent to prison, where they continued to work for their cause by staging hunger strikes. Bill after bill was introduced to the British Parliament during the 1800s and early 1900s with no success. Public support for women's voting rights slowly grew and, in 1918, an act was passed that allowed women age 30 or over to vote. In 1928, this age was lowered to 21, the same as men. After more than a century, women finally achieved equal voting rights with men.

5 Which of the following statements is a fact?

A Women were treated unfairly by the public.

B In 1928, the voting age for women was 21.

C Women were too aggressive in their fight for equal rights.

D The British Parliament acted unjustly toward women.

6 Which of the following is an opinion?

F Bills were introduced to Parliament.

G Women achieved equal voting rights with men.

H By 1918, women age 30 and over could vote.

J The British Parliament was unfair toward women.

Name ______________________________ Date ______________

Read the passage. Then, answer the questions.

> On April 25, 1990, the crew of the space shuttle *Discovery* placed the most sophisticated telescope ever created in orbit around Earth. The Hubble Space Telescope was named for Edwin Hubble, the most important American astronomer of the twentieth century. Unlike telescopes on Earth, the Hubble telescope can see deep into space without the interference of Earth's atmosphere. The images received by Hubble are much brighter and clearer than anyone could have imagined. With the Hubble Space Telescope, people are able to clearly see the breathtaking beauty of the universe.

7 Which of the following statements could be supported by facts?

A The *Discovery* crew placed the most sophisticated telescope into orbit.

B The *Discovery* crew performed a great service to humanity.

C The Hubble allows people to see the universe more clearly than ever imagined.

D The Hubble is a wonderful invention that will make the world a better place.

8 Which of the following statements best describes the author's opinion of the Hubble Space Telescope?

F It is an important invention that will benefit science and humanity.

G The Hubble took a great effort to put in place, but it was worth it.

H It is the most technologically advanced invention in the field of science.

J Without the Hubble, scientists would know very little about the universe.

Literary Analysis

Read the following questions. Then, choose the best answer.

9 What do biography and autobiography have in common?

A Both are told from a first-person point of view.

B Both are told from a third-person point of view.

C Both tell the story of a famous person's life.

D Both include important events and dates in a person's life.

10 In an autobiography, how can you get a better understanding of an author's perspective?

F by studying the author's tone

G by learning when and how the author lived

H by studying how the author uses figurative language

J by observing how the author's style fits his or her purpose

Name ______________________________ Date ______________

Read the passage. Then, answer the questions.

Emily Dickinson is considered one of America's greatest poets, but few of her poems were published in her lifetime. Born in 1830, Dickinson grew up in Amherst, Massachusetts, and attended school there and in nearby Holyoke. She was no doubt familiar with other popular New England writers of her day, especially Ralph Waldo Emerson. Dickinson had a fairly normal social life until she reached her mid-twenties, after which she rarely left the home she inherited from her parents. Instead, she seems to have been able to understand the world better by viewing it from a distance. With a sharp eye and keen intellect, she pondered nature, friendship, love, and death in poems of powerful simplicity. Only about seven of her poems were published during her lifetime, all without her consent. When she died in 1886, relatives found over 1,500 more of Dickinson's poems, many of them written on napkins and slips of paper neatly tied up with ribbons.

11 What does this biographical essay emphasize?

A Emily Dickinson's childhood and adolescence

B Emily Dickinson's love of nature

C Emily Dickinson's family and other personal relationships

D Emily Dickinson's odd habits and writing career

12 What is the author's attitude toward Emily Dickinson?

F amused

G sarcastic

H admiring

J indifferent

13 From this selection, what can you conclude about Emily Dickinson?

A She was talented but shy.

B She imitated other New England writers.

C She was clever but unfriendly.

D She wrote about topics she knew little about.

14 Which word best describes the author's style in this selection?

F poetic

G playful

H ironic

J serious

15 Which statement best explains why this selection is biographical, rather than autobiographical?

A It tells about important events in the subject's life.

B It tells about the writer's contacts with the subject, Emily Dickinson.

C It is one person's account of events in the life of another person.

D It gives the years of birth and death for Emily Dickinson.

16 Figurative language is characterized by the —

F use of formal or informal language

G way in which an author's style fits his or her purpose

H way in which an author feels about a subject

J use of hyperbole, personification, metaphor, or simile

17 Which term describes an author's use of vocabulary and word choice?

A tone

B purpose

C diction

D message

Name ________________________________ Date ______________

Read the passage. Then, answer the questions.

My Early Years
by Alexandra Pappas

I was born in Chicago, Illinois, on March 22, 1974, at 3:26 in the afternoon. It was one of those rare Chicago spring days, warm and beautiful enough for people to sail their boats out on Lake Michigan. I know this because my mother loves to tell the story about how she watched the boats from a hospital window while she was in labor with me. In fact, she feels compelled to repeat this story every year on my birthday at exactly 3:26 in the afternoon. It doesn't matter where I am or what I'm doing; my mother always calls in her chipper voice to reminisce over what must have been one of the most painful experiences of her life—childbirth.

I spent my earliest years in an apartment in Evanston until my parents moved us to a house in Oak Park. I loved the new house because it had a big backyard, and it was within walking distance of my cousin's house.

My cousin Jason and I were very close growing up. In fact, people often mistook us for twins. Our mothers would dress us alike, in matching sweaters with our names sewn across the front. We would have to wear the sweaters when our mothers dragged us to the house of someone important—usually another Greek woman. There we would be told to behave ourselves and sit still while the adults spoke Greek to one another. Of course, we felt silly in our matching sweaters, and we hated to sit still. It was boring.

When we didn't have to wear the matching sweaters, my cousin and I wore our outfit of choice: overalls with a T-shirt and Zip shoes. I loved my Zip shoes. They came in red, white, or blue and featured cartoon characters across the rims of the soles. We would run around outside in our Zip shoes, pretending to be Luke Skywalker and Han Solo. On rainy days, we would go to the basement and turn the old furniture upside down to form the cockpits of various spaceships that we had seen in the movies. We would carry out mock fights against invisible enemies.

In the 1970s, we didn't have DVD or videocassette players. We didn't even have cable, so there was never anything for us to watch on TV. We spent our days using our imaginations to entertain ourselves. Any piece of furniture at our disposal became a spaceship. Any blanket in the house became the wall of a fort.

18 What tells you that this selection is an autobiography?

F It includes important dates.

G It is told from first-person point of view.

H It is told from the third-person point of view.

J It offers details about wearing matching outfits.

19 What does the author tell you about the time period in which she grew up?

A Technology was available to few people.

B Girls were expected to behave differently from boys.

C The climate was much warmer than it is today.

D Children relied on imagination for entertainment.

Name ______________________________ Date ______________

20 **What kind of language does the author use in this selection?**

F critical

G poetic

H playful

J formal

21 **How does the author's style fit her purpose in writing an autobiography?**

A She uses an informal tone and vivid language.

B She uses an informative tone and important details.

C She uses a sympathetic tone with simile and metaphor.

D She uses a persuasive tone with long sentences.

Grammar

Read the following questions. Then, choose the best answer.

22 **Which of the following sentences uses a coordinating conjunction correctly?**

F Everyone in the club wanted to go to the home team's opening game.

G There were not enough tickets for all of them to go to the game.

H It rained in the morning, but the sun came out in the afternoon.

J It was a great day for the opening of the baseball season.

23 **Which of the following correctly combines the two sentences below by using a subordinating conjunction?**

My friend moved away last year. I miss her very much.

A But my friend moved away last year, so I miss her very much.

B Although my friend moved away last year, I miss her very much.

C My friend moved away last year, yet I miss her very much.

D My friend moved away last year, and I miss her very much.

Spelling

Read the following questions. Then, choose the best answer.

24 **Which of the following pairs of words are homophones?**

F bored/bared

G like/dislike

H bored/board

J fair/fair

25 **Which of the following sentences contains a homophone of the word *allowed*?**

A He was very proud to be one of the players on the team.

B They were not permitted to attend the game.

C Members of the losing team behaved in an aloof manner.

D She read the winners' names aloud.

Name ______________________________ Date ______________

Short Answer

Reading Skill: Differentiating Between Fact and Opinion

26 Explain why the statement "The polar ice caps have melted" can be considered a fact.

____

____

27 Explain how to tell a fact from an opinion.

____

____

Literary Analysis

28 What shapes an author's perspective?

____

____

29 How might the style of a letter to a friend differ from the style of a newspaper editorial? Explain.

____

____

Essay

Write on a separate sheet of paper.

30 Think of a historical figure or an acquaintance such as a teacher, friend, or family member who did something that you admire. Write a brief essay describing the event in that person's life that makes you admire him or her. Make sure that your essay clearly states why you admire the person's actions.

31 What current issue do you feel strongly about? Issues at school? Curfew? The environment? Write a brief newspaper editorial stating and defending your opinion on the issue. Be sure to include reasons and evidence to support your opinion and to address any counterarguments. Do not forget to use persuasive techniques to convey your message.

32 What makes you who you are? Write a brief essay about yourself in which you describe what has shaped your perception of the world. Allow the reader the chance to see the world through your eyes.

Name ______________________________ Date ______________

Mid-Year Test

Reading Skills and Literary Analysis

Read the following excerpt from Jack London's "Up the Slide." Then, answer the questions.

When Clay Dilham left the tent to get a sled-load of firewood, he expected to be back in half an hour. So he told Swanson, who was cooking the dinner. Swanson and he belonged to different outfits, located about twenty miles apart on the Stewart River, but they had become traveling partners on a trip down the Yukon to Dawson to get the mail.

Swanson had laughed when Clay said he would be back in half an hour. It stood to reason, Swanson said, that good, dry firewood could not be found so close to Dawson; that whatever firewood there was originally had long since been gathered in; that firewood would not be selling at forty dollars a cord if any man could go out and get a sled-load and be back in the time Clay expected to make it.

Then it was Clay's turn to laugh, as he sprang on the sled and *mushed* the dogs on the river-trail. For, coming up from the Siwash village the previous day, he had noticed a small dead pine in an out-of-the-way place, which had defied discovery by eyes less sharp than his. And his eyes were both young and sharp, for his seventeenth birthday had just cleared.

1 Which prediction is most likely to be correct, based on the details in the selection?

A Swanson will find wood before Clay does.

B Clay will forget where he saw the pine tree.

C Clay will find wood and return to camp soon.

D Swanson will be upset when Clay returns with wood.

2 Which detail helps you understand that the story is set in a remote area?

F Clay keeps dogs and has a sled.

G Swanson and Clay travel far to get the mail.

H Clay and Swanson work near a river.

J Swanson says that firewood is expensive.

3 You can tell that this selection is told from the third-person omniscient point of view because—

A Swanson guesses Clay's thoughts

B Clay is the story's narrator

C only Swanson's feelings are described

D both Swanson's and Clay's thoughts are described

4 In which part of the plot does this selection belong?

F exposition

G falling action

H resolution

J climax

Name ______________________________ Date ______________

Read the passage. Then, answer the questions.

The Price of Beauty

According to legend, the peacock did not always have such beautiful feathers. He was just an average bird who wanted to stand out. When the peacock's wish was granted and he got his new feathers, he visited his old friends. The pheasant, the swan, and the heron all admitted that the peacock was by far the most beautiful. On his way home, the peacock saw an eagle soaring overhead, as he used to do. Lifting his wings, the peacock tried to rise, but the weight of his new feathers held him down. He knew then that he would no longer fly up to greet the morning but instead walk the ground like a common beast.

5 What type of conflict does the peacock face?

A an internal conflict because he wants to be special

B an external conflict because he and the swan argue

C an external conflict because his home is too far to walk to

D an internal conflict because he wants to be an eagle

6 What lesson can be learned from this story?

F There is always someone less fortunate than you.

G The most precious things in life cannot be bought.

H Do not give up freedom for something less important.

J Avoid taking credit for something you did not do.

Read the passage. Then, answer the questions.

First Steps Concert

Jason watched with wide eyes as the four singers approached the stage. He had been looking forward to this moment for six weeks. Jason remembered the day when his choir director, Mr. Nelson, announced that the group First Steps would be performing for the school. Jason almost jumped out of his seat. He had all their CDs and dreamed of singing with the group someday. He often imagined himself on stage, singing in the spotlight as an audience of thousands clapped and sang along.

Because Mr. Nelson had told the class that they could watch the group warm up before the performance, Jason was the first one in the auditorium. He leaned forward, mesmerized, as they tuned to one another's voices. Suddenly they burst into an old spiritual. Jason had never heard anything so beautiful.

7 Through indirect characterization, you learn that Jason—

A prides himself on being punctual

B is a good judge of talent

C has a smooth singing voice

D is a daydreamer

8 Which phrase indicates a flashback in this selection?

F "with wide eyes"

G "Jason remembered the day"

H "before the performance"

J "Jason was the first one in the auditorium"

Name ______________________ Date ____________

Lake Louise

Lake Louise is part of Banff National Park in southern Alberta, Canada. The lake is about a mile and a half long and a third of a mile wide. Visitors find it quiet and peaceful at Lake Louise. The smooth waters mirror the surrounding mountains, creating breathtaking views. More people visit Lake Louise than anywhere else in the Canadian Rockies.

9 Suppose you are writing an essay persuading people to visit Lake Louise. Which of the following statements would be *most* effective?

A Lake Louise is part of Banff National Park in southern Alberta, Canada.

B The lake is about a mile and a half long and a third of a mile wide.

C The smooth waters mirror the surrounding mountains, creating breathtaking views.

D More people visit Lake Louise than anywhere else in the Canadian Rockies.

10 Which of these statements can be inferred from the paragraph?

F Lake Louise is close to the United States.

G People enjoy the spectacular scenery at Lake Louise.

H Lake Louise is the largest lake in Canada.

J The Canadian Rockies have many beautiful lakes.

The word *supermarket* was first used in the late 1920s in the United States. However, early supermarkets were not nearly as large as today's high volume, self-service stores. Several important developments mark this transition from small general stores to one-stop mega-supermarkets.

In 1910, the Great Atlantic and Pacific Tea Company opened the so-called economy store format. On their shelves, they placed attractive displays of such items as tea, coffee, and canned foods. This company kept their prices fairly low by selling in high volume. This practice became a feature of later supermarkets as well. The Great Atlantic and Pacific Tea Company also introduced the idea of "cash and carry." Customers had to pay cash, and delivery was not offered. This also helped keep grocery prices low.

Any discussion of the history of the supermarket must include mention of two more important developments. The introduction of the motor vehicle is one, and the invention of the home refrigerator is the other. Both of these products allowed people to buy large quantities of food at one time.

By the 1930s, the supermarket concept was becoming more and more popular. Convenient locations, parking lots, self-service, and low prices have kept shoppers flowing to stores for more than seventy years.

Name ________________________________ Date ____________

11 Why was the invention of motor vehicles important to the development of supermarkets?

A Shoppers would not go to stores without parking lots.

B People could carry more food home much more easily.

C Store owners had to charge more to pay for their vehicles.

D People needed all their products in one place to save gasoline.

12 What is the main idea of this selection?

F Supermarkets keep their prices low and sell in volume.

G Many factors influenced the development of supermarkets.

H The invention of home refrigerators helped supermarkets grow.

J The concept of a supermarket was introduced in the early 1900s.

Read the passage. Then, answer the questions.

Playing to Win

The student council held a meeting to decide which players on the school's sports teams would be given "Most Valuable Player" awards. While discussing the girls' softball team, the group could not decide which player had been the most outstanding member of her team.

"I think Pam Martin should get it," Lori said.

"My sister?" Jack asked. "No way. Terri O'Connor has hit more home runs than anyone else on the team."

"But Pam has the highest batting average and can run the fastest," Lori said.

Jack held up a hand to make a point. "The best thing about Terri is her great attitude. She encourages the other players with her sportsmanship."

Lori nodded in agreement. "Yes, Terri is enthusiastic. But Pam has played on the team for two years, and Terri has only played for one. That should count for something."

Jack had to admit that Lori's argument was strong. In the end, however, Jack and Lori were outnumbered when the student council voted to give the award to Anita Reynolds, who had played on the team for three years.

13 What is similar about how Jack and Lori approach their task?

A Each lists valid reasons why a player deserves the award.

B Each tries hard to make the other admit defeat.

C Each hopes that a family member will win the award.

D Each agrees to let someone else make the decision.

14 Which of the following is an example of situational irony from the selection?

F Jack and Lori debate Terri's and Pam's records, yet Anita wins the award.

G Jack agrees that Lori has a strong argument in favor of Pam.

H Lori wonders why Jack does not want his sister to win the award.

J Terri and Pam are both good players, and each deserves an award.

Name ______________________________ Date ______________

Read the passage. Then, answer the questions.

The Truth About *The Wizard Walks*

Recently, some parents tried to remove *The Wizard Walks* from the shelves of the local public library. These foolish people are entitled to decide for themselves what they will read, but *The Wizard Walks* should not be banned. The people who object to *The Wizard Walks* believe that it is unsuitable for children. However, a poll showed that most people who want to ban *The Wizard Walks* have not even read the book. They are mindlessly repeating what they have heard from others without taking the trouble to read the book themselves.

The main argument for banning *The Wizard Walks* is that it is almost a textbook on magic. But anyone who has actually read the book knows that it does not teach witchcraft. Although the main character of *The Wizard Walks* has magical powers, the story is obviously fictional. Most children have no trouble figuring out that this book describes an imaginary world.

Perhaps *The Wizard Walks* is not good for every child, but banning it from the public library goes too far. If ignorant people start banning books, soon our libraries will be empty. Every book is offensive to someone for some reason.

Parents who do not want children to read *The Wizard Walks* can ban it from their homes. To ban it from the public library would take away the right of other parents to make that decision for their own children.

15 What is the main idea of this selection?

A Everyone should read *The Wizard Walks.*

B *The Wizard Walks* is the author's favorite book.

C Most people who use the library are unintelligent.

D Banning books from public libraries is unfair.

16 The author's purpose in this selection is to—

F entertain people with a story about a wizard

G persuade readers to fight the ban

H inform readers about wizards

J encourage people to take polls

17 Based on the evidence in this essay, what can you infer that the author believes?

A Public libraries should have a wide variety of books.

B All children should be required to read *The Wizard Walks.*

C Only a few books should ever be banned from the library.

D *The Wizard Walks* is the best children's book of our time.

18 Which of these is the first clue of the author's disrespectful attitude toward the supporters of the ban?

F The author calls the supporters "foolish people."

G The author says that supporters are acting "mindlessly."

H The author says that the book is "not good" for all children.

J The author suggests that parents "ban [the book] from their homes."

Name ______________________________ Date ______________

Read the passages. Then, answer the questions.

John Wilkes Booth was born in 1838, one of ten children in a theatrical family. A talented actor, Booth took part in a successful acting tour through the Deep South in 1860. He became a strong supporter of the South and of slavery, and he often expressed his hatred of Abraham Lincoln. In 1864, Booth planned to kidnap President Lincoln, but his plans did not work. Finally, in 1865 he planned to murder the President. On April 14, 1865, Booth entered the presidential box at Ford's Theater in Washington, D.C., and shot the president in the head. After shooting Lincoln, Booth leapt onto the stage and shouted, "The South is avenged!" Although he broke his leg when he jumped, Booth was able to escape. However, on April 26, Federal troops found Booth hiding in a barn at a farm in Virginia. Booth refused to surrender and died of a gunshot wound.

19 Which of the following best explains why this selection is biographical?

A The writer tells about an important event in the life of another person.

B The selection describes an important event that the writer experienced.

C The writer describes events from his or her own lifetime.

D The selection gives the years of the birth and death of John Wilkes Booth.

20 The author's style can best be described as—

F poetic

G playful

H informative

J critical

San Francisco's Chinatown is the second-largest Chinese community in the United States. Rebuilt after the 1906 earthquake, it became a major tourist attraction in the 1920s. Today, tourists from all over flock to Chinatown to visit the many fascinating shops and superb restaurants that line the crowded streets.

Begin your tour at the Chinatown Gate. Stroll along Grant Avenue and peek into some of the crowded shops you pass along the way. You'll find that the shop windows have encased unusual objects of every description. Some shops sell everything from valuable antiques to inexpensive trinkets. Others concentrate on one specific kind of item. Of course, you don't have to enter every shop you see to find out what's inside. A quick peek at the window display will usually reveal the kinds of things being offered for sale.

The most interesting part of a visit to Chinatown, of course, is seeing the people who live there. Be sure to visit the teeming fruit and vegetable stands on Stockton Street. There, you will find many local people doing their daily grocery shopping.

21 **How does the writer make this selection about Chinatown more interesting to the reader?**

A by creating a visual tour with only words

B by comparing Chinatown to other neighborhoods

C by describing the people of Chinatown in great detail

D by pointing out both good and bad things about Chinatown

22 **Which detail best supports the statement that Chinatown's shops are unique and fascinating?**

F Chinatown was rebuilt after the 1906 earthquake.

G Some shops sell a wide variety of goods.

H Some shops sell only a specific kind of item.

J Shop windows display objects of every description.

Grammar

Read the following questions. Then, choose the best answer.

23 **Choose the correct personal pronoun to complete the following sentence.**

People like to take _______ dogs to the park on Saturday mornings.

A they

B us

C their

D yours

24 **Which of the following sentences contains correct subject/verb agreement?**

F Jake's two dogs licks my hand when I visit.

G The oak tree sway in the strong wind.

H Rude visitors walk loudly through the museum.

J One of those books have fallen to the floor.

25 **Which word or group of words belongs in the space shown in the sentence below?**

Of the two O'Connor brothers, Chris is the _______.

A more athletic

B athletic

C athleticest

D most athletic

26 **Choose the correct preposition for the following sentence.**

After finishing your lunch, please place your bag _______ your seat.

F within

G beside

H before

J about

Name ______________________ Date ______________

Vocabulary

Read the following questions. Then, choose the best answer.

27 Choose the best meaning of the underlined word.

Because Teresa misjudged the distance to the theater, the movie had started by the time she arrived.

A ran from
B left without directions
C acted unpleasantly
D estimated incorrectly

28 Which word comes from the Greek root that means "reason"?

F evidence
G logical
H conclusions
J similar

Spelling

Read the following questions. Then, choose the best answer.

29 Choose the correct homophones for the following sentence.

The boys went (threw/through) the turnstile before counting (their/there) change.

A threw, their
B threw, there
C through, their
D through, there

30 Choose the word that correctly completes the sentence.

The meeting was ______ for the day.

F adjourned
G ajourned
H adjurned
J ajorned

Essay

Write on a separate sheet of paper.

31 Imagine that the community center in your town will soon be adding something new. What do you think should be added? It may be a new piece of equipment, a new club, or a new class that you would like to take. It may be something that you can use or an activity that you can take part in after school, on weekends, or during summer vacation. Write to convince the director of the community center that your idea is the one that should be added. Be sure to be specific and explain your reasons.

Name ______________________________ Date ______________

Diagnostic Test 1 — Unit 4

Read the passages. Then, answer the questions.

The day is done, and the darkness
Falls from the wings of Night,
As a feather is wafted downward
From an eagle in his flight.

I see the lights of the village
Gleam through the rain and the mist,
And a feeling of sadness comes o'er me
That my soul cannot resist:

A feeling of sadness and longing,
That is not akin to pain,
And resembles sorrow only
As the mist resembles the rain.

Come, read to me some poem,
Some simple and heartfelt lay,
That shall soothe this restless feeling,
And banish the thoughts of day.

—from "The Day is Done" by Henry Wadsworth Longfellow

1 Which is the best paraphrase of lines 1–4 of Longfellow's poem?

A Nighttime has come.
B Feathers fall from the sky.
C Dark clouds cover the sky.
D An eagle with dark feathers is flying.

2 Which best restates lines 5–12 of Longfellow's poem?

F I feel sad and restless in the rain.
G I am unhappy because I am in pain.
H Lights from the village shine in the rain.
J The rain brings back unhappy memories.

3 Which is the best paraphrase of this entire excerpt from Longfellow's poem?

A I dislike getting caught in the rain.
B I feel a bit down, but poetry will brighten my mood.
C I am worried about things that happened during the day.
D I feel lonely walking around the village by myself at night.

4 Before you paraphrase a line or a passage, you should first —

F restate the details more simply
G identify the most basic information
H put the information into your own words
J replace the writer's original words with synonyms

Name ______________________________ Date ______________

Dark hills at evening in the west,
Where sunset hovers like a sound
Of golden horns that sang to rest
Old bones of warriors under ground,
Far now from all the bannered ways
Where flash the legions of the sun,
You fade—as if the last of days
Were fading, and all wars were done.

—"The Dark Hills" by Edwin Arlington Robinson

5 Which imagery from Robinson's poem appeals to the sense of hearing?

A evening in the west

B sunset hovers

C golden horns that sang

D flash the legions

6 The sunset symbolizes—

F war

G death

H music

J happiness

Read the following questions. Then, choose the best answer.

7 If *adaptation* comes from the Latin word *adaptare,* meaning "to fit," which word probably shares the same origin as *adapt*?

A addition

B address

C adapter

D advantage

8 If *reflectable* comes from the Latin word *reflectere,* meaning "to bend back," which word probably shares the same origin as *reflectable*?

F recur

G reflex

H reference

J relaxation

9 Which sentence uses a verb in the active voice correctly?

A The rabbit was chased by the hounds.

B We were led through the museum by a guide.

C A map showed us how to find our way to the park.

D Three songs were sung by David.

10 Which sentence uses a verb in the passive voice correctly?

F He gave me an interesting book on lighthouses.

G We were about to leave the restaurant when we saw Dave arrive.

H Margaret was encouraged by her parents to join the lacrosse team.

J Alexander has completed his research paper on Thomas Jefferson.

11 Which word is spelled correctly?

A dispensable

B classifing

C omiting

D readyness

12 What should you do to spell the italic word in this sentence correctly?

The teacher *specifyed* the materials needed for the assignment.

F Add and *f.*

G Add an *i.*

H Drop the *y* and add an *f.*

J Drop the *y* and add an *i.*

Name ______________________ Date ______________

Reading Skills: Paraphrasing

Reinforcement 4-2

Paraphrasing means restating a text in your own words. It is not the same as summarizing, which is telling the main ideas of a text. A paraphrase should be about the same length as the original text, while a summary should be considerably shorter. Paraphrasing involves two main tasks. First, find the essential information. This includes main ideas and details. Second, state that information in simple language that does not repeat the writer's words. To avoid repetition, you can use synonyms, rearrange sentence structure, or replace complicated language with simpler descriptions.

Read this passage from *Out of Tragedy: Art and Community.* Then, respond to the items that follow.

Art can express what words cannot, and it can bring people together. In memory of those who died in the attack on the World Trade Center, a memorial on the scale of the original towers was designed. The memorial, called *Reflecting Absence,* is a landscaped public plaza with two large one-acre gaps where the Twin Towers once stood. Around the edges of these gaps, water cascades into the voids to make two reflecting pools. Memorials of those who have died serve two purposes: they not only memorialize the dead but also create community.

1. What is purpose of *Reflecting Absence*?

____

____

____

2. Paraphrase the paragraph.

____

____

____

____

____

____

____

____

____

____

____

3. Use your paraphrase to identify the main idea of the paragraph.

____

____

Name ______________________________ Date ______________

Reading Skills: Paraphrasing

Extension 4-2

When you **paraphrase** poetry, you use the same steps as you would to paraphrase prose, but you apply the step a little differently. For example, to identify basic information, you must understand a poem's structure. If the poem has sentences, read them for main ideas. Look beyond the literal meaning of the words for the poet's key ideas. It is all right, at certain times, to include the poet's words when you paraphrase. For example, if a poem describes very specific items, use the poet's names for these items in your paraphrase to preserve the poem's meaning.

Read "The Song of the Old Mother" by William Butler Yeats and respond to the items that follow.

I RISE in the dawn, and I kneel and blow
Till the seed of the fire flicker and glow.
And then I must scrub, and bake, and sweep,
Till stars are beginning to blink and peep;
But the young lie long and dream in their bed
Of the matching of ribbons, the blue and the red,
And their day goes over in idleness,
And they sigh if the wind but lift up a tress.
While I must work, because I am old
And the seed of the fire gets feeble and cold.

1. Paraphrase the last sentence of the poem.

____

____

2. What do you think the poet means by the last sentence of the poem? Explain the sentence's literal and figurative meaning.

____

____

____

____

____

3. Paraphrase the second sentence of the poem.

____

____

____

____

____

____

Name ______________________ Date ____________

Vocabulary: Word Roots

Reinforcement 4-3

Many English words came from Latin or Greek. The Latin and Greek languages are both structured on *word families* and *root words*. A *word family* is a group of words that have all been constructed from the same *root word*, and all have similar meanings. You can guess the meanings of new words if you know the meaning of their root word, or of another word in their word family.

Language	Root Word	Meaning	Example
Latin	-aqua-	water	aquatic
Latin	-spec-	see	spectacular
Greek	-logos-	word or reason	logic
Latin	-mater-	mother	matriarch
Latin	-adapt-	to fit or adjust	adaptable

Choose words from the box below to complete the sentences. Use the table on root words and a dictionary to assist you.

maternity	illogical	aquarium	spectator	monologue
adapter	speculate	maternal	adaptation	aquamarine

1. The electrical plug wouldn't fit in the outlet, so we had to use an ____________.

2. I love seeing dolphin and seal shows at the ____________.

3. My teacher is out on ____________ leave, so we have a substitute.

4. Mom watches football on TV, but Dad says that ____________ sports bore him.

5. Tina spent hours perfectly memorizing her ____________ for the school play, because there would be no one else on stage to cover for her if she forgot it.

6. Our school play is an ____________ of Shakespeare's *Romeo and Juliet*.

7. Without any evidence, we could only ____________ about who could have started the rumor.

8. The Caribbean waters are a gorgeous ____________, my favorite color.

9. His reasoning made no sense and was completely ____________.

10. My neighbor, who is very ____________, always has snacks ready for us after school.

Name ________________________ Date ____________

Vocabulary: Word Origins

Extension 4-3

Suffixes *–ous* and *-ment*

A *word family* is a group of words that are constructed from the same root word and have similar meanings. Root words and word families are part of the basic structure of languages such as Latin and Greek. English has inherited many of these word families.

Examine the table below. Then, answer the questions.

Language	Root Word	Meaning	Example
Greek	-graphos-	to write	graph
Latin	-pater-	father	paternal
Greek	-pathos-	to suffer	sympathy

1. List as many English words as you can from the word family with the root *graphos*. Do not use a dictionary.

____

____

____

2. List as many English words as you can from the word family with the root *pater.* You may use a dictionary if necessary.

____

____

____

____

3. Think of at least 6 words from the word family with the root *pathos*, and write their meanings. You may use a dictionary if necessary.

____

____

____

____

____

____

Name ______________________________ Date ____________

Literary Analysis: Imagery

Reinforcement 4-4

Imagery is language that uses images—words or phrases that appeal to the senses of sight, hearing, smell, taste, and touch. Writers use imagery to do the following:

- create moods
- express emotions
- help readers imagine sights, sounds, textures, tastes, and smells.

An image can appeal to more than one sense. For example, "the icy snow crunched under Sally's boots" appeals to the senses of touch ("icy snow") and hearing ("crunched").

Read the poem and identify sensory language. List the language, the sense to which it appeals, and the part of speech used.

Waves crash and cry
As the daylight dives
Into the salty sea.

Commanding all eyes,
A new blue moon rises,
Orange as the blazing noon sun.

Sensory Language	Sense Appealed To	Part of Speech

Use sensory language appealing to the sense of taste and/or smell to describe each item listed. You may use similes and metaphors if you wish.

1. a spring day ______________________________

2. a busy street ______________________________

Name ______________________ Date ____________

Literary Analysis: Imagery

Extension 4-4

To create **imagery**, poets and prose writers construct descriptions using the five senses. This is known as **sensory language.** Writers may also use comparisons and word repetition in their descriptions to heighten the imagery.

Write a short poem using imagery and sensory language. Include at least one **metaphor** and one **simile**. Then, respond to the following questions.

1. Underline the simile and circle any metaphors.
2. How many of the five senses are included in the imageryof your poem? Give an example of each.

Write a metaphor and a simile for each item listed.

1. an autumn day
2. a traffic jam

Name ________________________________ Date ________________

Literary Analysis: Symbolism

Reinforcement 4-5

Symbols are people, places, or things that stand for something beyond their literal meaning. Writers use symbols, or **symbolism,** to communicate ideas.

- Universal symbols are those that most readers will recognize, such as a dove for peace.
- Specific symbols are those created by a writer for a particular context, such as a wintry garden representing a character's isolation.

Identify whether each symbol is a universal or specific symbol. Then, write the meaning of each symbol in the chart. If the symbol is specific, create your own possible meaning for the symbol.

	Symbol	Meaning	Universal or Specific
1.	a heart		
2.	the sun		
3.	one flower in a garden bed		
4.	the color black		
5.	a tattered flag on a flagpole		
6.	a baby		
7.	a car with a flat tire		
8.	a knife in a kitchen		

Name ______________________________ Date ______________

Literary Analysis: Symbolism

Extension 4-5

Symbols in literature and in life convey meaning that adds emotional depth to ideas. In literature, symbols help us understand characters. In life, symbols let us share emotions with others. Some works of literature are about symbols.

Read this poem about the Statue of Liberty, "The New Colossus," by Emma Lazarus. Then, respond to the items that follow.

Not like the brazen giant of Greek fame,
With conquering limbs astride from land to land;
Here at our sea-washed, sunset gates shall stand
A mighty woman with a torch, whose flame
Is the imprisoned lightning, and her name
Mother of Exiles. From her beacon-hand
Glows world-wide welcome; her mild eyes command
The air-bridged harbor that twin cities frame
"Keep, ancient lands, your storied pomp!" cries she
With silent lips. "Give me your tired, your poor,
Your huddled masses yearning to breathe free,
The wretched refuse of your teeming shore.
Send these, the homeless, tempest-tost to me,
I lift my lamp beside the golden door!"

1. What are some of the symbols in this poem? ______________________________

____

____

2. What does the Statue of Liberty stand for? ______________________________

3. What emotions does the use of symbolism in this poem evoke?

____

____

The Statue of Liberty itself contains many symbols, included by its creators to add meaning to the statue. Look up the Statue of Liberty and find out what the following symbols stand for.

4. broken shackles: ______________________________

5. seven-pointed crown: ______________________________

6. 25 windows in the crown: ______________________________

7. the tablet Liberty holds: ______________________________

Name ______________________________ Date ______________

Comparing Literary Works: Figurative Language

Reinforcement 4-6

Figurative language is language that goes beyond literal meaning to convey feelings, images, and values.

- **Personification** gives human traits to a nonhuman subject.
- **Simile** uses *like* or *as* to compare different ideas or things.
- **Metaphor** compares two ideas or things without *like* or *as*. Metaphors can be **direct,** in which the comparison is stated, **implied,** in which it is merely implied, or **extended,** in which several comparisons are connected.

In the chart below, you will find examples of figurative language from the poems "Dreams," "The City is So Big," "Slam, Dunk, and Hook," and "The Road Not Taken." Fill in the missing boxes to complete the chart.

Example	Type of Figurative Language	Explain the Comparison	Meaning
". . . Life is a broken-winged bird that cannot fly."		The author is comparing life without dreams to a bird that cannot fly.	
". . . Its bridges quake with fear . . ."	personification		The city is so big that even object that appear large to us, are scared of the city.
". . . we could almost last forever, poised in midair like storybook sea monsters."			The basketball players' moved with skill and grace, and could perform awe-inspiring lay-ups.
"Two roads diverged in a yellow wood, and sorry I could not travel both and be one traveler . . ."	extended metaphor	The author is comparing choice of roads to choice in life.	

Name ______________________ Date ______________

Comparing Literary Works: Figurative Language

Extension 4-6

Figurative language is often used in poetry to describe characters, settings, and ideas, where conveying levels of meaning with few words is particularly useful. For example, Emily Dickinson uses an **extended metaphor** to describe the feeling of hope in her poem "'Hope' is the thing with feathers." In the poem, "The City Is So Big," Richard Garcia uses metaphors and similes to describe a city setting.

Use figurative language to create your own descriptions of people, places, and ideas. After each example, tell what kind of figurative language you used.

1. despair: ______________________

2. your best friend: ______________________

3. your room or locker: ______________________

4. joy: ______________________

5. place you go to relax: ______________________

6. a stranger recently encountered: ______________________

7. anger: ______________________

8. activity you enjoy the most: ______________________

9. favorite movie or book: ______________________

10. favorite actor or book character: ______________________

11. setting from a book or film: ______________________

Name ______________________ Date ______________

Language Coach: Active and Passive Voice

Reinforcement 4-7 A

A verb can show action or link a subject to another word in the sentence. A verb can appear in the active voice or the passive voice.

- If the subject performs the action of the verb, the verb is in **active voice.**
  Example Maria *swallowed* a bug.
- If the subject receives the action of the verb, the verb is in **passive voice.** Passive voice always uses the verb form *to be + action verb.*
  Example A bug *was swallowed* by Maria.

The choice between the active and passive voice is usually a matter of preference, not correctness. The use of active voice is usually more powerful.

Underline the verb and circle the subject it refers to in the sentences below. Then, tell if each sentence is in the active or passive voice. Rewrite sentences that are in the passive voice in the active voice.

1. Memories of the trip were treasured by Enrique.

____

2. Andrew told everyone that Hawaii was amazing.

____

3. Plans were made by the travel group to go next year.

____

4. The mailbox was hit by a car.

____

5. Jeremy scored two goals during the championship game.

____

Apply Write a brief journal entry about things that have happened this week. In your journal entry include sentences written in both the active and passive voice.

____

____

____

____

____

____

____

____

Name ______________________________ Date ______________

Language Coach: Spelling Words With Suffixes

Reinforcement 4-7 B

Adding a **suffix** to a base word often involves a spelling change in the word.

A	C
Drop the e when adding a suffix that begins with a vowel. *move + -able = movable*	Double the final consonant of the base word when the base word has one syllable AND the suffix begins with a vowel. *rob + -er = robber*
B	**D**
Change the y to i when the base word ends with a consonant followed by y. *rely + -able = reliable* exception: if suffix begins with i *cry + -ing = crying*	Double the final consonant of the base word when the base word ends in a single vowel followed by a single consonant and the accent falls on the last syllable AND the suffix begins with a vowel. *rebel + ion = rebellion*

Add each base word and suffix to spell a new word. Write the letter of the spelling rule you used on the line provided.

1. drive + -ing ____________ Rule: ____________
2. operate + -or ____________ Rule: ____________
3. vary + -ing ____________ Rule: ____________
4. debate + -able ____________ Rule: ____________
5. defy + -ance ____________ Rule: ____________
6. slip + -ery ____________ Rule: ____________
7. control + -ing ____________ Rule: ____________
8. plan + -ed ____________ Rule: ____________
9. commit + -ed ____________ Rule: ____________
10. hop + -ed ____________ Rule: ____________
11. encourage + -ing ____________ Rule: ____________
12. beauty + -ful ____________ Rule: ____________

Name ______________________________ Date ____________

Language Coach: Active and Passive Voice

Extension 4-7

Grammar and spelling rules provide tools that help you write effectively. For example, once you know the difference between **active** and **passive voice** you can choose when depending on the effect you want. When you know how to change the spelling of a word to add a suffix, then the meaning of the new word will be clear.

Fill in the blanks with the correct spelling of the word, adding the indicated suffix. Rewrite every active voice sentence as passive voice and rewrite every passive voice sentence as active voice.

1. Tasha cooks a special dinner for her family once a week.

____

2. The wok that she uses was bought by her mother.

____

3. Woks are use (+ ed) __________ by many people for make (+ ing) __________ Asian food.

____

4. One day, the cooking was begun late by Tasha.

____

5. Annoyed with her tardy (+ness) __________, she quickly pile (+ed) __________ all of the ingredients in her arms.

____

6. Suddenly, everything was dropped.

____

7. The vegetables were ruined and the wok was broken by the calamity.

____

8. Sit (+ing) __________ down in the mess on the floor, Tasha cry (+ed) __________ tears of frustration.

____

9. The meal was ruined by Tasha.

____

Analyze Do you think any sentences should stay in passive voice? Explain?

____

____

____

____

Name ______________________________ Date ______________

Writers Workshop: Critical Review

Reinforcement 4-8

If you are uncertain whether you would enjoy the latest blockbuster movie or bestseller book, you might turn to a **critical review.** In a critical review, writers will give you information and their opinions. They use words such as *brilliant* or *dull* to convey strong or mild praise or disapproval.

Read the beginning of the critical review below and answer the questions.

I found the movie "Bridge to Terabithia" extremely weak in contrast to the book, which should be read by everyone. Although the movie's story line followed closely with the book's, it did not deliver the fantasies described in the book with the quality for which I'd hoped.

In the book, Jess and Leslie create a fantasyland where they can escape the pressures of school and life. No one can defeat them here. The descriptions given to the fantasies provide a wonderful image, which you hope to see transformed beautifully in the movie. To much disappointment, the fantasy scenes seemed carelessly created. For example, it is obvious in one scene that the main characters Jess and Leslie are running on a treadmill in front of a green screen instead of running in a real forest. With the amazing cinematography present in today's movies, the fantasy life created should be richer.

1. What similar theme exists between the movie and the book versions of "Bridge to Terabithia"?

____

____

2. Why does the writer of this critical review prefer the book to the movie?

____

3. What words does the writer use to show his or her opinion?

____

____

Conclude Write an ending to the critical review. Keep the writer's point of view.

____

____

____

____

____

____

____

____

Name ______________________ Date ______________

Writer's Workshop: Critical Review

Extension 4-8

Comparing two literary pieces on the same subject can help you identify the positive and negative attributes of each piece. Professional critics frequently use this technique in reviews.

The poem and prose piece below both address the same subject. Read both selections and answer the questions that follow.

"The Burning of Books" by Bertolt Brecht. This poem was written in 1933 prior to the Nazi Book Burnings.

When the Regime ordered that books with dangerous teachings
Should be publicly burnt and everywhere
Oxen were forced to draw carts full of books
To the funeral pyre, an exiled poet,
One of the best, discovered with fury, when he studied the list
Of the burned, that his books
Had been forgotten. He rushed to his writing table
On wings of anger and wrote a letter to those in power.
Burn me, he wrote with hurrying pen, burn me!
Do not treat me in this fashion. Don't leave me out. Have I not
Always spoken the truth in my books? And now
You treat me like a liar! I order you:
Burn me!

Excerpt from the speech "Areopagitica" by John Milton. This was prepared as a pamphlet for the Liberty of Unlicensed Printing and was presented to the Parliament of England in 1644.

"And yet, on the other hand, unless wariness be used, as good almost kill a man as kill a good book. Who kills a man kills a reasonable creature, God's image; but he who destroys a good book, kills reason itself, kills the image of God, as it were in the eye. Many a man lives a burden to the earth; but a good book is the precious life-blood of a master spirit, embalmed and treasured up on purpose to a life beyond life."

1. Which style did you prefer? Explain.

____

____

____

2. On a separate sheet of paper, list five words you could use in a critical review to show praise and five words you could use to show disapproval.

Write What are the positive and negative attributes of each piece? On a separate sheet of paper, write a critical review of both pieces.

Name ______________________________ Date ______________

Mid-Unit Benchmark Test — Unit 4

Reading Skill: Paraphrasing

Read the following questions. Then, choose the best answer.

1 What is paraphrasing?

A skimming the text to find main ideas

B restating the text in your own words

C analyzing the text to find connections

D reading through the text carefully

2 What can paraphrasing help you do?

F understand difficult vocabulary when you first read it

G write stories filled with colorful details

H use antonyms to explain the writer's meaning

J avoid plagiarism, or using someone else's words as your own

Read the passage. Then, answer the questions.

Announced by all the trumpets of the sky,
Arrives the snow, and, driving o'er the fields,
Seems nowhere to alight: the whited air
Hides hill and woods, the river, and the heaven,
And veils the farmhouse at the garden's end.
The sled and traveller stopped, the courier's feet
Delayed, all friends shut out, the housemates sit
Around the radiant fireplace, enclosed
In a tumultuous privacy of storm.

—from "The Snowstorm" by Ralph Waldo Emerson

3 Which is the best paraphrase of lines 1–2 of Emerson's poem?

A The sky is full of wonder.

B Great horns are blowing.

C A snowstorm has come.

D Wind blows over the fields.

4 Which best expresses the meaning of lines 3–5 of Emerson's poem?

F The snow falls softly on the land.

G The snow blots out everything.

H Snow falls but fails to stick.

J The weather is cold and gloomy.

5 Which best restates lines 6–9 of Emerson's poem?

A People are staying indoors during the storm.

B Travelers stop to admire the beauty of the woods.

C Families enjoy sitting around the fire together.

D Neighbors stay in contact during the storm.

Name ______________________________ Date ______________

Read the passage. Then, answer the questions.

Try these steps if your computer display goes blank or if your system freezes:

1. Unplug all external devices that are connected to your computer except the power adapter.
2. Simultaneously depress the Command and Control keys, as well as the Power button, to reactivate the system.
3. Allow the battery to charge at least 10 percent before plugging in external devices.

Note: Look at the Battery Status icon to determine how much the battery has recharged.

6 Which sentence is the best paraphrase of step 2?

F Press the Command key, followed by the Control key.

G Press the Command key, and then press the Control and Power buttons.

H Press the Power button, and then press the Command key.

J Press the Command, Control, and Power buttons, all at the same time.

7 Which is the best paraphrase of the last sentence?

A The Battery Status icon will tell you the charge of the batter.

B Check the Battery Status icon to see whether the battery has recharged.

C To determine how much the battery has recharged, look at the icon.

D View the battery icon to determine how much the battery has recharged.

8 Which paraphrase shows the steps described in the selection in the correct order?

F Unplug the power adapter. Recharge the battery to 10 percent. Then, hold down the Command and Control keys. Press the Power button to restart your computer.

G Plug in external devices to the computer. Then, hold down the Command, Control, and Power buttons to turn off the computer. Let the battery recharge to 10 percent.

H Unplug all devices except the power adapter. Hold down the Command, Control, and Power keys all at once to restart the computer. Let the battery charge to 10 percent before plugging in externals.

J Hold down the Command and Control keys to shut down the computer. Then, recharge the battery to 10 percent. Restart the computer.

Vocabulary

Read the following questions. Then, choose the best answer.

9 Which word probably shares the same origin as *aquatic*, which comes from the Latin word *aqua*, meaning "water"?

A aquarium

B acquire

C quart

D quality

10 Which word probably shares the same origin as *receive*, which comes from the Latin word *recipere*, meaning "to get"?

F reception

G recipe

H recite

J recount

Name ______________________________ Date ______________

11 **Which word probably shares the same origin as *gratify*, which comes from the Latin word *gratus*, meaning "pleasing"?**

A graduate

B congratulate

C migrate

D grating

12 **Which word probably shares the same origin as *reflector*, which comes from the Latin word *reflectere*, meaning "to bend back?"**

F flexible

G reflection

H infection

J reference

Literary Analysis

Read the following questions. Then, choose the best answer.

13 **Which of these best defines imagery in poetry?**

A pictures that accompany poetry

B comparison of one thing to another

C language that appeals to the senses

D imagination in poetry

14 **Which of these is an example of the use of imagery?**

F The icy snow crunched underfoot.

G Jack filled his plate with food.

H Two chimneys rose from the house.

J His mind was busily at work.

15 **Which of these is an example of the use of figurative language?**

A The breeze rustled the leaves of the tall elms.

B The grain stalks bowed to one another in the breeze.

C A sudden breeze cooled our hot faces as we worked.

D The wind chimes dinged and clanged in the breeze.

16 **Which choice contains a simile?**

F The sheriff was a hearty fellow.

G Amelia likes to jog before breakfast.

H The stream gurgled over the rocks.

J Pynchon's Pond was as smooth as glass.

17 **Which of the sentences is an example of personification?**

A A rusted stove crouched in the corner.

B In the race, Evan ran like a gazelle.

C The trail bent left, toward the creek.

D She sat sleepily, nodding her head.

18 **Which of these best defines the use of personification?**

F Two unlike things are compared by using *like* or *as*.

G Two unlike things are compared by saying that one is the other.

H A nonhuman subject is given human characteristics.

J Human behavior is described in terms of animal behavior.

19 I stared out the window of my drab, cramped room. A single bird soared across the sky, its wings spread wide and free.

The bird in these sentences symbolizes—

A boredom

B the sky

C freedom

D the window

20 **Which type of figurative language is used in this sentence?**

The surface of the pond was a mirror reflecting the summer clouds.

F personification

G simile

H hyperbole

J metaphor

Name ______________________ Date ______________

Read the passage. Then, answer the questions.

As Cara shuffled through the neglected, barren parking lot, she thought about the fight. Edie would never forgive her for what she had said. Their friendship was over.

Then Cara saw it. A small, brilliantly red flower had managed to grow through one of the many jagged cracks of the parking lot. It stood in the midst of the parking lot like a lone boat in the middle of the ocean. How it had survived in this wasteland, Cara would never know. But seeing this unlikely flower, she began to think that anything was possible. Maybe Edie would forgive her.

21 What does the flower symbolize?

A desperation

B excitement

C hope

D anger

22 Which of the following sentences contains a simile?

F "As Cara shuffled through the neglected, barren parking lot, she thought about the fight."

G "Edie would never forgive her for what she had said."

H "It stood in the midst of the parking lot like a lone boat in the middle of the ocean."

J "How it had survived in this wasteland, Cara would never know."

23 The "small, brilliantly red flower" appeals to the reader's sense of—

A touch

B sight

C smell

D hearing

24 "Jagged cracks" appeals to the reader's senses of—

F touch and smell

G hearing and taste

H smell and sight

J sight and touch

Grammar

Read the following questions. Then, choose the best answer.

25 Which of these best defines a verb in the passive voice?

A Its subject receives the action.

B The verb lacks strength.

C The performer is important.

D Its subject is unclear.

26 Which sentence correctly shows a verb in the active voice?

F A loud screech was heard in the tree.

G This street was paved yesterday.

H The baby is sleeping soundly.

J The new park was finished at last.

Name ______________________________ Date ______________

27 **How would you change this sentence to the active voice?**

The leaky faucet was repaired by my mother.

A The extremely leaky faucet was repaired by my mother.

B By my mother, the leaky faucet was repaired.

C The leaky faucet is repaired by my mother.

D My mother repaired the leaky faucet.

28 **Which sentence correctly shows a verb in the passive voice?**

F The ancient artifact was expertly crafted.

G Sawyer ate cereal and fruit for breakfast.

H The butterfly fluttered past our window.

J Josie walked by the classroom door.

Spelling

Read the following questions. Then, choose the best answer.

29 **In which sentence is the underlined word spelled correctly?**

A We brought an <u>inflateable</u> mattress for the camping trip.

B We found an <u>affordable</u> vacation.

C Clarence <u>modifyed</u> the team's remaining schedule.

D There was <u>resistence</u> to my idea.

30 **Which word would correctly complete this sentence?**

Samantha is ______ for notifying the newspaper of our book sale.

F responsable

G responsible

H responssible

J responseable

31 **Which word would correctly complete this sentence?**

An additional ______ of the play is scheduled for Sunday afternoon.

A performance

B performence

C performmence

D performince

32 **Which word would correctly complete this sentence?**

Shiann felt ______ after losing the tennis match.

F pityyful

G pityful

H pittyful

J pitiful

33 **In which sentence is the underlined word spelled correctly?**

A <u>Carrying</u> all of the boxes upstairs took longer than we thought.

B Dad couldn't believe the <u>filthyness</u> of my room.

C Keep dairy food cold so that it stays <u>consumeble</u>.

D Maria said that she was nervous before she <u>testifyed</u> in court.

34 **In which sentence is the underlined word spelled correctly?**

F Colonel Smith was famous for his <u>hardyness</u>.

G To make a better design, Jack <u>varyed</u> the colors he used.

H My favorite part of zoology is <u>classifying</u> the animals.

J Mrs. Henderson told me to try <u>modifiing</u> my formula.

Name ______________________ Date ______________

Short Answer

Reading Skill: Paraphrasing

35 **Paraphrase the following sentence.**

When Darien runs his mouth constantly, his mother's patience wears thin.

36 **Briefly explain how to paraphrase.**

Literary Analysis

37 **What is hyperbole?**

38 **Describe the comparison in the following sentence. What type of metaphor is used?**

Jerod mowed down my idea for a group project.

Essay

Write on a separate sheet of paper.

39 **Jot down notes for a study for a poem about a walk in the woods. Begin by listing some things you might see, hear, smell, touch, and taste in the woods. Then choose three items on your list and write phrases that make comparisons. Use one example each of a simile, a metaphor, and personification, such as *The tall pines look like sharpened pencils.***

40 **Choose one of the poems from this test and imagine that you have been asked to write a review of it. On a separate sheet of paper, write the headings "Word Choice" and "Imagery." Then write an example of each from the poem and tell whether you think the poet uses the word or words and images effectively. Give reasons for your opinions.**

41 **Think of an object or animal that symbolizes something for your nation or state. Write a paragraph describing and explaining this symbol and what it represents.**

Name ______________________ Date ____________

Diagnostic Test 2 — Unit 4

Read the passages. Then, answer the questions.

Mom thinks that I'm a chronic slob. My room has always been a mess because I never clean it. Mom nags me to straighten up my room, but I like it the way it is. It may seem like a mess to her, but the way that I have my room organized makes perfect sense to me. I've compiled a mental list of the room's furnishings. My desk chair holds my dirty clothes. The dresser in the corner is piled with my school books. One side of the bed is covered with clean towels and laundry that I never fold or put away. I always know where to find my things, so I don't think it's messy at all!

1 What is the meaning of *chronic*?

A huge

B awful

C constant

D annoying

2 Based on the passage's context, the idiom "straighten up" means—

F stand taller

G improve behavior

H organize carefully

J have good posture

3 What type of context clue is given for *compiled*?

A an idiom

B an antonym

C a synonym

D an explanation

4 Synonyms can help you determine the meaning of an unfamiliar word because they—

F mean the same as the unfamiliar word

G are idioms for the unfamiliar word

H mean the opposite of the unfamiliar word

J give information about the unfamiliar word

The tide rises, the tide falls,
The twilight darkens, the curlew calls;
Along the sea-sands damp and brown
The traveler hastens toward the town,
And the tide rises, the tide falls.

Darkness settles on roofs and walls,
But the sea, the sea in darkness calls;
The little waves, with their soft, white hands
Efface the footprints in the sands,
And the tide rises, the tide falls.

The morning breaks; the steeds in their stalls
Stamp and neigh, as the hostler calls;
The day returns, but nevermore
Returns the traveler to the shore.
And the tide rises, the tide falls.

—"The Tide Rises, the Tide Falls" by Henry Wadsworth Longfellow

Name ______________________________ Date ______________

5 **What subject is the speaker talking about?**

A the sound of the waves

B the passing of time

C the joys of traveling

D the beauty of nature

6 **How many feet are in line 3?**

F four

G five

H eight

J nine

7 **The repetition of line 1 is used to emphasize—**

A the call of the sea

B the busy activity of the town

C the long journey of the traveler

D the ceaseless movement of the tide

8 **This is a lyric poem because it—**

F has a plot

G lacks a set pattern of rhythm or rhyme

H expresses the feelings of a single speaker

J tells a story by using a character's own thoughts

Read the following questions Then, choose the best answer.

9 **Which of these sentences is a complex sentence?**

A We moved to a new neighborhood.

B Jackie loves the new house, but I miss the old house.

C We will get a dog after we have settled into the new house.

D Samantha drove to the store to buy some milk.

10 **What should you do to change the following sentence into a compound-complex sentence?**

We walked to the lake and back.

F Add a comma.

G Add a subordinate clause.

H Add a comma and a conjunction.

J Add another independent clause and a subordinate clause.

11 **Which of the following sentences uses an adverb correctly to add interest to the sentence?**

A Bella saw a spider.

B Bella saw a big, black spider.

C Suddenly, Bella saw a spider.

D Bella, my youngest sister, saw a spider.

12 **Which of these sentences uses a prepositional phrase correctly to add interest to the sentence?**

F Jon brushed the dog and then took a nap.

G Before his nap, Jon brushed the dog.

H Jon brushed the dog quickly and took a long nap.

J Jon wanted to take a nap so he brushed the dog.

Name ______________________________ Date ______________

Reading Skills: Using Context to Determine Meaning

Reinforcement 4-10

Context clues are the words surrounding a word or phrase that help to suggest its meaning. Read the following sentences.

John had improved his study habits by completing his homework before dinner. Then, spring and good weather came. He regressed; he started playing basketball until dinner every night and sometimes didn't get to his homework until right before class.

The word *regressed* means "moving backward." The context clue is the information about John not completing his homework before dinner like he did before. In this example, the context clue was an explanation. Context clues can also be synonyms or antonyms of the unfamiliar word.

Read the following paragraph. Then, answer the questions.

The tall towers of the old building reached skyward and glittered in the sun. They were golden turrets, built to defend against enemies. It was a castle from another era, when women wore corsets that were so tight under their clothing that they could barely breathe. As I approached the gate, visitors were peering over the parapet, clearly ignoring a sign that said, "Stay away from the edge of the wall."

1. a. What do you think *turrets* means?

   ____

   b. What context clues did you use?

   ____

   c. What type of context clue did you use to determine the meaning?

   ____

2. a. What do you think *corsets* means?

   ____

   b. What context clues did you use?

   ____

   c. What type of context clue did you use to determine the meaning?

   ____

3. a. What do you think *parapet* means?

   ____

   b. What context clues did you use?

   ____

   c. What type of context clue did you use to determine the meaning?

   ____

Name ______________________________ Date ______________

Reading Skills: Using Context to Determine Meaning

Extension 4-10

How do you find the meaning of an unfamiliar word? One way is to look at the words and phrases that surround the unknown word. In the sentence, "Albert has a litigious nature; he has sued his landlord, his employer, and his barber," if you didn't know the meaning of "litigious" you could figure it out by the explanation in the remainder of the sentence.

Context clues can be explanations, or synonyms, or antonyms that appear in surrounding words or phrases.

Find the context clues for the underlined words in the following poem. Then, complete the chart to include the meaning, context clue, and type of context clue. If you need more space, copy and complete the chart on a separate sheet of paper.

"Sea Mist"

A typical and normal day
Of fighting gale winds and brutal mist,
Of silence, interminable,
This unending life, the driven
We hold our life in our fists.
Near the ocean, we were muted, mum.
Forceful gusts and perpetual roar of waves
So loud in our thoughts, quiet in our ways.

Unfamiliar Word	Context Clue Type of Context Clue	Meaning
gale		
interminable		
mum		

Evaluate Use a dictionary to look up the unfamiliar words from the poem. Compare the definitions with the meanings you wrote. How accurate were you in determining the meaning of the words? Explain any differences between the meaning you derived and the dictionary definition of the word.

____

____

____

____

____

Name ______________________________ Date ______________

Literary Analysis: Sound Devices

Reinforcement 4-11 A

Sound devices are used to make poems to create a mood and make them more interesting to read. Often, poems have words, phrases, sounds, or sentences that are used more than once to emphasize an idea.

Alliteration	repetition of consonant sounds at the beginning of words ("*g*hostly *g*alleon")
Consonance	repetition of consonant sounds at the end of words ("gall*eon*" and "up*on*")
Assonance	repetition of vowel sounds in words ("m*oo*nlight" and "m*oo*r")
Internal Rhyme	repetition of sound within a line ("*r*oad was a *r*ibbon . . . ove*r* the pu*r*ple moo*r*")
End Rhyme	repeated sound at the end of lines ("tr*ees*" and "s*eas*")
Onomatopoeia	words that imitate sounds ("gusty")

Write the letter of the matching sound device for each of the examples from the poem above. Some devices may be used more than once and some examples may match more than one letter.

1. _____ "road was a ribbon"
2. _____ "highwayman came riding"
3. _____ "locked and barred"
4. _____ "there" and "hair"
5. _____ "clattered and clashed"
6. _____ "with his whip"

a. end rhyme
b. assonance
c. consonance
d. alliteration
e. onomatopoeia
f. internal rhyme

Name ______________________ Date ______________

Literary Analysis: Rhythm and Meter

Reinforcement 4-11 B

Rhythm in poetry is the pattern of beats in language. A specific pattern of stressed and unstressed syllables is the **meter** of a poem. To find the meter of a poem, count the stressed and unstressed syllables in a line. To mark a poem's meter, write a slanted line (´) above every stressed syllable and a horseshoe symbol (˘) above every unstressed syllable. Use vertical lines to divide weak and strong stresses into feet.

Read the following poem by Robert Frost that exhibits traditional forms of meter and rhyme. Answer the questions that follow.

Acquainted With the Night by Robert Frost

I have been one acquainted with the night,
I have walked out in rain — and back in rain.
I have outwalked the furthest city light.

I have looked down the saddest city lane.
I have passed the watchman on his beat
And dropped my eyes, unwilling to explain.

I have stood still and stopped the sound of feet
When far away an interrupted cry
Came over houses from another street,

But not to call me back or say good-bye;
And further still at an unearthly height,
One luminary clock against the sky

Proclaimed the time was neither wrong nor right
I have been one acquainted with the night.

1. Scan the poem by marking stressed and unstressed syllables and feet.
2. Is this poem made up of iambic (da DUM da DUM) or trochaic (DUM da DUM da) feet? ______________________
3. Discuss the interaction between the poem's rhythm and its message.

____

____

Name ______________________ Date ____________

Literary Analysis: Repetition

Extension 4-11

A well-written poem engages the reader on many levels. Imagery, **rhyme, meter,** and the sounds of words, all work together to send a particular message. **Repetition,** using the same word or words repeatedly, is another tool of the poet.

The poem "Alabanza: In Praise of Local 100," uses repetition to excellent effect. People unfamiliar with Spanish may not realize the extent of the repetition. The word *alabanza* means "praise" in Spanish, so when the poet says, "Alabanza. Praise . . . ," he is actually using the word "praise" twice.

Read the poem "Alabanza: In Praise of Local 100" from Lesson 4 aloud. Then, answer the questions below.

1. Discuss the effect of the poet's use of the words *alabanza* and *praise.*

2. This poem is divided into three sections. The second section uses the word *after* repeatedly. What does the word *after* refer to? What effect does the poet's use of the word have on the reader?

3. The poet repeats the image of the lighthouse in Fajardo. How is this image used? How do the two appearances of this image relate to one another?

4. In the second section of the poem, the poet repeats the word *soul* several times. Why do you think he did this?

Name ______________________ Date ____________

Listening and Speaking: Reading Poetry Aloud

Reinforcement 4-12

Reading a poem aloud requires an understanding of the meaning of the poem. To convey meaning, speak clearly and effectively.

Read the following stanza about daffodils from "I Wandered Lonely As a Cloud" by William Wordsworth and answer the questions that follow.

Continuous as the stars that shine
And twinkle on the milky way,
They stretched in never-ending line
Along the margin of a bay:
Ten thousand saw I at a glance,
Tossing their heads in sprightly dance.

1. What do you imagine when you read this stanza? What words help paint the picture? ______________________

____

2. What tone of voice would you use when reading this stanza aloud? Why?

____

____

Read the following stanza from "If" by Rudyard Kipling and answer the questions about how to effectively read this stanza aloud.

If you can keep your head when all about you
Are losing theirs and blaming it on you;
If you can trust yourself when all men doubt you,
But make allowance for their doubting too:
If you can wait and not be tired by waiting,
Or, being lied about, don't deal in lies,
Or being hated don't give way to hating,
And yet don't look too good, nor talk too wise;

3. What do you think is the meaning of this stanza? How would you convey this meaning when you read the poem aloud? ______________________

____

____

____

4. Where would you pause when reading this stanza aloud?

____

Name ______________________________ Date ______________

Listening and Speaking Workshop: Reading Poetry Aloud

Extension 4-12

Reading poetry aloud can enhance your perception of the meaning of the work. You can hear many things in a poem—the rhythm, the sounds of the words, the rhymes. Knowing how to read a poem aloud to convey meaning is an important skill.

In the following lines of poetry notice the rhythm, sounds of words, and rhymes that might be emphasized when you read the poem aloud. Then, answer the questions below.

This is the first stanza from "I Wandered Lonely As a Cloud" by William Wordsworth.

I wandered lonely as a cloud
That floats on high o'er vales and hills,
When all at once I saw a crowd,
A host, of golden daffodils;
Beside the lake, beneath the trees,
Fluttering and dancing in the breeze.

1. Count the syllables in each line. Are they all the same? If not, which ones are different? ______________________________

____

2. Which lines rhyme? ______________________________

3. What picture do the images create? ______________________________

____

Synthesize Write notes on how you would present a reading of this poem. Which words would you emphasize? Where would you pause? Is your tone of voice happy, sad, or sentimental?

____

____

____

____

____

____

____

Name ______________________ Date ____________

Literary Analysis: Forms of Poetry

Reinforcement 4-13 A

Poems come in many forms. They can be short or long. They may rhyme or they may not. They may have an established meter or no recognizable meter. **Narrative** poems tell a story with a plot, characters, and a setting. **Lyric** poems are short poems that express the speaker's feelings. **Concrete** poems are set in the shape of their subject.

The following poem contains some nautical terms, that is, words relating to boats. Here is a list of the words you'll see:

Prow: the bow, or front of a boat

Heel: to lean to one side, which a sailboat does in a good wind

Sheet: the rope that controls a sail

Hull: the body of the boat

Read the poem and answer the questions that follow it.

Give
me wind
and I will fly
unleashed and free.
My prow a knife,
My sail my strength.
I yearn to heel,
My sheet held
tight.
My hull, my sleek wood home, asks only this.
Release my chain and let me slake my
thirst on rushing sea.

1. What type of poem is this? How do you know? ______________________

2. Do you think the poet made the right choice in choosing this type of poem? Why or why not?

____

3. Who is the speaker of this poem? How do you know? ______________________

4. How does the speaker feel about sailing? Use details from the poem to support your answer.

____

Name ______________________________ Date ______________

Literary Analysis: Speaker

Reinforcement 4-13 B

The **speaker** of a poem is the imaginary voice assumed by the writer of a poem. The speaker is similar to a narrator, however, a speaker may only express thoughts or feelings. To better understand the speaker's views of ideas and events is to **infer the speaker's attitude.**

Read the first verse of Walt Whitman's "O Captain! My Captain!" then answer the following questions about the speaker of the poem.

O CAPTAIN! my Captain, our fearful trip is done,
The ship has weather'd every rack, the prize we sought is won,
The port is near, the bells I hear, the people all exulting,
While follow eyes the steady keel, the vessel grim and daring;
But O heart! heart! heart!
O the bleeding drops of red,
Where on the deck my Captain lies,
Fallen cold and dead.

1. Who is probably the speaker of the poem?
   - a. the captain of a ship
   - b. a sailor
   - c. a fish
   - d. a ship

2. What is the subject the speaker is talking about?
   - a. a broken heart
   - b. sailing
   - c. treasure
   - d. a ship's captain

3. How does the speaker probably feel?
   - a. overjoyed to see land
   - b. afraid the crowd will steal their prize
   - c. helpless he or she is unable to save the captain's life
   - d. excited to see the cheering crowds at the port

4. What is the speaker's tone?
   - a. fearful
   - b. friendly
   - c. tired
   - d. indifferent

5. What words convey the subject of the poem? Explain.

____

____

____

____

____

Name ______________________________ Date ______________

Literary Analysis: Speaker

Extension 4-13

Who or what is the voice in a poem? The poet is the writer, but the poet is not necessarily the voice, or speaker, of the poem. Determining a poem's speaker may not always be possible, but clues to his or her attitudes and feelings are present in the word choices and tone of a poem.

Alice Walker and Yusef Komunyakaa are only a few years apart in age, but their poems "At First, It Is True, I Thought There Were Only Peaches & Wild Grapes" and "Slam, Dunk, & Hook" reveal speakers at different stages of life.

Reread the poem "At First, It Is True, I Thought There Were Only Peaches & Wild Grapes." Then, answer the questions below.

1. What do you know about the speaker's attitudes and feelings? How do you know it?

____

____

2. Does the fruit described have a meaning beyond itself? What meaning is that?

____

____

3. What can you infer about the age of the speaker in this poem?

____

____

Reread the poem "Slam, Dunk, & Hook." Then, respond to the following.

4. Komunyakaa provides a lot of information about the earlier life of the speaker of this poem. Write a short paragraph describing the speaker and his friends at the time described in the poem.

____

____

____

____

5. How do you think the speaker described in "Slam, Dunk, & Hook" would respond to the message of "At First, It Is True, I Thought There Were Only Peaches & Wild Grapes"? Explain.

____

____

Name ______________________________ Date ______________

Language Coach: Sentence Structure

Reinforcement 4-14 A

A **simple sentence** is one independent clause—a group of words that has a subject and a verb and can stand by itself as a complete thought.

Example The dog chased the ball.

A **compound sentence** consists of two or more independent clauses linked by a word such as *and, but,* or *or.*

Example Mr. Roberts was a teacher, but he also coached soccer.

A **complex sentence** contains one independent clause and one or more subordinate clauses—a group of words that has a subject and a verb but is not a complete thought.

Example Although he was a science teacher, Mr. Roberts also taught math.

Read the following sentences. Identify each as either *simple, compound,* or *complex.* Write your answer on the line.

1. ____________ Barry played football.
2. ____________ Alicia lived in the city, and one of her cousins live in the country.
3. ____________ I am the student government president this year.
4. ____________ Our tour guide showed us the house, and she demonstrated cooking on a cast iron stove.
5. ____________ Although it was a holiday, Sheena worked on her science assignment.
6. ____________ Tiffany forgot to water the plants.

Write a sentence using the phrase provided. Label your sentences by writing *simple, compound,* or *complex* in parentheses after each one.

7. liked to write poetry

____

8. although he was

____

____

9. but she fell asleep

____

____

Name ______________________________ Date ______________

Language Coach: Revising to Vary Sentence Patterns

Reinforcement 4-14 B

If most of your sentences begin with nouns followed by verbs, you can vary the beginnings of your sentences to make your writing more interesting. By adding an adjective, adverb, or prepositional phrase to the beginning of a sentence, you can vary your sentence patterns.

dull sentence:	Joshua's team lost the soccer game.
+ adjective:	*Disappointed,* Joshua's team lost the soccer game.
+ adverb:	*Unfortunately,* Joshua's team lost the soccer game.
+ prepositional phrase:	*After practicing all week,* Joshua's team lost the soccer game.

Revise the following paragraph by filling in the blanks according to the directions in the parentheses.

______________________, Lisette and Sunny wanted to start a recycling
(prepositional phrase)

program. ______________, Sunny's mom suggested they have a meeting
(adjective)

after school. ______________, several students volunteered to help them.
(adjective)

______________, they needed money to buy recycling bins for the
(adverb)

cafeteria. ______________________, they earned enough money to buy the
(prepositional phrase)

bins. ______________, the principal congratulated them on their success.
(adjective)

Name ______________________ Date ____________

Language Coach: Revising to Vary Sentence Patterns

Extension 4-14

A paragraph full of sentences that begin with nouns followed by verbs can seem repetitive and boring. You can add interest to your writing by starting a sentence with a different part of speech—for example, an adjective, adverb, prepositional phrase, or infinitive phrase. Inverting the subject and verb can add interest, too.

Complete the following activities.

1. Revise the following paragraph so that most sentences start with an adjective, adverb, prepositional phrase, or infinitive phrase. Leave the beginning of one sentence as it is, but add an appositive or appositive phrase to it. You may add words or reorganize the existing words to revise each sentence.

   My grandfather is one of my favorite people in the world. He never gets tired of listening. He always gives me good advice. My grandmother and he live next door to us. We go to their house for waffles on Sunday nights.

   ____

   ____

   ____

   ____

   ____

2. Make any changes you can think of to improve the following paragraph. Add adjectives, adverbs, prepositional phrases, infinitives phrases, and appositive phrases. You can add them anywhere in the sentences, not just at the beginnings. You may change the word order of the sentences, and you may combine sentences, if that will improve the paragraph. Do not remove any sentences.

   My class went on a field trip to the art museum last week. I didn't think I would enjoy it. I was wrong. I thought it would be wall after wall of boring, old paintings. That wasn't how it was. There were big, bold canvases. They were full of color. The painter seemed to reach inside me and grab my attention. I poked my head into the next room. I couldn't wait.

   ____

   ____

   ____

   ____

   ____

   ____

   ____

Name ______________________________ Date ______________

Writer's Workshop: Writing for Assessment

Reinforcement 4-15

When you **write for assessment,** start by reading the prompt carefully. You need to understand what you are being asked to write. Next, decide on your topic. If possible, choose something you feel knowledgeable about. Organize your thoughts using a diagram or outline, and then write a draft. The opening sentence of your essay should state the main idea. Read your draft over, and refer back to the prompt to ensure that it answers the question. Check to see that you have backed up your ideas with details, and organized your thoughts in a logical way. Finally, check for spelling and grammatical errors.

Read the following two prompts. Choose a prompt and use the lines below to organize your response. Then, on another sheet of paper, write your exposition.

A. Poetry, more than other literary forms, focuses on calling up specific feelings in its readers.

Choose a poem you have read in or out of school that calls up specific feelings in its readers. In a well-developed composition, identify what feelings the poem evokes and explain how one of the tools (imagery, figurative language, sound devices) helps communicate those feelings.

B. A poem is like an intimate conversation between the poem's speaker and its reader.

Choose a poem you have read in or out of school. select a character that is honorable. In a well-developed composition, identify who the speaker is, the subject he or she is talking about, and how the speaker feels about the subject. How does the identity of the speaker affect your response to the poem's subject?

____

____

____

____

____

____

____

____

____

____

____

____

Name ________________________________ Date ______________

Writer's Workshop: Writing for Assessment

Extension 4-15

Writing well under pressure requires focus, the ability to draw your thoughts together in a limited amount of time, and mastery of the mechanics of good writing. The first step is to zero in on what you are being asked to write. Next, choose a topic you can examine thoroughly. Organize your thoughts logically, and then revise.

Read the following poem, note, and prompt. Then, complete the items that follow.

"I Have Heard the Sunset Song of the Birches"
By Stephen Crane

"I have heard the sunset song of the birches,
A white melody in the silence,
I have seen a quarrel of the pines.
At nightfall
The little grasses have rushed by me
With the wind men.
These things have I lived," quoth the maniac,
"Possessing only eyes and ears.
But you—
You don green spectacles before you look at roses."

Note If you look at something red through green glass, it will appear gray.

Prompt In no more than 30 minutes, write an essay analyzing two key elements of the poem. These key elements may include the following: imagery, symbolism, figurative language, sound devices, or rhythm.

1. Time yourself so that you finish these prewriting questions in 8 minutes or less.
   a. Choose two elements and take notes on a separate sheet of paper.
   b. Which type of organization will you use for your essay? Why?

   ____

   ____

2. Time yourself, allowing 14 minutes to write your draft on separate paper.

3. Time yourself to make sure you spend 8 minutes or less revising your essay. You can mark up the draft instead of rewriting it.

Reflect Tell what you found easy or difficult and what you might do differently next time.

____

____

Name ______________________________ Date ____________

End-of-Unit Benchmark Test — Unit 4

Reading Skill: Using Context to Determine Meaning

Read the following questions. Then, choose the best answer.

1 What is a word's context?

A the other words or phrases that surround it

B a synonym or word close in meaning

C the dictionary definition of a word

D an easy way to explain a word's meaning

2 Antonyms can help you determine the meaning of an unfamiliar word because they—

F give information about the unfamiliar word

G mean the same as the unfamiliar word

H give the literal meaning of a word

J mean the opposite of the unfamiliar word

Read the passage. Then, answer the questions.

> My life is cold, and dark, and dreary;
> It rains, and the wind is never weary;
> My thoughts still cling to the mouldering Past,
> But the hopes of youth fall thick in the blast,
> And the days are dark and dreary.
> Be still, sad heart! and cease repining;
> Behind the clouds is the sun still shining;
> Thy fate is the common fate of all,
> Into each life some rain must fall,
> Some days must be dark and dreary.
>
> —from "The Rainy Day" by Henry Wadsworth Longfellow

3 Which of these is the most likely definition of *mouldering* in the poem?

A burning

B decaying

C inspiring

D darkening

4 Which of these best helps you determine a possible meaning for *mouldering*?

F the word *past,* which suggests something that has died or is dying

G the phrase *dark and dreary,* which suggests sadness

H the phrase *hopes of youth,* which suggests inspiration

J the phrase *thick in the blast,* which suggests fire or burning

5 Which of these is a possible meaning for the word *repining* in the poem?

A expressing uncertainty

B expressing determination

C expressing happiness

D expressing discontent

6 In the poem, what type of context clue for *repining* is the word *shining*?

F explanation

G definition

H synonym

J antonym

Name ______________________________ Date ______________

Read the passage. Then, answer the questions.

THE RIVER calmly flows,
Through shining banks, through lonely glen,
Where the owl shrieks, though ne'er the cheer of men
Has stirred its mute repose,
Still if you should walk there, you would go there again.

The stream is well alive;
Another passive world you see,
Where downward grows the form of every tree;
Like soft light clouds they thrive:
Like them let us in our pure loves reflected be.

—from "Boat Song" by Ralph Waldo Emerson

7 Which of these is the best definition of *repose* in Emerson's poem?

A silence
B depth
C rest
D liveliness

8 Which word in the first stanza of Emerson's poem is a clue to the meaning of *repose*?

F calmly
G mute
H shining
J lonely

9 What is the most likely meaning of *passive* in Emerson's poem?

A flowing
B inactive
C calming
D busy

10 Which of these is a context clue to the meaning of *passive* in Emerson's poem?

F downward grows
G soft light clouds
H well alive
J reflected be

Read the passage. Then, answer the questions.

Whisk together the flour and eggs until they are thoroughly mixed. Gradually add the milk and water, stirring to combine. Add the salt and butter, and beat until smooth. Then heat a lightly oiled frying pan over medium-high heat. Pour the batter into the pan. Tilt the pan with a circular motion so that the batter coats the surface evenly. Cook the crêpe for about 2 minutes. Then loosen the crêpe with a spatula, turn, and cook the other side.

11 What context clue best helps you figure out the meaning of *whisk* in the selection?

A gradually
B mixed
C add
D heat

12 Based on the context in which it is used, what is the most likely meaning of *spatula*?

F a tool for heating food
G a tool for frying food
H a tool for mixing food
J a tool for lifting food

Name ______________________ Date ____________

Literary Analysis

Read the following questions. Then, choose the best answer.

13 The sound device that uses words to imitate sounds is—

A onomatopoeia

B rhythm

C alliteration

D rhyme

14 What type of sound device is used in this line of poetry?

A tapering turret overtops the work

F onomatopoeia

G alliteration

H rhyme

J rhythm

15 Which line contains an example of internal rhyme?

A Yellow-happy sun shines high in the sky.

B I spy a tiny inch-worm crawling, creeping home.

C At the edge of the sea, a shell splashed in the tide.

D The river calls the birds with drip, slosh, gurgle.

16 Which of these is the best example of the use of rhythm as a sound device?

F A snail trail streamed across the summer porch.

G The water in the hot pan hissed and sputtered.

H When I wished upon a star, the star winked back at me.

J Four farmers toiled tirelessly in their fields.

17 The main purpose of a narrative poem is to—

A express a feeling

B tell a story

C describe a character

D describe a setting

18 What form of poetry looks like its subject?

F lyric

G haiku

H free verse

J concrete

Read the passage. Then, answer the questions.

When my mother died I was very young,
And my father sold me while yet my tongue
Could scarcely cry "Weep! weep! weep! weep!"
So your chimneys I sweep, and in soot I sleep.
There's little Tom Dacre, who cried when his head,
That curled like a lamb's back, was shaved; so I said,
"Hush, Tom! never mind it, for, when your head's bare,
You know tht the soot cannot spoil your white hair."

—from "The Chimney-Sweeper" by William Blake

Name ______________________________ Date ______________

19 **What sound device is used in line 4 of the poem?**
A onomatopoeia
B end rhyme
C internal rhyme
D consonance

20 **What is the rhyme scheme of this poem?**
F AABBCCDD
G ABABCDCD
H ABCDEFGH
J ABBACDDC

need poem

21 **The speaker in the poem is most likely a—**
A mother
B lamb
C child
D father

22 **What is the speaker's tone?**
F bored
G sorrowful
H confused
J informal

23 **Which of these is an example of end rhyme from the poem?**
A young/weep
B sleep/head
C said/bare
D bare/hair

need poem

24 **Which of these phrases from line 4 is an example of alliteration?**
F So your chimneys
G chimneys I sweep
H I sweep and
J in soot I sleep

Read the passage. Then, answer the questions.

> Shall I compare thee to a summer's day?
> Thou art more lovely and more temperate.
> Rough winds do shake the darling buds of May,
> And summer's lease hath all too short a date.
>
> —from "Sonnet 18" by William Shakespeare

25 **What form of poetry are the lines by William Shakespeare?**
A lyric poetry
B humorous poetry
C concrete poetry
D narrative poetry

26 **Which of these best describes the overall impression of Shakespeare's sonnet?**
F The speaker loves summer more than autumn.
G The speaker is expressing tender love for someone.
H The speaker appreciates the different moods of summer.
J The speaker feels that summer days pass too quickly.

Name ______________________________ Date ______________

Grammar

Read the following questions. Then, choose the best answer.

27 Which of the following is a simple sentence?

A Yesterday I cleaned my room, and I went to the store.

B I visited my aunt's house, which is where I ate dinner.

C I took the bus home from school today.

D Todd took an extra cookie because he was hungry.

28 Which is the best way to vary the dull pattern in the following sentence?

The cyclists pedaled to the top of the hill.

F The cyclists pedaled quickly to the top of the hill.

G The three cyclists pedaled to the top of the steep hill.

H Huffing and chuffing, the cyclists pedaled slowly up the steep hill.

J Several cyclists rode slowly up the steep hill.

29 Which is the best way to combine these sentences to form a compound sentence?

Luis enjoys gardening. Luis can't wait for spring.

A Because he likes gardening, Luis can't wait for spring.

B Luis wants spring to come so that he can garden.

C When spring arrives, Luis will be able to garden.

D Luis enjoys gardening, so he can't wait for spring.

30 Choose the variation of the sentence that begins with an adjective.

F Sleepy, Shelley took a long nap that afternoon.

G Shelley was so sleepy that she took a long nap.

H In the afternoon, Shelley took a long nap.

J Because she was sleepy, Shelley took a long nap.

31 What is the best way to vary the pattern by using a prepositional phrase?

A dog ran onto the soccer field.

A While its owner chased it, a dog ran onto the soccer field.

B Barking, a dog ran onto the soccer field.

C At the park, a dog ran onto the soccer field.

D A dog ran onto the soccer field and scared the players.

32 Which is the best way to combine these sentences into a complex sentence?

Jen's dad traveled to Alaska. Jen's dad went on a fishing trip.

F Jen's dad went on a fishing trip in Alaska.

G Jen's dad traveled to Alaska, and he went on a fishing trip.

H Jen's dad went on a fishing trip when he was in Alaska.

J Jen's dad traveled to Alaska to go fishing.

Name ______________________ Date ______________

Short Answer

Reading Skill: Using Context to Determine Meaning

33 Identify the idiom in the following passage, and explain how its context helps you determine its meaning.

Alice won't come outside to play because she's too busy reading. She's such a bookworm!

____

____

34 Describe two of the three types of context clues that help you determine the meaning of unfamiliar words.

____

____

Literary Analysis

35 What is the speaker in a poem?

____

____

36 What is an iamb in poetry?

____

____

Essay

Write on a separate sheet of paper.

37 Imagine that you want to write either a lyric or narrative poem about a river. Decide whether you want to describe your impressions of the river or tell a story about it. On a separate sheet of paper, write the first line of a poem you might write. If you are writing a lyric poem, make sure to include at least two details about the river's qualities; if you are writing a narrative poem, include information about the setting and a character in the poem.

38 Imagine that you have been asked to write an introduction for a favorite recorded song that you will play for other students. You want to draw students' attention especially to the words of the song and their effect on you. On a separate sheet of paper, jot down two or three ideas about how you will explain why the words of this song are important to you. Mention any use of sound devices such as alliteration, onomatopoeia, rhyme, or rhythm in the song.

39 Imagine that you are writing for assessment and have expressed the following main idea in response to a writing prompt.

Poetry often reassures us that someone else shares our thoughts and feelings.

On your paper, list at least three details that you might use to support this main idea.

Name ______________________ Date ____________

Diagnostic Test 1 — Unit 5

Read the passage. Then, answer the questions.

Sarah Breedlove, an African American woman better known as Madame C. J. Walker, founded her own business in the first decade of 1900. Within 15 years she was a millionaire—the first black woman to attain that achievement.

What propelled Breedlove along her road to success was what you might call a disastrous hair day! She developed a scalp problem and lost patches of hair. She was ashamed of her appearance and, in her embarrassment, she began mixing and experimenting with hair products to find a cure. In the process, she discovered not only the source of her future company but her skill as a businesswoman.

In 1905, Breedlove married Charles Joseph Walker. She took his name—initials and all—and began producing "Madame Walker's Wonderful Hair Grower." Soon she had a line of hair care products for African American women and was presenting them door-to-door. She visited with women in their homes, demonstrating her products and always looking for new ways to sell them. Madame Walker was the picture of hard work and industry, and before long her business was thriving.

At the high point of Walker's success, more than 3,000 people, many of them women, were dependent on her for employment, and Walker supported them with good jobs.

1 Sarah Breedlove experimented with hair care products because she

A had a problem with her hair

B had her husband's support to start a business

C wanted to become wealthy and famous

D liked visiting other women in their homes

2 What inspired Sarah Walker to develop more hair care products after she invented "Madame Walker's Wonderful Hair Grower"?

F successful sales of her Hair Grower

G the need to keep her employees busy

H her love of selling things door-to-door

J her husband's unquestioning support

3 What effect did Madame C. J. Walker have on the hair care industry?

A Madame C. J. Walker realized that only women could make products for other women.

B She identified the need for products made specifically for African American women.

C Walker saw the future in selling hair care products door-to-door.

D She started the trend in using her husband's name to identify her products.

4 What background information could help you link the causes and effects in the passage?

F a book on how to marry a millionaire

G an article on chemical hair processing

H a film on Sarah Breedlove's childhood

J a multimedia presentation on selling products door-to-door

Name ______________________ Date ______________

Read the passage. Then, answer the questions.

Act 1, Scene 1

[It is early morning in a large city. The sounds of automobiles and buses can be heard through an open window. The home is small—a three-room flat. The furnishings are sparse, but the place is tidy. A gray-haired man stands in the tiny kitchen, cracking eggs into a bowl and scrambling them. A teenage girl is sitting at the kitchen table.]

Grandfather: Are you running this morning, little one?

Marianna: I don't know yet, Grandfather. It's hot already, and I could use a little extra sleep. (*She rubs her eyes.*)

Grandfather: You don't know what this day will bring, Mari. You'd better run now, before school. You'll be at the hospital this afternoon. Your mom should be out of surgery by then.

5 What information is included in the stage directions in the selection?

A the characters' thoughts

B the theme of the play

C the characters' costumes

D the description of the setting

6 The dialogue in this selection reveals that

F Grandfather always fixes breakfast.

G traffic in the city is heaviest in the morning.

H three-room flats in the city are expensive.

J Marianna's mom is having surgery that day.

Read the following questions. Then, choose the best answer.

7 What is the meaning of the root shared by *circumvent* and *circumference*?

A all

B narrow

C around

D human

8 What is the participle in the sentence?

Shaken by the news of his team's loss, Kyle walked slowly toward the coach.

F Shaken

G news

H walked

J slowly

9 What is the best way to combine these sentences with a gerund or a participle?

Jamal likes to sing. He sings folk songs.

A Jamal likes singing folk songs.

B Jamal likes to sing, and he sings folk songs.

C Jamal sings folk songs.

D Folk songs are what Jamal likes to sing most.

10 Which word in the sentence is a gerund?

Ming enjoys walking early in the morning.

F Ming

G walking

H early

J morning

Name ______________________________ Date ______________

Reading Skills: Cause and Effect

Reinforcement 5-2

Causes are what make something happen. **Effects** are the events that happen as a result. For example, rain causes the ground to get wet. The rain is the cause. The wet ground is the effect. A cause-and-effect relationship does not always exist when one event happens after another. For example, the sun comes out after the rain ends, but the rain doesn't cause the sun to come out. In fact, the rain could end and the sun could remain clouded. When a cause-and-effect relationship exists you can describe it with a sentence—*The ground is wet because it rained.*

Read each pair of events. Write *C-E* if the events are linked by a cause-and-effect relationship. Write *No C-E* if the events are merely sequential. If the events have a cause-effect link, combine the two sentences to describe the link.

1. __________ It began to rain outside. We were at the mall.

____

____

2. __________ Heavy rain continued for many hours. There was water on the basement floor.

____

____

3. __________ The power went out. The rain fell even harder.

____

____

4. __________ The ground became soggy. A newly-planted tree tipped over in our yard.

____

____

5. __________ We ran out in the rain to set the tree upright. The power came back on.

____

____

6. __________ The storm ended and the rain stopped. The ground began to dry out and the water began to recede.

____

____

Name ______________________________ Date ______________

Reading Skills: Cause and Effect

Extension 5-2

Not only can cause-and-effect relationships form links, they can also form webs. Webs occur when a **cause** has more than one **effect** or several causes work together to create a single effect. For example, read the first paragraph in "Amigo Brothers" by Piri Thomas.

> Antonio Cruz and Felix Vargas were <u>both seventeen years old</u>. They were so together in friendship that they felt themselves to be brothers. <u>They had known each other since childhood, growing up on the lower east side of Manhattan in the same tenement</u> building on Fifth Street between Avenue A and Avenue B.

The underlined text shows several causes for the boys' strong friendship. No single cause explains the friendship, but together they create the effect. As this story does not use cause-and-effect signal words, knowledge of people and behavior can help you see the links.

Read the rest of "Amigo Brothers" from Unit 1, Lesson 7. Look for effects with multiple causes and causes that have multiple effects. Complete the webs below or create new ones on a separate sheet of paper to record cause-and-effect webs from the story.

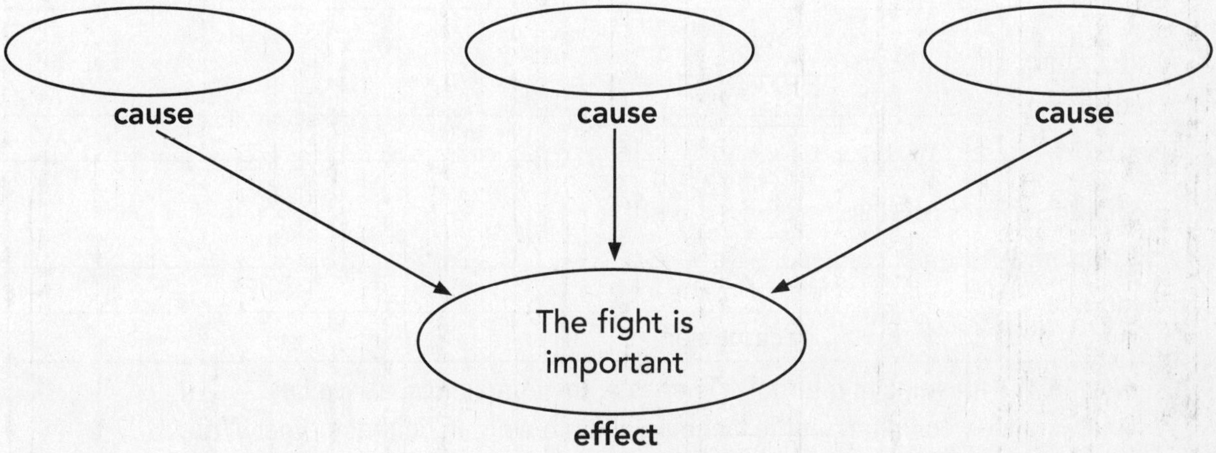

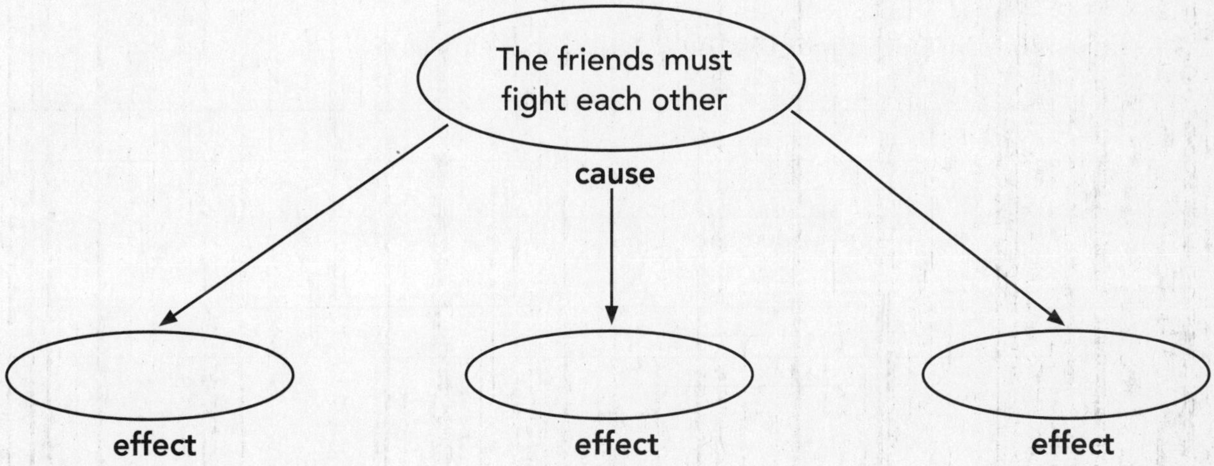

Name ______________________________ Date ______________

Vocabulary: Using a Dictionary

Reinforcement 5-3

Word Roots

A word **root** is the basic meaning in a word. Knowing word roots will help you understand new words and also choose the correct word when you write. For example, if you know that *-fac-* means "to make" you can figure out that a *factory* is a place where things are made. You can then use the word in a sentence—Please visit our *factory* to see how we make our toys.

Look at each word root and word. Then think about the situation clue in parentheses. Define the word, then write a sentence about the situation. Use a dictionary if necessary.

1. ***-fac-*** manufacturer (furniture)
   Definition: ______________________________
   Sentence: ______________________________
2. ***-sum-*** resume (homework)
   Definition: ______________________________
   Sentence: ______________________________
3. ***-val-*** valiant (firefighters)
   Definition: ______________________________
   Sentence: ______________________________
4. ***-sequ-*** consequence (doing well on a test)
   Definition: ______________________________
   Sentence: ______________________________

Review the meaning of the roots. Then, use their meanings, as well as context clues, to figure out the meaning of each word in boldface type. Write your definitions on the lines provided.

5. It started to rain. **Consequently**, the field day was canceled.

   ____

   ____

6. This photograph is clear **validation** that Fran was at the top of the Eiffel Tower while she was in France.

   ____

   ____

Name ______________________________ Date ______________

Vocabulary: Using a Dictionary

Extension 5-3

One word **root** can be used to build many different words. Still, all words containing a particular root share some relationship in meaning. For example, the Greek root *graph* means "write." It occurs in words such as *telegraph, photograph, phonograph,* and *autograph.* Each contains the meaning of "write," but in a different way. A telegraph sends writing far away. A photograph writes light. A phonograph writes sound. An autograph is writing by the self.

Work in pairs to create words for a new secret language using the roots below. Use a dictionary to find the meanings of the roots you have not yet learned. Then, write a definition for each new word and a sentence containing it.

1. circum ______________________________
2. morph ______________________________
3. brev ______________________________
4. acri ______________________________
5. poly ______________________________
6. omni ______________________________
7. anthrop ______________________________
8. chrom ______________________________

Compare Some words appear to share a root but in fact do not. As an example, use a dictionary to compare the roots and meanings of the words "assumption" and "summary."

____

____

Name ______________________________ Date ______________

Literary Analysis: Dialogue and Stage Directions

Reinforcement 5-4 A

Dialogue and **stage directions** help you learn about character motivation. They suggest how characters think and feel, which helps you understand why they act certain ways. Dialogue is what characters say on stage. Stage directions are the playwright's notes that describe a scene's setting and the movements of actors on stage, and suggest emotions actors should show.

Read this excerpt from *The Diary of Anne Frank* by Frances Goodrich and Albert Hackett. The Frank family is hiding from the Nazis during World War II. Mr. Kraler is helping them hide in the warehouse that Mr. Frank owns. Then, answer the questions that follow.

MR. KRALER: *[He rises]* If we could go downstairs . . . *[*MR. FRANK *starts ahead;* MR. KRALER *speaks to the others.]* Will you forgive us? I won't keep him but a minute. *[He starts to follow* MR. FRANK *down the steps.]*

MARGOT: *[With sudden foreboding]* What's happened? Something's happened! Hasn't it, Mr. Kraler?

*[*MR. KRALER *stops and comes back, trying to reassure* MARGOT *with a pretense of casualness.]*

MR. KRALER: No, really. I want your father's advice . . .

MARGOT: Something's gone wrong! I know it!

MR. FRANK: *[Coming back, to* MR. KRALER*]* If it's something that concerns us here, it's better that we all hear it.

MR. KRALER: *[Turning to him, quietly]* But . . . the children . . . ?

MR. FRANK: What they'd imagine would be worse than any reality.

1. What information do the stage directions provide about the movements of Mr. Kraler and Mr. Frank? ______________________________

____

____

2. What do you learn from the stage directions about Mr. Kraler's reason for returning to speak with Margot? ______________________________

____

____

3. Why does Mr. Frank ask Mr. Kraler to share his news with everyone? ______________

____

____

4. What do the stage directions and dialogue suggest about the play's mood?

____

____

Name ______________________________ Date ______________

Literary Analysis: Character Motivation

Reinforcement 5-4 B

The reason or reasons a character acts one way or another is called **character motivation.** A character's motivation can be external, internal, or both.

External motivation comes from situations that arise in the character's external world, such as needing to pass a midterm. Internal motivation, on the other hand, comes from the character's own emotions, such as anger or compassion.

Character's Action	External Motivation	Internal Motivation
A girl enters a skateboarding contest.	Her friends dare her to enter the contest.	She wants to prove that she is a better skater than her older brother.

Write an external and internal motivation for each character's action in the chart.

Character's Action	External Motivation	Internal Motivation
1. A student refuses to complete a science lab.		
2. A lifeguard swims in shark-infested waters.		
3. A boy quits the band the night before a big concert.		
4. A taxi driver runs a red light.		

Name ______________________________ Date ______________

Literary Analysis: Dialogue and Stage Directions

Extension 5-4

Because drama has no narration, readers must make inferences to understand plot, conflict, and character motivation. They must put together clues from what characters say and do and from their own knowledge or experience. Read this scene from *The Piano Lesson,* in which a brother and sister are discussing what to do with the family's piano.

BERNIECE: . . . Now set that piano back over there. I done told you a hundred times I ain't selling that piano.

BOY WILLIE: I'm trying to get me some land, woman. I need that piano to get me some money so I can buy Sutter's land.

BERNIECE: Money can't buy what that piano cost. You can't sell your soul for money. It won't go with the buyer. It'll shrivel and shrink to know that you ain't taken on to it. But it won't go with the buyer.

BOY WILLIE: I ain't talking about all that, woman. I ain't talking about selling my soul. I'm talking about trading that piece of wood for some land. Get something under your feet. Land the only thing God ain't making no more of. You can always get you another piano. I'm talking about some land. What you get something out the ground from. That's what I'm talking about. You can't do nothing with that piano but sit up there and look at it.

BERNIECE: That's just what I'm gonna do. Wining Boy, you want me to fry you some pork chops?

Think about what Berniece and Boy Willie say and do. Think about how people you know speak and act in similar situations. Record both kinds of clues in the chart.

Story Clues:	→	Life Clues:	→	Inferences:

Make inferences to answer these questions about plot, conflict, and character.

1. What are the conflicts in this play? ______________________________

2. How does the dialogue reveal the conflict? ______________________________

____

3. Does the dialogue suggest that the characters' motivations are external, internal, or both? ______________________________

____

Name ______________________________ Date ______________

Language Coach: Participles and Participial Phrases

Reinforcement 5-5 A

A **participle** is a form of verb that acts as an adjective.

Present participles end in –ing.

Example: *Smiling,* Kira accepted her award.

Past participles end in –ed, unless they are irregular verbs.

Example: Chavez, *annoyed,* didn't make the basketball team.

A **participial phrase** is a present or past participle that is modified by an adverb or adverb phrase.

Example: *Thinking about her test next period,* Rita felt ill.

Example: *Concerned about his grade,* Sebastiano asked the teacher for extra help.

Underline the participial phrase in each sentence and draw an arrow from the phrase to the word it modifies. Then, write PrP if the participle is a present participle or PaP if it is a past participle on the line provided.

1. ______ Looking at his watch, Brian waited for the bell to ring.
2. ______ Yolanda dribbled the soccer ball down the field, scoring the winning goal.
3. ______ Relieved, Jaya let her brother get back onto his bike.
4. ______ Training for a track meet, the team ran an hour after school.
5. ______ Obligated to mow the lawn, Raoul stayed home.
6. ______ The baked pie smelled wonderful.
7. ______ Evan, dodging the kickball, slid into third base.
8. ______ Roberto, exhausted, couldn't stay up and study any longer.
9. ______ Finished with their homework, the children played outside.
10. ______ The family, excited about their trip, packed their suitcases.

Name ______________________________ Date ______________

Language Coach: Sentence Combining

Reinforcement 5–5 B

Participles and **gerunds** are both created from verbs. Participles function as adjectives in sentences. Gerunds function as nouns. Verbs that end in *-ing,* such as *cooking,* can be either participles or gerunds depending on how they are used in a sentence.

For each verb, write the present participle, past participle, and gerund. Remember that some past participles are formed in irregular ways.

1. lead: participle ________ past participle ________ gerund ________
2. enjoy: participle ________ past participle ________ gerund ________
3. raise: participle ________ past participle ________ gerund ________
4. follow: participle ________ past participle ________ gerund ________
5. shake: participle ________ past participle ________ gerund ________
6. plod: participle ________ past participle ________ gerund ________

You can use participles and gerunds to combine sentences. Circle the verbs in each pair of sentences. Then, create a participle or gerund from one verb in order to combine the sentences.

7. George plays soccer. It is his best sport.

____

8. The dog barked. He ran away from his owner.

____

9. K.C. bakes cakes. She likes to bake for her friends.

____

10. Hugh's science project was a success. He designed it very carefully.

____

11. Suso trained his dog well. He won first prize in the dog show.

____

____

12. The play was a huge success. The auditorium was packed.

____

____

Name ______________________ Date ____________

Language Coach: Sentence Combining

Extension 5-5

Participles and **gerunds** can help you craft interesting sentences. For example, you can rearrange the same ideas and words in many different ways. This changes the style of your writing, which is influenced by sentence length and variety. Look at these sentences that use the same words.

Trembling with fear, the puppies slowly walked toward me.
The puppies were trembling with fear as they slowly walked toward me.
As they walked slowly toward me, the puppies were trembling with fear.

Combine each pair of sentences at least two ways. Use a past or present participle.

1. Hallie's baby brother napped all afternoon. He kept the family home.

____

____

2. The winter sky got dark in the storm. It closed in on the trapped family.

____

____

3. At last, the storm broke. The family emerged into the sun and smiled at each other.

____

____

4. The cat stopped howling. It was finally calmed.

____

____

5. Make a story from one sentence in each cluster. Experiment with different sentence forms to create variety. Write your story on a separate sheet of paper.

Write Choose from these gerunds and participles. Form and include the plural of a tricky word. Then, write five of your own sentences on another sheet of paper.

Gerunds and Participles				Tricky Words		
playing	passing	shaken	cooking	glass	fly	man
cut	concerned	jogging	pleased	leash	beach	mouse
inquiring	lost	sleeping	arrested	fox	potato	
trembling	reduced	written	pleased	pantry	berry	
noticed	discouraged	studying	broken			

Name ______________________________ Date ______________

Writer's Workshop: Manual

Reinforcement 5-6

How-to manuals explain a process by giving directions for each step. Directions must be very specific. To be useful, directions must also clearly show the sequence, or order, in which steps are completed. They must use time order transition words, such as *first, next, second, later, then, finally, the next day,* and *after that,* to emphasize the sequence.

Complete the following activities.

1. General steps for making spaghetti are listed below in random order. In the right column of the chart, record the steps in sequential order. In the left column, write time order words that emphasize the sequence of steps.

Place the spaghetti noodles in the water.
Pour water into a pot.
Bring the water to a boil.
Drain the water from the noodles.
Boil the noodles for 10 minutes, or until they are tender.
Put the noodles back into the pot, and add the sauce.

Time Order Words	Steps

2. Practice getting specific. Choose two of the steps used to make spaghetti. Add words to the instruction to make it more specific.

Example: Bring the water to a boil.
Second, bring the water to a *rapid* boil.

____

____

____

____

Name ______________________________ Date ______________

Writer's Workshop: Manual

Extension 5-6

The most important element in how-to directions is clarity. Use these elaboration tools to increase clarity.

- Adverbs can help you tell how much, how long, or how to complete a step. Look at this example: *Stir the sauce slowly until it thickens*. The adverb *slowly* tells how to complete the stirring action. The adverbial phrase *until it thickens* tells how long to continue the action.
- Diagrams or illustrations can show processes when words aren't enough. Consider carefully which steps might be hard to understand from words alone. Make diagrams simple and straightforward, with clear labels and numbers where appropriate.

Complete the following activities.

1. Record three steps from your directions that you wrote in your work text. Then, list adverbs or adverbial phrases that will tell how much, how long, or how to complete a step. Add these to your steps as you revise.

Step: ______________________________

Adverb/Phrase: ______________________________

____

Step: ______________________________

Adverb/Phrase: ______________________________

____

Step: ______________________________

Adverb/Phrase: ______________________________

____

2. Record one step from your directions below. Create a diagram or illustration that explains it. Then, trade papers with a classmate. Try to follow your partner's written and visual directions, then exchange feedback.

Step: ______________________________

Diagram or Illustration:

Name ______________________________ Date ______________

Mid-Unit Benchmark Test — Unit 5

Reading Skill: Cause and Effect

Read the following questions. Then, choose the best answer.

1 Which of these are transitional words that signal causes and effects?

A because, therefore
B sometimes, always
C however, also
D in, over

2 Which of these is a transitional phrase that signals an effect?

F in the meantime
G as a result
H along the way
J over time

3 Which question is important to ask when looking for a cause-and-effect relationship in a literary work?

A What happens to the main characters?
B What is the central theme of the work?
C Why did this event or situation happen?
D How does the work affect the reader?

4 Which of these statements is true in analyzing causes and effects in a work?

F One effect always has only one cause.
G An effect cannot become a cause.
H Every cause has at least two effects.
J Causes and effects can connect as a chain.

5 Which of the following best describes the cause-and-effect relationship in the following situation?

The endangered falcons eventually used the human-made nest boxes, which led to their raising young falcons in the nests; also because of the nest boxes, the falcons began establishing their own nests on the nearby bluffs of the Mississippi.

A One cause produced one effect.
B Two causes produced two effects.
C Two effects caused two more effects.
D One cause produced two effects.

Read the passage. Then, answer the questions.

In the 1970s, after a period of calm and prosperity, demands for reform in Guatemala were increasing. A military dictatorship had been established and the popularly elected president was forced to leave. In addition, peasant cooperative farms were destroyed, and political parties and unions were crushed. Thousands of people were killed, and thousands fled Guatemala for their lives. Still, movements for reform continued to flourish, in spite of continued efforts to stamp them out. One man, a United States citizen and a priest, decided to put his life on the line for justice for the peasants and other oppressed people in the country.

Name ______________________ Date ____________

6 **What caused the popularly elected president to leave?**
- **F** He was forced out after the establishment of a dictatorship.
- **G** Peasant cooperative farms were destroyed.
- **H** He disrupted a period of calm and prosperity.
- **J** His oppressive rule caused the citizens to revolt.

7 **The priest is most likely in danger because of his work. What background information best helps you link this effect with a cause in the selection?**
- **A** Thousands of people have fled the country.
- **B** People are being punished for working for reforms.
- **C** The man is a United States citizen as well as a priest.
- **D** Movements for reform continue to flourish.

Literary Analysis

Read the passage. Then, choose the best answer.

> *[It is evening on the front porch of a small cabin in the woods. A lantern placed on a porch table gives off a soft glow. The buzzing of insects and croaking of frogs can be heard in the distance. Now and then there is the sound of water splashing, as if a fish has jumped in a pond. A gray-haired woman in her sixties rocks back and forth in a rocking chair on the porch. Her granddaughter, an 8-year-old girl, sits nearby, eating a cookie. It is obvious that there is great affection between the grandmother and girl, in the way they speak to each other.]*

8 **What information is included in the stage directions in the selection?**
- **F** a description of sounds
- **G** the characters' lines
- **H** the central theme
- **J** the characters' costumes

9 **What can you tell about the setting of the play from the selection?**
- **A** The setting is afternoon, on a porch.
- **B** The setting is evening, in a kitchen.
- **C** The setting is night, on a cabin porch.
- **D** The setting is morning, near a pond.

10 **What do you learn about the characters from these stage directions?**
- **F** how they feel about each other
- **G** why they are at the cabin
- **H** what is important to them
- **J** how they will solve a problem

11 **To whom might these stage directions be most useful?**
- **A** to an actor in the play
- **B** to someone reading the play
- **C** to a reviewer of the play
- **D** to a viewer of the play

Name ______________________________ Date ______________

Read the passage. Then, answer the questions.

Lindy: *[approaches the new student, who is eating lunch at a table by himself in the cafeteria]* Hi there! My name is Lindy. Welcome to the United States and to Crockett School.

Luis: *[looks surprised and a little flustered; wipes his mouth with his napkin]* Hello. I . . . uh . . . my name is Luis. I—*[sighs deeply]* . . . well . . . it's a hard day. So much is new. Please excuse my English.

Lindy: *[smiles warmly]* Your English is very good. You should hear my Spanish! *[she rolls her eyes]* My family has moved a lot, so I know how hard it is to be the new kid. You feel like a sore thumb at first!

Luis: *[looks a little baffled]* Did you say *sore thumb*? Now I am *really* confused.

12 Which of these most likely motivates Lindy to approach Luis in the school cafeteria?

F curiosity

G sympathy

H confusion

J frustration

13 Which of these most likely motivates Luis to sit alone in the cafeteria?

A anger

B illness

C discomfort

D unfriendliness

Read the passage. Then, answer the questions.

Churchill: *[growing more impatient]* We have *got* to try harder to come up with a solution, or else England will fall to Hitler. I won't stand for having my country handed over to the Nazis.

Mr. Soames: *[taking off his glasses and rubbing his weary eyes]* But, sir, it is nearly two in the morning, and we've all been working since just after breakfast—

Mr. Wright: *[glaring at Churchill]* Except for the Prime Minister, who indulged in a nap—

Churchill: *[drawing a deep breath and exhaling slowly before speaking]* All right, gentlemen. I don't wish to deplete my finest resources. Let us end this meeting and resume tomorrow at nine.

14 Which of these best describes the selection?

F dialogue

G biography

H narration

J nonfiction

15 What does this selection reveal about the character of Churchill?

A He cares deeply about the safety of his country.

B He has difficulty tolerating criticism or disagreement.

C He does not appreciate the hard work of his advisors.

D He expects others to work harder than he does.

Name ________________________________ Date ______________

Grammar

Read the following questions. Then, choose the best answer.

16 Which of these best defines a participial phrase?

F a phrase consisting of a verb form ending in *-ing* that acts as a noun

G a phrase composed of a preposition and its object

H a verb form commonly ending in *-ing* or *-ed*

J a group of words that begins with a participle and forms a unit of meaning

17 What is the participle in the following sentence?

The bald eagle, spotting a fish in the river, plunged headfirst into the water.

A spotting

B in

C plunged

D into

18 What is the best way to combine these sentences using a participial phrase?

The crowd encouraged the team. The team scored ten points.

F The team, encouraged by the crowd, scored ten points.

G When the crowd encouraged the team, they scored ten points.

H The team scored ten points, because they were encouraged by the crowd.

J The crowd encouraged the team to score ten points.

19 What is the participle in the following sentence?

Frightened, the kitten ran and hid behind the chair.

A frightened

B ran

C hid

D behind

20 What is the best way to combine these sentences using a participial phrase?

The hiker whistled as he walked. The hiker thought he was on the right trail.

F While the hiker thought he was on the right trail, he whistled as he walked.

G As he walked, the hiker whistled and thought he was on the right trail.

H Thinking about the easy trail, the hiker whistled as he walked.

J The hiker thought he was on the right trail, so he whistled as he walked.

21 Which of these is the best definition of a gerund?

A a verb form ending in *-ed* that is used as an adjective

B a verb form ending in *-ing* that is used as a direct object

C a verb form ending in *-ing* that is used as a noun

D a verb form ending in *-ed* that is used as a past participle

22 Which word in the following sentence is a gerund?

Tania prefers drinking filtered water.

F prefers

G drinking

H filtered

J water

23 Which word in the following sentence is a gerund?

Talking on a cell phone is rude when you are in a restaurant or movie theater.

A talking

B phone

C rude

D restaurant

Name ______________________________ Date ______________

24 **What is the best way to combine the following sentences using a gerund or a participle?**

Steve reached a conclusion. The conclusion was a surprise.

F Steve reached a conclusion that was a surprise.

G Steve reached a surprising conclusion.

H Steve reached a conclusion, and it was surprising.

J Steve reached a conclusion, a surprise.

25 **What is the best way to combine these sentences using a gerund or participle?**

Celina likes to read. She reads mysteries.

A Celina reads mysteries.

B Celina likes to read, and she enjoys mysteries.

C Celina likes reading mysteries.

D Mysteries are what Celina likes to read the most.

Vocabulary

Read the following questions. Then choose the best answer.

26 **What is the meaning of the root shared by *circumvent* and *circumference*?**

F small, unimportant

G far away

H available

J around, about

27 **What is the meaning of the root *anthrop* in *anthropology*?**

A history

B human being

C cultural beliefs

D health

28 **What is the most likely meaning of *anthropoid* in this sentence?**

Fingers and toes gave the strange creature almost anthropoid features.

F unreal

G elegant

H humanlike

J frightening

29 **What is the meaning of the root *acri* in *acrid*?**

A tall

B warm

C easy

D bitter

30 **What does *omnipresent* mean in this sentence?**

The omnipresent chill made the evening uncomfortable for all the participants.

F misbehaving all of the time

G avoiding punishment

H present in all places at all times

J unable to find out the truth

31 **What is the most likely meaning of *acrimony* in this sentence?**

When his father scolded us, his words were filled with acrimony.

A remarkable cleverness

B unmistakeable boredom

C unexpected praise

D biting sharpness

32 **What is the most likely meaning of *circumnavigation* in this sentence?**

Sir Ranulph Fiennes and his team completed a polar circumnavigation expedition in 1979 and again in 1982.

F a journey through the air

G a trip all around Earth

H a mission that failed

J a lesson in survival

Name ____________________ Date ____________

Short Answer

Reading Skill: Cause and Effect

33 Identify the cause, effect, and signal word in the following sentence.

Toby studied for two hours, so he did well on the test.

34 Identify the cause, effect, and signal words in the following sentence.

As a result of her poor eyesight, Chandra squints when looking at distant objects.

Literary Analysis

35 What are stage directions in a play?

36 What is character motivation in a literary work?

Essay

Write on a separate sheet of paper.

37 Think of an event in your past that consisted of a cause-and-effect chain. Write each cause and effect, placing arrows to display the chain. Then write a paragraph or two describing the event. Make sure to include cause-and-effect signal words.

38 Imagine that you are preparing to write a scene with dialogue for a play. The scene will involve two characters speaking to each other. On a separate sheet of paper, write a sentence that describes the situation that will set up your scene, such as "Two friends who will enter projects in a school science fair discover that they are both preparing identical science projects." Then write the first lines of dialogue for the scene.

39 Playwrights often borrow dialogue from real life to use in their plays. Think of a humorous situation that happened to you or to someone you know and that involved more than one person. Imagine that you are using this situation in a play you are writing. On a separate sheet of paper, write three lines of dialogue based on the humorous situation in which two or more people speak to each other.

Name ______________________________ Date ______________

Diagnostic Test 2 — Unit 5

Read the passages. Then, answer the questions.

History is filled with tragic examples of cities going up in flames. Among the first recorded major fire disasters is the burning of Rome in July of 64 A.D. A fire broke out in one of the wooden shops near the Circus Maximus, a large stadium. The fire raged for six days before it was brought under control. Then it started again and burned for three more days. Accounts of the time report that strong winds fanned the flames. In the narrow streets, the fire spread quickly, causing many deaths.

The role of Emperor Nero is a side story to this great fire. According to a famous myth, "Nero fiddled while Rome burned." He was accused of being outside the city, playing music while watching the fire. Although Nero was known as an entertainer, the thought that he might sing a ballad of Rome's destruction at such a time seems unlikely. In fact, Nero was hailed for his response to the fire. His actions included opening his royal gardens and surviving public buildings to the homeless. He also directed the rebuilding of Rome. Following the fire, builders relied on marble and stone for rebuilding the city.

1 Which conclusion is best supported by the first paragraph?

A Fires are more easily controlled in large cities than in small villages.

B A crowd from the Circus Maximus set Rome on fire.

C Fires that start at night are more dangerous than those that begin during the day.

D Fewer people would have died in the fire if the streets had been wider.

2 Why are the dates of the Rome fire important in understanding why the fire was difficult to control?

F The dates indicate that equipment to fight fires was primitive.

G The dates indicate that many tourists were in Rome and hindered firefighting efforts.

H Historians know that Emperor Nero played the fiddle on those particular dates.

J Historians know that the shops in Rome were closed for business on those days.

3 From the second paragraph, what can you conclude about myths and history?

A Myths are easier to remember than facts.

B Myths are humorous, and facts are boring.

C Myths are unreliable, but history records the facts.

D Myths and history usually offer similar interpretations of events.

4 An assumption is best defined as—

F a decision made by reasoning

G a judgment of the worth or strength of something

H a guess that something is a fact without proof

J an idea based on a series of inferences

Name ______________________________ Date ______________

[Scene: The stage is divided in two. Downstage left is a school gymnasium being decorated for a dance. Teens are making large, colorful flowers and hanging them throughout the gym. A sign on the wall reads: **Dance Tonight!** Upstage right is a teenage girl's bedroom. Several trophies are lined on a shelf above a desk. The lights are brought up in the bedroom. Samantha Jackson is in her bedroom, attempting to pirouette. Her right ankle is taped.]

Samantha Jackson: Ouch! I'll never be able to go to the dance tonight. Why did I think skating the day before the biggest dance of the year was a good idea? I have to go tonight! I'll do anything!

[Her mother enters the bedroom, carrying a pair of crutches.]

5 Which of these is a prop?

A the stage

B Samantha's mother

C Samantha's movements

D the crutches

6 Samantha's words in this scene are—

F an aside

G a monologue

H a soliloquy

J a point of view

7 Which of these is a stage direction from the selection?

A "I'll never be able to go to the dance tonight!"

B "Why did I think skating the day before the biggest dance of the year was a good idea?"

C [Her mother enters the bedroom, carrying a pair of crutches.]

D A sign on the wall reads: **Dance Tonight!**

8 The sentences "I have to go tonight! I'll do anything!" are an example of—

F suspense

G scenery

H foreshadowing

J dramatic irony

9 Which of these genres is most likely to be dramatized?

A sonnet

B editorial

C short story

D nonfiction article

10 The purpose of a soliloquy is to allow a character to—

F talk privately with the other characters so that the audience cannot hear

G reveal plot details

H have more time on stage

J talk privately to the audience without other characters overhearing the remarks

Read the following questions. Then, choose the best answer.

11 Which sentence contains a subordinate clause?

A Most of the books that Jesse donated to the library were paperbacks.

B That computer game has amazing animation!

C Tamika ran toward first base, but she failed to touch the bag.

D Isaiah wants to pick up his car early in the morning.

12 Which of these sentences contains both an independent clause and a subordinate clause?

F Perched on the windowsill was my cat, Spike.

G In three days Maria and her family will leave on vacation.

H When Pete dropped the vase, the broken pieces scratched the floor.

J The players ran happily across the field and surrounded their coach.

Name ______________________ Date ____________

Reading Skills: Drawing Conclusions

Reinforcement 5-7

A conclusion is a reasonable opinion or decision you reach by analyzing several facts and details. To **draw conclusions** about characters in a play, notice what the characters say and do. Pay attention to how characters interact with each other. Then, use your own experience and knowledge about people to assess this information and make a decision about the characters.

Read the example. Then, answer the questions.

Maria: Could you please get the cake pan from the upper shelf? I can't reach it.

Carla: Here it is. Is that everything we need?

Maria: Let me check the recipe. I think we're ready to start mixing.

Carla: Shouldn't we turn the oven on now? Mom usually does that so the oven preheats while she's mixing the batter.

Maria: You're right, she does. In fact, that's what the recipe says, too.

1. What do you think Maria and Carla are doing? Circle the letter of the best answer.
   A. performing an experiment
   B. playing a trick on their mother
   C. baking a cake
   D. fixing dinner

2. Who do you think is taller, Maria or Carla? ______________________

3. Why do you think so? ______________________

   ____

4. Which of the following conclusions does not seem correct, based on the interaction of the characters? Circle the letter of the best answer.
   A. Maria and Carla work well together.
   B. Maria and Carla are sisters.
   C. The girls are skilled bakers.
   D. The girls have learned from their mother.

5. What do you think Maria and Carla's relationship is like?

   ____

   ____

6. Which of these best describes a conclusion? Circle the letter of the best answer.
   A. a prediction
   B. a decision
   C. an argument
   D. a cause

Name ______________________________ Date ______________

Reading Skills: Drawing Conclusions

Extension 5-7

To effectively **draw conclusions,** you identify details the author emphasizes. You also rely on previous experience to help make sense of those details. For example, when you see two people embracing and smiling, you **conclude** that they have a close relationship. You use the details they emphasize—their actions and expressions—AND your own experience with how people feel when they demonstrate such actions and expressions. Drawing conclusions from reading works the same way. After pulling together details from the reading, you must factor in your previous experience with similar or related situations.

Read the section "A Breakthrough at Tuskegee" in "The Red Tail Angels" from Lesson 2. Use the chart to gather information for drawing conclusions. List details that the author emphasizes and information from your previous experience that relates to these details. Then, draw a conclusion.

Details Emphasized in Text

Previous Experience That Relates

Conclusion

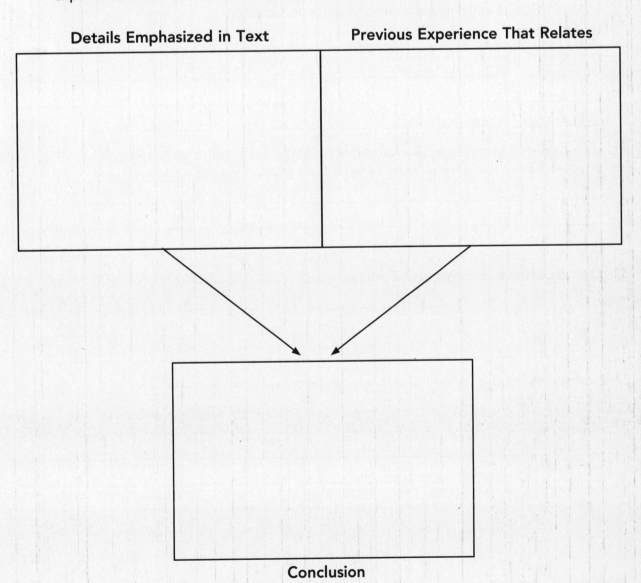

Name ______________________________ Date ______________

Literary Analysis: Suspense

Reinforcement 5-8

Suspense is the tension or uncertainty that readers feel about how a story will turn out. One way that writers create suspense is with **foreshadowing.** Foreshadowing hints at events that may—or may not—happen later in the story. This creates suspense by inviting readers to imagine that dangerous events will happen or to eagerly wonder if positive events will happen. Foreshadowing can be hard to recognize. As you read, ask yourself "What do I expect to happen because of what I am reading now?" For example, if you read that the river is rising as a character is driving toward a bridge, you might expect a problem to arise when the character reaches the bridge.

Read the paragraph from "Thank You M'am" by Langston Hughes that begins "The water dripping from his face" on page 390. Then, answer the questions that follow. Remember that in this story, Mrs. Jones has caught a boy trying to snatch her purse. She has brought the boy back to her home in order to wash his face and perhaps to punish him for his behavior.

1. What is happening in this paragraph?

____

____

____

2. Based on this paragraph, ask and answer the question *What do I expect to happen later in the story because of what I am reading now?* Explain.

____

____

____

3. How does this paragraph create suspense?

____

____

____

4. Does the suspense created in this paragraph make readers worry or wonder? Explain.

____

____

____

____

Name ______________________ Date ______________

Literary Analysis: Suspense

Extension 5-8

Sometimes authors try to keep the **suspense** strong almost to the very end of a story. Some authors try to keep the suspense strong after the story ends by not resolving the conflicts in the plot. These strategies allow authors to accomplish two goals. They keep readers thinking about the story after they are finished reading. They also shift the important resolution from plot events to changes in one of the characters. The author may want the reader to be more focused on how a character develops and grows as a result of an experience, rather than in the experience itself.

Think back to "Amigo Brothers" by Piri Thomas, then read this passage from the story's ending. Answer the questions that follow.

> Finally the referee and the two trainers pried Felix and Antonio apart. Cold water was poured over them to bring them back to their senses.
>
> They looked around and then rushed toward each other. A cry of alarm surged through Tompkins Square Park. Was this a fight to the death instead of a boxing match?
>
> The fear soon gave way to wave upon wave of cheering as the two amigos embraced.
>
> No matter what the decision, they knew they would always be champions to each other.
>
> BONG! BONG! BONG! "Ladies and Gentlemen. Señores and Señoras. The winner and representative to the Golden Gloves Tournament of Champions is . . ."
>
> The announcer turned to point to the winner and found himself alone. Arm in arm the champions had already left the ring.

1. What is the main conflict in the story?

____

2. What creates suspense in this story?

____

3. Why is the suspense at its greatest point at and after the story's end?

____

____

4. What aspect of suspense is resolved at the end of the story?

____

Synthesize Now let's see how well you understand the literary element of suspense. With a partner, create a storyboard that includes all elements of plot as well as suspense.

Name ______________________ Date __________

Literary Analysis: Staging

Reinforcement 5-9 A

Staging includes all the elements required to bring a drama to life. The main pieces of staging describe **sets,** costumes, movements of characters, **props,** lighting, and sound effects. In some plays, the script actually lists each staging element at the beginning of each scene. In other plays, directors and actors must read through the text for clues to what props might be needed.

Read the excerpt from *Let Me Hear You Whisper* by Paul Zindel. Think about sets, props, costumes, and sound effects that are suggested, but not named, by the actions, characters, and settings of the play. Then, answer the questions.

Setting: *The action takes place in the hallway, laboratory and specimen room of a biology experimentation association located in Manhattan near the Hudson River.*

Time: *The action begins with the night shift on a Monday and ends the following Friday.*

Act I, Scene 1

[DR. CROCUS and MR. FRIDGE are leaving the laboratory where they have completed their latest experimental tinkering with a dolphin, and they head down a corridor to the elevator. The elevator opens and MISS MORAY emerges with HELEN.]

MISS MORAY: Dr. Crocus. Mr. Fridge. I'm so glad we've run into you. I want you to meet Helen.

HELEN: Hello.

[DR. CROCUS and MR. FRIDGE nod and get on elevator.]

MISS MORAY: Helen is the newest member of our Custodial Engineering Team.

[MISS MORAY and HELEN start down the hall.]

1. What does the main location suggest to you about what the set should look like for Act 1, Scene 1? ______________________

____

2. What kind of clothing would you expect workers in a science laboratory to wear? ______________________

3. What sounds would you expect to hear as people walk down the hallway and enter or exit the elevator? ______________________

____

____

Create Suppose you were asked to write a play about lunchtime in the cafeteria. On a separate sheet of paper, describe the sets, props, costumes, and sound effects that you would need.

Name ______________________ Date ____________

Literary Analysis: Dramatization

Reinforcement 5-9 B

A play that has been adapted by another source is called a **dramatization. Dialogue** and **stage directions** help bring the same story to life for an audience.

On March 6, 1876, Alexander Graham Bell sat in a room at his residence in Ontario, Canada fiddling with one of his new inventions as his assistant, Watson, waited in the other room. Finally, Bell uttered the first words ever to be heard over a telephone.

Scene 9. [Victorian house in Ontario, Canada, 1876.]

BELL. Darn it! Why won't this silly thing work already! Watson!

WATSON. [shouting from the other room] What? I can't hear you!

BELL. [slamming his invention on the table] Watson! I need you in here!

WATSON. [shaking the telephone, still shouting] What?

BELL. [shouting into the telephone] Come here, Watson! I want to see you!

stage directions

dialogue

Write a dramatization for the following passage in the space provided. Be sure to include dialogue and stage directions.

Original	Dramatization
Late one night, on their way home from their Aunt Rita's fiftieth birthday party, Pilar and her brother, Jorge, were driving down a desolate highway when all of sudden, a blinding light penetrated the black night sky. Jorge slammed on the breaks and Pilar screamed. When the dust settled around the car, they looked up in disbelief as an alien ate a cactus and waved hello.	

Name ______________________________ Date ______________

Literary Analysis: Staging

Extension 5-9

When playwrights dramatize another kind of writing, they have to make many choices. They may expand the focus on one scene and leave out another part of the story. They may move a scene indoors or into a different room to minimize the number of sets on the stage. They may move narration into dialogue or even add a narrator in order to get important information across to the audience. Playwrights may also adapt works across different kinds of drama, for example, making a dramatic play into a musical or a stage play into a film. These adaptations also require choices.

1. Reread the excerpt from *Pygmalion* from Lesson 4, along with the Background. Think about the **staging** described in the text. Then, use the table below to describe the sets, props, costumes, sound effects, and lighting you would use for the scene.

Sets and Props	
Costumes	
Sound Effects	
Lighting	

Synthesize *Pygmalion* was adapted as a stage musical called *My Fair Lady* and then again adapted as a musical film of the same name. Consider the scene you have just read and describe how you would stage it differently for a musical on stage or on film. Write your description on a separate sheet of paper.

Name ______________________________ Date ______________

Comparing Literary Works: Dramatic Speeches

Reinforcement 5-10

In a play, the characters talk to each other in a natural conversation. This is called dialogue. Sometimes a character's dialogue is not part of a conversation. These moments of dialogue are called **dramatic speeches.** A dramatic speech may be presented as one of the following.

- In a **monologue,** the character is speaking to another character or to the audience.
- In a **soliloquy,** the character is speaking as if to himself or herself—as if the audience can hear what the character is thinking, or like the character is thinking out loud.
- In an **aside,** the character makes a short remark, either to another character or to the audience, but the other characters in the play do not hear it.

Read the selection below. Then, respond to each question that follows.

Yeah, it's tough trying to live in Chinatown. But it's tough trying to live in Torrance, too. It's true. I don't like being alone. You know, when Mom could finally bring me to the U.S., I was already ten. But I never studied my English very hard in Taiwan, so I got moved back to the second grade.

1. Whom is the character speaking to? ______________________________

2. Which type of dramatic speech is this? ______________________________

3. Which clues in the speech help you identify it? ______________________________

____

____

Now, read this selection. Respond to each question that follows.

You're right, Chen. It's tough trying to live in Chinatown. But do you know what? It's tough trying to live in Torrance, too. I know, Chen. You like being alone. But me? I don't like being alone at all. You came here when you were a baby. Me? When Mom could finally bring me to the U.S., I was already ten. I never studied my English very hard in Taiwan, so I couldn't speak it like someone who grew up here. I got moved back to the second grade. Second grade, Chen! Can you imagine?

4. Whom is the character speaking to? ______________________________

5. Which type of dramatic speech is this? ______________________________

6. Which clues in the speech help you identify it? ______________________________

____

____

Name ______________________ Date ______________

Comparing Literary Works: Dramatic Speeches

Extension 5-10

In a **monologue,** only one actor speaks but the other characters are still on the stage, often reacting to the speech. They may respond with facial expressions, actions, or gestures. This means that when you read a monologue, you must try to imagine how the other characters are responding. The monologue may offer clues. For example, punctuation may suggest that the speaker pauses. Questions may suggest that the speaker pauses to wait for a nonverbal response from other actors or that the speaker is recounting another person's speech. Studying these clues in a monologue will help you visualize the entire conversation, not just the words spoken.

Read this monologue from *The Diary of Anne Frank.* Recall that Mr. Kraler is talking with Mr. Frank and his daughter Margot. Then, answer the questions that follow.

MR. KRALER: That's the man. A couple of weeks ago, when I was in the storeroom, he closed the door and asked me . . . how's Mr. Frank? What do you hear from Mr. Frank? I told him I only knew that there was a rumor that you were in Switzerland. He said he'd heard that rumor too, but he thought I might know something more. I didn't pay any attention to it . . . but then a thing happened yesterday . . . He'd brought some invoices to the office for me to sign. As I was going through them, I looked up. He was standing staring at the bookcase . . . your bookcase. He said he thought he remembered a door there . . . Wasn't there a door there that used to go up to the loft? Then he told me he wanted more money. Twenty guilders more a week.

Answer these questions about the passage.

1. What do the ellipses (. . .) tell you about Mr. Kraler's speech?

____

2. Find the two questions in the passage. What kind of voice would Mr. Kraler use for these questions? Why? ______________________________

____

____

3. What do you think Mr. Frank and Margot are doing while Mr. Kraler is speaking? ______________________________

____

Perform Work with two partners to create a dramatic reading of Mr. Kraler's monologue. Remember that even the two actors who are listening participate in the scene. Take turns presenting the monologue.

Name ______________________________ Date ______________

Listening and Speaking: Reading Drama Aloud

Reinforcement 5-11

A play has two groups of participants. The first group are the actors and behind-the-scenes people who organize and perform the play. The second group is the audience, the people who watch the play. Each group has its own responsibilities.

- The actors and behind-the-scenes people must be able to work together. They must organize the play into an enjoyable event. They must be able to convey the play in such a way that people understand what the play is about. In addition, the actors must perform so people can understand and hear them.
- The audience must pay attention to the play. The people in an audience must listen closely to the words spoken on stage, as well as follow the action on stage. They must also respond with the appropriate responses, such as laughter, applause, or even silence.

Read each question below. Determine if the question reflects good speaking on the part of the actors and the behind-the-scenes people, or if it reflects good listening on behalf of the audience. Write S for Speaking and L for Listening.

1. _____ How well did the group demonstrate eye contact?
2. _____ How organized was the group when presenting their scene?
3. _____ How well did the group focus attention on the performance?
4. _____ How well did the group work together?
5. _____ How well did the group's presentation reflect the content of the scene?
6. _____ How well did the group demonstrate pitch and volume?
7. _____ How well did the group demonstrate they were paying attention by responding appropriately?
8. _____ How well did the group follow stage directions and know their lines?

Synthesize Do you agree or disagree with the following? *The speakers and the audience have equally important roles.* Explain.

____

____

____

Name ______________________ Date ____________

Listening and Speaking: Reading Drama Aloud

Extension 5-11

When you read dramatically, it's like performing a play without sets or costumes. The challenge is to imagine yourself inside the character you portray. This means you must create the character from your voice, gestures, movements, thoughts, and so on. You must also explore and understand how your character will react to the actions and words of other characters. Understanding the character inside and out will help you become that person.

Complete the following activities.

1. Complete a character web to learn about your character.

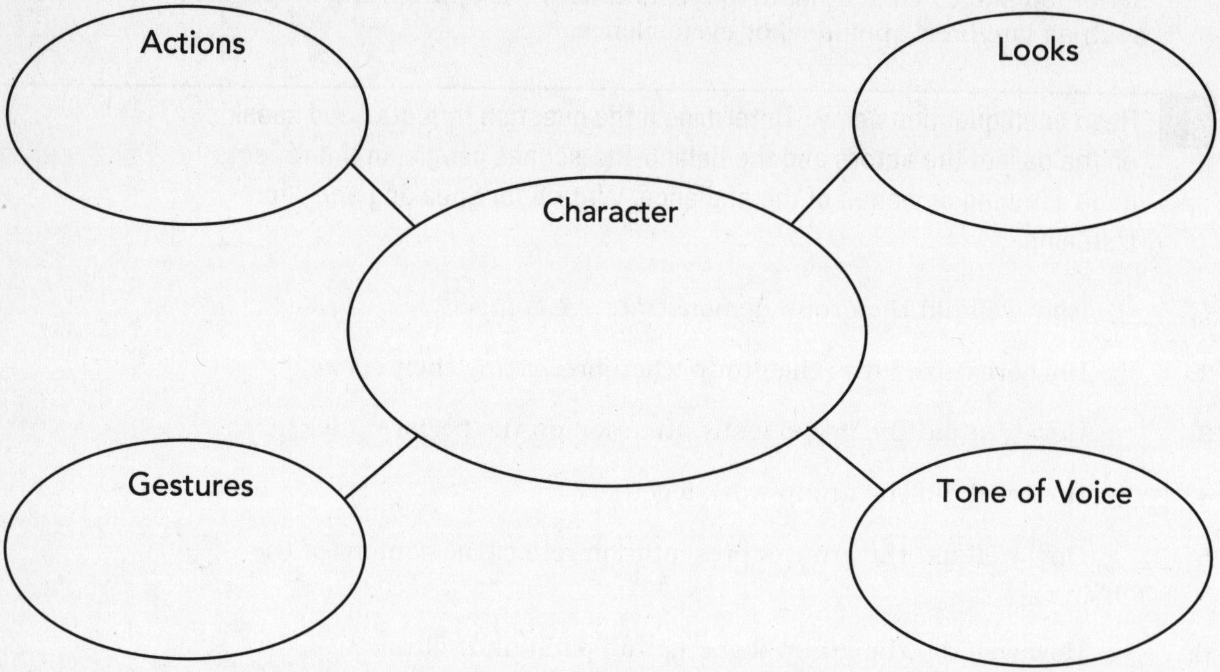

2. Now complete a cause-and-effect chart to explore how your character will react to other characters. As you rehearse, record what other characters do. Consider and record what your character might say, think, or do in response. Use your own experiences and the text to help you decide.

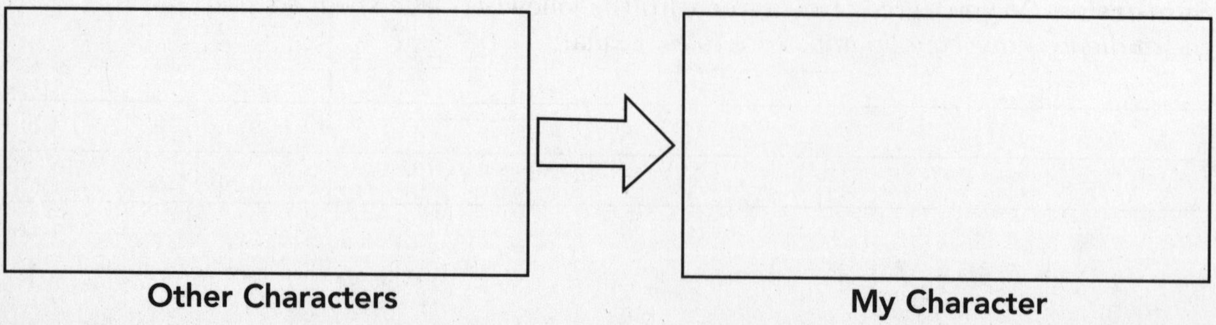

Name ______________________ Date ____________

Language Coach: Independent and Subordinate Clauses

Reinforcement 5-12 A

A group of words that have a subject and a verb is called a **clause.**

- An **independent clause** must have a subject and a verb as well as express a complete thought. It is the essential part of a sentence and can stand alone as a complete sentence.
- A **subordinate clause** usually begins with a conjunction such as *while, once, even though, when, after, since, if,* and *because.* It has a subject and verb but it is not a complete sentence. A subordinate clause makes the reader want or need additional information to finish the thought. Using subordinate clauses is one way of combining two ideas into a single sentence, in order to make your writing more interesting.

Circle the subordinate clause in each sentence.

1. When a garden snake slithered across the sidewalk, Dina gasped and ran.
2. She was worried, as she did not see it slink away.

Use one of the following conjunctions to combine the following sentences.

because, which, since

3. The Havasupai tribe lives at the base of Havasu Canyon. It is part of the Grand Canyon.

____

____

4. It is difficult to reach the village. Supplies are brought in by horse or mule train.

____

____

5. It is called the "Shangri-la of the Grand Canyon." It has towering cliffs and spectacular waterfalls.

____

____

Write On a separate sheet of paper, write two sentences that use subordinate clauses.

Name ______________________ Date ______________

Language Coach: Sentence Combining With Subordinate Clauses

Reinforcement 5-12 B

One way to vary your writing is to combine 2 short related sentences into one sentence with a **subordinate clause.** A subordinate clause is a group of words that has its own subject and verb but cannot stand as a complete sentence by itself.

Example Sihu rollerblades in the park. It is a block from her apartment.

Sihu rollerblades in the park, *which is a block from her apartment.*

Example Jonah ate his lunch with Shelby. Shelby had a tuna sandwich.

Jonah ate his lunch with Shelby, *who had a tuna sandwich.*

In the examples above, *which* refers to the park and *who* refers to Shelby.

Use a subordinate clause to combine each pair of sentences.

1. Marta had gym class on the baseball field. She hit a home run there.

____

____

2. Chanté visited her grandmother. Her grandmother lives in Chicago.

____

____

3. Sean doesn't like to ride the bus. He gets motion sick.

____

____

4. We watched the movie. It was a documentary about penguins.

____

____

5. Anisa ate dinner. Then, she finished her social studies project.

____

____

6. Naeem played a video game. His mom gave it to him.

____

____

Name ________________________ Date ____________

Language Coach: Independent and Subordinate Clauses

Extension 5-12

Writers often add a subordinate clause to a sentence to make it more specific or to add extra information. To be more specific about a thing or a group, use either *that* or *which*. For information that is essential to the sentence, use *that*:

I don't eat foods that are high in fat.

Without the underlined clause, the reader would not know which foods the writer is talking about. So the information is essential. To add extra information to a sentence, use *which*:

The bicycles at the store, which are mostly mountain bikes, are on sale.

Even without the underlined clause, the reader still knows which bicycles the writer is talking about. So the information is not essential. When using which, always place the subordinate clause between commas.

To be more specific about a person or group of people, use *who* instead of *which* or *that*:

The barber who cuts my hair is as bald as a bowling ball.

You can use *who* to provide either essential or extra information. You can also use *who* to refer to animals (usually pets).

Complete the sentences using *who, that,* or *which.*

1. William Shakespeare, ____________ wrote both plays and poetry, was born in 1564.
2. The plants ____________ I gave you should be watered every week.
3. Wilbur must be the only monkey in Tanzania ____________ doesn't like bananas.
4. Jenny's ice cream, ____________ was chocolate, melted quickly in the hot sun.
5. Are those the cicadas ____________ only appear once every seventeen years?
6. Puerto Rico, ____________ is a U.S. territory, is an island in the Caribbean Sea.
7. The book ____________ Ricardo read was about the American Revolution.
8. The photographer ____________ took our class portraits, will be taking pictures at the school dance.

Name ______________________________ Date ______________

Writer's Workshop: Business Letter

Reinforcement 5-13

Business letters can be written when you want to request information, order a product, make a complaint, or share your opinion on a subject. The basics of good business letter writing are easy to learn. In a standard business letter you should describe who you are and why you are writing the letter, using appropriate voice and style. Always present facts, examples, and details to support your opinion or request.

Read the letter, and then complete the activities that follow.

Dear Ms. Lee:

I am an eighth-grade student. I believe that students in our school should wear uniforms. We need to spend less time and money worrying about what we wear to school and spend more time on our studies.

Parents would spend less money on clothes, if students were allowed to wear uniforms. Students wouldn't be pressuring them to buy new clothes to fit in with everyone. It would free parents up to spend their money on other things for their families.

Wearing uniforms would help everyone feel that they are a part of this school. It would help avoid bad feelings among students and lessen the possibility of cliques based on what people wear. Students would be able to look beyond what people are wearing and judge them for who they are.

There are many reasons why this is important. I feel that this is something that we should put before the students in our school to discuss.

Thank you, Ms. Lee, for reading my letter. I hope you will consider my suggestion.

Sincerely,

Timothy Johns

1. What is the purpose of this letter? ______________________________

____

2. Underline at least three details the writer uses to support his argument.

3. Write the opening paragraph as a response to this letter.

____

____

____

____

____

____

____

____

____

Write On a separate sheet of paper, complete the reply to this letter.

Name ______________________________ Date ______________

Writer's Workshop: Business Letter

Extension 5-13

After sending a **business letter** to a possible employer, job searchers need to follow-up. This often includes making phone calls and sending e-mails or letters. After an interview, a thank you letter or e-mail is also expected. Writers should approach these tasks using skills and strategies for **workplace writing.** Read these follow-ups from Chantelle Baron.

Phone call or e-mail:

> This is Chantelle Baron. I wrote a letter to you last week to apply for an internship in the Cloisters Summer Internship Program. I'd like to answer any questions you have about my qualifications and talk about how I can help the program. When would be a good time for you to meet?

Thank you letter or e-mail:

> Thank you for taking the time yesterday to meet with me. I enjoyed hearing more about the Cloisters Summer Internship. I am sure that I can be helpful to the program, especially in the demonstrations you described. I know I would be good at helping with demonstrations because of my experience with teaching art projects. I would welcome the chance to join your team and I hope to hear from you soon.

---

1. Write the text for a phone or e-mail follow-up and a thank you letter or e-mail. Use specifics from your business letter.

____

____

____

____

____

____

____

____

____

____

____

____

____

2. Work with a partner. Exchange your business letters and follow-ups. Then, role-play an interview that reflects the information from the letters. Perform your interview for the class. Ask your classmates for comments.

Name ______________________ Date ____________

End-of-Unit Benchmark Test — Unit 5

Reading Skill: Drawing Conclusions

Read the following questions. Then, choose the best answer.

1 Which of these is most important in drawing conclusions while reading?

A identifying main ideas
B connecting important details
C recognizing author's purpose
D identifying key details

2 Which of these best describes a conclusion?

F a decision
G a reason
H a prediction
J an effect

Read the passage. Then, answer the questions.

Thomas: Come on, Patrick, you'll have fun. You'll learn a lot, and you'll be helping a family have a home that they otherwise couldn't afford.

Patrick: I don't know, Thomas. I've never built anything before, much less a house.

Thomas: You don't have to build the whole thing by *yourself*. There are dozens of people donating their time. Someone will show you just what to do.

Patrick: What if a piece of wood falls on me or I step on a nail . . .?

Thomas: What if, what if. *What if* you just said yes to the project?

Patrick: Well, I don't know. . . .

Thomas: Come for three hours on Saturday. If you're not having fun by then, you can leave. And I won't tease you like I did when you quit the baseball team.

3 Which conclusion about the building project is supported by the selection?

A It is for a company that builds houses.
B It will be a good source of money.
C It is a volunteer project to help others.
D It was organized by Thomas.

4 Which conclusion is best supported by the selection?

F Thomas knows that Patrick will avoid the project.
G Patrick thinks that Thomas is trying to trick him.
H Thomas feels that Patrick will benefit from helping on the project.
J Patrick is trying to appear braver than he really is.

Name ______________________________ Date ______________

Literary Analysis

Read the questions. Then, choose the best answer.

5 Which best shows an example of comparing a primary source with a dramatization?

A comparing a biography and a novel based on the biography

B comparing a diary and a short story based on the diary

C comparing a news account with a documentary based on the account

D comparing a journal and a play based on the journal

6 Which of these best defines staging?

F the act of putting on a play

G a script written for a movie

H a story written to be performed by actors

J the directions that guide the performance of a play

7 How is a play adapted from another form of writing?

A The set replaces the setting of the story.

B A character's words are transformed into speeches.

C The same story is told by using stage directions and dialogue.

D A character's dialogue is introduced with the character's name.

8 Which is a brief remark that a character directs privately to the audience or to another character?

F an aside

G dialogue

H a prop

J monologue

Read the passage. Then, answer the questions.

[Scene 1. Hallway in a cozy and cheerful house. Morning sunlight is pouring in, and a soft breeze is blowing from two open French doors in the background.]

Mom: Are you sure you're going to be okay here by yourself until I get home from work?

Gillian: *[She looks annoyed.]* Yes, Mom. If I'm old enough to babysit, I'm old enough to be home alone until six o'clock. Besides, I'm not feeling as sick today as I was yesterday. I'll be fine; I promise.

Mom: All right, but call me if you need anything.

Gillian: I'll be fine. You're such a worrywort.

Mom: *[She looks annoyed at* GILLIAN, *then seems to remember something.]* Oh, don't forget to close the doors down here. I left the French doors open to let in a little breeze, but if you're going to be upstairs in your room, you should just close them. *[She looks at her watch and grabs her briefcase.]* I'm running late. Gotta go!

*[*MOM *exits.* GILLIAN *sighs with relief and picks up the tiny black kitten that has been watching her from a bench in the hallway.]*

Gillian: I was beginning to think she'd never leave. Why do mothers always worry so much? Huh, Piper? *[*PIPER *purrs as* GILLIAN *scratches the kitten's head.]* Let's go back upstairs. *[As* GILLIAN *climbs the stairs with* PIPER, *a squirrel creeps in through the French doors, which have been left open.]* We're going to enjoy a nice, quiet day in the house by ourselves.

Name ______________________ Date ____________

9 **Which of the following items is a prop in this scene?**

A the squirrel

B French doors

C sunlight

D Mom's briefcase

10 **Which of the following events foreshadows another event in the plot?**

F Gillian looks annoyed at Mom.

G Mom realizes that she is late for work.

H Piper purrs as Gillian scratches her head.

J Mom reminds Gillian to close the French doors.

11 **What dramatic irony is at work in scene 1?**

A Gillian thinks that she is going to enjoy a quiet day alone, but the audience sees the squirrel creep through the French doors.

B Gillian forgets to close the French doors before going upstairs, but the audience sees the breeze blowing through the hallway.

C Mom looks at her watch and rushes off to work, but the audience knows that she is already very late.

D Mom worries about leaving Gillian home alone all day, but the audience knows that Gillian babysits.

Read the passage. Then, answer the questions.

[Scene 3. Gillian's bedroom. The sun has set, and the room is lit by a lamp on Gillian's desk. A phone sits next to the lamp.]

Gillian: *[She appears frightened.]* I really don't want to go downstairs. Who knows what I'm going to find down there? I really wish that Mom would get home. She said that she'd be home by six o'clock, but she must be running late. *[She hears a loud bang coming from downstairs and is visibly startled.]* There it is again! It can't be Piper. She's hiding under the bed. Ohhhh, why do these things always happen to me when I'm alone? Maybe I should call the police. Okay, that's what I'll do. I'll call the police. Better safe than sorry. Then again, what if it turns out to be nothing? I'll feel ridiculous if the police come here and don't find anything. They'll think I'm paranoid. *[She hears something move across the hardwood floor below and the sound of glass breaking.]* That's it! I've got to do something; I can't just stand here shaking. I'm calling the police right now. I can't take such chances. What if there's a burglar down there . . . or worse? *[She rushes to the phone on her desk and picks up the receiver.]*

12 **Which of the following terms best describes the selection?**

F aside

G dialogue

H soliloquy

J monologue

13 **At which point in the plot does Scene 3 probably take place?**

A the rising action

B the climax

C the exposition

D the end

Name ______________________________ Date ______________

Read the passage. Then, answer the questions.

[Scene 4. The red and blue lights of a police vehicle are flashing on the walls of the hallway. The front door opens as Mom walks in, followed by two police officers.]

Mom: What is going on? Gillian? Where are you?

Gillian: *[She rushes down the stairs, looking excited.]* Mom!

Police Officer 1: Ma'am, please wait right here while we look around.

Mom: Go ahead. Gillian, what happened? Why are the police here?

Gillian: I went back upstairs with Piper after you left this morning. I still felt dizzy, so I got back into bed. I slept, and then I did some homework. Around six o'clock, I heard a crash downstairs. At first, I thought Piper was making noise. I figured she'd knocked something over. I was about to go downstairs when I saw Piper dash under my bed. Then I heard another crash. Mom, I got really scared! I called the police because I didn't know what to do!

*[*MOM *is about to speak but she is interrupted when* POLICE OFFICER 2 *enters.]*

Police Officer 2: *[He is smiling.]* We've solved the mystery; you've got a squirrel in your kitchen.

Mom: Oh, Gillian! Did you forget to close the French doors when you went upstairs?

Gillian: *[She covers her face with her hands.]* Oh, no! I completely forgot!

Mom: *[She laughs.]* And who's the worrywort now?

Police Officer 1: *[He laughs.]* We'll arrange to have someone get the squirrel.

Gillian: *[She is smiling sheepishly.]* Boy, I feel foolish.

14 Which of the following terms best describes Gillian's account of events?

F prop
G aside
H monologue
J foreshadowing

15 Which is part of the set?

A the front door
B Piper
C the police officers
D the squirrel

Grammar

Read the following questions. Then, choose the correct answer.

16 Which of the following is a complete sentence?

F When I write, I prefer pen and paper.
G If the bicycle chain had not come off.
H Because the stove was on fire.
J In order to get to class on time.

17 Which sentence contains a subordinate clause?

A After the heavy meal, Gil took a long nap.
B When Ian finished the book, he gave it to Sean.
C You can reach me on my cell phone, if necessary.
D Shortly before noon, the sky darkened and the air cooled.

18 What is one reason to use a subordinate clause to join two short sentences?

F to show two important ideas

G to complete an incomplete thought

H to show a connection between ideas

J to express a complete thought

19 Which of these contains both an independent clause and a subordinate clause?

A The children scrambled up the ladder and slid down the chute.

B In less than an hour, Manny cleaned his bedroom.

C Coiled under a rock was a large rattlesnake.

D Lijia kept yelling until someone finally rescued her.

20 Which of these best defines a clause?

F a group of words that has a subject and a verb

G a group of words that expresses a complete thought

H a group of words that stands by itself as a complete sentence

J a group of words that tells more about a noun

21 Which of these best defines a subordinate clause?

A a clause that stands alone as a complete sentence

B a clause that has a verb without a subject

C a clause that has a subject without a verb

D a clause that cannot stand by itself as a sentence

Short Answer

Reading Skill: Drawing Conclusions

22 What does it mean to draw a conclusion?

____

____

23 What is one thing that can help you draw conclusions about characters in a play?

____

____

Literary Analysis

24 What is suspense in a literary work?

____

____

25 What is a dramatic speech? Name three types of dramatic speeches.

____

____

Name ______________________ Date ______________

Essay

Write on a separate sheet of paper.

26 Imagine that you are writing a scene with a monologue for a play. On a separate sheet of paper, begin your scene with the stage directions in which you describe the setting of the play. Then write the monologue.

27 Imagine that you are writing scene 1 of a play. The scene will foreshadow the outcome of events in a later scene. On a separate sheet of paper, begin your stage directions with a description of the set and the props needed for scene 1. Then write a dialogue.

28 Imagine that you are applying for a summer job. The job application requests a letter of recommendation. Think of a person who can confirm that you are qualified for the job. On a separate sheet of paper, write a letter to that person in which you give three reasons why you want the job.

Name ______________________________ Date ______________

Diagnostic Test 1 — Unit 6

Read the passage. Then, answer the questions.

Early Theories

Alexander Graham Bell's invention of the telephone developed from his observing the trials of communication for his mother and wife, both of whom were deaf. Bell had a theory that he could communicate with his mother through vibrations from his voice. He tested his idea by speaking near her forehead in low, deep tones.

New Inventions

Wanting to help his wife, mother, and others communicate better, Bell was determined to continue his studies of the ear and his experiments with sound. In 1875, he successfully transmitted the first sounds over a wire, and in 1876, he invented the telephone. The telephone was born from a world of silence.

1 Before reading this selection, what action will help you set a purpose?

A critiquing the selection's contents
B scanning the selection's headings
C adjusting your reading rate
D revising your ideas of what you want to know

2 Which of the following states a valid purpose for reading this selection?

F to understand how a phone works
G to find out how to be an inventor
H to learn why Bell invented the telephone
J to be entertained by a story about Bell's childhood

Read the passage. Then, answer the questions.

In the 1800s, cheap labor was needed to build the new Canadian Pacific Railroad. More than 5,000 Chinese workers were recruited from China and another 7,000 from California. The Chinese were excellent workers who deftly performed whatever tasks were required of them. Their employers, however, had little concern for their comfort or safety. The Chinese workers were housed in flimsy canvas tents, and many workers were killed each night by falling rocks. In addition, non-Chinese workers were earning five times as much for their labor while the Chinese worked on the most dangerous sections of the railroad! Those who lived to tell about their experiences vividly recalled the long days of back-breaking labor that was the plight of the Chinese railroad workers.

Name ______________________ Date ______________

3 **While researching the Canadian Pacific Railroad, a student found this selection. To what specific topic might the student narrow his or her research using this selection?**

A the plight of Chinese railroad workers

B the history of California

C the search for cheap labor in the 1800s

D the dangers of construction jobs

4 **Which sentence best avoids plagiarism?**

F Cheap labor was required to build the Canadian Pacific Railroad in the 1800s.

G The Chinese, who did whatever was asked of them, were good workers.

H The railroad employers ignored the Chinese workers' safety and comfort.

J Although they took the most risks, the Chinese were poorly paid for their work.

5 **Which main idea and supporting detail would you write on a note card for this source?**

A Chinese workers treated unfairly (dangerous conditions)

B railroads difficult to build (cheap labor needed)

C California's population high in 1800s (7,000 Chinese)

D no hotels in 1800s (people slept in tents)

6 **If the student's report were to cite a primary source, which of the following might it be?**

F an encyclopedia entry about railroads

G a newspaper article from the 1800s

H a diary of a Chinese worker

J a nonfiction book about China's history

Read the following questions. Then, choose the best answer.

7 **Choose the borrowed word that completes this sentence.**

Susan stayed until the end of the play so that she wouldn't miss the ______.

A finale

B gumbo

C gung-ho

D incognito

8 **Choose the best revision of the sentence fragment and sentence.**

Forgot the date. Julio was late for his appointment.

F Julio was late for his appointment he forgot the date.

G Because he forgot the date, Julio was late for his appointment.

H Forgot the date, and Julio was late for his appointment.

J When Julio forgot the date. He was late for his appointment.

9 **Which is the best revision of this quotation?**

Nikki Carter said more people buy chocolate ice cream than vanilla.

A Nikki Carter said, "More people buy chocolate ice cream than vanilla."

B More people buy chocolate ice cream than vanilla, Nikki Carter said.

C Nikki Carter said More people buy "chocolate" ice cream than "vanilla."

D "Nikki Carter said," more people buy chocolate ice cream than vanilla.

10 **Choose the borrowed word that completes this sentence.**

We used the ______ to cross the river.

F yoga

G kayak

H leprechaun

J moccasin

Name ______________________ Date ______________

Reading Skills: Setting a Purpose for Reading

Reinforcement 6-2

Setting a purpose for reading helps the reader understand why he or she needs to read a selection and what information is to be gained from the reading. Before you begin reading it is a good idea to think about the reason for reading.

When you read *The World Book Encyclopedia* entry, you were given a guiding question that asked about the importance of heroic characters and authors. This allowed you to set your purpose for reading the text.

Circle the letter of the best answer.

1. What is the best definition of a *purpose for reading*?
   - A. a reason for opening a book
   - B. a specific reason for reading a selection
   - C. to be entertained
   - D. to be informed
2. Which of the following would be most helpful in setting a purpose for reading a specific work?
   - A. understanding where to locate the work
   - B. asking questions about the topic of the work
   - C. hoping to have a positive response to the work
   - D. knowing what the author's purpose was in writing the work

Answer the following question.

3. How is setting a purpose for reading helpful to the reader?

____

____

____

Apply Imagine that you have been given a research assignment to investigate the history of something we use every day. Choose a topic to research, then complete the following chart.

Topic:		
What I Think I Know	**What I Want to Know**	**Five Possible Sources**

Name ______________________________ Date ______________

Reading Skills: Setting a Purpose for Reading

Extension 6-2

When reading a new assignment or text, a quick survey of the material will enable you to gain an understanding even before you begin. In many cases, the title is likely to provide you with a general sense of the selection. However, some texts require a more thorough scan to determine the purpose. The structure or format of the text can also help you determine what you will learn.

Read the selection below. Then, respond to each item.

Welcome to Sweet Meadow Farm

Sweet Meadow Farm is dedicated to ensuring the health, safety, and quality of life of our horses. We are equally committed to the satisfaction of our customers and our students.

Below is a list of stable policies, effective January 2008.

- Helmets must be worn at all times when handling a horse.
- Unsupervised children under age 12 are not allowed in the stables or indoor arena.
- Horses must be properly groomed before and after riding.
- Before entering the indoor arena, visitors must first announce themselves by calling "Door!" to alert riders and horses.
- Horses must not be left unattended on the crossties.
- Horses are to be turned out with their halters on.
- Guests are welcome to visit, but please refrain from feeding the horses.
- The stables are open from 8 a.m. to 10 p.m.

1. At first glance, what did you assume to be the purpose of the text?

____

____

2. List the types of information you learn by reading this selection.

____

____

____

____

3. What features might be added to reinforce important information?

____

____

Synthesize On a separate sheet of paper, discuss how this informational text can be read for different purposes. Give examples.

Name ______________________ Date ____________

Vocabulary: Words from Mythology and Borrowed Words

Reinforcement 6-3

The word *mythology* comes from the Latin word *mythos*, meaning narrative. Myths are stories that a particular culture uses to explain or describe its worldview. Many are about ancestors, gods, and heroes. Because myths are so important to the culture that made them, mythological words are often used to describe everyday things.

As people from different cultures with different languages come together, it is natural for their words to intermingle. As a result, English has adopted many words from other languages. Some of them have mythological origins, and some of them describe things or concepts that did not originally have names in English.

Read the descriptions of the god and goddess listed below. Then, answer the questions about them.

Ceres: Roman goddess of the harvest

Hypnos: Greek god of sleep

1. Identify an English word that relates to Ceres, and define it.

____

____

2. Identify an English word that relates to Hypnos, and define it.

____

____

Use each of the following borrowed words in a sentence.

3. igloo (Inuit)

____

4. hula (Hawaiian)

____

5. rodeo (Spanish)

____

6. opera (Italian)

____

7. denim (French)

____

Name ______________________ Date ____________

Vocabulary: Words from Mythology and Borrowed Words

Extension 6-3

Since English is such a diverse language, many of our words have their origins in other languages. Some borrowed words in the English language are used just as they are in their original language. Others have been adjusted slightly in terms of their spelling, pronunciation, or part of speech.

Review the list of borrowed words below. Look in the dictionary to find the language of origin and write it next to the word. Then, match the definition to the correct word.

1. petite	____________	**a.** ring-shaped bread roll
2. bungalow	____________	**b.** a temple
3. pagoda	____________	**c.** a severe rain storm
4. monsoon	____________	**d.** a small house
5. adobe	____________	**e.** something done alone
6. armada	____________	**f.** small
7. bagel	____________	**g.** a fleet of ships
8. solo	____________	**h.** a type of brick used for building

Review the words below. Then, write the English version of the word on the space provided. If you have difficulties, try saying the word aloud.

9. renegado (from Spanish) ____________

10. flamengo (from Italian) ____________

11. maschera (from Italian) ____________

12. bronzo (from Italian) ____________

13. appartement (from French) ____________

14. mitaine (from old French) ____________

Read the passage, then answer the question.

In Greek mythology, the River Lethe was one of five rivers that separated the living from the underworld. Those who drank from the river experienced complete forgetfulness and forgot all troubles of life.

15. If you are feeling lethargic, what might you want to do?
a. take a nap **b.** talk a walk **c.** eat dinner

16. Define the word *lethargic*. ____________

Name ______________________ Date ______________

The Research Process: Choosing Your Topic

Reinforcement 6-4

Each step of the research process involves making choices, and each choice has its own results and challenges. It is important to make choices that will lead to the best research and the fewest problems. For example, a topic that fascinates you but yields few research materials will cause more problems than a second-choice topic that yields plenty of research materials. You may find that you prefer researching the second choice topic.

Answer each question below.

1. Pedro wants to research ways that teens can earn money. Circle the key words that will work best for him in an electronic search, and tell why.

   a. *teens, jobs*

   b. *teens, money*

   ____

2. Rachel wrote down two ideas for questions she could use to guide her research on the following website. Read the information about the Web site, then circle the question that would be most helpful to Rachel, and tell why.

   Teen Job Clearinghouse
   Sponsored by Work Changes Lives
   Links to local business and organizations that hire teen workers for summer and continuing work. Reference information for teen workers. Contact Hailey Argiston at Work Changes Lives . . .
   www.WorkforLife.org/teens/jobs

   a. Who hires teen workers?

   b. Why should teens work at all?

   ____

   ____

3. Circle the book you would use for a report on how Americans today feel about the Vietnam War, and tell why.

   a. *The Media During the Vietnam War*
   Henry, Jamal
   Enterprise Press, New York City,
   © 2000

   b. *Vietnam and the Memorial*
   Chap, James
   Enterprise Press, New York City,
   © 2000

   ____

   ____

Name ______________________________ Date ______________

The Research Process: Choosing Your Topic

Extension 6-4

Narrowing Your Research Topic

When doing research it is important to focus on specific information. Once you have narrowed your topic, you must find information that does not extend beyond the scope of your narrowed topic. At every step of the way, you have to ask yourself which information is most important to focus on in the time you have available.

Suppose you have to do research for an oral history project.

1. Write three topics that you could do your oral history project on.

____

____

____

2. Choose one of your topics and describe how you could narrow its focus. Be specific.

____

____

____

____

3. Do preliminary research to decide how to narrow your topic. Explain how your research helped you narrow your topic.

____

____

____

4. Before you research your topic, it helps to come up with topic specific questions. The research you do should aim to answer these questions. You can use these questions to create introductory and topic sentences in your presentation. List three specific questions that you would like to answer about your topic.

____

____

____

5. On a separate sheet of paper, write a research proposal for this topic in a few paragraphs. Use the information above to support your ideas. Include ways you plan on presenting your topic. Then, present your research proposal to the class.

Name ______________________ Date ____________

The Research Process: Finding Reliable Sources

Reinforcement 6-5

Note-taking is a critical step in the research process. If your information is not accurate or well-organized, you will have difficulty drafting your research paper. You may miss key information, present incorrect information, or accidentally **plagiarize** your source. Remember to list complete information about each source, then to reference that source with each note card or note entry.

Complete the following activities.

1. On a separate sheet of paper, draw a Cornell Method format and an index card. As you read the following passage, take notes using both methods, then answer the following questions. Be careful not to plagiarize.

From *The Surrender in the Bear Paw Mountains* by Chief Joseph. This speech was given by Chief Joseph of the Nez Percé Indians in 1877 when he surrendered his army and his people's land to U.S. forces.

> Tell General Howard I know his heart. What he told me before, I have it in my heart. I am tired of fighting. Our chiefs are killed; Looking Glass is dead, Too-hul-sote is dead. The old men are all dead. It is the young men who say yes or no. He who led on the young men is dead. It is cold, and we have no blankets; the little children are freezing to death. My people, some of them, have run away to the hills, and have no blankets, no food. NO one knows where they are—perhaps freezing to death. I want to have time to look for my children, and see how many of them I can find. Maybe I shall find them among the dead. Hear me, my chiefs! I am tired; my heart is sick and sad. From where the sun now stands, I will fight no more forever.

2. Would this source be relevant for a paper on the struggle for land between Native Americans and white settlers? Why?

____

____

____

3. How current is this source? How important is the date for this source?

____

____

4. In what ways is Chief Joseph's speech a reliable source? What other sources should the researcher look for?

____

____

____

____

Name ______________________ Date ____________

The Research Process: Finding Reliable Sources

Extension 6-5

In many cases, you will come across source material reprinted in another source. For example, in your work text you have read many passages that come from other sources. Sometimes you are told the original source and sometimes you are not. When researching for a report, you will need to find that original source and evaluate it. You may also need to look up an author to determine if he or she is unbiased.

Read "Kids on the Bus: The Overlooked Role of Teenagers in the Civil-Rights Era" by Jeffrey Zaslow in Lesson 10. Use the title and author as key terms to search for information on the source. Supply information appropriate for a source card, then answer the questions.

______

Author: Jeffrey Zaslow
Title: Kids on the Bus: The Overlooked Role of Teenagers in the Civil-Rights Era

Publisher: ______________________

Date/Place of Publication: ______________________

Web Address: ______________________

Site Sponsor: ______________________

Page Name: ______________________

Date of Last Revision: ______________________

Date of My Visit: ______________________

1. Do you think this source offers credible and accurate information? Explain.

____

____

2. What is another way to verify the information about Barbara Johns? ______________________

____

3. Is the date of this source current for a paper about the civil-rights era? Explain.

____

____

4. Can you determine if Jeffrey Zaslow is biased from the information you have? Explain.

____

____

____

Name ______________________ Date ____________

The Research Process: Primary and Secondary Sources

Reinforcement 6-6

The materials that researchers use to gather information are called sources.

- **Primary sources** are written about events or experiences that the writer personally observed or participated in. For example, you create primary sources whenever you write diaries or letters.
- **Secondary sources** are written about events or experiences that the writer has researched. They may cite primary source material. For example, you create secondary sources whenever you write a research paper.

Ashanti found the following passages, but she needs both a primary and a secondary source about each topic. Read the selections, then help her by answering the questions that follow.

"Water Man Comics" by artist Dav Pilkey

I first started drawing the Water Man Comics in 1977, when I was eleven years old. . . . [O]ver the next few months [I] compiled twenty issues of my Water Man Epic Saga. These comics featured not only Water Man and his crime-fighting pals Molecule Man and Mr. Shape-O, but also a cast of famous bad guys, including King Kong, the Invisible Man, and Jaws 2. . . . I made my comics up as I went along. I started with the title, then made up the stories as I drew the pictures (much the same way I do today). Sometimes it worked out great . . . other times it didn't.

"Always to Remember" by Brent Ashabrenner

In 1980, Congress authorized the building of the Vietnam Veterans Memorial in Washington, D.C., between the Washington Monument and the Lincoln Memorial. The answer . . . was to hold a national design competition open to all Americans. The winning design would receive a prize of $20,000, but the real prize would be the winner's knowledge that the memorial would become a part of American history on the Mall in Washington, D.C. . . . Announcement of the competition in October 1980, brought an astonishing response. The Vietnam Veterans Memorial Fund received over five thousand inquiries. They came from every state in the nation and from every field of design; as expected, architects and sculptors were particularly interested.

1. Which type of source does each passage represent? How do you know?

____

____

____

____

2. For each topic, tell where you might look for the other type of source.

____

____

Name ______________________ Date ____________

The Research Process: Primary and Secondary Sources

Extension 6-6

Secondary sources often contain **primary source** material such as quotations. You may not realize, however, that primary source materials often contain secondary source material. For example, a collection of letters or speeches might have background or context information written by an editor. In some case, such as an interview, the primary and secondary materials may be blended almost seamlessly.

Read these excerpts from an interview with horror novelist Stephen King. Then, complete the questions and activities.

LESLEY STAHL (CO-HOST): There's hardly anybody in America who hasn't read a Stephen King novel or seen a Stephen King movie. Let's face it, he's the world's best-selling novelist, the most successful horror writer in history. As we reported in February last year, even including entertainers, King is one of the highest paid in the country, earning more than $30 million in a single year. . That's all because his mind works this way: A man screams . . .

STEPHEN KING (NOVELIST): . . . and this rat jumps into his mouth and gets halfway down his throat. And if you can imagine, OK, not just the taste of it and the rear legs sort of kicking in air, but the feel of the whiskers way back in your throat as it sort of gobbles away at your soft palate.

STAHL: You know what? I'm completely grossed out. You've accomplished . . .

KING: I'm sorry.

STAHL: No, you're not. That's what you wanted to do.

1. What kind of source is an interview typically? ______________________

2. In what way is this first paragraph secondary source material? Explain. ____________

____

3. Would you define Stahl's final comment as primary or secondary source material? Explain. ______________________

____

4. Read the rest of the interview from lesson 7. Identify another example of secondary and primary source material. Explain your choices.

____

____

____

____

____

____

____

Name ______________________ Date ____________

Analyzing an Informational Text: Interview Transcript

Reinforcement 6-7

You are probably familiar with **interviews** from TV, magazines, or the radio. How do you know the difference between an interview and a conversation? In a conversation, two or more people talk about a topic and ask one another questions. In an interview, there are two distinct roles. The *interviewer* asks questions to obtain information from the *subject*, and the subject tries to provide helpful answers. Often, the interview is created for an audience to see or hear, so the interviewer may sometimes talk to the audience as well as to the subject. When you hear or see an interview, you know this is happening because the interviewer looks toward the audience or changes his or her tone of voice. If you are reading a **transcript** of an interview, however, it can be confusing.

Read the following interview transcript from a youth TV program, then answer the questions.

Meg Riley (host): So, you're going to audition for the circus tomorrow . . .

Jamie Spokes (Meg's neighbor): Oh yeah!

Meg: Are you nervous?

Jamie: Only when I'm not practicing. I know my routine so well, I relax as soon as I get into it.

(footage of Jamie juggling while riding a unicycle and spinning a hula hoop on one arm)

Meg: (voiceover) Thanks to Jamie, all the kids on my street know how to hula hoop, juggle, and stilt walk. But I'm pretty sure Jamie is the only one who can do them all at once!

Jamie: (laughs) I just love playing with stuff, and I'm a multi-tasker. I'm never doing only one thing at a time. In the circus, I'll get to play around all the time, and get paid for it!

1. Why are there ellipses (3 periods) at the end of Meg's first line?

____

2. Does Meg ever talk directly to the audience? If so, when?

____

____

3. What does the interview reveal about Jamie?

____

____

____

____

____

____

Name ______________________________ Date ______________

Analyzing an Informational Text: Interview Transcript

Extension 6-7

When preparing to interview a subject, it is helpful to first familiarize yourself with the person you will be questioning. For example, if you are asked to interview a football coach on his championship season, it is a good idea to research some basic facts about the league, and perhaps some key highlights from his career. These pieces of information enable an interviewer to ask appropriate questions and engage the subject in conversation.

In the Stephen King interview, Lesley Stahl states some facts and background information about King's past and personal life. This helps the audience learn more about King. It also prompts King to add his thoughts and reflections without being asked a direct question.

In addition to gathering background information on a subject, it is helpful to plan out the interview in advance. While conversations make take their own turns, a skilled interviewer is able to keep the discussion on track by planning questions in advance and setting goals.

Complete the following activities.

Analyze Review the King interview. List at least four facts Stahl brings into the interview and explain how they affect the interview.

____

____

____

____

____

____

____

____

____

____

____

____

Analyze the structure of the King interview. On a separate sheet of paper, compose an outline Lesley Stahl might have used when interviewing King.

Name ______________________ Date ____________

Language Coach: Run-on Sentences and Sentence Fragments

Reinforcement 6-8 A

A sentence is a complete idea. It contains a subject and a verb. Two main problems with sentences are fragments and run-ons. **Sentence fragments** do not express a complete thought. **Run-on sentences** contain two or more complete sentences without the correct punctuation.

Tell if each sentence is a fragment or a run-on. Then, revise the sentences, adding words or punctuation as needed.

1. ____________ When Tanya finally got home. It was very late at night.

____

2. ____________ The traffic when she left.

____

3. ____________ The flight was badly delayed in Philadelphia there was bad weather.

____

4. ____________ Because she had extra time in Philadelphia.

____

5. ____________ The buses had stopped running she took a cab.

____

6. ____________ Her trip was successful she was exhausted.

____

Write two fragments and two run-ons.

7. ____
8. ____
9. ____
10. ____

Exchange papers with a partner. Revise each other's sentences, adding words or punctuation if appropriate.

11. ____
12. ____
13. ____
14. ____

Name ______________________ Date ______________

Language Coach: Revising to Use Quotation Marks and Block Quotes

Reinforcement 6-8 B

When you use someone else's exact words in your writing, you must signal this to your reader with quotation marks. There are two types of quotations, brief quotations and block quotations.

> **Capitalize!**
> The first letter of a direct quote or the beginning of a new sentence
>
> **Use Commas!**
> to separate the speaker from the quoted words

If a quotation has fewer than 5 lines, it is called a **brief quotation.**

Brief Quotation Example:

"Mom? Can I go to Heather's house," Nisha begged.

If a quotation is longer than 5 lines, it is called a **block quotation.** Block quotations must be indented.

Block Quotation Example:

In the following excerpt, Chief Joseph describes his physical and emotional fatigue at the battle in the Bear Paw Mountains.

> "I am tired of fighting. Our chiefs are killed; Looking Glass is dead, Tu-hul-hil-sote is dead. The old men are all dead. It is the young men who say yes or no. He who led the young men is dead. It is cold and we have no blankets. The little children are freezing to death."

It is easy to see how his state of mind led to the surrender.

Rewrite the following brief quotations, correcting capitalization and punctuation.

1. Hi, Mrs. Tobin, Jamil said.

____

2. "Good afternoon, Jamil," have you seen your mother, she asked.

____

3. "Yeah. She's at Mrs. Papetti's house he replied."

____

4. Mrs. Tobin asked if you see her, "can you please ask her to call me.

____

5. Jamil told her, sure, "No problem."

____

Name ______________________ Date ______________

Language Coach: Revising Run-on Sentences and Sentence Fragments

Extension 6-8

Good writers think about style when they correct **run-on sentences** or **sentence fragments.** If you find a run-on sentence in a passage that has many long sentences, use two short sentences for variety. When you want to show a particular relationship, use a comma and a conjunction. When you want to combine sentences in a more neutral way, use a semi-colon.

Good writers also think about style when weaving quotations into their writing. For example, writers can use more descriptive words than said to describe how a quotation was spoken or intended. They can also position linking text before, in the middle of, or after the quotation.

Complete the following activities.

1. Revise the following paragraph to correct sentence fragments and run-ons. Vary the kinds of corrections you make so that the revised paragraph flows smoothly. Write your revised paragraph on a separate sheet of paper.

   When the meeting began. Abby believed the problem could be solved. She proposed a new way to organize the recycling program at school she suggested electing recycling officers for each grade. These officers would come up with at least two ways. To get classmates involved in recycling. Abby and the other leaders of the program would then explain all the options to the whole school community. She thought her idea was a good one the others voted against it. They wanted to keep the program the way it was.

2. Revise the following paragraph to weave in the quotations more effectively. Look at both the language and placement of the linking text. Add or change words if you need to so that the revised paragraph flows smoothly. Write your revised paragraph on a separate sheet of paper.

   There are very few jobs available this year for teens. Bob Philbrick, the head of the Chamber of Commerce, said, "teens will have to look long and hard this year to find good jobs." He said teens should "start looking early" and be creative. He said, "Young people may want to identify a need in the community and find a way to fill that need." Bob gave the example of a young man who noticed that several of his neighbors' homes were empty. He offered to water lawns and keep an eye on the houses. The young man said before long, I had a booming house-sitting business.

Name ______________________ Date ____________

Writers Workshop: Interview Report

Reinforcement 6-9

A compelling **interview** begins with the interviewer's curiosity about the subject of the interview or about what the subject knows or has done. An interview report worth reading combines an interesting interview with background material. It should consist of a clear organizational format, and lively, varied, error-free writing to provide something people want to read and want to know more about.

Review the elements of an effective interview report, then answer the following questions.

1. Imagine that you are interviewing your favorite musician. Write three questions you would ask about his or her background.

____

____

____

2. Write three questions you would like to ask about music.

____

____

____

3. Imagine that the following is part of a transcript of your interview with a musician. Write a brief interview report based on it on a separate sheet of paper. Reorganize the questions into a format that makes sense. Check for spelling and grammar, and add an opening to the interview. Give the musician a name and use some of the questions and responses as background information. You might want to make notes on this page about what information you are using and what order you will follow.

What are you working on now?
I'm writing some songs about people I met when I went to New Orleans to help out after the hurricane.

Who was your first musical influence?
My mom sang me lullabies every night. So I'd have to say she was.

Which do you like best: writing songs, touring, or performing?
Performing is really fun, and I like meeting people on tour, but nothing is as satisfying as song-writing at those times when the song seems to write itself.

When and where were you born?
I was born just outside of Boston, Massachusetts, about thirty years ago.

Name ____________________ Date ____________

Writer's Workshop: Research: Interview Report

Extension 6-9

An **interview** report takes the questions and answers from a dialogue between two people and turns them into an account of the exchange that is interesting, coherent, and informative. The report should open with background information, then move on to the most insightful, surprising, and interesting questions and answers.

Work with a partner and imagine that you are going to interview a fictional character about one of his or her accomplishments.

1. Who will you interview and what is his or her accomplishment?

2. Research and write three pieces of background information about the topic of your subject's accomplishment. Also include background information about the character as it relates to that accomplishment.

3. Write five specific questions you could ask. Then, answer the questions from the character's perspective on a separate sheet of paper. Be creative! Ask questions that would keep the attention of the interviewee.

   I. ____________________

   II. ____________________

   III. ____________________

   IV. ____________________

   V. ____________________

Present Introduce your character's background information to the class and act out the interview with your partner. One should be the interviewer and the other the character being interviewed. You may choose to really become your character by doing voices and wearing a costume!

Name ______________________________ Date ______________

Mid-Unit Benchmark Test — Unit 6

Reading Skill: Setting a Purpose for Reading

Read the following questions. Then, choose the best answer.

1 When should you set a purpose for reading?

- **A** before you read
- **B** after you finish reading
- **C** only when you read to be entertained
- **D** only when you read to be informed

2 Once you set a purpose for reading, what should you do about your rate of reading?

- **F** Adjust your rate of reading to match your mood.
- **G** Read more slowly when you enjoy what you are reading.
- **H** Read more slowly when you are reading a difficult text.
- **J** Always read at the same speed, no matter what you are reading.

Read the passage. Then, answer the questions.

Today, we associate the Wright brothers with the development of flying, but they were not the first to try to fly. The person expected by the scientific community to perform the feat was a prominent scientist named Samuel Pierpont Langley. Langley had a whole team of other scientists working with him as well as the financial backing of organizations such as the Smithsonian Institute. Working in the Washington, D.C., area, he built a series of experimental flying machines. The only problem was that every time he launched one, it would crash. Wilbur and Orville Wright, in contrast, had no formal scientific training. To earn a living, they ran a bicycle shop in their hometown of Dayton, Ohio. Intrigued by the possibility of flight, they studied aerodynamics, built their flying machine, and flew it successfully. Even after their landmark success, it took years for them to get credit for the achievement.

3 Which sentence best helps you set a purpose for reading?

- **A** Today, we associate the Wright brothers with the development of flying, but they were not the first to try to fly.
- **B** Working in the Washington, D.C., area, he built a series of experimental flying machines.
- **C** Wilbur and Orville Wright, in contrast, had no formal scientific training.
- **D** To earn a living, they ran a bicycle shop in their hometown of Dayton, Ohio.

4 The most valid purpose for reading the selection is to learn about—

- **F** the early history of flying
- **G** the history of Dayton, Ohio
- **H** the history of Washington, D.C.
- **J** the laws of aerodynamics

5 In addition to learning new information, what other purpose might you have for reading this selection?

- **A** to investigate products before buying them
- **B** to escape to an imaginary world of adventure
- **C** to be entertained with interesting historical anecdotes
- **D** to appreciate the poetry written about flying

Name ______________________________ Date ____________

Vocabulary

Read the following questions. Then, choose the best answer.

6 Which of these words comes to English from Italian?

F moccasin
G gung-ho
H leprechaun
J incognito

7 Which of these words comes to English from Hindi?

A yoga
B gumbo
C finale
D kayak

8 Which English word for a windstorm do you think has its origins in the Chinese *tai-fung*, which means "big wind"?

F hurricane
G blizzard
H tornado
J typhoon

9 In Persian, the word *khak* means "dust" or "earth." What color would you guess that *khaki* pants are?

A white
B yellow brown
C violet blue
D green

10 In Spanish, a *corro* is a circle or a ring. What part of a ranch do you think a *corral* is?

F the farmhouse
G the stable
H the enclosure for holding the animals
J the field where crops are grown

Literary Analysis

Read the following questions. Then, choose the best answer.

11 For every source that you gather while researching, you should create a—

A transcript
B self-interview
C rough draft
D source card

12 When using the Cornell method of note taking, what should you write on the bottom 1/4 of the paper?

F the author's name
G a summary
H prompts
J notes

13 If you find differences in the information of two sources, you should—

A check a credible third source to verify the information
B assume that the most current source is correct
C check a .com Web site to verify the information
D ask a parent or guardian about the information

14 Which type of writing is a primary source?

F encyclopedia entry
G newspaper article
H textbook
J diary entry

Name ______________________ Date ____________

15 What is plagiarism?

A paraphrasing with proper citation

B obtaining information from an outdated source

C presenting someone else's research, ideas, or opinions as your own

D using a search engine to help narrow your research topic

16 An unbiased source is —

F one written by an author without special ties to the subject

G one that has little information on your research topic

H one that is outdated and therefore unreliable

J one published on a personal website

The passage below shows the results of a student's preliminary Internet search on endangered species. Study the results and then answer the questions.

SEARCH: endangered species

Save **Endangered** Species

The purpose of our organization is to provide the public with information about various endangered species and give people the tools to . . .
www.saveendangered.org

The **Endangered** Siberian Tiger

We must come together to protect the endangered Siberian tiger. Although all tigers are at risk, the majestic Siberian tiger is at an especially high . . .
www.endangeredsiberian.com

Endangered Birds of the Mariana Islands

This Web site features firsthand accounts from Theodore Malcheski, a prominent field biologist. His accounts detail his research findings while living among the endangered birds of the Mariana Islands in 2008 . . .
www.marianabirds.org

17 Why would you consider the first result a reliable source?

A It promotes a worthy cause.

B It has a Web address ending with .org.

C It provides information.

D It promotes the survival of more than one species.

18 Which topic provides a narrower focus for your research?

F Fascinating animals

G The endangered Siberian tiger

H Various endangered species

J Providing the public with information

19 The third result is considered—

A a primary source

B an unreliable source

C a secondary source

D an outdated source

20 Why should you avoid using the second result for your research?

F The source is irrelevant to the topic.

G The source contains outdated information.

H The source may be unreliable.

J The source is a magazine article.

Name ______________________________ Date ______________

Read the following excerpt from a nonfiction book that was published in 1956. Then, answer the questions.

> Born in England to an English mother and an American father, Agatha Christie grew up at a time when women from wealthy families did not work for a living. World War I, however, changed all that. During the war, Christie worked at a local hospital, helping to dispense medicines. Then, after the war, she decided to try writing mysteries. Soon she was creating stories featuring one of two popular detectives—Hercule Poirot, an eccentric former Belgian policeman working as a detective in London, and Miss Jane Marple, an elderly spinster who had an uncanny understanding of human nature. Christie's first marriage, to World War I pilot Archibald Christie, ended in divorce, but in 1930 she married British archeologist Max Malloran, whom she sometimes accompanied on digs in the Middle East.

21 What type of source is this passage?

A primary

B current

C secondary

D autobiographical

22 Suppose that you developed an idea map of this passage. What might you write in the middle oval?

F Born in England

G Agatha Christie's remarriage to Max Malloran

H Famous characters in her stories.

J Agatha Christie's personal life and work

23 What might you write in one of the outside ovals of an idea map?

A Who was Agatha Christie's father?

B Christie distributed medicine at a hospital during World War I.

C Citizens were forced to make great sacrifices during World War I.

D Christie's books remain popular today.

24 Why is it unacceptable for a student to use this sentence in a research paper?

Miss Jane Marple was an elderly spinster who had an uncanny understanding of human nature.

F The student is including information that is false.

G The sentence is grammatically incorrect.

H The sentence is too short to be in a research paper.

J The student is plagiarizing the author's work.

25 What key word would you write on the top of a note card about this source?

A Archibald Christie

B women writers

C Agatha Christie

D World War I

Name ______________________________ Date ______________

Grammar

Read the following questions. Then, choose the best answer.

26 Revise this run-on sentence.

Sophia is coming over for dinner my father is making spaghetti.

F My father is making spaghetti, Sophia is coming over for dinner.

G Sophia is coming over for dinner. My father is making spaghetti.

H Sophia is coming over for dinner and my father. Is making spaghetti.

J Sophia is coming over for dinner, my father is making spaghetti.

27 Revise this sentence fragment.

Before my mother mows the lawn. We have to pick up the large sticks.

A Before my mother mows the lawn, we have to pick up the large sticks.

B Before my mother mows the lawn, and we have to pick up the large sticks.

C Before my mother mows the lawn; we have to pick up the large sticks.

D Before my mother mows the lawn; and we have to pick up the large sticks.

28 Revise this run-on sentence.

Toby enjoys reading detective books he finds them exciting.

F Toby enjoys reading detective books, he finds them exciting.

G Toby enjoys reading detective books and he finds. Them exciting.

H Toby enjoys reading detective books, but he finds them exciting.

J Toby enjoys reading detective books; he finds them exciting.

29 Revise this sentence fragment.

During the bus ride. The person next to me would not stop talking.

A During the bus ride and the person next to me would not stop talking.

B During the bus ride; the person next to me would not stop talking.

C During the bus ride, the person next to me would not stop talking.

D During the bus ride the person, next to me would not stop talking.

30 When should you use quotation marks for quotations that you include in an essay or another paper?

F for shorter quotations only

G for longer quotations only

H whenever you quote material exactly

J whenever you introduce a quotation with a colon

31 What is a block quotation?

A any words within quotation marks

B a longer quotation that is set off by indenting

C any words that follow a colon

D a quotation that does not use the exact words of the speaker or writer

32 Which quotation is punctuated correctly?

F Tony said, We are out of milk.

G "Tony said," We are out of milk.

H Tony said, We are out of "milk."

J Tony said, "We are out of milk."

Name ______________________ Date ______________

Short Answer

Reading Skill: Setting a Purpose for Reading

33 When setting a purpose for reading, explain how to preview unfamiliar text to identify the topic.

34 After you read a selection, what should you ask yourself about your purpose for reading?

Literary Analysis

35 Name the four strategies for choosing a general topic for a research paper.

36 What is an interview transcript?

Essay

Write on a separate sheet of paper.

37 Think of a specific topic for a research report—one that is not too broad or too narrow. On a separate sheet of paper, write the topic. Then write four questions that you would like to answer about the topic.

38 Use the following question to help you think of a possible general research topic. In what place in the world would you find it fun or interesting to live? Write a paragraph explaining why it would be interesting or fun to live there. Then, write three questions that could help you narrow your research topic.

39 Think of a historical figure whom you would like to interview. Write a list of at least ten questions to ask your subject. Arrange the questions in an order that will allow the interview to go smoothly.

Name ______________________________ Date ______________

Diagnostic Test 2 — Unit 6

Read the passage. Then, answer the questions.

Imagine a wall of brick and stone, 15 feet wide and 25 feet high. Imagine that it spans some 1,500 miles. That's roughly the distance from New York City to Omaha, Nebraska. Imagine a wall so vast that astronauts orbiting Earth can see it from space! Believe it or not, you've just imagined one of the seven wonders of the world—the Great Wall of China.

Built entirely by hand, the Great Wall was begun around the seventh century B.C.E. It took many hundreds of years to complete. The first segments were built thousands of years ago to keep out invaders from the north. Nearly paralyzed by the fear of being overrun by barbarians, Chinese emperors ordered that a wall be built to protect the people.

1 If you were writing a summary of this selection, which of these details would you be most likely to include?

- **A** China was once threatened by invaders from the north.
- **B** The Great Wall is 1,500 miles long.
- **C** There are seven wonders of the world.
- **D** Chinese emperors feared barbarians.

2 If you were writing a summary of this selection, which of these details would you be least likely to include?

- **F** The Great Wall of China is 25 feet high.
- **G** Building on the wall began in the seventh century B.C.E.
- **H** The Great Wall was built for protection.
- **J** Chinese emperors were nearly paralyzed by fear.

Read the passage. Then, answer the questions.

(1) The International Space Station Alpha orbits Earth 16 times a day. (2) The Alpha astronauts use equipment. (3) The equipment is scientific. (4) They study conditions on the planet. (5) Because of the astronauts' unique perspective, governments should use their observations when making decisions about facing changes in Earth's climate.

(6) Alpha crews worry about troubling developments. (7) Astronaut Frank Culbertson piloted shuttle missions in the early 1990s. (8) He took command of ISS Alpha in 2001. (9) An immediate surprise was the change in what he could observe of Earth's face. (10) Pollution now creates a far more cloudy view than in the decade before. (11) "There is smoke and dust in a wider-spread area than we have seen before," he explained in an interview. (12) He also recalled the magnificent light shows on Earth's surface at night.

Name ______________________________ Date ______________

3 The sentence that contains the thesis statement for this student paper is—

A sentence 1

B sentence 3

C sentence 5

D sentence 7

4 Which is the best way to revise sentences 2, 3, and 4 to avoid a choppy rhythm?

F The Alpha astronauts use scientific equipment to study conditions on the planet.

G The Alpha astronauts study conditions on the planet. They use scientific equipment.

H The Alpha astronauts have equipment. They study conditions on the planet.

J The Alpha astronauts use scientific equipment. The equipment studies conditions.

5 The sentence that is irrelevant in this first draft of a student report on the International Space Station is—

A sentence 5

B sentence 9

C sentence 10

D sentence 12

6 How should this student give credit to the source of the quotation?

F (author's name) "There is smoke and dust in a wider-spread area than we have seen before," he explained in an interview.

G "There is smoke and dust in a wider-spread area than we have seen before," he explained in an interview (title of the work and page number).

H "There is smoke and dust in a wider-spread area than we have seen before," he explained in an interview (author's name and page number).

J "There is smoke and dust in a wider-spread area than we have seen before," (author's name) he explained in an interview. (page number)

Read the following questions. Then, choose the best answer.

7 In which sentence are all words capitalized correctly?

A Trey's favorite History Museum is in New york city.

B Sheryl cried, "hey! you forgot your shoes!"

C Jim and Judy greeted Ms. Phillips, the innkeeper at White Rose Inn.

D After i went to bob's Market, I took the bread home to Mother.

8 In which sentence is the punctuation correct?

F Samantha had a list of chores: mow the lawn, rake the leaves, and wash the car.

G After the party; I went to the beach.

H The Fourth of July is my favorite holiday: I like Thanksgiving too.

J Please hand in your reports take out some paper, and begin your homework.

Name ________________________________ Date ______________

Reading Skills: Summarizing

Reinforcement 6-10

A **summary** is a short statement that presents the main ideas and most important points in a piece of writing. Follow these steps to summarize a section of text or a whole work:

- Read the piece of writing all the way through.
- Reread to identify main events or ideas. Jot them down.
- **Organize** your notes by first identifying the **sequence** of events. Then, put the main events or ideas in order and cross out minor details that are not important for an overall understanding of the work.
- Summarize by identifying **pertinent** information and restating the main ideas *briefly* in your own words.

Read this passage. Then, reread it, focusing on the main ideas. Finally, answer the questions.

(1) Many paleontologists, the scientists who study dinosaurs, believe that the smallest dinosaur of all time was probably *Compsognathus*. (2) It was a slender, flesh-eating dinosaur that lived during the last part of the Jurassic period. (3) Fossils and skeletal remains have been found in southern Germany. (4) This dinosaur was only about 2 feet long, and most of its length was in the form of a long, whip-like tail. (5) About the size of a turkey, *Compsognathus* probably weighed no more than 22 pounds.

1. What is the main idea of this passage?

____

2. Which sentence gives the most important information?

____

____

3. Which is pertinent information that should appear in a summary of this passage?

A. It was a flesh-eating dinosaur.

B. It was only about two feet long.

C. It had a long, whip-like tail.

D. Its remains have been found in Germany.

4. Which is a minor detail that should *not* appear in a summary of this passage? ____

____

Write On a separate sheet of paper, write a brief summary of the passage. Include only the main ideas, expressed in your own words.

Name ______________________________ Date ______________

Reading Skills: Summarizing

Extension 6-10

Summarizing is an important reading tool. Summarize when you need to understand information to answer questions, when you need to record key ideas to discuss in a paper, or when you want to identify key persuasive points in order to respond.

Complete the activities below.

1. Read this "Letter to the Editor" and summarize it.

Dear Editor:

Cars are everywhere. We have 130 million cars on U.S. roads right now, and add 15 million more each year. But there is another transportation option, bicycles, and it seems that most motorists are unaware of them. People should realize that bicycles are often a better way of getting around than cars.

There are a lot of benefits to traveling by bicycle. Bicycles are powered by muscle, not non-renewable fossil fuels. When you ride a bike for half an hour, you could burn almost as many calories as if you were working out at a gym for the same amount of time. Plus, there is nothing more relaxing than riding a bicycle on a sunny afternoon.

The problem is that cars and bicycles cannot always share the same space. Roads can be a dangerous place for bicyclists. Motorists are exclusively at fault in 60 percent of car-bike collisions, compared to 17 percent for cyclists. I am not suggesting that automobiles be banned from roads, but I feel that people on bicycles will feel safer when there is coordination between automobile and bicycle traffic. We need to encourage bicycling, not discourage it.

A Concerned Citizen

____

____

____

____

____

____

____

____

____

____

____

2. On a separate sheet of paper, write a response to this letter. You may agree or disagree with its main points, but you must identify them in your response. Use your summary to help you.

Name ______________________ Date ____________

The Research Process: Drafting

Reinforcement 6-11

Developing a thesis statement can be challenging. Recall the process used in Lesson 4 about narrowing your topic. You can adapt those same steps to create a **thesis statement.** For example, asking questions can help you uncover the thesis statement "hidden" in your topic. As each question leads to other questions, you generate the information you need in your thesis statement.

Study this diagram created for a student's paper about Alexander the Great. Then, complete the items that follow.

Topic: Alexander the Great

↓

Question: Was he great?
Answer: Yes, I think so.

↓

Question: Why was Alexander great?
Answers: **1.** He conquered many empires.
2. He used brilliant battle strategies.
3. He was a decisive leader.

↓

What is my view?
Alexander was great for many reasons.

↓

Any background needed in thesis?
Alexander became King of Macedonia at an early age.

↓

Thesis Statement: Alexander became King of Macedonia at the young age of twenty and commenced to conquer the Persian Empire and part of modern-day India using brilliant battle strategies and a quickness to act that kept his enemies guessing.

1. How does this diagram serve to sum up the main idea of the report?

____

____

____

2. Why is it helpful to have the background in the thesis statement?

____

____

Apply On a separate sheet of paper, copy the diagram with its headings and questions only. Complete the diagram for your topic as you generate a thesis statement.

Name ________________________________ Date ______________

The Research Process: Drafting

Extension 6-11

Instead of a **standard outline,** it may be helpful to create a **sentence outline,** including more detail so that you can flesh out your ideas as you plan. You can then move easily to drafting by linking the sentences together, then smoothing out the flow of the paragraph.

Below is a sample standard outline.

Standard Outline

II. Alexander's first 20 years

A. Parents: Philip II of Macedonia; Olympias, princess of Epirus

1. Close with mother
2. Religious influence of mother
3. Military genius; bravery of father

Sentence Outline

II. Alexander's first twenty years show important influences in his life.

A. Alexander's parents were Philip II, King of Macedonia, and Olympias, a princess of Epirus.

1. Alexander was very close to his mother.
2. Olympias taught Alexander her religious views.
3. Philip II was a military genius. He was a brave man.

Paragraph: Alexander's first twenty years show important influences in his life. His parents were Philip II, King of Macedonia, and Olympias, a princess of Epirus. Alexander was very close to his mother, who taught him her religious views. In his father, he saw a military genius and a brave man.

In the space provided below, adapt another main heading of the sample outline into a sentence outline. Alternatively, use an outline you have created for your research report. Use the Roman numeral and capital letter of the outline section. Then, on a separate sheet of paper, expand it into a paragraph.

Outline Section: Roman Numeral ______, Capital Letter ______

Sentence Outline:

Main Heading: ______________________________

Subhead: ______________________________

1: ______________________________

2: ______________________________

3: ______________________________

4: ______________________________

Name ______________________ Date ____________

The Research Process: Revising Your Research Report

Reinforcement 6-12

Revising is an important step in any kind of writing. It allows you to fine tune your ideas and how you express yourself. When working on your first draft, you can focus on organizing and writing down your research. Afterward, when you revise, it is easier to see where you may need more research and how you can improve your writing to better express your ideas.

Read this rough draft about Darius III, the king that Alexander the Great defeated. Then, answer the questions that follow.

Darius became king of the Achaemendid dynasty through treachery. He belonged to a branch of the royal family and was placed on the throne by Bagoas, who murdered the two previous kings, Artaxerxes III and Arses. Bagoas had hoped to control the decisions that Darius made while on the throne, but when Darius made his own decisions, Bagoas tried to kill him with poison. His plan backfired when Darius forced him to drink the poison himself. It is also believed that Darius called for the assassination of Alexander the Great's father, Philip II. He was trying to free the Greek cities from Achaemendid rule. Alexander the Great took over the fight against the empire. Darius was unprepared to defend his empire. He was eventually defeated by Alexander the Great. <u>Darius was a poor leader. He was not a coward.</u> Darius fled the empire, leaving his family behind. He sent Alexander two letters offering ransom in return for an alliance. Alexander rejected the offers. Darius headed toward Bactria for safe retreat, but he was dethroned and murdered by the Bactrian satrap Bessus.

1. Where would be an appropriate place to add this sentence? "Darius III was the final ruler of a long dynasty."

____

2. How could you use a conjunction *but* to link the underlined sentences? Why does such a link clarify the ideas?

____

____

3. Find two places where you can combine sentences to avoid choppiness, and write your combined sentences below.

____

____

____

4. Make another suggestion for how this passage could be improved.

____

____

____

Name ________________________________ Date ________________

The Research Process: Revising Your Research Report

Extension 6-12

Primary source material is a key component to a strong research paper. Weaving in this material is an important part of the revision process. Whether you use brief quotations or block quotations, it is important to connect this material to nearby text and to your main ideas and thesis. Pay attention to placement and to transitions both into and out of quoted material. Remember that you can weave quotations into a sentence or allow them to stand independently after an introductory sentence.

Read these passages from the student model "Alexander the Great." Underline the transition that introduces each quotation. Then, reread the full essay in your work text and explain how the transitional text links the quotation to nearby ideas.

Even as a child, Alexander had enough ambition for several men, as shown by his comments after his father had conquered a city, "My father will have everything, and I will have nothing left to conquer."

1. ____

____

____

As the ancient historian Arrian reports, Darius fled in such a panic, he abandoned his royal chariot. "He even left his bow in the chariot, and mounting a horse continued his flight."

2. ____

____

____

Apply Find a paragraph in your report that contains a quotation. Add transitional text to reinforce the links between the quotation and nearby sentences and ideas. Write your revised paragraph here, underlining the new text and explaining the links you have created.

____

____

____

____

____

____

____

____

____

Name ______________________________ Date ______________

The Research Process: Sources and Publishing

Reinforcement 6-13

Sources must be cited in a bibliography according to specific rules. The order of information and the punctuation must be the same as below.

- Book, film or long musical piece:
  Author last name, Author first name. *Title of book.* City published, state published: publisher, copyright date.

  Example: Hamilton, Edith. *Mythology.* Boston, MA: Warner Books, 1999.
- If the work cited is a short story, newspaper article, or poem, the title should go in quotes instead of italics.

Below each citation, write what the mistake is.

1. Julio H. Moro. *Encyclopedia of Home Businesses.* New York City, NY: Enterprise Press, 1999.

   ____

2. *Self-Starters Tell Their Secrets.* Deane, Terrence C. and Guy York. New York City, NY: Enterprise Press, 1999.

   ____

3. Roosevelt, Lisa J. *Surprise! Stories of Teen Achievement in Business.* Rocket Publishers, Philadelphia, PA: 2004.

   ____

4. Jameson Chamber of Commerce. *Young People's Guide to Business Success.* New York City, NY. Enterprise Press, 1999.

   ____

Answer the following questions about the citations above.

5. If *Young People's Guide to Business Success* was actually a newspaper article, how would you change the citation?

   ____

6. Who is the author of *Young People's Guide to Business Success*?

   ____

7. In the bibliography, how should this list of citations be ordered?

   ____

8. If Lisa J. Roosevelt's book did not have an author listed, how would you change the citation? Where would you place it in the bibliography?

   ____

Name ______________________ Date ____________

The Research Process: Sources and Publishing

Extension 6-13

In today's world, you will likely do a lot of your research using a computer. You may find Web sites, or online versions of print media, such as magazine articles. When citing these reference sources, there are special rules.

Read the examples below and answer the questions that follow.

Website: 1) author if available; 2) title of the web page and the name of the web site; 3) name of the organization that hosts the site; 4) date the page was created or updated; 5) place and date you viewed the site; 6) URL or Web address.

Malcarne, Donald. "A Brief History of Essex, Connecticut." Essex, Connecticut, The Best Small Town in America. May 2007. Centerbrook, CT. 18 May 2007 <http://www.essexct.com/Index.htm>.

Newspaper/Magazine Article on the Internet: 1) author if available; 2) name of the article with original publication source, date, and page numbers; 3) database that collected the article and its publisher; 4) library or other organization where you read the article, with its location; 5) date you read the article; 6) URL or web address.

"Two thousand years later, the world takes its first look at King Philip II of Macedonia. (medical illustrator recreates his likeness). People Weekly Vol. 20 (Dec. 19, 1983): 121. InfoTrac OneFile. Thomson Gale. Deep River Public Library, Deep River, CT. 18 May 2007. <http://www.iconn.org>

1. What information is not included in the citation from *People Weekly*? Why? ______________________

____

____

2. Which publication does Thomson Gale publish, *People Weekly* or InfoTrac One File? ______________________

3. Which of these citations should appear first in an alphabetized bibliography? Explain. ______________________

____

Apply Find a Web site or online article for your report. Create a citation for your new source below.

____

____

____

____

____

____

____

Name ______________________ Date ______________

Listening and Speaking: Analyzing Media Messages

Reinforcement 6-14

When evaluating a media message, it is important to distinguish facts from opinions and assess both kinds of statements.

- A *fact* is a statement that can be proven by experiment or confirmed by reliable sources. Sometimes facts can be misleading, often because they come from unreliable sources or are taken out of context.
- An *opinion* cannot be proven. It expresses someone's viewpoint or feeling about a subject. An opinion can be supported by facts or by other opinions. If an opinion is not supported, or is supported only by other opinions, it is a good idea to examine it more closely before deciding if you agree with it or not.

Read the following advertisement and answer the questions that follow.

Feel good in your own skin! Try new and improved DermaClean soap for the cleanest, healthiest skin you've ever had. 99% of people surveyed use soap in the shower, but only 20% are happy with their skin. Daniela Lagos, from Athens, Georgia, says, "I love new and improved Derma Clean. It makes my skin feel just like an angel's!" And dermatologists agree. In fact, no other soap approved by the American Association of Dermatology is proven to give you softer, smoother skin. You and your family deserve great skin. Try new DermaClean soap today!

1. Write two facts presented in the ad. Then, explain why each fact could be misleading.

   Fact: ______________________

   Why misleading: ______________________

   ____

   ____

   Fact: ______________________

   Why misleading: ______________________

   ____

   ____

2. Write two opinions presented in the ad. Then, explain whether each opinion is supported or not.

   Opinion: ______________________

   Supported? ______________________

   ____

   Opinion: ______________________

   Supported? ______________________

   ____

Name ______________________ Date ____________

Listening and Speaking: Analyzing Media Messages

Extension 6-14

When making points, writers must back up their conclusions with convincing evidence and language. Often, they will include statistics, counter opposing viewpoints, and use persuasive language to create a certain effect. Strong readers carefully evaluate the evidence, making sure the passage does not omit key facts or viewpoints and reach faulty conclusions. In this way, strong evidence can make a message more powerful, and weak evidence can make a message less powerful.

Read the following newspaper editorial and answer the questions that follow.

Some people say that schools should extend the school day, so students can attend class for more time each day. This is a ridiculous idea. Clearly, anyone who favors this idea is crazy. A longer day does not mean students learn more. Students are already given too much to do. As it is, many do not have time to do their homework. And they are already overscheduled. When would they have time to relax?

1. What is the writer's purpose?

____

2. The writer states, "Clearly, anyone who favors this idea is crazy."

   a. What evidence is there for this claim?

   ____

   b. Does the word choice make the argument stronger or weaker? Why?

   ____

   ____

   c. Rewrite this statement to make the message stronger.

   ____

   ____

3. What evidence does the writer use to back up the overall message?

____

____

4. What evidence could the writer have included to make the message more convincing?

____

____

____

____

____

____

Name ______________________________ Date ______________

Language Coach: Capitalization

Reinforcement 6-15 A

Capital letters are important signals in your writing because they draw attention to specific people, places, or things.

When to Use Capital Letters

1. geographical names
2. at the beginning of sentences
3. the first word of a quotation
4. the pronoun *I*
5. organizations
6. titles of people

I was born in Atlanta, Georgia (1). Today (2) is my birthday. Mom said, "Happy (3) birthday!" After cake, I (4) opened my present. My party is on Saturday. Alejandro from The Boys and Girls Club (5) came. Even my neighbor, Mr. Fisher (6) came.

Underline all the proper nouns in the passage below. Rewrite and capitalize all the proper nouns in the box provided.

______________________________ ______________________________ ______________________________ ______________________________ ______________________________ ______________________________ ______________________________ ______________________________ ______________________________ ______________________________ ______________________________ ______________________________ ______________________________ ______________________________ ______________________________ ______________________________ ______________________________	The ps 122 middle school went on a trip to the american museum of natural history in new york city. it is right by central park. mrs. beasley's class went to the milstein hall of ocean life where they saw a 94-foot-long blue whale suspended from the ceiling. leo johnson and i wanted to go see the stegosaurus skeleton in the dinosaur exhibit but mr. nelson said, "not until after lunch."

Name ______________________ Date ______________

Language Coach: Commas, Semicolons, and Colons

Reinforcement 6-15 B

A **comma** indicates a brief pause. The following table shows the situations in which it should be used.

Situation	Example
Items in a series	He bought peas, beans, and pears.
Adjectives in a series	Her elegant, fast, high leaps thrilled us.
After introductory material	Before yesterday, I'd never seen such a thing.
With parenthetical expressions	I ran, even in the heat, and won the race.
To set off appositives	My brother, a nine-year-old, loves games.
With participial phrases	Running hard, we arrived just as the bus did.
With adjective clauses	Janet, who started school, has a sister.

Semicolons join independent clauses that are not connected with a conjunction like *and, but, or, nor, for, so,* or *yet.*

Example: The bus drove past; we were too late to get on.

Colons introduce a list that comes after an independent clause.

Example: She bought the following things: grapefruit, fish, and carrots.

Rewrite the sentences. Add commas, semicolons, and colons where needed.

1. Carrots which get soft when cooked are high in Vitamin A.

____

____

2. A person holding binoculars told us that the tall long-legged bird was a heron.

____

____

3. I got an A in math last term you'd never guess it used to be hard for me.

____

____

4. To knit a sweater you need these things yarn knitting needles and a pattern.

____

____

5. Even though it was raining we decided to take a walk.

____

Name ______________________ Date ______________

Language Coach: Commas, Semicolons, and Colons

Extension 6-15

Commas, semicolons, and colons all indicate pauses in written English. **Commas** are the most widely used.

- It separates adjectives and items in a series
  The weather was cloudy, muggy, and rainy.
- It sets an appositive apart
  The insect, a spider, scurried across the floor.
- It can be used after the introduction of a sentence
  After we realized we had nothing to eat, we went to the store.
- It separates phrases and adjective clauses from the rest of the sentence
  Spinach, which children often leave uneaten, is delicious.

Semicolons are used to join complete sentences together when no conjunction is in use.

The water was choppy and cold; our boat almost tipped over.

Colons come at the end of a complete sentence to introduce a list.

My favorite sports are the following: baseball, basketball, and tennis.

Revise each sentence according to the directions in parentheses. Use proper punctuation.

1. Jon showed his artwork in the city-wide show. (Add an adjective clause.)

   ____

2. The kinds of books I like to read have the following elements. (Add a list.)

   ____

3. The speaker talked for about forty minutes. (Add an appositive or an appositive phrase.)

   ____

4. We went swimming. (Add introductory material.)

   ____

5. The fair lasted until sunset. (Join with another complete sentence.)

   ____

Apply On a separate sheet of paper, write a brief paragraph about a favorite hobby that uses commas, semicolons, and colons incorrectly. Then, exchange papers with a partner and revise each other's paragraphs by using the correct punctuation. Cross out any commas, semicolons, and colons that are used incorrectly and add them where they are missing.

Name ______________________ Date ____________

Writers Workshop: Multimedia Report

Reinforcement 6-16

If you enhance an oral or written report with other media, you will have a **multimedia report.** The other media may include any of the following: music, artwork, charts, maps, posters, live performance, slides, or video. A multimedia report should include the following elements.

- a topic that can be covered thoroughly in the time allowed
- a main idea that shows a clear focus
- facts, details, examples, and explanations to support the main idea
- media that effectively support the topic and main idea
- careful and accurate research

Read this plan for a multimedia report. Then, answer the questions.

Sara wants to do a multimedia report on animals of Africa. She wants to cover mammals, birds, fish, reptiles, and insects. She went to the library and consulted several encyclopedias and about twenty books. She plans to include video of the animals, recordings of the animals' sounds, and charts showing genus and species relationships. She is hoping to get a zoo worker to present some live animals for members of her audience to observe and pet.

1. What is the problem with Sara's topic? Give specific examples.

____

____

____

____

2. How could Sara change her topic to improve its focus?

____

____

____

3. Give at least two examples of how Sara could change her plan so she would have a more effective presentation.

____

____

____

____

____

____

____

Name ______________________________ Date ______________

Writers Workshop: Multimedia Report

Extension 6-16

A **multimedia report** includes video, photos, slides, maps, audio, along with written material. Multimedia reports use sight and sound in creative ways to hold the audience's attention. In choosing a topic for a multimedia report, consider whether you will be able to find information in both print and non-print sources. Also, make sure that your topic is not too broad. In preparing your multimedia report, keep your audience and purpose in mind when deciding which media to incorporate.

Complete the following activities.

1. Imagine this is your multimedia assignment: Prepare a lesson on the color red for a preschool class. List some of your ideas for what to include in this presentation. ______________________________

2. Imagine this is your multimedia assignment: Prepare a presentation with the topic "A Day in the Life of an Eighth Grader." List some of your ideas for what to include in this presentation. ______________________________

3. Suppose you are planning a multimedia report about a topic of interest from science, social studies, literature, or another school subject. Fill in the information below. Then, write a description of the multimedia report you will present.

My topic:

My main idea: ______________________________

Three examples of media I can use to support my ideas: ______________________________

Brief description of my multimedia report: ______________________________

Name ______________________ Date ______________

End-of-Unit Benchmark Test — Unit 6

Reading Skill: Summarizing

Read the following questions. Then, choose the best answer.

1 A paragraph summary of a selection should include—

A all the details that appear in the selection

B precisely the same phrases as appear in the selection

C the main idea and the sequence of pertinent details or events of the selection

D the main idea of the entire selection rather than the main idea of each paragraph

2 Which of these types of writing would be a good example of a summary?

F a description of a TV show in a magazine

G a news story in a local or national newspaper

H an instruction manual that comes with a new automobile

J a story that appears in an anthology of short stories

3 Which statement is the best one-sentence summary of this information about a Chicago museum?

Among the huge number of things you can see at the Art Institute of Chicago are the Harding collection of medieval armor and the Thorne collection of miniature rooms, handmade to the smallest detail. The museum's paintings, which go back to the thirteenth century, include a particularly fine collection of European impressionist and post-impressionist works. The museum is also known for its American art and furniture, including the famous paintings *Nighthawks* by Edward Hopper and *American Gothic* by Grant Wood.

A The Art Institute of Chicago displays works dating all the way back to the thirteenth century.

B Highlights at the Art Institute of Chicago include a collection of medieval armor and a collection of miniature rooms.

C The Art Institute of Chicago has a huge collection of works from many cultures and eras.

D At the Art Institute of Chicago you can find many famous works of art, including *American Gothic* by Grant Wood.

Read the passage. Then, answer the questions.

Janine and I were out collecting specimens for a science project, although we were not finding many items that we needed. Suddenly, the sky grew dark and the wind grew fierce. Realizing that a storm was coming, we turned and headed for home. We had not gone far, however, when the rain began to pour. I ushered Janine into a cave on the side of the mountain to use as a shelter. Never having been in a cave, she was very frightened. The cave was damp and dark and smelled of decay. Luckily, we had a flashlight with us, although its light was rather dim. We remained there until the storm ended. Janine was glad to leave the cave—and frankly, so was I!

Name ______________________ Date ______________

4 If you were writing a summary of this selection, which of these details would you be most likely to include?

F We found few science specimens.

G During the storm, we found shelter in a cave.

H The cave was damp and dark and smelled of decay.

J Luckily we had a flashlight, although it was rather dim.

5 If you were writing a summary of this selection, which of these details would you be least likely to include?

A Janine and I were collecting specimens for a science project.

B Janine and I found few specimens for our project.

C We went into a cave to find shelter from the storm.

D After the storm, we headed for home.

Literary Analysis

Read the following questions. Then, choose the best answer.

6 What type of organization might you use in a biography of Queen Elizabeth I?

F chronological order

G cause-and-effect

H order of importance

J compare-and-contrast

7 For which of the following topics would you use a Venn diagram to help you organize your information?

A oak trees

B school sports

C cheetahs

D a football game

8 Why would chronology be one good way to organize an essay about how people become infected with the flu virus, get sick, and get better?

F You could explain where the flu virus comes from and how vaccines can be used to prevent the flu.

G You could explain the step-by-step process of what happens when the virus enters a human body and then makes a person sick.

H You could explain each of the symptoms that a person gets and how it affects the way the person feels.

J You could explain how the flu virus affects different parts of the body and how the person's immune system reacts.

9 Which is the correct way to list the title of a newspaper article in a bibliography?

A in italics

B underlined

C in parentheses

D in quotation marks

10 How do you cite a source in a bibliography when the author's name is unknown?

F List the citation by its title.

G List the name of the organization that wrote the work.

H List only the publisher.

J List only the publisher and the year of publication.

11 Which sentence contains a correctly formatted internal citation?

A According to scientist Josh Johnson, research into "the potentially harmful" side effects is necessary. Wilson 33

B According to scientist Josh Johnson (Wilson 33), research into "the potentially harmful" side effects is necessary.

C According to scientist Josh Johnson, research into "the potentially harmful" side effects is necessary (Wilson 33).

D According to scientist Josh Johnson, research into "the potentially harmful" (Wilson 33) side effects is necessary.

Name ______________________ Date ____________

Read the passage. Then, answer the questions.

(1) Maya Angelou is one of the most popular poets of recent times. (2) She has enjoyed great success, although not just as a poet. (3) She is also known as an author, a playwright, an actress, a dancer, a director, a producer, and an educator. (4) Angelou is a fluent speaker of half a dozen languages and uses them as she travels around the world, spreading her message of love and social equality. (5) Millions of people have been touched by Angelou's expressive readings of her work on television and at live performances. (6) Her powerful and animated reading of her poem "On the Pulse of Morning" was a highlight of President Clinton's 1993 inauguration. (7) The poem asks the people of America to work together to build a more loving nation.

(8) In her poetry, Maya Angelou uses short lines and everyday vocabulary to describe the great joy and terrible sadness she has known in her life. (9) The words she prefers to use may not be very fancy. (10) The feelings and ideas she expresses through her poetry are anything but bland. (11) Her poems are filled with strong emotions and powerful images. (12) Maya Angelou clearly understands that language is a gift to be cherished and used wisely.

12 Which of the following could be the thesis statement of this selection?

F Maya Angelou is a talented woman who uses her skills with language to spread her message of love and social equality.

G Maya Angelou has found success as a poet because she uses simple language that is easy for most people to read.

H Maya Angelou has often put her acting talent to great use by giving outstanding public readings of her poems.

J Maya Angelou is such a popular poet because she travels widely and often appears on television.

13 What is the main idea of paragraph 2?

A Angelou has had a difficult life.

B Angelou is an understanding person.

C Angelou's poetic style is simple but expressive.

D Angelou's poetry has touched many people.

14 Where could the writer have used a transition to connect ideas more clearly?

F between sentences 2 and 3

G between sentences 5 and 6

H between sentences 9 and 10

J between sentences 11 and 12

15 Which of the following details from the selection best shows the writer's perspective on Maya Angelou?

A Angelou has filled many roles including author, actress, and educator.

B Angelou uses short lines and everyday vocabulary in her poems.

C Angelou's poetry reading was a highlight of Clinton's inauguration.

D Angelou is a fluent speaker of several languages and uses them as she travels the world.

Name ______________________________ Date ______________

Read the passage. Then, answer the questions.

(1) The life of the racing greyhound can be a difficult one. (2) Valued only for their speed, many greyhounds are treated inhumanely. (3) Awareness of this inhumane treatment has grown and more efforts have been made to rescue greyhounds. (4) Adoption groups around the country collect thousands of dogs from racetracks and place them in homes as pets. (5) However, finding suitable homes for greyhounds can be difficult.

(6) One reason for the homelessness of so many greyhounds is that they are not a common or popular breed. (7) According to Jack Thomason from Michigan Greyhound Adoption, many people do not think to adopt a greyhound. (8) "People rarely see greyhounds walking around their neighborhoods or parks, so when people want to get a dog, they do not think to get a greyhound. (9) Greyhound are an uncommon pet breed because until recently, greyhounds largely belonged to the racing industry," explains Thomason.

(10) Greyhounds can require more care than other dog breeds. (11) This is in part because of the lack of socialization they receive at the track (Burns 12). (12) When a greyhound enters its first home, so much is new and frightening. (13) The stress of being in a new environment can lead to behavior problems. (14) People who adopt a greyhound must be patient and help the dog adjust to its new surroundings. (15) Many people consider the process of adjustment too much work.

(16) People assume that greyhounds need a great deal of exercise or require a large yard because of their size and speed. (17) This is not true. (18) In fact, greyhounds can be very lazy and spend most of their day sleeping (Burns 14). (19) Great Danes are also a large breed, but they do not require much exercise.

16 Which type of organization is used in this selection?

F chronological order

G cause-and-effect

H order of importance

J compare-and-contrast

17 What must be added at the end of this quotation to give credit to its source?

"People rarely see greyhounds walking around their neighborhoods or parks, so when people want to get a dog, they do not think to get a greyhound. Greyhounds are an uncommon pet breed because until recently, greyhounds largely belonged to the racing industry," explains Thomason.

A the page number in parentheses

B the author's name in parentheses

C the author's name and the page number in parentheses

D the author's name, title, and page number in parentheses

18 Which of the following could be the topic sentence of paragraph 4?

F Mistaken beliefs also surround the greyhound breed.

G Little is known about the greyhound breed.

H Greyhounds are much like other large-breed dogs.

J Only wealthy people can afford to own greyhounds.

19 Which sentence in the selection is irrelevant and should be removed?

A sentence 4

B sentence 9

C sentence 13

D sentence 19

Name ______________________________ Date ______________

Grammar

Read the following questions. Then, choose the best answer.

20 How should this sentence be rewritten so that commas are used correctly?

Touring Spain we visited the cities of Madrid Granada, and Seville but never reached Barcelona.

F Add a comma after *Spain, Madrid,* and *Seville* and keep the comma after *Granada.*

G Add a comma after *Spain* and *Madrid* and remove the comma after *Granada.*

H Add a comma after *Madrid* and *Seville* only and keep the comma after *Granada.*

J Add a comma after *Spain* and *Madrid* and keep the comma after *Granada.*

21 Which of these sentences is punctuated correctly?

A The zoo which opens at ten stays open late on Thursdays, Saturdays, and Sundays.

B Beautifully landscaped it is a large, impressive zoo with thousands of animals.

C If you visit on a busy weekend, you will probably wait in line at opening time.

D A visit usually costs seven dollars for adults but on Thursdays the zoo is free to all.

22 Which of these sentences is punctuated correctly?

F My little brother lost his hat, I found it the next day.

G I dressed him in: a hat, gloves, and a scarf.

H The Lost and Found contains these items; an umbrella and five gloves.

J I went to the Lost and Found; the hat was there.

23 In which sentence are all words capitalized correctly?

A Last thanksgiving, my parents and i visited the City of atlanta.

B last thanksgiving, my parents and I visited the city of atlanta.

C Last Thanksgiving, my Parents and I visited the City of Atlanta.

D Last Thanksgiving, my parents and I visited the city of Atlanta.

24 In which sentence are all words capitalized correctly?

F Yesterday Miss Duncan asked the class, "How many of you like to read poetry?"

G Yesterday Miss Duncan asked the class, "how many of you like to read poetry?"

H Yesterday miss Duncan asked the class, "how many of you like to read poetry?"

J Yesterday miss Duncan asked the class, "How many of you like to read poetry?"

25 Read the following sentence.

my family goes to beaufort, south carolina, every summer.

Choose the correct revision.

A My Family goes to Beaufort, South carolina, every Summer.

B my family goes to Beaufort, South Carolina, every summer.

C my family goes to Beaufort, South Carolina, every Summer.

D My family goes to Beaufort, South Carolina, every summer.

Name ______________________________ Date ______________

Short Answer

Reading Skill: Summarizing

26 What four steps must you take before writing the summary of a passage?

____

____

27 You often read summaries at school. Where else do you encounter summaries?

____

____

Literary Analysis

28 When you are revising your report, what can you do to write more effective sentences?

____

____

29 When do you need to cite sources in your report?

____

____

Essay

Write on a separate sheet of paper.

30 Write a one-paragraph summary of the passage on greyhounds in your own words.

31 Think of a play, a movie, or a television show that you have watched recently. Write a two-paragraph summary of the work. Be sure to include any pertinent details about the plot or characters in your summary.

32 Imagine that you have been assigned to write a report on a topic of your choice. On a separate sheet of paper, write your thesis statement at the top of the page. Then, describe your audience, how you will present your topic to your audience, and what type of organization you will use. Finally, list the types of sources you plan to use.

Name ______________________ Date ______________

End-of-Year Test

Reading Skills and Literary Analysis

Read the following questions. Then, choose the best answer.

1 Which of the following sentences contains a metaphor?

A The long hall was dark, dreary, and frightening.

B Sun shone through the south window of the little house.

C The spotlight was a great eye looking down upon us.

D Marlene flung her clothes carelessly over the furniture.

2 Why does the poet repeat the word *knock* so often in these lines of poetry?

What was the constant knock,
knock, knocking
Waking me before dawn?

F to show that the speaker is expecting a visitor

G to show that the speaker has been asleep

H to show that there is no doorbell

J to show that the knocking is continuous

3 What is the correct meaning of the underlined phrase in the sentence below?

If you string him along, he may get angry when he finds out the truth.

A give him a job

B ask him to volunteer

C make fun of him

D fool or deceive him

4 Which of the following sentences contains a simile?

F The ball connected crisply with Lily's bat and shot into center field like a jet.

G Red and yellow apples were piled in brown bushel baskets.

H Across the gym, the "away" team's fans filled the bleachers, an array of colors, lacking features.

J Savory meat, flavorful beans, crisp lettuce, even a crunchy taco shell—they're nothing without salsa.

Read the passage. Then, answer the questions.

It is autumn; not without,
But within me is the cold.
Youth and spring are all about;
It is I that have grown old.

Birds are darting through the air,
Singing, building without rest;
Life is stirring everywhere,
Save within my lonely breast.

There is silence: the dead leaves
Fall and rustle and are still;
Beats no flail upon the sheaves
Comes no murmur from the mill.

"Autumn Within" by Henry Wadsworth Longfellow

Name ______________________ Date ______________

5 **What does autumn symbolize in this poem?**
A a mill
B old age
C the air
D energy

6 **What type of poem is "Autumn Within"?**
F narrative
G lyric
H free verse
J dramatic

Read the passage. Then, answer the questions.

The Pink Ribbon Gourmet Hand Mixer

(1) Congratulations! (2) You have purchased The Pink Ribbon Gourmet Hand Mixer. (3) Not only do you have the assurance of a quality hand mixer, but you also have the knowledge that you have helped someone in need. (4) A portion of your purchase is being donated to the Hope for All Cancer Treatment Center.

(5) Before using your mixer for the first time, wash and dry the beaters and the mixing bowl. (6) Make sure that the speed control is in the OFF position and the mixer is not plugged in. (7) Insert the beaters into the openings on the bottom of the mixer. (8) Push until each beater clicks into position. (9) Then plug the cord into a standard household electrical outlet (120 volt, 60 Hz AC).

7 **Which is the best paraphrase of sentence 6?**
A Make sure that the mixer is not plugged in.
B Check that the mixer is turned off and unplugged.
C The speed control should be in the OFF position.
D Be careful when using electronic devices.

8 **What should you do before using the mixer for the first time?**
F Wash and dry the cord.
G Wash and dry the speed control.
H Wash and dry the electrical outlet.
J Wash and dry the beaters and mixing bowl.

9 **Which of the following is the best explanation of the purpose of this passage?**
A The passage informs how to use The Pink Ribbon Gourmet Hand Mixer.
B The passage describes the features of The Pink Ribbon Gourmet Hand Mixer.
C The passage informs how to plug in The Pink Ribbon Gourmet Hand Mixer.
D The passage describes how to wash The Pink Ribbon Gourmet Hand Mixer.

10 **Based on the information in the passage, what can you conclude?**
F People who buy this mixer want to avoid cooking.
G The mixer should be operated by professional chefs.
H People who buy this mixer want to donate to charity as well.
J The mixer should be operated outdoors.

Name ______________________________ Date ______________

Read the passage. Then, answer the questions.

Modern Bandage

Although many people do not even know his name, Earle Dickson was responsible for creating one of today's most common household items. Dickson was the genius behind the self-stick bandages we use today.

In 1917, Dickson was a newly married man and a cotton buyer for a successful bandage company in New Jersey.

As the story goes, Dickson's wife, Frances, was accident-prone. She often cut herself or nicked her fingers doing various household tasks. Regular bandages were too big and clumsy for Frances, so Dickson devised something better.

He folded pads of cotton gauze and placed them on long strips of surgical tape. He covered this with a material called crinoline. This prevented the tape from sticking to itself when it was rolled back together. Frances could unroll the bandage and cut off as much as she needed.

One day, Dickson mentioned his creation to a friend at work. Soon, Dickson was before the Johnsons, showing them what he had come up with. The Johnsons were especially impressed with the fact that you could put the new bandage on yourself. Up until that point, bandages had been difficult to apply without help.

The company began producing self-stick bandages, but the bandages did not take off until the mid-1920s, when the company gave thousands of samples to the Boy Scouts. After that, they were a hit. Dickson was made vice president of the company, and when he died in 1961, the company was selling $30 million worth of self-stick bandages a year.

11 What caused Earle Dickson to create a new type of bandage?

A He wanted to become vice president of the company.

B He wanted to use his invention to impress a friend at work.

C His wife was having trouble using bandages.

D He knew that it would be a hit if he created it.

12 The most valid purpose for reading the selection is to learn about —

F the history of the modern bandage

G the profits of the company

H the way to put on the modern bandage

J the history of the Boy Scouts

13 Which statement is the best one-sentence summary of this passage?

A The company made self-stick bandages a successful product by presenting a large sample of bandages to the Boy Scouts.

B The older bandages were difficult to use.

C A cotton buyer becomes head of a company.

D Earle Dickson presented his homemade bandage to the company that successfully developed this product into the modern bandages we use today.

Name ______________________________ Date ______________

Read the passage. Then, answer the questions.

[Daylight is disappearing on a quiet street. A young boy is timidly walking up the front steps of a large, eerie house. He is carrying a box of candy bars with him. His older brother stands at the end of the driveway. The young boy has a fearful look on his face. His older brother looks irritated.]

Vincent: *[anxiously tapping his foot]* Go on! You're the one who wants the prize for selling the most candy bars. Get up there.

Noah: *[taking a deep breath]* I'm going. *[He slowly makes his way up to the front door and knocks. There is no response.]* I don't think anyone's home. *[Suddenly a large dog jumps up to the front window, barking loudly and pressing against the screen. It looks as if the dog could jump through the screen. Noah screams loudly.]*

Vincent: *[running up onto the porch and stepping in front of his brother]* Okay, nobody's home. *[protectively guiding Noah down the steps and off the porch]* Besides, we should get home. Dinner's probably ready.

Noah: *[looking gratefully up at his brother as they walk onto the sidewalk]* Yeah, you're right.

Vincent: *[smiling down at his brother]* Race you home! *[The boys run down the street.]*

14 Which of these most likely motivates Vincent to run onto the porch?

F irritation

G concern

H fatigue

J curiosity

15 What do you learn about Noah from the stage directions at the beginning of the passage?

A He is tired.

B He is frightened.

C He is excited.

D He is depressed.

16 Which of the following details adds to the suspense of the passage?

F Noah is approaching a large, eerie house.

G Vincent guides Noah off the porch.

H Vincent suggests that they go home.

J Noah feels grateful toward his brother.

17 What can you conclude about Vincent from the passage?

A He is afraid of the dark.

B He dislikes selling candy bars.

C He feels responsible for his brother.

D He is afraid of large, barking dogs.

18 Which is the most logical conclusion about the relationship between Noah and Vincent?

F Vincent has to watch over Noah.

G Noah likes to compete with Vincent.

H Vincent dislikes taking care of Noah.

J Noah is frightened of Vincent.

19 The box of candy bars could best be described as a—

A prop

B stage direction

C dialogue

D aside

Name ________________________________ Date ________________

The passage below shows the results of a student's preliminary research for a report about winter sports. Study the results, and then answer the questions.

Database Search Results

SEARCH: winter sports

The Evolution of **Winter Sports** in Olympic Competition
Chalders, Harriet
Jeffries' Press, New York City, ©2007

Enjoying **Winter Sports:** Now's the Time
Tachard, Marcus
New Rocking Publishers, Boston, ©1972

Winter Is the Only Season for **Sports**
Kastor, Sebastian
Hantora Publishers, New York City, ©2006

20 Why should you avoid using the second result for your research?

F The topic is irrelevant.

G The source is not an Internet site.

H The source is outdated.

J The search results do not give enough information.

21 Which topic provides a narrower focus for your research?

A Enjoying winter sports

B Sports seasons

C Winter sports in the Olympics

D Time for winter sports

Read the following excerpt from a nonfiction book that was published in 2008. Then, answer the questions.

At the dawn of the twentieth century, few people dared to speculate that human beings would ever be able to fly. Yet, two brothers named Orville and Wilbur Wright were about to make that dream come true.

The adventurous Wright brothers had never been afraid of a challenge. Together, as young men, they opened a bicycle shop in Dayton, Ohio. Their business was a commercial success, but simply making money was not enough to satisfy the Wright brothers. Their curiosity led to an interest in flying, and they started building a series of gliders. Fearing that the gliders would be unable to withstand strong winds, they built a sturdier airplane powered by a lightweight gasoline engine. They took their new airplane to Kitty Hawk, North Carolina, to test it.

On December 17, 1903, the brothers tossed a coin to see who would go up first. Orville won. He flew for 12 seconds and traveled 120 feet. Although the farthest the plane flew that day was only 825 feet, the airborne brothers were rightfully proud of their extraordinary aerial feat. It did not take very long for people around the world to realize that the Wright brothers' invention could change the course of history.

Name ____________________ Date ____________

22 **What type of source is this passage?**

F autobiographical

G secondary

H outdated

J primary

23 **Suppose that you developed an idea map of this passage. What might you write in the middle oval?**

A Owned a bicycle shop in Dayton, Ohio

B Thought that gliders would not withstand powerful winds

C First flight in Kitty Hawk, North Carolina

D The Wright Brothers' invention of a gasoline-powered airplane

Read the passage. Then, answer the questions.

Presidents must deal with intense situations that test their leadership capabilities. Herbert Hoover met one of the greatest presidential challenges of all time. He was President of the United States when the country slid into the Great Depression.

The Great Depression began in October 1929 when the stock market crashed. The price of stocks in companies all over America fell dramatically. An estimated $30 billion was lost. Many individuals' savings were wiped out. Companies cut back or closed, and people lost their jobs. The country was stricken with fear of financial catastrophe.

President Herbert Hoover lacked a deep understanding and clear recognition of what had happened. He believed that the country's problems were caused primarily by the normal ups and downs of business and would resolve on their own. As a result, President Hoover did little to change things.

Soon, 25 percent of able workers were unemployed. Banks also failed. In December 1931, the Bank of the United States went broke, losing $200 million in depositor's savings.

24 **Which of the following could be the thesis statement of this selection?**

F Herbert Hoover's underestimation of the United States' economic situation caused an already unstable situation to worsen.

G The Stock Market Crash of 1929 sent the United States into a financial crisis.

H The Great Depression led to massive unemployment for the citizens of the United States.

J When the Bank of the United States collapsed, people who had deposited money there were hit with heavy losses.

25 **In an outline of this selection, which would be the best main heading for paragraph 2?**

A People losing life savings

B Companies forced to close

C $30 billion lost

D Beginning of the Great Depression

26 **Which would be the best main heading for paragraph 3?**

F The President Speaks

G Big Changes Ahead

H The Ups and Downs of Business

J President Hoover Fails

Name ______________________________ Date ______________

Grammar

Read the following questions. Then, choose the best answer.

27 Which punctuation mark belongs in the space shown in this sentence?

Devon failed to pass the lifeguard test the first time ___ therefore, he studied harder before his second attempt.

A semicolon
B exclamation mark
C period
D colon

28 Revise this sentence fragment.

After you clean the kitchen. You can sweep the back deck.

F After you clean the kitchen; you can sweep the back deck.
G After you clean the kitchen you can. Sweep the back deck.
H After you clean the kitchen, you can sweep the back deck.
J After you clean. The kitchen you can sweep the back deck.

29 Which is the best way to combine the following sentences by using a gerund or a participle?

The dog raced to the door. It barked loudly.

A The dog raced to the door and barked loudly.
B Barking loudly, the dog raced to the door.
C The dog raced to the door; it barked loudly.
D It barked loudly as it raced to the door.

30 In the sentence, "Maria read many books," which of the following words is the direct object?

F Maria
G read
H many
J books

Vocabulary

Read the following questions. Then, choose the best answer.

31 What does the origin of *reflection* mean?

A to adjust
B to bend back
C to receive
D pleasing

32 Choose the borrowed word that completes this sentence.

My father's recipe for ____________ is fantastic.

F incognito
G yoga
H finale
J gumbo

33 Based on your understanding of the prefixes *non-* and *un-*, which word is a synonym of *nonessential*?

A uncertain
B unlimited
C unnecessary
D unthinkable

34 From your knowledge of prefixes, what do you think you call someone who does not behave in a conventional way?

F a nonresident
G a dishonor
H a uniform
J a nonconformist

Name ______________________________ Date ______________

Spelling

Read the following questions. Then, choose the best answer.

35 Which word correctly completes this sentence?

I enjoy the ______ of a day at the swimming pool.

A laziness

B lazieness

C lasiness

D lazyness

36 Which word correctly completes this sentence?

Baked ______ with broccoli make an excellent meal.

F potatose

G potatoes

H potatos

J potatoze

Essay

Write on a separate sheet of paper.

37 Think of a school field trip that you have taken. Write a business letter to the organization or business that you visited or to the person who guided you on your field trip. The purpose of your business letter should be to thank this organization, business, or person.

Name ______________________________ Date ______________

Venn Diagram

Teaching Aid 1

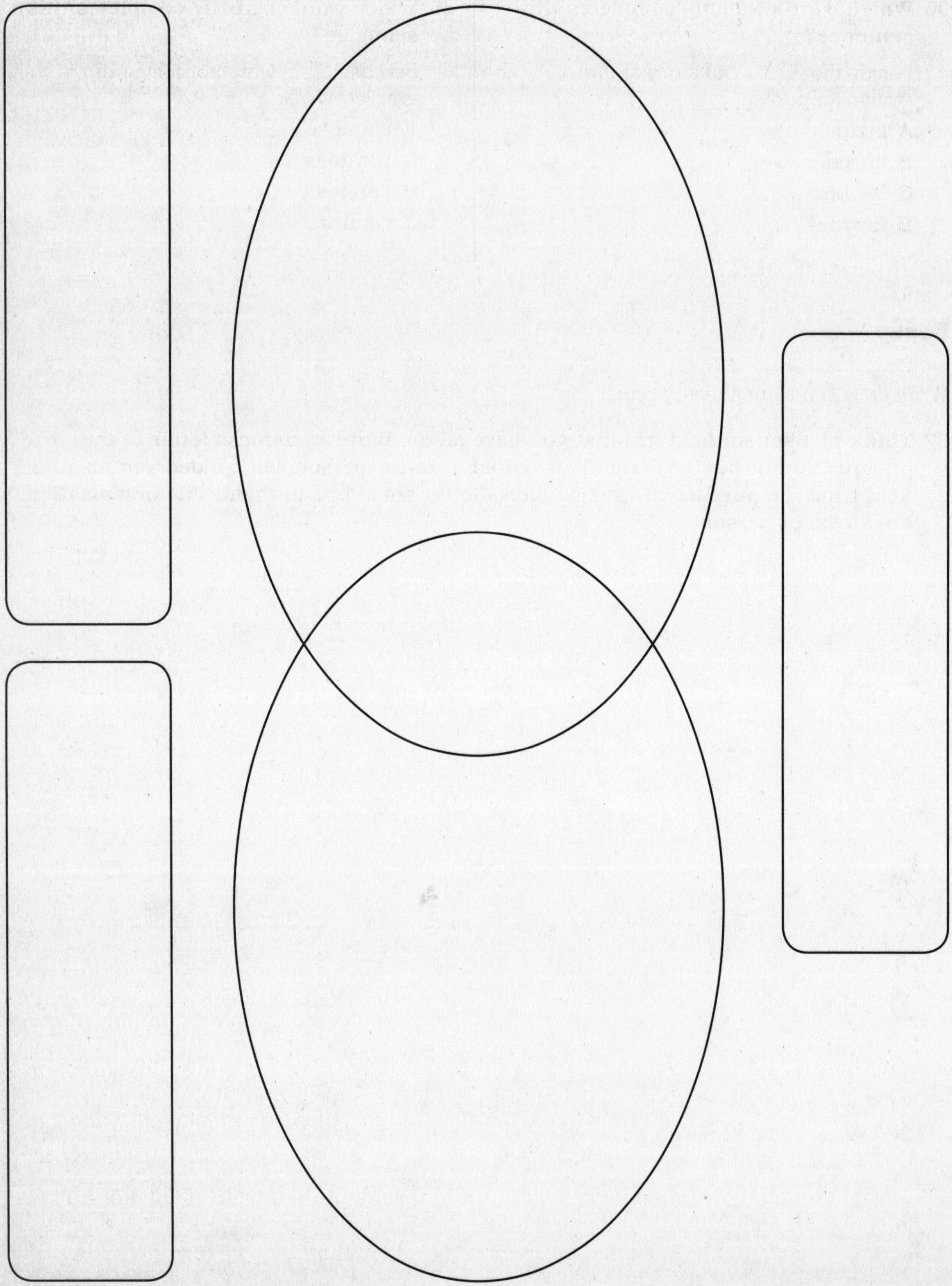

Name ______________________ Date ______________

Narrative Elements

Teaching Aid 2

Directions: *Fill in the following table as you read the selection.*

Narrative Element	Question	Details of the Story
Character(s)	Who was involved?	
Conflict	What was the problem, challenge, or obstacle?	
Plot	What happened?	
Setting	Where and when did the event happen?	

Name ______________________________ Date ______________

Plot Diagram

Teaching Aid 3

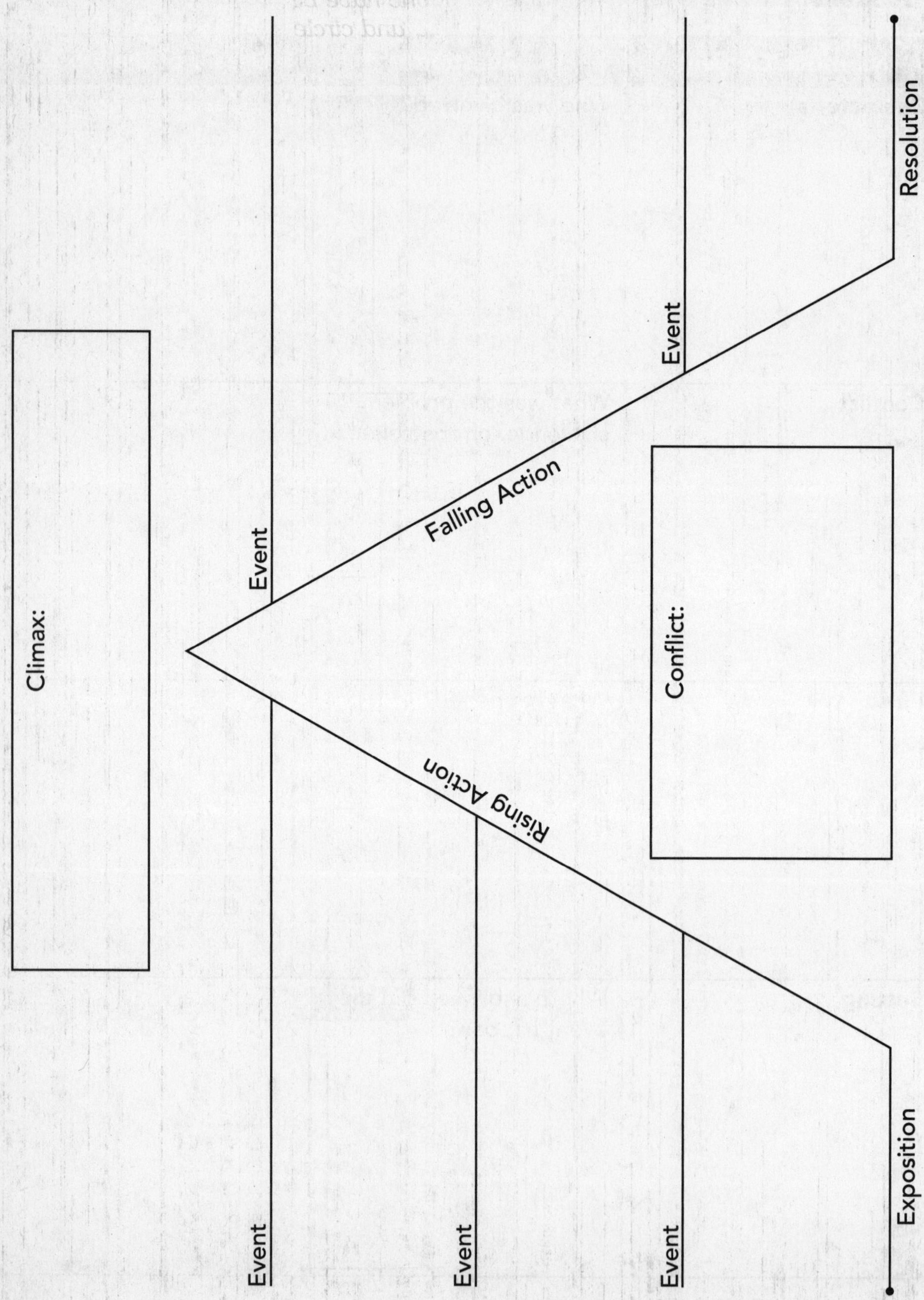

Name ______________________________ Date ______________

Essay Organizer: Descriptive

Teaching Aid 4

Directions: *In the table below, list people who have been important influences in your life. Then, review your list, and circle the person you would like to describe in your essay.*

Family	Friends	Teachers	Coaches	Other

Directions: *Use your five senses to build a physical description of the person you chose.*

Touch	Taste	Smell	Hear	Sight

Directions: *Help your readers understand the characteristics that your person possesses.*

Character:

Actions	Character Traits	Behavior

Name ______________________ Date ____________

Vocabulary Journal

Teaching Aid 5

Word	Word Parts	Context Clues	Meaning

Name ______________________ Date ______________

Cluster Diagram

Teaching Aid 6

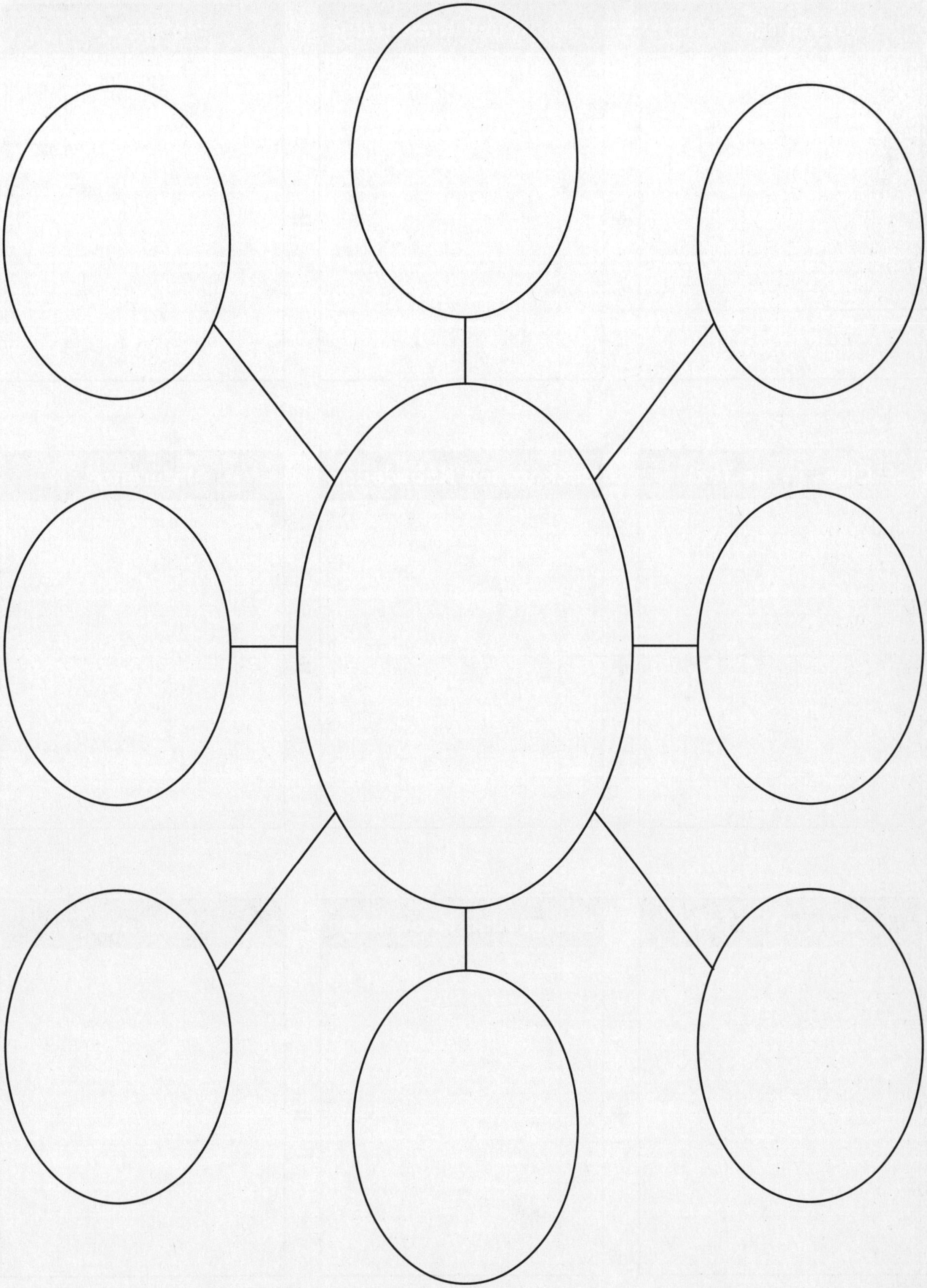

Name ______________________ Date ______________

Making Inferences

Teaching Aid 7

Clues in the Text		Background Knowledge		Inference
	+		=	

Clues in the Text		Background Knowledge		Inference
	+		=	

Clues in the Text		Background Knowledge		Inference
	+		=	

Name ______________________________ Date ______________

Building Character

Teaching Aid 8

Three Adjectives to Describe Him/Her Physically:	Three Adjectives to Describe His/Her Personality:	Three Things that He/She is Good At:

Write one sentence from this character's point of view (something he or she might say).

Write one sentence about the character from a third-person point of view.

Imagine that the person is confronted with a crisis. What would he or she do?

Name ______________________ Date ______________

Character Wheel

Teaching Aid 9

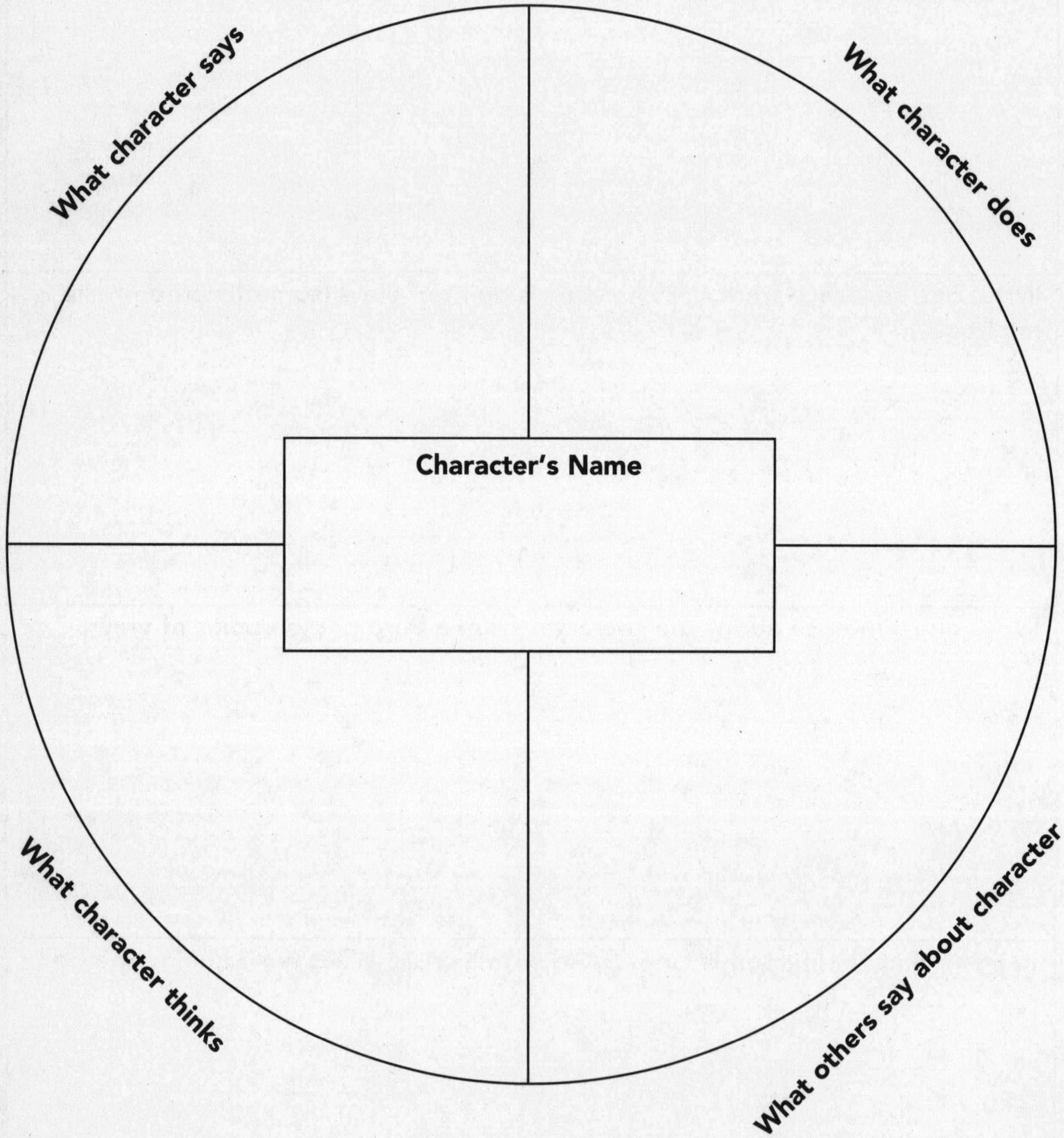

Name ______________________________ Date ______________

Organizing Your Presentation

Teaching Aid 10

Literary Term:	Definition:
Short Story Title:	Key Words:

Visual:

Description of Assessment:

Name ______________________ Date ____________

Outline

Teaching Aid 11

Topic	I. ______
Subtopic	A. ______
Supporting details	1. ______
	2. ______
	3. ______
	4. ______
Subtopic	B. ______
Supporting details	1. ______
	2. ______
	3. ______
	4. ______
Topic	II. ______
Subtopic	A. ______
Supporting details	1. ______
	2. ______
	3. ______
	4. ______
Subtopic	B. ______
Supporting details	1. ______
	2. ______
	3. ______
	4. ______

Name ______________________ Date ______________

Self-Assessment Form

Teaching Aid 12

Directions: *The following questions assess your performance in the literature circles. Try to give answers that are honest and detailed.*

1. Name the members of your group. ______________________

2. What was your role in the group? ______________________

3. Describe something you did well in the group, and something you'd like to do better the next time you work in a group. ______________________

____

____

4. Did you have any concerns or problems while working with your group? Explain. ______________________

____

____

5. Would you like to recognize anyone in your group for doing an outstanding job? If so, who? Explain. ______________________

____

6. What are some things you like and dislike about working in literature circles? ______________________

____

____

____

Name ______________________________ Date ______________

Essay Organizer: Cause and Effect

Teaching Aid 13

Directions: *List 5 topics that interest you enough to write about. Circle the topic you are most knowledgeable about, and can write about in depth.*

1. ______________________________

2. ______________________________

3. ______________________________

4. ______________________________

5. ______________________________

Directions: *After you have chosen your topic, begin gathering facts, examples, and details.*

K-W-L Chart		
What I Know	What I Want to Know	What I Learned

Directions: *Brainstorm cause and effect relationships you will address in your essay.*

1.	2.	3.
Cause / **Effect**	**Cause** / **Effect**	**Cause** / **Effect**

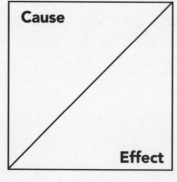

Name ______________________________ Date ______________

Cause and Effect Match-up

Teaching Aid 14

Directions: *Cut out the events in the* **Cause** *and* **Effect** *columns. Match the causes and effects until all the events have been used. More than one cause can be used for an effect, and more than one effect can be used for a cause.*

Causes	Effects
My alarm did not go off.	I couldn't watch my favorite TV show.
It was raining.	The game was canceled.
The dog started barking.	My mother got angry with me.
The electricity went out.	My little sister got scared.
Because I sprained my ankle.	The cat hissed, then ran away.
The baseball broke our window.	I couldn't play in the game.
I did not finish my homework.	I was late to school.
There was thunder and lightning.	I could not participate in the outside activities.

Name ______________________ Date ____________

Analyzing Facts and Opinions

Teaching Aid 15

STATEMENT: ____

____

Can the statement be proved true or false?

Yes. The statement is a fact.

What sources of information are (or could be) cited to prove the fact true or false?

Source: ______________________

Source: ______________________

Source: ______________________

No. The statement is an opinion.

What facts are (or could be) used to justify the opinion?

Fact: ______________________

Fact: ______________________

Fact: ______________________

Name ______________________ Date ____________

Author's Style Clues

Teaching Aid 16

Title	Style	Clues in the Text

Name ______________________ Date ______________

Essay Organizer: Persuasive

Teaching Aid 17

Directions: *Plan your persuasive essay by completing the following table based on your chosen topic.*

Topic	
Who?	
What?	
When?	
Where?	
How?	

Directions: *In the chart below, fill in the left column with arguments others may have against your position. Then, fill in the right column with counterarguments of your own.*

Arguments	Counterarguments

Directions: *Use the information above to guide your writing for the first draft of your persuasive essay. When you finish, read your essay to a peer and have that peer fill out the following.*

Does this essay convince you of the author's opinion? If not, what could the author do, to make his or her essay more persuasive? ______________

____

Name ______________________ Date ______________

Imagery—Using the Five Senses

Teaching Aid 18

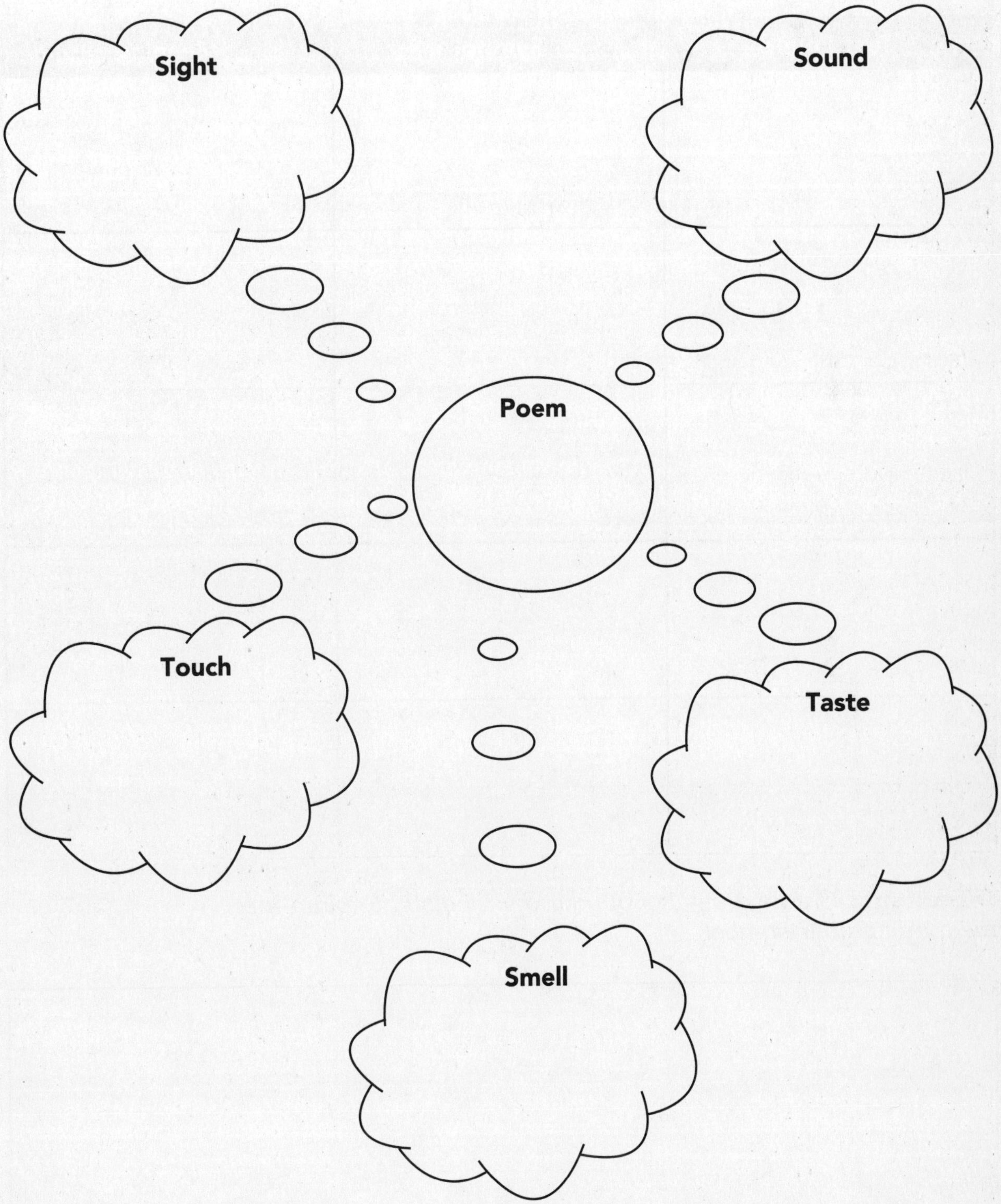

Name ______________________ Date ______________

Symbolism

Teaching Aid 19

Directions: *In the following table, show examples of symbolism you found while reading. Use the text to form a meaning for the symbol.*

Text Found	Symbol	Meaning

Directions: *Create a symbol of your own, below. Explain the meaning of your symbol.*

Name ______________________ Date ______________

Shape Your Writing: Block Organizer

Teaching Aid 20

Introduction

↓

Body

↓

Body

↓

Conclusion

Name ______________________ Date ____________

Asking Questions

Teaching Aid 21

In this Literature Circle, you and your group members will be asking different kinds of questions about your anchor book. The following graphic organizer shows four kinds of questions you can ask about your anchor book.

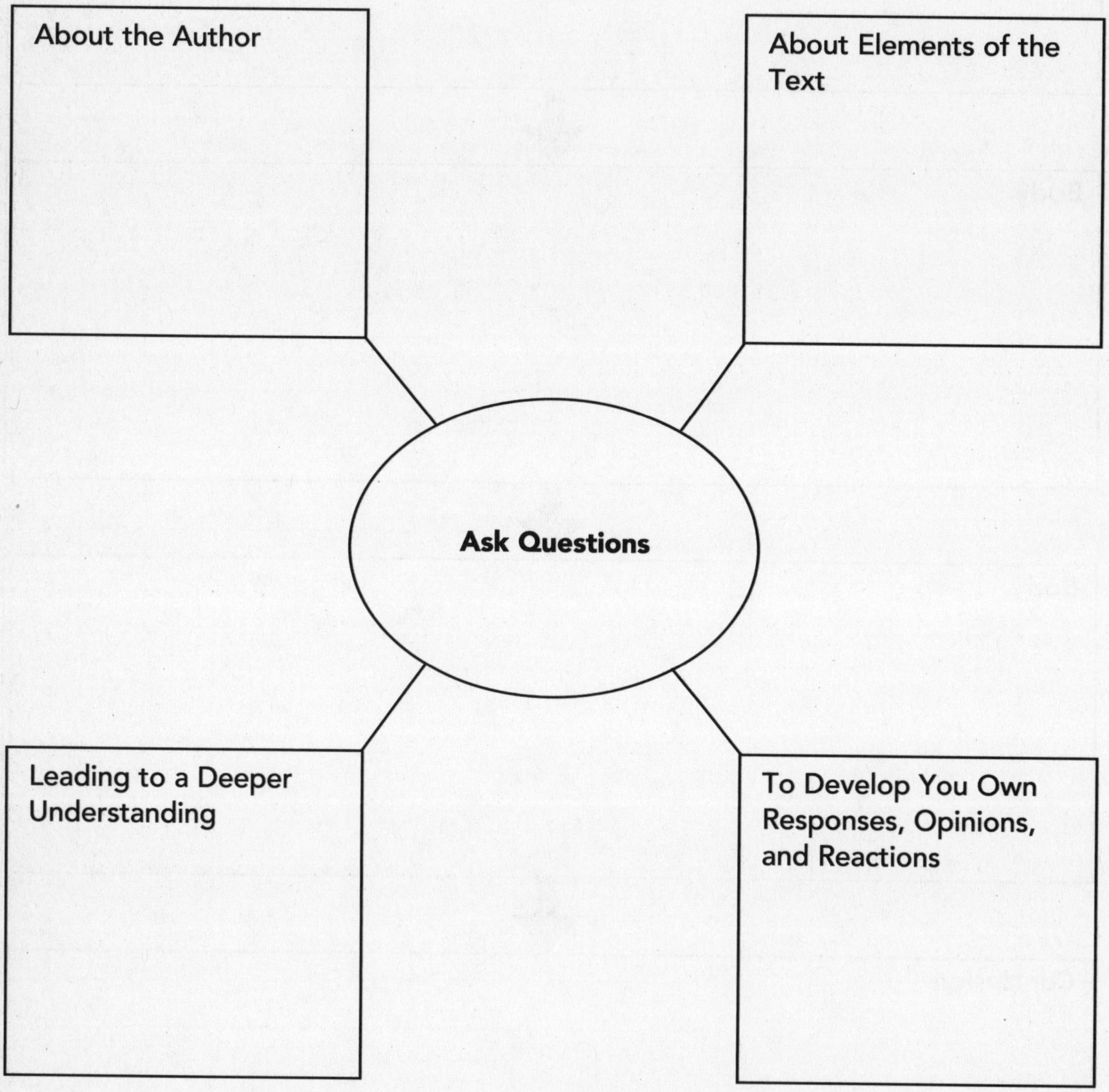

Name ______________________________ Date ______________

Context Clues

Teaching Aid 22

Word or Phrase	Definition	Context Clues	Context Clue Type

Name ______________________ Date ____________

Cause-and-Effect Relationships

Teaching Aid 23

Cause:	→	Effect:
Cause:	→	Effect:
Cause:	→	Effect:

Name ______________________________ Date ______________

Creating Words

Teaching Aid 24

A.

1. ____________ + ____________ = ____________

real word   real word   made-up word

Definition of made-up word:

____

Use the made-up word in a sentence.

____

2. ____________ + ____________ = ____________

real word   real word   made-up word

Definition of made-up word:

____

Use the made-up word in a sentence.

____

B.

____________ + ____________ = ____________

real word   real word   made-up word

Definition of made-up word:

____

Use the made-up word in a sentence.

____

Name ______________________ Date ______________

Verbs, Participles, and Gerunds

Teaching Aid 25

Verb	Participle	Gerund
We are laughing.	Laughing, the crowd clapped.	Laughing feels good!

Name ______________________ Date ______________

K-W-L Chart

Teaching Aid 26

What I *K*now	What I *W*ant to Know	What I *L*earned

Name ______________________ Date ____________

Proofreading Marks

Teaching Aid 27

Symbol	Meaning	Example	Corrected Example
≡	Capitalize a letter.	Mr. houng is a teacher at my school.	Mr. Houng is a teacher at my school.
/	Make a capital letter lowercase.	Washington D.C. is our Nation's capital.	Washington D.C. is our nation's capital.
⊙	Insert (add) a period.	My dog is brown and white⊙ He has spots.	My dog is brown and white. He has spots.
ℓ	Delete (take out).	Mary she wants to be an astronaut.	Mary wants to be an astronaut.
∧	Insert a word or letter.	The baseball team ∧ (received) new uniforms.	The baseball team received new uniforms.
∧,	Insert punctuation.	We went to Raleigh∧, North Carolina for vacation.	We went to Raleigh, North Carolina for vacation.
◯ sp.	Correct a spelling error.	Holly is the main (charcter) sp. in the story.	Holly is the main character in the story.
¶	Start a new paragraph.	Michael received a letter from his grandfather.¶One afternoon his dad . . .	Michael received a letter from his grandfather. One afternoon his dad . . .

Name ______________________ Date ____________

Learning About Research: Topic

Teaching Aid 28

Directions: *Use the questions in the box to brainstorm ideas for your research topic. Circle the topic you find most interesting or relevant to your life.*

Topic Ideas:

1. ______________________
2. ______________________
3. ______________________
4. ______________________
5. ______________________

- **What people or places fascinate me?**
- **What objects or events have a special meaning to me?**
- **What interests would I like to learn more about?**

Directions: *Now that you have choosen a topic for your research paper, focus on the questions you would like to answer about the topic and where you might find the answers. Complete the table below.*

Topic Question	Type of source

Name ____________________ Date ____________

Learning About Research: Drafting

Teaching Aid 29

The Thesis Statement: Follow the steps below to create a thesis statement for your research report.

Main Idea		Perspective		Thesis Statement
	+		=	

Organizing Your Report: Use the boxes below to organize the main ideas and details that support your thesis statement.

Main Idea 1:

Detail	Detail	Detail

Main Idea 2:

Detail	Detail	Detail

Main Idea 3:

Detail	Detail	Detail

On the back, create an outline for your report, using the information above.

Name ______________________ Date ______________

Bingo Grid

Teaching Aid 30

		Bingo		

Name ______________________ Date ____________

Reader's Journal Questions

Teaching Aid 31

Throughout the year you will be keeping a Reader's Journal for your Anchor Book. In your Reader's Journal, you will answer questions asked in your student book and questions assigned by your teacher from the list below.

Plot

1. Describe what happened in your reading. Which events seemed important? Explain why.
2. Describe the major problem or conflict in the work. When and how does the conflict reach its crisis, and how is it resolved?

Setting

3. What is the importance of the setting? How would the story be different if it occurred in a different time and place?

Character

4. Describe an interesting character and explain what motivates him or her to think and behave as he or she does.
5. Is there a specific character with which you can identify? Does a character remind you of someone you know? How? Why?

Point of View

6. From whose point of view is the story told? Why do you think the author selected this particular point of view?
7. How might the narrative have been different if another character had told the story?

Theme

8. What general truth does the author seem to be stating about human nature? How is this theme revealed in the book?
9. Do you agree with the author's major theme(s)? Why or why not?

Author's Perspective and Style

10. Discuss the author's literary style. Give examples of the kind of language the author uses.

Evaluation

11. What effects did reading the book have upon you? Did you have any particular thoughts or emotional responses as you read? What were they?
12. Offer your assessment of the work. Did you enjoy it or not? Give specific reasons.
13. Did this book remind you of any other work you have read? How? Explain.

Name ______________________________ Date ______________

Literature Circle Roles

Teaching Aid 32

Directions: *You are responsible for asking questions about your Anchor Book based on your assigned role. Record your group's answers to these questions in your Reader's Journal.*

Role	Questions to Ask
Summarizer Summarize the reading discussed. Be certain to include important details, characters, and events in your summary for future review.	• What important events happened? • Why were they important? • What were the effects of these events? • What important changes in the plot and the character did you observe?
Connector Find connections between your book and the world outside of your book. Think about connections to your own experiences, current and historical events, and other books.	• What did the text make you think about? • Have you had a similar experience? • What other people, events, or books could you compare this to?
Word Wizard Identify words you don't know the meaning of and words that seem important. Words that reflect careful choices of the author should be analyzed for how they add meaning.	• What new words did you discover? • What is the meaning and part of speech of these words? • Which words seem important to the characters or author? Why?
Illustrator Describe what you read through drawn images, or create a collage using images from magazines. Think about both the literal meaning and the theme and symbols of the reading.	• What did the reading make you think about? • What images would best reflect the important details and meaning of the reading?
Excerpts Expert Find quotations from your Anchor Book that are important to discuss with your Literature Circle. Write down the quotation and its page number so that your group members can look at it in context.	• What did the quotation make you think about? • Why is this quotation important to the reading? • What do you think the author's purpose was in writing this passage?
Questioner Write down a few questions that you have about the reading. Focus on the big ideas and what is most interesting about the reading.	• What were you wondering about while you were reading? • If you could ask the author or a character a question, what would it be? • What message is the author trying to communicate?

Name ______________________________ Date ______________

Observation Sheet

Teaching Aid 33

Student Name	Date	Observations (Record observations such as "prepared," "participated," "had difficulty with task," "shows improvement," "assisted other student.")
1.		
2.		
3.		
4.		
5.		
6.		
7.		
8.		
9.		
10.		
11.		
12.		
13.		
14.		
15.		
16.		
17.		
18.		
19.		
20.		

Answer Key

Screening Test

MULTIPLE CHOICE

1. B	10. J	19. D	28. J
2. J	11. D	20. G	29. D
3. B	12. H	21. B	30. H
4. J	13. D	22. G	31. D
5. C	14. H	23. C	32. F
6. F	15. A	24. H	33. B
7. A	16. G	25. D	34. F
8. G	17. B	26. F	35. C
9. C	18. F	27. A	

Unit 1

Unit 1 Diagnostic Test 1

MULTIPLE CHOICE

1. B	4. G	7. A	10. H
2. F	5. D	8. F	11. C
3. A	6. G	9. D	12. J

1-2 Reading Skills: Making Predictions

1-2 Reinforcement

1. *Students will most likely predict that the story will be about a dog that surfs. Other predictions are acceptable as long as they are based on some prior knowledge—"surf" could be used in the context of surfing the Internet, for example.*
2. C
3. *Students will revise their predictions using new information. Knowing that the main character, the dog named Milo, fell off a fishing boat gives more details for forming predictions.*
4. *Possible answer:* chunk of driftwood (this detail would support a prediction that Milo will use something as a surfboard); driftwood caught a wave (this detail would support a prediction that Milo would actually surf); rode it in to shore (this detail supports a prediction that Milo will surf).

1-2 Extension

Possible responses:

"The Greenhouse Effect"

- The text will compare two models of global warming.
- The diagram will explain how natural and amplified warming occur and how each affects the greenhouse effect.
- Read slowly, carefully analyzing how the numbered statements relate to the diagram.
- What causes the greenhouse effect? Is global warming the result of human activity?

"Occupation: Conductorette"

- The text will be about a female trolley conductor.
- The text will recount Maya Angelou's struggle against prejudice in San Francisco
- Read faster, taking in Maya Angelou's story while noticing details about her personality and her struggle.
- What is Maya Angelou like? Why does she want to become a conductor? Who might try to stop her, and why?

1-3 Vocabulary: Prefixes and Suffixes

1-3 Reinforcement

1. review
2. precaution
3. prejudge
4. reprogram
5. previews
6. intend; intention
7. modernize; modern
8. revise; revision

1-3 Extension

1. misinterpret + -ed = misinterpreted; incorrectly understood
   misinterpret + -tion = misinterpretation; an incorrect understanding of something
   misinterpret – mis- = interpret; + re- = reinterpret; to understand in a new way
   reinterpret + -tion = reinterpretation; a new understanding of something
   misinterpret – mis = interpret; + -tion = interpretation; the process of understanding something
2. exclude + -sion = exclusion; the state of being left out or kept out
   exclude – ex- = -clude-; + in- = include; to make part of a group
   include + -sion = inclusion; the state of being part of a group
3. review – re- = view; to look at something again
   view + pre- = preview; to look at something before
   view + inter- = interview; a meeting in which two or more people look at and talk to each other
   Other possible answers include reviewed, previewed, interviewed.

4. international + -ize = internationalize; the process of making international
internationalize – inter- = nationalize; to make national
nationalize + -tion = nationalization; the state of being nationalized
Other possible answers include internationalization, nation.

1-5 Analyzing an Informational Text: Reading a Diagram

1-5 Reinforcement

1. C
2. D
3. A
4. B

1-5 Extension

1. *Diagrams and legends will vary but should be accurately executed, clearly labeled and numbered, and logically explained. Legends should contain 4–8 steps and cover the main elements of the process.*

2–5. *Answers will vary but should reflect accurate reading of the specific diagram and legend. Students should provide answers to the questions they write.*

1-6 Literary Analysis: Narrative Texts

1-6 Reinforcement

1. The characters are the writer/narrator Paul Zindel, his sister, and his mother. "I" is Paul Zindel.
2. The family's new house has cockroaches in it. The narrator is unhappy about the cockroaches.
3. It takes place at a new home for the narrator and his family. The narrator is excited to have a new home.

1-6 Extension

1. Frederick Douglass was an enslaved African American who was born on a plantation in Maryland. He learned to read and write and became an important abolitionist voice.
2. *Possible answer:* Frederick Douglass is determined, patient, generous, and wise.
3. *Possible answer:* He believes that people are generally good, but that slavery is an evil institution that oppresses certain people while corrupting the hearts of others.
4. *Possible answer:* The reader learns the most about Frederick Douglass by what he writes about other people. We learn that while he has a strong sense of right and wrong, he does not want to judge other people unfairly. We also learn from his actions: his making friends with the poor white children and giving them bread in exchange for teaching; his reading in defiance of his master.
5. *Possible answer:* Frederick Douglass and Maya Angelou both have the strength and determination needed to overcome discrimination and improve their lot in life. Both have a strong sense of injustice, but Maya Angelou finds in humor society's problems, while Frederick Douglass tends to analyze the root of the problem.
6. *Possible answer:* Maya Angelou uses more personal reflections and dialogue to show the reader how and why she is the way she is. Frederick Douglas spends more time criticizing the people around him and describing his relationships with them.

1-7 Literary Analysis: Conflict

1-7 Reinforcement A

1. B
2. C
3. A
4. C
5. D
6. *Answers will vary. Check that students support their ideas with examples from the text.*

1-7 Literary Analysis: Understanding Plot

1-7 Reinforcement B

1. rising action
2. exposition
3. climax
4. resolution
5. falling action

Chart: exposition, rising action, climax, falling action, and resolution.

1-7 Language Coach: Common and Proper Nouns; Concrete, Abstract, and Possessive Nouns

1-7 Extension

Check students' work. Poems should use the type of nouns specified in each line.

1-8 Language Coach: The Writing Rules

1-8 Reinforcement A

1. (B) The Grapes of Wrath is considered to be one of the best works of American literature.
2. (C) Ms. Sullivan's class read several different Irish poets' poems.

3. (A) The student wanted to listen carefully to the teacher's lecture since it would be on the exam.
4. (E) Romance novels' main characters are often broken-hearted heroines.
5. (D) Herman Melville's novel, Moby Dick, opens with one of the most famous lines in literature.

1-8 Language Coach: Common and Proper Nouns

1-8 Reinforcement B

Common nouns: members, future, document, colonies, ruler, declaration, bell, streets, nation

Capitalized proper nouns: July, 4, 1776, Second Continental Congress, Thirteen Colonies, Thomas Jefferson, King George III, Great Britain, Declaration of Independence, John Hancock, Ben Franklin, President of the United States of America, John Adams, Independence Hall, Philadelphia, Liberty Bell

1. France
2. Toronto Maple Leafs
3. February
4. Wednesday
5. Robot Dreams
6. Bono
7. Valentine's Day
8. National Geographic
9. J.K. Rowling
10. The Sandlot
11. Boston
12. White House
13. Nobel Prize

1-8 Language Coach: Concrete, Abstract, and Possessive Nouns

1-8 Reinforcement C

1. Italy is known for its rich cultural heritage.
2. Visitors are drawn by the beauty of its beaches, vineyards, and mountains.
3. Cities such as Florence, Rome, and Venice also attract tourists.
4. People find inspiration in the great artworks displayed at the museums.
5. They seek relaxation in the Italian countryside.
6. Teresa's
7. Joneses'
8. bloodhound's
9. children's
10. artist's
11. parents'
12. men's
13. teachers'

1-8 Language Coach: Spelling Plural Nouns

1-8 Reinforcement D

1.	boxes	A
2.	families	B
3.	leaf	C
4.	wishes	A
5.	glass	A
6.	cliffs	C
7.	feet	D
8.	beaches	A
9.	mouse	D
10.	spy	B

1-8 Language Coach: Common and Proper Nouns; Concrete, Abstract, and Possessive Nouns

1-8 Extension

Check students' work. Poems should use the type of nouns specified in each line.

1-9 Writer's Workshop: Descriptive Essay

1-9 Reinforcement

1. *Possible response:* The writer's grandfather is much weaker than he used to be when he was younger.
2. *Possible response:* Lila is very friendly and cares about other people.
3. *Students should supply evocative details by using words with strong connections to several of the five senses.*

Extension

1. *Answers will vary but students should include both adjectives and verbs and should list at least one detail for each sense and at least two details in each character category.*
2. *Answers will vary but students should have accurately added sensory details to their sentences.*

Unit 1 Mid-Unit Benchmark Test

MULTIPLE CHOICE

1. D	9. B	17. A	25. A
2. G	10. J	18. J	26. G
3. C	11. C	19. A	27. C
4. J	12. F	20. G	28. G
5. B	13. C	21. D	29. D
6. F	14. G	22. G	30. H
7. D	15. A	23. A	31. B
8. J	16. G	24. J	32. F

SHORT ANSWER

33. Use the details and your own experience to make predictions as you read, keep reading to see whether your predictions are accurate, and change a prediction if new details point to something different.
34. A diagram is a graphic design that explains the relationships between parts of a whole.
35. It is the high point of the plot, the point at which the suspense or tension is greatest and the likely outcome is determined.
36. A narrative contains the elements of character, conflict, plot, and setting.

ESSAY

37. Students may recount the story or retell it in summarized form. They may include details that point to the new ending or create a surprise ending, but the ending should be consistent with events and characterizations that came before.
38. Students' descriptive essays should include detailed and sensory descriptions of the place and should explain why visiting the place is enjoyable.
39. Students should use a consistent first-person point of view. They should present a clear sequence of events that centers around a particular conflict or problem. Students should include their feelings about the incident and make clear why the incident is significant for them.

Unit 1 Diagnostic Test 2

MULTIPLE CHOICE

1. C	4. G	7. B	10. J
2. G	5. A	8. H	
3. B	6. J	9. B	

1-11 Reading Skills: Author's Purpose

1-11 Reinforcement

1. to inform
2. *Students should list any two details that are informative.*
3. to entertain
4. *Students should list any two details from the paragraph that are entertaining.*

1-11 Extension

1. a. to persuade someone not to give up
   b. to inform someone of what happened and how it felt
   c. to reflect on a difficult situation
2. *Possible answer:* In anecdote a, the narrator uses entertainment to draw the learner into the story so that the learner will expect to experience the same triumph that the writer did. This convinces the learner to keep trying, like the writer did.
3. *Answers will vary, but each anecdote should be interesting and have a clear purpose.*

1-12 Literary Analysis: Setting and Mood

1-12 Reinforcement

1. in a fictional future time
2. *Students might underline references to going to work in a Jetstar; landing on a pod; the unusual time reference; the blue-and-white shower.*
3. on the planet Andaron
4. *Students might circle the name Andaron on one or both of the places it is mentioned.*
5. The mood varies; the narrator seems a little annoyed by the weather and by hurrying to get to work, but he or she is also amused by Commander Voss. The rain and the traffic contribute to a rushed mood; the last paragraph suggests that Commander Voss shouldn't be taken too seriously.

1-12 Extension

1. The author is standing at the railing of a ship heading for America. The ship is shuddering on a turbulent sea, and the air is cold and damp.
2. Hana Omiya remembers her old village home, with its colorful flowers and trees rice fields, thatched roofs, and mountains. The setting on the boat is cold, grey, threatening, and in constant unsteady motion, while the setting in Oka village is pleasant, colorful, and stable.
3. Hana Omiya has chosen to leave her home in Japan for a new and uncertain life in America, and she has conflicted thoughts about her decision, because she misses her home and is afraid of the future.
4. The unsteady setting at the railing of the pitching boat parallels the fear and uncertainty in Hana Omiya's mind; the colorful tranquility of her home village express the homesick feelings she has about leaving it.

1-13 Comparing Literary Works: Theme

1-13 Reinforcement

1. A; laziness does not lead to success.
2. *Possible responses:* People who play tricks on others often get caught; People are smarter than you think; Don't trick a trickster; Pride often leads to defeat.
3. *Possible responses:* If opportunity knocks, open the door; Make the most of what life offers.

1-13 Extension

1. *Possible answers:* Family gives you strength; family teaches important lessons; family gives us lifelong burdens; without family, we may fail in life; family includes everything good and everything bad in life; we need humor to deal with our families.
2. *Possible answer:* The theme of "Waterman Comics" is that our families help us be our best and reach our dreams. This theme relates to the themes of "The Grass Harp" and "The Child of the Owl" because all three works have themes related to family. All three themes show positive effects of family and suggest that family helps us face challenges and solve problems. The two stories show that family can be anyone, not just parents, while "Waterman Comics" focuses specifically on parents as family.

1-14 Language Coach: Personal Pronouns

1-14 Reinforcement A

1. I (N) asked my (P) friends, "Have you (N) found the calculator today?"
2. "Oh, so the strange object we (N) found is yours?" (P) Ben kidded me. (O)
3. "Why isn't your (O) name on the back?" his (P) brother Jack said.
4. I (N) said it (O) was not mine; (P) my (P) brother Julio owned the calculator.
5. "You (N) should feel lucky it (O) was found by us," (O) Mara said.
6. "Its (P) cased is ripped, but I (N) bet your (P) father could repair it." (O)
7. Later, she (N) and we (N) boys discussed our (P) summer plans.
8. "Are you (N) going to try out for our (P) community play?" Ben asked.
9. "Yes, I (N) would like the hero's role. Are you (N) two trying out?" I (N) asked him (O) and his (P) brother.
10. They (N) said they (N) would rather try their (P) luck as villains.

1-14 Language Coach: Reflexive Pronouns

1-14 Reinforcement B

1. B
2. A
3. myself; I, we; incorrect
4. herself; Yvette; correct
5. yourselves; They; incorrect
6. yourself; you; correct

1-14 Pronoun Agreement

1-14 Reinforcement C

1. it—moon
2. me—I
3. its—Neither
4. they—children
5. his or her—Everyone
6. Ask someone on the girls' swim team to show you her technique.
7. Nobody on the boys' soccer team ever forgets his cleats.
8. The drawer had two pencils and a notepad inside it.

1-14 Spelling Tricky and Difficult Words

1-14 Reinforcement D

1. 3
2. 3
3. 2
4. 3
5. 3
6. mischievious: mischievous
7. opra: opera
8. blustry: blustery
9. wintery: wintry
10. choclate: chocolate

1-14 Language Coach: Personal and Reflexive Pronouns

1-14 Extension

Enrico, Yolanda and *I* ~~myself~~ are traveling deep into the Congo. Every traveler should do *his or her* ~~their~~ research and find a skilled guide before setting out. Our *Watching who? The guide, or Enrico?* guide told Enrico that there were monkeys watching him. They threw sticks down at us. Monkeys love *Even big sticks, or even big monkeys?* throwing sticks, even when they are big. ~~Me and~~ Yolanda *and I* spotted a baby monkey clinging to his mother's back. There were parrots everywhere. The tropical parrot*s* ~~was~~ *were* gorgeous, but their noisy chatter made it impossible to talk. At dusk, we hung our mosquito nets around ourselves, and listened to ~~their~~ *the mosquitoes* frustrated buzzing. I had promised myself I would see the Congo, and I love it.

1-15 Writer's Workshop: Personal Narrative

1-15 Reinforcement

1–3. My family and I drove to the Grand Canyon this summer. (At first I didn't want to go.) Slowly, though, I changed my mind. We drove through the incredible scenery of the desert. The sunsets were astonishing, coloring the faraway mountains with shades of gold and orange. Even before we got to the Grand Canyon, (I realized that I would not have wanted to miss this for the world.)

4. *Students should name a personal experience suitable for a personal narrative.*
5. *Students should give a descriptive detail from the experience.*
6. *Students should give one of their reactions to the experience, such as a thought or feeling they had at the time.*

1-15 Extension

1. *Answers will vary.*
2. *Answers will vary.*
3. *Answers will vary.*

Unit 1 End-of-Unit Benchmark Test

MULTIPLE CHOICE

1. A	8. J	15. B	22. J
2. H	9. B	16. F	23. C
3. D	10. G	17. D	24. H
4. F	11. D	18. J	25. A
5. A	12. J	19. D	26. H
6. J	13. B	20. F	27. C
7. C	14. G	21. A	28. H

SHORT ANSWER

29. To persuade readers to believe in one side of an issue.
30. Humorous, suspenseful, or exciting details.
31. The time and place of the action.
32. Responses will vary. Students should include that a person grows with each challenge that he or she overcomes.

ESSAY

33. Students should include sensory details and colorful adjectives that convey the setting's appearance, smells, and sounds. The details should work together to capture the confused, hectic mood that the story must convey.
34. Students should identify the work under consideration and clearly state the theme or life lesson that they drew from the work. They should then explain how the theme or lesson applies to one or more real-life situations drawn from their own experience.
35. Students should state the theme they wish to convey. They should also indicate the characters in their story, the setting in which the story unfolds, the plot events centering around a conflict that a main character faces, and the outcome of that conflict. They may also include dialogue and the thoughts of particular characters.

Unit 2

Unit 2 Diagnostic Test 1

MULTIPLE CHOICE

1. B	4. F	7. A	10. F
2. J	5. B	8. G	
3. C	6. F	9. C	

2-2 Reading Skills: Making Inferences

2-2 Reinforcement

1. Lana feels anxious, nervous, restless, impatient, or stressed.
2. "paced back and forth"; "flipping through the pages impatiently"; "continued her pacing"
3. The brother had a bad day at work.
4. She doesn't really want to lend her roller skates to anyone.
5. "she never mentions the skates"; "she looks away from you"; "probably the wrong size for you"

2-2 Extension

Answers will vary.

2-3 Vocabulary Building Strategies:

2-3 Reinforcement

similar, inspect, similarities, differences, aspect, differ, spectators, differentiate, spectacular

similis: similar, similarities
differre: differences, differ, differentiate
spec: inspect, aspect, spectators, spectacular

2-3 Extension, p. 69

facsimile—Latin
logo—Greek
spectrum—Latin
apology—Grek
conclusive—Latin
trilogy—Greek
spectators—Latin
dialogue—Greek
simulation—Latin

1. conclusive
2. logo
3. trilogy
4. facsimile
5. spectators

1. epilogue
2. indifferent

2-5 Literary Analysis: Flashback

2-5 Reinforcement A

1. The flashback begins "It was nearly sixty years ago"; Grandma is described as having wrinkled hands in the present and as being a slim, young woman in the past; the setting changes: Grandma is in her rocker and then she is in the kitchen.
2. The flashback begins "as she remembered . . ."; in the present, Shaniqua has no problem stepping onto the subway car and in the past, she nearly misses getting on the subway car; the flashback ends "snapped her back to the present".
3. The flashback begins "Images of childhood fill my head"; the setting changes: narrator is blowing out a cake in the present and then sitting on the stoop in the past.

2-5 Literary Analysis: Foreshadowing

2-5 Reinforcement B

1. B. *Answers will vary.*
2. B. *Answers will vary.*
3. C. *Answers will vary.*

2-5 Extension

dialogue, action, comment by narrator

Answers will vary.

2-6 Language Coach: Action and Linking Verbs

2-6 Reinforcement A

1. visit
2. chases
3. laugh
4. read
5. play
6. drives
7. After the bell, the hallways looked crowded. looked
8. My backpack feels heavier than yesterday. feels
9. The school bus sounds like a lion. sounds
10. The pigeons look fatter than ever! look
11. The basketball courts seem busier than last time. seems
12. I was our team captain. was
13. The other team is much faster. is
14. The roasted peanuts smell delicious! smell
15. Sadly, the peanuts taste burnt. taste
16. They were absolutely terrible. were

2-6 Language Coach: Principal Parts of Regular Verbs

2-6 Reinforcement B

1. he fixes; he fixed; he has/had fixed; he is fixing
2. I step; I stepped; I have/had stepped; I am stepping
3. you explain; you explained; you have/had explained; you are explaining
4. we deny; we denied; we have/had denied; we are denying
5. she combines; she combined; she has/had combined; she is combining
6. they hurry; they hurried; they have/had hurried; they are hurrying
7. For centuries the house cat has lived with humans. past participle
8. An Egyptian tomb painting showed a house cat. past
9. The great cats roam wild on the African plains. present
10. The lions and tigers are hunting their prey. present participle
11. The cat has hunted alone since prehistoric times. past participle

12. People sometimes capture small wild cats for pets. present
13. Some governments have stopped this practice. past participle

2-6 Language Coach: Grammar, Vocabulary, and Spelling

2-6 Reinforcement C

1. rise
2. did
3. gone
4. saw
5. did
6. did
7. went
8. brought
9. drunk
10. chosen

2-6 Language Coach: Subject/Verb Agreement

2-6 Reinforcement D

1. dog, barks, dogs, bark
2. teacher, listens, teachers, listen
3. student, writes, students, write
4. basketball player, jumps, basketball players, jump
5. girl, steps, girls, step
6. child, plays, children, play
7. librarian, whispers, librarians, whisper
8. tree, grows, trees, grow
9. glide
10. collapses
11. run
12. work
13. plants
14. sow
15. lives
16. want
17. play
18. was

2-6 Language Coach: Grammar, Vocabulary, and Spelling

2-6 Extension

1. laid
2. lay
3. lay
4. lain
5. laid

2-7 Writer's Workshop: Narration—Short Story

2-7 Reinforcement

1. The Sampson family.
2. They can't leave their house because of the storm and their power went out.
3. *Answers will vary.*

2-7 Extension

Answers will vary.

Unit 2 Mid-Unit Benchmark Test

MULTIPLE CHOICE

1. A	9. A	17. A	25. D
2. H	10. G	18. F	26. F
3. D	11. C	19. A	27. C
4. F	12. H	20. H	28. J
5. B	13. A	21. C	29. B
6. G	14. G	22. G	
7. C	15. D	23. B	
8. G	16. H	24. G	

SHORT ANSWER

30. Hope is nervous.
31. Noah is a very good swimmer.
32. Possible responses: "I remember," "There was a time," "I recall"
33. The team finally may win a game.

ESSAY

34. Students should have the detective make logical inferences to solve the mystery. Students should make sure that the detective uses clues along with background knowledge to solve the mystery.
35. Students should describe a surprise event and the clues that foreshadowed this event. A student's parents may have kept secret a visit from a beloved relative. Clues might include the fact that the student had to clean his or her bedroom and that the parents made a special dinner.
36. Students should give a vivid description of the flashback and should relay what the flashback reveals about the character that it focuses on.

Unit 2 Diagnostic Test 2

MULTIPLE CHOICE

1. A	4. H	7. B	10. J
2. G	5. B	8. H	11. C
3. B	6. J	9. A	

2-9 Reading Skills: Compare and Contrast

2-9 Reinforcement

1. A. the Olympic athletes
   B. comparison
   C. They "both" had patience and had trained; "they" are grouped together as the subject of the passage.
2. A. San Francisco and New York City
   B. contrast
   C. "however" indicates a contrast; San Francisco was "enjoying weather" whereas New York City was "in the midst of a frosty chill".

2-9 Extension

1. Possible anno: Foxes are least likely to be a nuisance in a city because they do not attack cats, dogs, or children. Also, they eat pests and rodents instead of garbage.
2. Possible anno: Coyotes are the most dangerous animals because coyote attacks on pets and children are increasing.
3. Possible anno: Bears and geese both pollute cities. Bears go through dumpsters, leaving garbage in the streets and geese pollute parks and water with their droppings.

2-10 Learning About the Novel: Character

2-10 Reinforcement A

1. B
2. *Possible Answers:* Leonard: insensitive; Ginger: sensitive, intelligent, sly; Mr. Cruthers: grumpy, unfriendly
3. Simon and Leonard are flat characters because we do not know anything else about them besides the fact that they are jokesters. Mr Cruthers is also a flat character because we only know he is grumpy and unfriendly.
4. Ginger is a round character because we know she likes playing jokes on people but she does not like to hurt others' feelings. We also know she is clever and has a sense of justice because she is planning to teach Simon and Leonard a lesson.

2-10 Literary Analysis: Characterization

2-10 Reinforcement B

1. jock/athletic; indirect—describes character's appearance
2. shy; indirect—describes character's actions
3. confident; indirect—describes character's thoughts
4. fearful; direct—narrator states character trait
5. smart/intelligent; indirect—another character's dialogue describes him

2-10 Learning About the Novel: Character

2-10 Extension

1. *Answers will vary. Possible answers:*

   Selfish—The narrator doesn't care about Doodle's health or limitations, he only wants someone with whom to race and play. Perhaps they would have stayed inside that day if the narrator didn't want to play outdoors.

   Proud—The narrator wants to take credit for Doodle's success so when Doodle fails, the narrator leaves Doodle by himself in the woods out of anger. If the narrator wasn't proud, he might have helped Doodle immediately after he falls.

   Ashamed/Embarrassed by his brother -- If the narrator didn't attempt to train Doodle to run, swim, and climb, then Doodle might have had enough energy to return home.

   Ignorant – Doodle doesn't feel well all week but the narrator ignores Doodle's poor health. If the narrator paid attention, they might not have done so much activity that week.
2. *Answers will vary.*

2-11 Learning About the Novel: Point of View

2-11 Reinforcement A

1. T-P
2. F-P
3. F-P
4. T-P
5. T-P

2-11 Literary Analysis: Irony

2-11 Reinforcement B

1. D. *Answers will vary.*
2. C. *Answers will vary.*
3. A. *Answers will vary.*

2-11 Learning About the Novel: Point of View

2-11 Extension

1. The story is told from the limited third-person point of view.
2. Possible Answer: Since the narrator believes Hamadi is odd, the narrator purposely pays close attention to his strange actions and behavior. If the story was told from the first-person point of view, Hamadi probably wouldn't comment on his own behavior or actions because he does not think he is different.
3. Possible answer: Although Susan is a member of Hamadi's community, she does not know him well, similar to the reader. Susan and the reader share the same point of view.

2-12 Listening and Speaking Workshop: Conflict and Resolution

2-12 Reinforcement

1. internal and external conflict
2. external conflict
3. internal conflict

Group answers will vary.

2-12 Extension

Answers will vary.

2-13 Language Coach: Verbs—Simple Tenses

2-13 Reinforcement A

1. play, played, will play
2. pretend, pretended, will pretend
3. live, lived, will live
4. hike, hiked, will hike
5. sail, sailed, will sail
6. try, tried, will try
7. plan, planned, will plan
8. learn, learned, will learn

<u>fascinates</u> (P), <u>started</u> (PT), <u>described</u> (PT), <u>created</u> (PT), <u>explained</u> (PT), <u>launched</u> (PT), <u>make</u> (P), <u>will continue</u> (F), <u>will build</u> (F)

2-13 Language Coach: Grammar, Vocabulary, and Spelling

2-13 Reinforcement B

1. present perfect; have heard
2. past perfect; had thought
3. future perfect; will have read
4. past perfect; had been
5. present perfect; have been
6. past perfect; had sunk
7. present perfect; have looked
8. future present; will have searched
9. future present; will have discovered
10. present perfect; has found

2-13 Language Coach: Vowel Sounds in Unstressed Syllables

2-13 Reinforcement C

1. B
2. C
3. D
4. B
5. D
6. B
7. A
8. C
9. C

2-13 Language Coach: Choosing the Right Word

2-13 Reinforcement D

1–13 *Answers will vary.*

2-13 Language Coach: Grammar, Vocabulary, and Spelling

2-13 Extension

1. (*Sentences will vary*)
   Bring: has brought; had brought; will have brought
   See: has seen; had seen; will have seen
   Search: has searched; had searched; will have searched
2. 1. had answered
   2. have talked
   3. will have read
   4. has chosen

2-14 Writer's Workshop: Comparison and Contrast Essay

2-14 Reinforcement

1. block
2. companionship; ability to be trained
3. *Answers will vary. Possible answers:* feeding habits, size/color/breeding
4. *Answers will vary*

2-14 Extension

Answers will vary.

Unit 2 End-of-Unit Benchmark Test

MULTIPLE CHOICE

1. C	9. B	17. D	25. D
2. G	10. H	18. F	26. J
3. A	11. A	19. B	27. C
4. F	12. H	20. H	28. F
5. B	13. A	21. A	29. C
6. G	14. F	22. H	30. F
7. D	15. D	23. B	
8. F	16. H	24. G	

SHORT ANSWER

31. Students should write any sentence that states one or more similarities.
32. Students should write any sentence that states one or more differences.
33. A round, dynamic character is the most complex.
34. the perspective from which a story is told

ESSAY

35. Students should list details that clearly address the writing prompt. They should include at least two similarities and two differences for each mode of travel. The similarities might include that both modes of travel can be exciting and that both afford interesting perspectives; differences include that travel by car is slower and less convenient than travel by plane and that travel by car affords a better sense of changing country than does travel by plane.
36. Students should describe the character's main traits and indicate his or her situation and actions. They should attempt to explain why the character acts or thinks the way he or she does.
37. Students' stories should include details that set up an ironic ending. An event must occur that contradicts what the reader or a character expects will happen.

Unit 3

Unit 3 Diagnostic Test 1

MULTIPLE CHOICE

1. C	4. F	7. D
2. G	5. A	8. H
3. D	6. G	9. C

3-2 Reading Skills: Identifying Main Ideas and Supporting Details

3-2 Reinforcement

1. The main idea is that a baby penguin was born.
2. The main idea is directly stated. The writer says in the first paragraph that a baby penguin was born.
3. The chick was born at 7:45 a.m., weighed 4 ounces, and was named Zeki.
4. *Possible response:* the origin and meaning of Zeki

3-2 Extension

1. *Possible response:* Grizzly bears are much larger than other bears.
2. *Possible response:* Clarissa is a good friend to the writer.
3. *Possible response:* A tsunami is a very dangerous natural disaster.

3-3 Vocabulary: Synonyms and Antonyms

3-3 Reinforcement

1. Some days my sensible friend Gloria isn't always level-headed.
2. It's hot and humid today, but not as muggy as yesterday.
3. She was accused of prevaricating, but she was not lying.
4. Those two have remained friends, even though they were once bitter enemies.
5. The kitchen was spacious, while the den was cramped.
6. Some of the songs are traditional and others are modern.
7. *Consistent* means "same," so inconsistent means changing.
8. *Correct* means "right," so incorrect means *wrong*.
9. *Connected* means "linked," so unconnected means not joined.
10. *Earned* means "gained by work," so unearned means *not deserved*.

3-3 Extension

1. *Possible response:* The task that the runners faced was effortless and undemanding; however, many found it trying.
2. *Possible response:* At first the news was heartbreaking and gloomy, but after other reports came in, everyone grew cheerful.
3. *Possible response:* The horse proved that he was brawny and muscular despite the frigid conditions.
4. *Possible response:* The inside of the car was grimy and filthy; still after a lot of work, it came out spotless.
5. *Possible response:* The landscape in front of them seemed appealing and attractive, although the road ahead would soon be hideous.

3-4 Literary Analysis: Expository Writing

3-4 Reinforcement

1. *Students should circle* factor, effect, because*; The method is* cause and effect.
2. *Possible response:* I am tall because my parents are tall.
3. *Possible response:* First add the eggs, then add the flour.
4. *Possible response:* Unlike my parents, I have red hair.
5. *Possible response:* One solution to the problem is recycling.

3-4 Extension

1. *Students should choose the Flow Chart organizer. Answers may vary, but should be similar to the following:*
   Box 1: The pistons move up and down, moving the piston rods.
   Box 2: Which causes the piston rods to turn the crankshaft.
   Box 3: Which causes the crankshaft to turn the up-and-down motion into a spinning motion.
   Box 4: Which causes the flywheel to spin, carrying the power to the rear wheels that move the car.
   Possible explanation: I chose this chart because the causes and effects are connected. One leads to another, then another, and so on.
2. *Student answers may vary, but should be similar to the following:*
   Problem-and-Solution

   [Problem] → [Event] + [Event] = [Solution]

   Inferences

   [Event] + [Event] = [Inference]

3-5 Literary Analysis: Persuasive Writing

3-5 Reinforcement A

1. He says that a favorite thing to do is throw stuff away.
2. *Possible response:* The sentence appeals to a sense of pride in being American. It advances the writer's position by suggesting that we all feel this pride, but the pride is misplaced because in this case, the American way is a harmful way.
3. negative; *Possible response:* positive: collectible treasures; neutral: things

3-5 Literary Analysis: Propaganda

3-5 Reinforcement B

1. B; answers will vary
2. C; answers will vary
3. C; answers will vary
4. A; answers will vary

3-5 Literary Analysis: Understanding Tone

3-5 Reinforcement C

1. alien and cold, unknown lanes that twisted with malicious intent

   (D) The denotation of alien is foreign, strange; the connotation of cold is unfriendly; the connotation of unknown and twisted lanes is that they are unwelcoming.
2. difficult to escape, The only things Americans do more than watch television are work and sleep.

   (B) In both instances, the author uses denotations to establish tone.

3-5 Literary Analysis: Persuasive Writing

3-5 Extension

1. The emotional appeal is to readers' sense of fairness and the belief that everyone should have the same rights.
2. The writer's position is that voting rights are precious and that people should use them.
3. *Possible response:* She wants readers to value their voting rights and recognize how precious they are. Her tone is uplifting. Language like "downright feeling of pride" creates a community with readers and urges them to feel good about valuing voting rights. Broad concepts such as "the course of our lives" and "country's history" elevate the writing to a grand scale and make readers feel involved in something important.
4. *Possible response:* While some people in the United States may take it for granted that women in this country have the right to vote, it is important to appreciate the significance of this. The right to vote should be a source of pride to all women and considered a license to have a voice and make a difference in the community in which they live. Women across the country should take full advantage of their right to vote to truly make a difference in their country and in the world.

5. *Possible Response:* The emotional appeal is to the readers' belief that women should fully utilize the rights that they have been given. The tone is stirring. A sense that women can hold a place of power in the world by voting is conveyed through language like "truly make a difference in their country and in the world."

3-6 Listening and Speaking Workshop: Delivering a Persuasive Speech

3-6 Reinforcement

1–5 *Possible topics will vary based on students' interests. Topic chosen should show that students gave thought to the questions at the right of table.*
Answers will vary opinions and facts should support the topic chosen.

6. *Answers will vary according to topic. Tone can be satirical, serious, and so on.*
7. *Answers will vary according to topic. Students can use Venn diagrams, webs, charts, pictures or illustrations, and so on.*

3-6 Extension

Topic

- Choose a topic or do both.

Should people on skateboards, roller-blades, or bicycles use the sidewalks on school grounds?

Position

- What opinion will you be presenting?
- Will you present more than one position?

I will argue that people riding on wheels do not belong where people are walking.

I will also argue that the school should set aside an area for people on wheels to use.

Possible Audience

- Who will hear your speech?
- Who is likely to agree or disagree?

Many students and faculty will want to hear my speech because riders of all kinds have bothered many of them. They will agree with me because they have been hurt or frightened.

Key Points

- Cite at least three reasons for your opinion.

1. Wheel riders are dangerous to themselves and to everyone.
2. The sidewalks have other purposes than providing tracks for wheel riders.
3. A safe and secure park for wheel riders will provide plenty of fun and challenges.

Information and Facts

- Supporting evidence
- Facts, quotes, anecdotes

1. Statistics show the number of injuries from wheel riders is up.
2. I took a survey and 80% of those questioned agreed with my position.
3. My friend, Sadie, ended up in the hospital after a skateboarder knocked her down near the gym.

Possible Visual Elements

- Pictures, illustrations, charts, or artwork

1. Chart showing the increase in injuries.
2. A map of campus showing problem areas.
3. Photos of wheel riders on sidewalks.
4. A poster calling for a rally.

Possible Form of Organization

- Opening, supporting statements, and summary

1. Open with statistics of the danger.
2. Show photos and read anecdotes.
3. Summarize with possible solutions.

3-7 Language Coach: Adjectives, Articles, and Adverbs

3-7 Reinforcement A

Possible responses:

1. The young (girl) dropped her ice cream cone.
2. There are five (jars) on the shelf.
3. Did you speak to the newspaper (reporter)?
4. I watched a tiny (fly) get eaten by a spotted (bullfrog).

Possible responses:

5. Today I am going to the fair with my friends.
6. The plate went crashing to the floor.
7. The long column of soldiers marched rapidly through the pass.
8. Jed's experiment went horribly wrong.
Possible paragraph: A [large] tree came down in the recent storm. The tree [completely] crushed a power line. The houses on Henry's block were left without electricity. Henry quickly called the [power] company. The repair crews were [extremely] busy. It took them a [long] time to come and fix the power lines. The power was [safely] restored.

3-7 Language Coach: Comparative and Superlative Forms

3-7 Reinforcement B

1. taller, C
2. latest, S
3. worse, C

4. better, C
5. most, S
6. harder, C
7. fastest, S
8. happiest, S
9. worst, S
10. best, S
11. less, C
12. more, C

3-7 Language Coach: Modifiers

3-7 Reinforcement C

1. Taz and Linus sang loudly along to Travis's guitar.
2. Taz smelled the chicken sizzling on the grill
3. He threw that ball barely thirty feet.
4. A dog that sang like an angel appeared in my dreams.
5. I was told by my professor that I won the scholarship.
6. To raise a good dog, one must have patience.
7. After eating dinner, the family left the kitchen.

3-7 Language Coach: Prepositions and Prepositional Phrases

3-7 Reinforcement D

1. From the meeting we strolled into the restaurant.
2. We listened intently throughout the manager's presentation.
3. A group of students demonstrated in front of the building.
4. The sound of falling rain can be very soothing.
5. At dawn we attempted to cross the river.
6. The investigators from the police station found evidence under the bridge.

Students' sentences will vary.

3-7 Language Coach: Modifiers

3-7 Extension

Adjectives: real, primary, arched, small, early, slight, distinct, salty, irritating, useful, clear; All examples of *a*, *an*, and *the* should be underlined. Prepositions and Prepositional Phrases: out of the eyes; of our eyebrows; of the hair growth; to the sides; of the face; in the fight; for survival; for shelter; from the eyes.

1. *Possible response:* Someone desperately looking for shelter or trying hard to outrun a predator.....
2. *Possible response:* In addition, our brows catch snow, dust, and even smaller debris.
3. *Possible response:* Today, humans don't depend on eyebrows for survival, but our brows still perform their most useful function of helping to keep our vision clear.
4. *Possible response:* In my first sentence, desperately showed how the person looking for shelter felt and hard showed the difficulty of outrunning a predator. In my second sentence, smaller showed the variety of debris eyebrows can catch. In my third sentence, most useful showed my belief about the importance of eyebrows keeping our vision clear.

3-8 Writer's Workshop: Exposition: Cause-and-Effect Essay

3-8 Reinforcement

1. many causes/single effect; *Web should show three cause cells:* Jorge's results, editorial argues for later start time, parents push for less homework*; and one effect cell*: committee will look into increasing sleep for teens
2. single cause/many effects; *Web should show one cause cell*: lead actress was ill; *and three effect cells*: Ilana took over the role, programs changed to reflect new cast, band changed music to fit Ilana's voice.
3. chain of causes and effects; *boxes should show, in order*: dropped eggs, went to store, left purse, went to store again for purse, locked the door with key inside, couldn't get in, father came home, let Erin in
4. same week, also, as a result of these many factors
5. because, several changes resulted
6. series of accidents, first, as a result, this meant that, when she returned, Finally

3-8 Extension

1. *Answers will vary. Possible response:* The essay is about the affects of sound on sleep. The author first addresses the amount of people with sleep deprivation, then moves on to problems people have due to lack of sleep, and provides information on the types of sound available to help people with sleep deprivation.
2. *Answers will vary. Students' paragraphs should address a subhead from section B and have supporting evidence similar to what is mentioned in the outline.*
3. *Outlines will vary, but should follow the model provided. Students should create outlines that reflect the information in their research.*
4. *Students should be able to identify problem areas in a partner's outline and reword or research additionally to correct problem areas in their own outlines.*

Unit 3 Mid-Unit Benchmark Test

MULTIPLE CHOICE

1. D	8. F	15. A	22. G
2. G	9. B	16. H	23. C
3. C	10. G	17. A	24. J
4. H	11. B	18. F	25. A
5. A	12. H	19. C	26. J
6. G	13. D	20. J	27. D
7. A	14. H	21. B	28. G

SHORT ANSWER

29. Ask yourself what the author is trying to tell you about the topic.
30. The main idea usually appears in the introduction.
31. Students should choose *chronological*, and give specific reasons for the choice.
32. Your children appreciate every time you buckle up.

ESSAY

33. Students' essays should contain a clear step-by-step explanation of the process.
34. Students' evaluations should include a description of the commercial, the persuasive techniques used, and an evaluation of the commercial's effectiveness.
35. Students' K-W-L charts should reflect what they know, what they want to know, and what they learned. Students' essays should reflect the benefits of a healthful diet.

Unit 3 Diagnostic Test 2

MULTIPLE CHOICE

1. C	4. G	7. B	10. F
2. F	5. A	8. J	
3. D	6. H	9. B	

3-10 Reading Skills: Differentiating Between Fact and Opinion

3-10 Reinforcement

But, what is the real reason for eyebrows? Most scientists believe the primary purpose is to keep moisture out of the eyes. The arched shape of our eyebrows and the direction of the hair growth help to divert rain and sweat to the sides of the face. In addition, our brows catch snow, dust, and other small debris. This may have given early humans a slight edge in the fight for survival. Someone looking for shelter or trying to outrun a predator would have had a distinct advantage if salty, irritating sweat were diverted from the eyes.

1. You could prove (or disprove) the statement by pouring water on someone's forehead to see where the water goes.
2. The shape of our eyebrows and the direction of hair growth help to divert rain and sweat from our eyes, and our brows catch snow, dust, and other small debris.
3. "Most scientists believe the primary purpose is to keep moisture out of the eyes." The word "believe" shows that this is an opinion rather than a fact.
4. Yes. The opinions given are surrounded by facts that can be proven.

3-10 Extension

1. *Possible response:* Exercising can be a lot of fun; Exercise is a good way to pass time; Exercise makes you feel better.
2. *Possible response:* Riding a bike or going for a walk can be a fun way to exercise on a regular basis. In addition to being fun, exercising rather than watching television or playing video games can be a good way to pass the time. Exercising on a regular basis is also good because it can make you feel better.
3. *Possible response:* Exercise lowers the risk of heart disease; Exercise increases energy levels; Exercising increases optimism and enthusiasm.
4. *Possible response:* The benefits of exercising on a regular basis are numerous. In addition to lowering the risk of heart disease, regular exercise can help a person feel better all around by increasing optimism and enthusiasm, as well as raising energy levels. Because many activities, such as riding a bike, running, or swimming are considered exercise, exercise can also be a fun and healthy way to pass the time!
5. *Possible response:* My second paragraph was more convincing. Rather than simply stating my opinion that exercising can be fun, my second paragraph supported this opinion with several facts, making my opinion more valid.

3-11 Literary Analysis: Biography and Autobiography

3-11 Reinforcement A

1. A
2. B
3. NA
4. A and B
5. B
6. A and B
7. Autobiographical because the author talks about experience sledding using the words "I" and "our."
8. Biographical because the author is describing his or her opinion of someone else using the words "Mr. Barns," "he," and "his."
9. *Check students' passages.*

3-11 Literary Analysis: Author's Perspective

3-11 Reinforcement B

1. Possible answer: As a young adult who was responsible for contributing to family finances.
2. Possible answer: As a young adult with spending money and free time who has interests and hobbies unique to being a teenager.

3-11 Maya Angelou's Autobiography

3-11 Extension

1. The key event is Maya's decision to get a job as a conductorette on the San Francisco streetcars.
2. Because Maya's mother supported her decision to go for the job, and because she provided food and cash, she made it possible for Maya to go after the job unreservedly.
3. *Sample response:* What does this selection tell you about the treatment of African Americans in San Francisco during the 1940s? Give examples from the selection.; They did not receive fair treatment. First, Maya learned that African Americans couldn't get jobs on the streetcar. The receptionist lied to her to get her to go away. The conductor on the trolley didn't treat her with respect. Once Maya was hired, she was given bad shifts.
4. *Possible response:* If you had been in Maya's place, how would you have handled the initial interview with the receptionist? How would that have affected your future actions?; *Answers will vary. Students may say that they would also have fought for the job, or they may say that they would have tried to get a different job that was easier to come by. They might further report that the initial interview would have demoralized them, or it might have spurred them on as it did Maya.*
5. *Possible response:* Compare the life of the fifteen-year-old Maya and yours; Maya had a lot more independence and responsibility than I do.
6. *Possible response:* What lesson do you draw from this selection?; If you have faith in yourself and a willingness to persevere, you can accomplish the goals you set.

3-12 Comparing Literary Works: Author's Style

3-12 Reinforcement

1. They both aim at making Smithfield seem like a great place to visit, and reference the Ava Gardner museum.
2. the second piece
3. the first selection
4. Yes. *Possible response:* The first piece is more informal, like what you would tell a friend. The second is more formal, like what you would tell someone if you wanted him or her to visit Smithfield.
5. *Students' preferences and reasons will vary.*

3-12 Extension

Possible response:

tone
- informal; friendly
- formal; straightforward

sentence length
- varied; suits purpose and audience
- varied; suits purpose and audience

vocabulary
- informal; may include figurative language and show emotion
- formal; straightforward; unemotional

purpose
- to inform a friend about a place
- to inform a person who might travel to a place

Create *Students' work will vary based on destination of the trip, and the purpose chosen. Make sure students realize they should create a letter or an advertisement. They can use the paragraphs in the lesson as models, and refer to the information on their charts as they work.*

3-13 Language Coach: Combining Sentences with Conjuntions

3-13 Reinforcement A

1. so
2. when
3. if
4. however
5. after
6. and
7. nor
8. or
9. when
10. since
11. but
12. while
13. unless
14. although
15. until

3-13 Language Coach: Homophones

3-13 Reinforcement B

1. *Answers shown in brackets:*

   My first marathon was a race I'll remember for a long time. To start with, I [wore] new running shoes, which was a big mistake. They gave me a terrible blister on my [heel]. Even though I took it easy, partway through the race, I got a [knot] in my calf. It tensed right up! The [road] was pretty good, though, since it didn't have too many potholes. The fans lining the road were great! The sound of [their] cheers really kept me going. When I was done, my coach gave me a big hug and said, "Now you're a [real] runner!
2. too
3. caught
4. peek
5. ceiling
6. haul
7. taut, stake

3-13 Language Coach: Spelling Homophones

3-13 Extension

1. Meet
2. Bare
3. Flour
4. Hey
5. Pole
6. Fair
7. *Possible response:*

   Our school took a poll decide the function we would have to celebrate the end of the year. A school fair was decided upon. My friends and I decided to meet at my house and go together. I asked my mother for money to cover the fare.

   When we arrived, a clown greeted us and handed us flowers. We said "hey" to some friends and then went to play games. My friend, Amber, won a stuffed bear. After games we ate meat on a stick and watched a mime pretend to climb a pole. He was very talented.

   The petting zoo was fun, but smelly. Donkeys were eating from stacks of hay and goats were lounging in the sun. We were leaving the petting zoo when we spotted a game that looked interesting. Two teams were throwing paper balls filled with flour at each other. White clouds puffed into the air. If you were tagged with a ball, you had to leave the game. Kids were running around, dodging behind little wooden walls.

   After a while, we decided to leave. The cool air was becoming too much for my bare arms and legs. I wanted to go home and curl up in a blanket.

3-14 Writer's Workshop: Persuasion: Persuasive Essay

3-14 Reinforcement

1. *Students should check boxes 1, 2, and 5. Topics selected, arguments, and counterarguments will vary.*
2. *The completed chart should show an understanding of how to organize persuasive ideas.*
3. People cause global warming.
4. "Our cars and fossil fuel plants emit greenhouse gases and cause climate patterns to change... These scientists tell people to stop cutting down trees and to stop air pollution."
5. *Students should underline the following sentence.* Some scientists state that global warming is the result of natural factors.

3-14 Extension

1. *Possible response:* that it is a good idea to hire players of a variety of racial backgrounds
2. *Students should underline any but the first and last sentences.*
   Facts students write will vary. Be sure they explain their choice.
3. *Check students' essays. Students should have supported their opinions with facts about the role model they chose.*

Unit 3 End-of-Unit Benchmark Test

MULTIPLE CHOICE

1. B	8. F	15. C	22. H
2. H	9. D	16. J	23. B
3. C	10. G	17. C	24. H
4. G	11. D	18. G	25. D
5. B	12. H	19. D	
6. J	13. A	20. H	
7. A	14. J	21. A	

SHORT ANSWER

26. The information in the statement can be proved true and supported with research.
27. A fact is something that has actually happened or that can be justified or proved; however, an opinion is a person's bias, or judgment or belief about something or someone. An opinion cannot be proved.
28. the author's experiences, age, gender, social position, and surroundings
29. *Possible response:* The style of a letter to a friend would use informal and perhaps playful language, whereas the newspaper editorial would use formal, informative language.

ESSAY

30. Students' essays should clearly state the event in a well-organized manner and why they admire the person for his or her actions.
31. Students' editorials should include a clear statement of the issue, credible support, and a response to opposing arguments.
32. Students' essays should reflect their perspectives and attitudes toward the world in which they live. They should describe the setting and the culture in which they live, and how they feel about their environment.

Mid-Year Assessment

MULTIPLE CHOICE

1. C	9. C	17. A	25. A
2. G	10. G	18. F	26. G
3. D	11. B	19. A	27. D
4. F	12. G	20. H	28. G
5. A	13. A	21. A	29. C
6. H	14. F	22. J	30. F
7. D	15. D	23. C	
8. G	16. G	24. H	

ESSAY

31. Students should write a letter that describes a solution or suggestion and uses persuasive language.

Unit 4

Unit 4 Diagnostic Test 1

MULTIPLE CHOICE

1. A	4. G	7. C	10. H
2. F	5. C	8. G	11. A
3. B	6. G	9. C	12. J

4-2 Reading Skills: Paraphrasing

4-2 Reinforcement

1. *Possible response:* To provide a shared experience of remembering for visitors at the site of the World Trade Center
2. *Possible response:* Art can help people understand shared experiences in unspoken ways. For example, a memorial was designed to remember those who died when the World Trade Center was attacked. *Reflecting Absence* as it is called, includes a public plaza with two large gaps where the buildings were. On the sides, water falls into the gaps and makes ponds that reflect back at visitors. The memorial remembers the dead and gives visitors a chance to share their experience of remembering.
3. *Possible response:* Art helps people share common experiences.

4-2 Extension

1. If I do not work, the fire will not be kept up.
2. *Possible response:* Unlike the young, the old woman has little time left. She is aware of the reality of things and must respond to them.
3. *Possible response:* I must work before dawn while the young sleep and dream of things of no importance. Then, when they awake, they occupy themselves with these things and are apt to get upset over nothing.

4-3 Vocabulary Building Strategies: Word Origins

4-3 Reinforcement

1. spectacles
2. aquarium
3. maternity
4. spectator
5. monologue
6. speculate
7. aquamarine
8. illogical
9. maternal

4-3 Extension

1. graph, graphing, autograph, monograph, paragraph, graphic, phonograph, polygraph, geography, photography, topography, grapher, graphite
2. paternity, paternal, patriarchy, patricide, patriot, patriotic, patriotism, patrilineal, patrimony, patriarchal, patriarch
3. *sympathy*: sorrow over another's pain; *sympathize*: to feel sorrow about another's pain; *sympathetic*: having the capacity to feel sorrow about another's pain; *empathy*: feeling another's pain as one's own; *empathize*: to feel another's pain as one's own; *empathic*: having the capacity to feel another's pain as one's own; *pathetic*: contemptibly inadequate; *pathetically*: performed with contemptible inadequacy; *sociopath*: a person who has no feeling of moral responsibility toward others; *psychopath*: a person who can commit violent crimes against other people and have no empathy or remorse; *pathology*: the study of the origins of disease; *telepathy*: the ability to read minds or communicate without speech or gestures; *telepath*: one who can read minds or communicate without speech or gestures

4-4 Literary Analysis: Imagery

4-4 Reinforcement

1. Sensory Language:
   light, dropped, green, latticework, branches, shining, drifting, clean, white, sand, sawing, song, high, empty, air, glass, overflowing, water
   Sense Appealed To:
   sight: light, dropped green, latticework, shining
   touch: sand, empty, air, water overflowing
   sound: sawing, song
   Part of Speech:
   noun, verb, adjective, noun, verb
   noun, adjective, noun, noun, adjective
   adjective, noun
2. *Possible response:* Crisp air perfumed by blossoms, welcomed the first day of May.
3. *Possible response:* The wind carried the aroma of seared corn on the cob and smoky hot dogs throughout the park.

4-4 Extension

1. Similes: chrysanthemums staring up like accusers; elms plunging and tossing like horses
   Metaphors: none
2. *Possible response:*
   Sight: flashing with sunlight
   Sound: pointing and shouting
   Touch: feet crackling splinters of glass and dried putty
   Taste: none
   Smell: none
   Taste and smell were left out because the scene is about climbing on a greenhouse and the consequences of that activity. Taste and smell are not as important to this experience as sight, sound, and touch.
3. *Possible response:* The repetition of "everyone" makes the reader pause on that word, showing its importance to the child. The repetition also makes the last line a more realistic exclamation that a child might make.
4. *Possible response:* Using "ing-verbs" implies that everything is happening all at once and shows how overwhelmed the child is.

4-5 Literary Analysis: Symbolism

4-5 Reinforcement

Possible Answers:

Answers will vary. The list that follows identifies words and phrases students may have underlined.

Symbol
- Fences
- The Kitchen Table

Meaning
- Less important; restricted; segregated
- Being included; acceptance

Universal or Specific
- Universal
- Specific

4-5 Extension

1. brazen giant, mighty woman, torch, lamp, golden door
2. the mother of all immigrants and a guide to freedom and safety
3. Answers will vary but may include, hope, a new life, freedom.
4. oppression
5. seven seas and continents
6. gemstones around the world
7. America's history of independence

4-6 Comparing Literary Works: Figurative Language

4-6 Reinforcement

Answers will vary. Possible responses:

Ex. ". . . Life is a broken-winged bird that cannot fly."
- **Type of Figurative Language:** *direct metaphor*
- **Meaning:** *Without dreams you will not live a full life and strive for something higher or better.*

Ex. ". . . Its bridges quake with fear . . ."
- **Explain the Comparison:** *The size of the city to the size of the bridges within the city.*

Ex. ". . . we could almost last forever, poised in midair like storybook sea monsters."
- **Type of Figurative Language:** *simile*
- **Explain the Comparison:** *The author is comparing the basketball players' lay-ups to storybook sea monsters.*

Ex. "Two roads diverged in a yellow wood, and sorry I could not travel both and be one traveler . . ."
- **Meaning:** *That although we may have many choices in life, you can only choose one path.*

4-6 Extension

Student responses will vary, but they should reflect students' understanding of figurative language and should include correct identification of each example by type of language. In addition, you may want to assess students on the creativity of their language and the depth of meaning they are able to suggest.

4-7 Language Coach: Active and Passive Voice

4-7 Reinforcement A

1. Memories of the trip were treasured by Enrique. Passive; Enrique treasured memories of the trip.
2. Andrew told everyone that Hawaii was amazing. Active.
3. Plans were made by the travel group to go next year. Passive; The travel group made plans to go next year.
4. The mailbox was hit by a car. Passive; A car hit the mailbox.
5. Jeremy scored two goals during the championship game. Active.

Answers will vary. Check for proper use of verbs in the active and passive voice.

4-7 Language Coach: Spelling Words with Suffixes

4-7 Reinforcement B

1. driving; A
2. operator; A
3. varying; B
4. debatable; A
5. defiance; B
6. slippery; C
7. controlling; D
8. planned; C
9. committed; D
10. hopped; C
11. encouraging; A
12. beautiful; B

4-7 Extension

1. A special dinner is cooked by Tasha for her family once a week.
2. Her mother bought the wok that she uses.
3. used, making; Many people use woks for making Asian food.
4. One day, Tasha began the cooking late.
5. tardiness, piled; Annoyed with her tardiness, all of the ingredients were quickly piled in her arms by Tasha.
6. Suddenly, she dropped everything.
7. The calamity ruined the vegetables and broke the wok.
8. sitting, cried; Sitting down in the mess on the floor, tears of frustration were cried by Tasha.
9. Tasha ruined the meal.
10. *Possible response:* I think sentence 3 should stay in passive voice because the subject is the wok not the people using it.

4-8 Writers Workshop: Response to Literature

4-8 Reinforcement

1. Both the movie and the book are about Jess and Leslie's fantasy life.
2. Although the movie followed the book closely, the fantasy scenes were not presented well in the movie.
3. *Disappointment, extremely weak, carelessly created, and so on*
4. *Answers will vary. Responses should favor the book over the movie version of "Bridge to Terabithia."*

4-8 Extension

1. *Students' preferences will vary. Be sure they explain why they prefer the style they chose.*
2. *Possible responses:* **Praise**—brilliant, hilarious, entertaining, accurate, intelligent, sad; **Disapproval**—confusing, dull, predictable, biased, pointless, misguided
3. *Critical reviews will vary. Be sure students address, and show an understanding of, the topic.*

Unit 4 Mid-Unit Benchmark Test

MULTIPLE CHOICE

1. B	10. F	19. C	28. F
2. J	11. B	20. J	29. B
3. C	12. G	21. C	30. G
4. G	13. C	22. H	31. A
5. A	14. F	23. B	32. J
6. J	15. B	24. J	33. A
7. A	16. J	25. A	34. H
8. H	17. A	26. H	
9. A	18. H	27. D	

SHORT ANSWER

35. Responses will vary. *Possible response:* Darien's mother grows impatient when he talks a lot.
36. Reread the text to clarify the writer's meaning. Then, identify the most basic information. Finally, restate the details more simply. Use synonyms for the writer's words.
37. Hyperbole is the exaggeration of speech for emphasis or effect.
38. The writer uses an implied metaphor to compare Jerod to a lawn mower.

ESSAY

39. Students' notes should include items that appeal to the senses. For three of the items on the lists, students should show examples of comparisons that use figurative language, demonstrating an understanding of and distinctions among similes, metaphor, and personification.

40. Students should identify one example of specific word choice and imagery from one of the poems in this test. They should clearly state whether they think the poet uses these effectively in the poem and should give supporting reasons for their opinions.
41. Students should write a paragraph describing an object or animal and explaining what this object symbolizes for the nation or state.

Unit 4 Diagnostic Test 2

MULTIPLE CHOICE

1. C	4. F	7. D	10. J
2. H	5. B	8. H	11. C
3. D	6. F	9. C	12. G

4-10 Reading Skills: Using Context to Determine Meaning

4-10 Reinforcement

1. a. towers
   b. "tall towers"
   c. synonym
2. a. old-fashioned women's undergarments
   b. "another era" and "under their clothing"
   c. explanation
3. a. the edge of a castle wall
   b. "peering over" and "edge of the wall"
   c. explanation

4-10 Extension

Possible responses:

Meaning

- Strong wind
- Endless
- Silent

Context Clue; Type of Context Clue

- Winds; synonym
- This unending life; explanation
- Muted; synonym

Answers will vary.

4-11 Literary Analysis: Sound Devices

4-11 Reinforcement A

1. d
2. b, f
3. c
4. a
5. e, d
6. b, d

4-11 Literary Analysis: Rhythm and Meter

4-11 Reinforcement B

1. Scanning should show that each foot has an unstressed syllable followed by a stressed syllable. The lines have 4, 2, 4, 4, 4, 4, 4, 2, 2 feet.
2. iambic
3. *Possible response:* The rhythm of the poem is comforting and familiar and seems at odd with the poem's message.

4-11 Literary Analysis: Repetition

4-11 Extension

1. *Possible response:* The repeated use of those words makes clear his admiration for the restaurant workers who died on September 11.
2. *Possible response:* The word *after* refers to after the planes hit the buildings. He uses it to describe what happened when the planes hit and just after they hit. The repeated use seems to slow down time and force the reader to imagine the scene.
3. *Possible response:* The first time, the poet praises the lighthouse as something noteworthy in Puerto Rico. By extension, he shows that Puerto Rico is a special place. He likens the lighthouse to a candle lighted in a church for a sacred purpose. The second time, he compares the stoves staying lit to the lighthouse. This ties the lighted stoves to the image of a candle lighted for a sacred purpose. And he further compares them to the cook's soul, making that holy as well.
4. *Possible response:* He mentions the word *soul* repeatedly to emphasize that the people who died, no matter their backgrounds, have a universality of experience; they are joined in death and perhaps there will be enlightenment in that union.

4-12 Listening and Speaking: Reading Poetry Aloud

4-12 Reinforcement

1. *Possible response:* I see a field full of daffodils, blowing in the wind, stretched along the horizon, and near water; stars, shine, twinkle, milky way, stretched, never-ending line, along, bay, ten thousand, sprightly, dance.
2. *Possible response:* inspired, passionate, cheerful

3. *Possible response:* The writer is talking about how to be well mannered and level-headed in a world that is unkind. The meaning could be conveyed through emphasizing words or phrases such as losing, blaming, trust yourself, doubt, make allowance, tired, lied, hated, good, and wise.
4. I would pause when I get to a comma, semicolon, or colon.

4-12 Extension

1. No, last line has nine syllables.
2. 1 and 3, cloud- crowd; 2 and 4, hills-daffodils; 5 and 6, trees-breeze
3. *Possible responses:* a beautiful day by a lake; it is bounded by trees and many daffodils
4. *Student responses will vary, but they should include students' analysis of the poem.*

4-13 Literary Analysis: Forms of Poetry

4-13 Reinforcement A

1. concrete poem
2. *Possible response:* Yes, because the shape of the poem adds to the effect
3. a sailboat
4. The speaker yearns to be sailing.

4-13 Literary Analysis: Speaker

4-13 Reinforcement B, p. 199

1. b
2. d
3. c
4. a
5. The title and first line indicate the subject of the poem is the captain. The lines, "O the bleeding drops of red,/Where on the deck my Captain lies,/Fallen cold and dead," indicate the captain is dead on the deck.

4-13 Literary Analysis: The Speaker in Poems

4-13 Extension

1. *Possible response:* The speaker is someone who is happy to have learned something of value over time. He or she mentions being delighted, uses the words "at first" to talk about his or her early life, and ends with "But now" showing that time has passed and he or she has gained knowledge.
2. *Possible response:* The fruit may stand for the idea that there are a lot more things in the world than you realized as a child. It is a much more interesting, diverse place than you might initially think.
3. *Possible response:* The speaker has lived long enough to uncover some new truths. The speaker seems to have lived a fairly long life, considering the way he or she uses the word "Child" to address the reader.
4. *Possible response:* The speaker is a man who used to be part of a group of young men who play basketball a lot and played it well. They had not reached their full growth, they liked having girls watch them. They were strong and quick. They knew trouble, and they knew loss. They thought well of themselves.
5. *Possible response:* He might not have much interest in what an older person had to say. He may think he and his friends knew everything they needed to know.

4-14 Language Coach: Sentence Structure

4-14 Reinforcement A

1. simple
2. compound
3. simple
4. compound
5. complex
6. *Possible response:* The student teacher liked to write poetry. (simple)
7. *Possible response:* Although he was a poet, Lewis Carroll also wrote novels. (complex)

4-14 Language Coach: Revising to Vary Sentence Patterns

4-14 Reinforcement B

Answers will vary.

4-14 Language Coach: Revising to Vary Sentences

4-14 Extension

1. *Possible response:* To tell the truth, my grandfather is one of my favorite people in the world. Luckily, he never gets tired of listening. Wise, he always gives me good advice. My grandmother and he, immigrants from Germany, live next door to us. On Sunday nights, we go to their house for waffles.
2. *Possible response:* Last week, my eighth-grade class went on a field trip to the art museum. I didn't think I would enjoy it, but I was totally wrong. Foolishly, I thought it would be wall after wall of boring, old paintings. As soon as we walked in, I saw that that wasn't how it was. In the main exhibit hall, there were big, bold canvases full of color. The painter, a young artist, seemed to reach inside me and grab my attention. Excitedly, I poked my head into the next room. I couldn't wait to look inside.

4-15 Writer's Workshop: Exposition: Writing for Assessment

4-15 Reinforcement

Answers will vary. Students' exposition should be well organized and answer all aspects of the prompt chosen.

4-15 Writer's Workshop: Writing for Assessment

4-15 Extension

1. *Students should choose 2 elements and write short notes about how they are used in the poem.*
2. *Any response is correct as long as it shows thought. Possible response:* I will use chronological order to write my ideas in the order they appear in the poem.
3. *Student drafts should discuss the use of their chosen elements in the poem. They should show about 15 minutes of work.*
4. *Student drafts should be marked up with well thought-out revisions from beginning to end.*
5. *Any response is correct as long as it shows thought. Possible response:* I had a hard time finishing my draft in only 15 minutes, but it was easy to revise it in less than 8 minutes. Next time I think I will give myself a little longer to write and not quite as long to revise.

Unit 4 End-of-Unit Benchmark Test

MULTIPLE CHOICE

1. A	9. B	17. B	25. A
2. J	10. H	18. J	26. G
3. B	11. B	19. C	27. C
4. F	12. J	20. F	28. H
5. D	13. A	21. C	29. D
6. J	14. G	22. G	30. F
7. C	15. A	23. D	31. C
8. F	16. H	24. J	32. H

SHORT ANSWER

33. The idiom is *bookworm.* The context "too busy reading" helps readers understand that *bookworm* means someone who likes to read very much.
34. Students should describe two of the three following types of context clues: A synonym is a word that means the same as an unfamiliar word. An antonym is a word that means the opposite of the unfamiliar word. An explanation is words that give information about the unfamiliar word.
35. The speaker is not the poet but the person, animal, or other entity that tells the poem's story or expresses thoughts and feelings in a poem.
36. An iamb is a form of poetic meter containing one unstressed and one stressed syllable.

ESSAY

37. Students' first lines should clearly show whether the poem is to be a lyric or narrative poem. The first line for a lyric poem should create an impression of the river by describing at least two details about it; the first line for a narrative poem should describe the setting and a main character.
38. Students' ideas should clearly give supporting reasons why the song is important and should cite one or more examples of the use of sound devices in the song.
39. Students should list three ways that poetry helps us connect with others, such as by expressing feelings that we might share about the power of nature, about the difficulties of growing up, or about the satisfaction of doing a job well.

Unit 5

Unit 5 Diagnostic Test 1

MULTIPLE CHOICE

1. A	4. G	7. C	10. G
2. F	5. D	8. F	
3. B	6. J	9. A	

5-2 Reading Skills: Cause and Effect

5-2 Reinforcement

1. No C-E; no sentence needed.
2. C-E; Heavy rain continued for many hours, so there was water on the basement floor.
3. No C-E; no sentence needed.
4. C-E; The ground became so soggy that a newly-planted tree fell over in our yard.
5. No C-E; no sentence needed.
6. C-E; When the storm ended and the rain stopped, the ground began to dry out and the water began to recede.

5-2 Extension

Possible response shown. Students may choose to pull additional examples of cause-and-effect scenarios from the story and create webs on a separate sheet of paper.

Causes may include:

The boys are good friends.

The boys share a common dream.

The community is very focused on the fight.

Effects may include:

Felix lies awake at night worrying.

The boys decide not to train together until after the fight.

Felix moves to South Bronx until the fight.

5-3 Vocabulary: Using a Dictionary

5-3 Reinforcement

Definitions should be consistent, but sentences will vary.

1. A manufacturer makes finished products from raw materials, usually on a large scale; Manufacturers make furniture from lumber and other materials.
2. To resume is to start again or use again after stopping; I will resume my homework after we eat dinner.
3. To be valiant is to show strength and bravery; Despite the valiant work of the firefighters, some people were injured in the fire.
4. A consequence is an event that happens because of another event before it in time; As a consequence of studying over the weekend, Sam did very well on his science test on Monday.
5. *Possible response:* as a result
6. *Possible response:* proof

5-3 Extension

1. *Possible response:* circumstand; to stand around in a circle; The teacher asked the students to circumstand for the activity.
2. *Possible response:* animorph; to shape like an animal; Josie animorphed the piece of clay for her art project.
3. *Possible response:* brevature; a short piece of writing; Paul was asked to submit a brevature for the arts section of the school newspaper.
4. *Possible response:* acriflave; something bitter tasting; The arciflave herbs were not to my liking.
5. *Possible response:* polysible; having many siblings; The polysible girl was always late because she had to fight for the bathroom every morning.
6. *Possible response:* omnimusical; liking all types of music; Because the choral director was omnimusical, he taught the class a variety of songs.
7. *Possible response:* statanthrop; a statue of a human; The city streets were covered in statanthrops in honor of its many historical leaders.
8. *Possible response:* chromoliphic; having intense color; The chromoliphic poster Cho made for the election campaign commanded a lot of attention.

Students should discover that the word *summary* in fact has a different root than *assumption*. In *summary*, the root *-sum-* means "highest" rather than "take" or "use."

5-4 Literary Analysis: Dialogue and Stage Directions

5-4 Reinforcement A

1. They describe how Mr. Frank and Mr. Kraler start down the steps, and then how they return to talk to Margot.
2. You learn that he returns in order to reassure Margot, who is upset.
3. Mr. Frank thinks the children will imagine worse news than any Mr. Kraler could share.
4. The mood is anxious and filled with danger and foreboding.

5-4 Literary Analysis: Character Motivation

5-4 Reinforcement B

Answers will vary.

5-4 Extension

Story Clues: They are arguing. Boy Willie wants to sell the piano. Berniece does not.

Life Clues: People argue when they disagree. They don't listen to each other well in such moments. People want to keep things they value and will sell things they don't value.

Inferences: box is blank.

1. Boy Willie wants to sell the piano. Berniece does not. Boy Willie does not value the piano. Berniece does.
2. The characters are arguing and reveal that they disagree over whether to sell the piano and over whether the piano has any real value.
3. The conflict over selling the piano comes from the external motivation that Boy Willie needs money and his internal motivation of wanting to have land. The conflict over the piano's value comes from Berniece's internal motivation of valuing the piano and her external motivation to keep that piano because she values it.

5-5 Language Coach: Participles and Participle Phrases

5-5 Reinforcement A

1. PrP, looking at his watch, Brian
2. PrP, scoring the winning goal, Yolanda
3. PaP, relieved, Jaya
4. PrP, training for a track meet, team
5. PaP, obligated to mow the lawn, Raoul
6. PaP, baked, pie

7. PrP, dodging the kickball, Evan
8. PaP, exhausted, Roberto
9. PaP, finished with their homework, children
10. PaP, excited about their trip, family

5-5 Reinforcement B

1. lead: leading, led, leading
2. enjoy: enjoying, enjoyed, enjoying
3. raise: raising, risen, raising
4. follow: following, followed, following
5. shake: shaking, shaken, shaking
6. plod: plodding, plodded, plodding
7. George plays soccer. It is his best sport.
   Playing soccer is George's best sport.
8. The dog barked. He ran away from his owner.
   The barking dog ran away from his owner.
9. K.C. bakes cakes. She likes to bake for her friends.
   K.C. likes baking cakes for her friends.
10. Hugh's science project was a success. He designed it very carefully.
    Hugh's science project, designed very carefully, was a success.

5-5 Extension

1. *Possible responses:* Hallie's baby brother, napping all afternoon, kept the family home; Napping all afternoon, Hallie's baby brother kept the family home.
2. *Possible responses:* The winter sky, darkened by the storm, closed in on the trapped family; In the storm. the winter sky darkened and closed in, trapping the family.
3. *Possible responses:* Emerging into the sun as the storm broke at last, the family smiled at each other; Smiling at each other, the family emerged into the sun as the storm broke at last.
4. *Possible responses:* The howling cat stopped and was finally calmed; Finally calmed, the howling cat stopped.
5. *Paragraphs will vary but should be created from the various ways to combine the sentences in items 1–4.*
6. *Sentences will vary but should include at least one gerund or participle and one irregular plural.*

5-6 Writer's Workshop: Manual

5-6 Reinforcement

1. **Time Order Words**
   - First
   - Second
   - Next
   - Then
   - After that
   - Finally

   Steps
   - Pour water into a pot.
   - Bring the water to a boil.
   - Place the spaghetti noodles in the water.
   - Boil the noodles for 10 minutes, or until they are tender.
   - Drain the water from the noodles.
   - Put the noodles back into the pot, and add to the sauce.
2. *Students' answers will vary, but should show that they understand where it is appropriate to add specific words to enhance a sentence.*

5-6 Extension

1. *Answers will vary, but students should correctly list adverbs or adverbial phrases that describe the actions in their steps.*
2. *Answers will vary, but diagrams or illustrations should be neatly and clearly rendered, should be accurately labeled, and should convey the written directions they accompany.*

Unit 5 Mid-Unit Benchmark Test

MULTIPLE CHOICE

1. A	9. C	17. A	25. C
2. G	10. F	18. F	26. J
3. C	11. B	19. A	27. B
4. J	12. G	20. H	28. H
5. D	13. C	21. C	29. D
6. F	14. F	22. G	30. H
7. B	15. A	23. A	31. D
8. F	16. J	24. G	32. G

SHORT ANSWER

33. The cause is that Toby studied for two hours. The effect is that he did well on the test. The signal word is *so*.
34. The cause is Chandra's poor eyesight. The result is that Chandra squints when looking at distant objects. The signal words are "as a result."
35. notes that tell how a play should be performed
36. It is the reason a character takes a particular action.

ESSAY

37. Students should arrange the causes and effects in a chain of at least three events. Students' paragraphs should reflect the cause-and-effect chain and should include cause-and-effect signal words.
38. Students' sentences should clearly state the situation on which the scene with dialogue will be based. Opening lines should show a character's name, followed by the character's words.

39. Students' responses should clearly show the characters' names, followed by lines of dialogue in which two or more characters are interacting.

Unit 5 Diagnostic Test 2

MULTIPLE CHOICE

1. D	5. D	9. C	13. B
2. F	6. F	10. J	14. F
3. C	7. C	11. A	15. C
4. H	8. H	12. H	16. H

5-7 Reading Skills: Drawing Conclusions

5-7 Reinforcement

1. C
2. Jean is probably taller.
3. Sarah cannot reach the top shelf for the cake pan; Jean can.
4. C
5. B

5-7 Extension

Text details should show emphasis on African American qualifications and willingness to serve: Some African Americans already knew how to fly; Since 1881, African Americans had studied science and technology there; Hundreds of African American men applied; Many had college degrees from top universities; scores on a qualifying test were so high; scored just as high on a second test.

Previous experiences will be different for students, but overall should reflect ideas that: those who have learned difficult tasks, such as flying, have worked hard and are capable; those who study science and technology are probably well educated; those who attend top universities are well educated; when people score highly on tests, they are usually well prepared.

Conclusions will vary, but should include the idea that the African American pilots were dedicated, willing to learn, and extremely qualified to be pilots.

5-8 Literary Analysis: Suspense

5-8 Reinforcement

1. *Possible response:* The boy is wondering if he can escape.
2. *Possible response:* Because I am reading that the boy wonders if he can escape, I expect that he might try to escape. People often consider whether they can succeed at something before they attempt to do it.
3. *Possible response:* This passage creates suspense because readers wonder if the boy will try to escape, and if he does try to escape, if he will succeed.
4. *Possible response:* The suspense in this passage makes readers worry.

5-8 Extension

1. The boys are close friends who must fight each other for an important honor.
2. Readers want to know who will win the fight and how the fight will affect the boys' friendship.
3. The winner of the fight is revealed, but the author does not share that information with readers. Readers are left to wonder who wins.
4. The boys are clearly still friends and will not let the fight come between them.
5. *Storyboard's will vary, but should clearly exemplify students' understanding of the elements of plot and suspense.*

5-9 Literary Analysis: Staging

5-9 Reinforcement A

1. The set should include a science lab, a hallway that is clean, brightly lit, and contains an elevator, and an area of employee lockers. A river should be visible through any windows that can be included.
2. They should wear white coats.
3. People walking will create the clacking of their shoes on hard floors. Miss Moray's shoes will make a sharper sound due to pointier heels. The elevator doors opening and closing should also be accompanied by a bell to announce the arrival of the elevator at that floor.
4. *Possible response:* The set would be a section of the cafeteria that included two tables and eight chairs along each side. Students would be sitting at the table eating their lunches. Some lunches would be on trays, others would be in brown paper bags and lunch boxes. Everyone would be wearing regular school clothes. There would be a lot of loud talking, including faint talking in the background.

5-9 Literary Analysis: Dramatization

5-9 Reinforcement B

Answers will vary.

5-9 Extension

1. *Possible answers:*

Sets and Props

- Inside a city home with elaborate furnishings, fireplace, piano, windows onto city street with row houses, bouquet of flowers for The Flower Girl to carry.

Costumes

- The Flower Girl wears street clothing. She should look poor. Depending on the time period chosen, she can be in a simple, flowered dress or in blue worker's pants with a shirt and flowered vest. She might have a kerchief in her hair. Professor Higgins should be dressed in teacher's clothing and possibly have a beard.

Sound Effects

- No music in the scene but a piano crash at the point when The Flower Girl runs away in terror.

Lighting

- The room should be evenly lit as a home den would be, with soft lighting. When the Flower Girl runs away to the piano the lighting should focus in on her with a spotlight.

2. *Possible response:*
The Flower Girl could sing a song about her desire to have a shop. The rest of the scene stays about the same, but instead of spotlighting on the girl at the piano, the camera would narrow for a close up.

5-10 Comparing Literary Works: Dramatic Speeches

5-10 Reinforcement

1. The character is speaking to the audience.
2. This is a soliloquy.
3. The character is speaking as if to himself with no mention of any other character. The repetitive use of "I" and "Me" are clues that this is a soliloquy. The words are directed at the audience.
4. The character is speaking to someone named Chen.
5. This is a monologue.
6. Chen's name within the speech helps me identify it as a monologue. Also the character's words are directed at Chen with such comments as "I know, Chen. You like being alone." and "Second grade, Chen! Can you imagine?"

5-10 Extension

1. He is pausing.
2. Questions include "how's Mr. Frank?" and "Wasn't there a door there that used to go up to the loft?" Mr. Kraler might speak these questions in another voice to show that they are the words of the worker.]
3. *Answers will vary. Possible answers:* Listening very intently, looking horrified, leaning forward to encourage Mr. Kraler, and so on.
4. *Performances will vary, but students should recognize the importance of interaction during a monologue. The speaker isn't just talking, he's talking to someone.*

5-11 Listening and Speaking: Reading Drama Aloud

5-11 Reinforcement

1. S
2. S
3. L
4. S
5. S
6. S
7. L
8. S

5-11 Extension

1. *Answers will vary. Students' webs should reflect a convincing picture of their chosen character.*
2. *Answers will vary. Students' charts should reflect perceptive and accurate listings of other character's behavior and logical inferences about the students' characters' behavior as a result.*

5-12 Language Coach: Independent and Subordinate Clauses

5-12 Reinforcement A

1. When a garden snake slithered across the sidewalk,
2. as she did not see it slink away.
3. The Havasupai tribe lives at the base of Havasu Canyon, which is part of the Grand Canyon.
4. Since it is difficult to reach the village, supplies are brought in by horse or mule train.
5. Because it has towering cliffs and spectacular waterfalls, it is called the "Shangri-la of the Grand Canyon."

5-12 Language Coach: Sentence Combining with Subordinate Clauses

5-12 Reinforcement B

1. Marta had gym class on the baseball field where she hit a home run.
2. Chanté visited her grandmother who lives in Chicago.
3. Sean doesn't like to ride the bus because/since he gets motion sick.
4. We watched the movie, which was a documentary about penguins.
5. After Anisa ate dinner, she finished her social studies project.
6. Naeem played a video game that his mom gave to him.

5-12 Extension

1. who
2. that
3. who or that
4. which
5. that
6. which
7. that

5-13 Writer's Workshop: Business Letter

5-13 Reinforcement

1. To share an opinion on school uniforms.
2. *Underlined details may vary but should include spending less money on clothes, getting to school on time and not worrying about fitting in.*

Answers will vary. Check to see that students have written letters correctly. Have students share their letters with classmates.

5-13 Extension

1. *Answers will vary. Students' letters, e-mails, and phone call texts should reflect the formal tone of business letters, should clearly reflect the purpose of getting a job, should follow up on information from the first letter or from meetings, and should offer specifics wherever possible.*
2. *Role-plays will vary but partners should create dialogue that derives from each student's writings. For example, if a thank you letter refers back to discussion of demonstrations, that discussion should appear in the role-play.*

Unit 5 End-of-Unit Benchmark Test

MULTIPLE CHOICE

1. B	7. C	13. A	19. D
2. F	8. F	14. H	20. F
3. C	9. D	15. A	21. D
4. H	10. J	16. F	
5. D	11. A	17. B	
6. F	12. H	18. H	

SHORT ANSWER

22. to arrive at an overall judgment or idea by evaluating several details
23. Responses will vary. *Possible responses:* Listen for statements that show characters' ideas and attitudes; watch characters' interactions; notice actions that show a pattern of behavior
24. the growing tension or uncertainty that the reader or audience feels about the outcome of events
25. a speech or remark that a character makes during a play; monologue, soliloquy, aside

ESSAY

26. Students' stage directions should clearly describe the set and the required props. Opening lines should reveal the character's name, followed by the character's words. The scene must include a long speech by one character that is addressed to another character or characters. The character giving the speech may also address the audience directly.
27. Students' stage directions should clearly describe the set and name the props needed for scene 1. Opening lines should reveal the character's name, followed by the character's words. The scene should clearly foreshadow the future outcome of events in the play.
28. Students' sentences should reflect appropriate language for a business letter and should clearly state three reasons why they want the job.

Unit 6

Unit 6 Diagnostic Test 1

MULTIPLE CHOICE

1. B	4. J	7. A	10. G
2. H	5. A	8. G	
3. A	6. H	9. A	

6-2 Reading Skills: Setting a Purpose for Reading

6-2 Reinforcement

1. *Possible response:* The article does a good job explaining the characteristics of a detective story. Many of the characteristics are listed at the very beginning. Then the pattern is given, the relationship with the reader is explained, and type of detective is discussed.
2. Both critiqued how well the article was written. No matter what type of information you are looking for, you need the article to be well-written.
3. *Possible response:* This informational text gives a broad overview of the topic, providing facts and details. Readers can focus on any of the details in it. They can focus on the history of detective stories, or the first detective story ever written, or the most famous detective stories.

6-2 Extension

1. *Possible response:* The title suggests the text will provide general information about the farm.
2. safety information, barn procedures, visiting information, hours of operation
3. *Possible response:* words in bold, images (helmet, horse with halter on, a carrot with an X through it)

6-3 Vocabulary: Words form Mythology and Borrowed Words

6-3 Reinforcement

1. cereal—a breakfast food
2. hypnotize—to put in a sleep-like state
3. *Possible response:* The igloo is a round house made of snow.
4. *Possible response:* Hula dancers wear grass skirts.
5. *Possible response:* There are several horse events at the rodeo.
6. *Possible response:* People say you will either love opera or you will hate it.

6-3 Vocabulary: Borrowed Words

6-3 Extension

1. f
2. d
3. b
4. c
5. h
6. g
7. a
8. e
9. alligator (from Spanish)
10. flamingo (from Italian)
11. mascara (from Italian)
12. bronze (from Italian)
13. apartment (from French)
14. mitten (from old French)
15. a
16. *Possible response:* tired, slow

6-4 The Research Process: Choosing Your Topic

6-4 Reinforcement

1. a. *Possible Response:* To focus on ways to earn money, you need the word *jobs*, which will yield more specific sites.
2. a. *Possible Response:* This web site will have links to local businesses and organizations that hire teens, but will probably not have opinions on whether or not teens should work, since it is designed to aid teens who have already decided to work.
3. b. *Possible Response:* Book *b.* focuses on remembering the Vietnam War and, since it was written recently, will probably include information about how people today feel about the war. Book *a.* focuses on events during the war, so it probably will not have information on how people today feel about it.

6-4 Extension

1. *Possible response:* Early America; World War II; Ottoman Empire
2. *Possible response:* Early America; I could research Early America online or find books about it in the library and search their tables of content and indices.
3. *Topics and research will vary, but students' should explain that while doing their research they discovered a major focus on a specific aspect of their topic. Students may also say that their research lead to the curiosity of a certain aspect.*
4. *Questions will vary but should be specific and crucial enough that they could stand alone as introductory and topic sentences.*
5. *Proposals should encompass all of the important points students plan to make in their history project. They should also include how they plan to present their topic (props, posters, video, and so on).*

6-5 The Research Process: Finding Reliable Sources

6-5 Reinforcement A

1. *Notes will vary but should follow the specified format of index cards and the Cornell Method.*
2. *Possible Response:* Yes; It gives a first hand account of one group's struggle.

3. *Possible Response:* The source is not current. Because it is a historical document, it is helpful in that it dates back to the event.
4. *Possible Response:* The speech is very reliable in recounting the actual experiences of Chief Joseph and the Nez Percé. The researcher should also look for sources explaining the historical background and for accounts from the U.S. forces.

6-5 Extension

Possible response:

CARD:

Author: Jeffrey Zaslow

Title: Kids on the Bus: The Overlooked Role of Teenagers in the Civil-Rights Era

Publisher: The Wall Street Journal Classroom Edition

Date/Place of Publication: January 2006; place not relevant for a web site

Web Address: http://wsjclassroomedition.com/archive/06jan/deja_civilrights.htm

Site Sponsor: The Wall Street Journal [WOL]

Page Name: Current Issue January 2006: Deja Vu

Date of Last Revision/Copyright Date: 2007

Date of My Visit: May 8, 2007

1. *Possible response:* Yes, the Wall Street Journal is a reputable news organization. Even though the site is a .com, it is reasonable to rely on a reputable news organization for accurate reporting.
2. *Possible response:* You could look her up in an encyclopedia.
3. *Possible response:* Yes. The source is about two years old, but the content is about events of more than fifty years ago, so the facts have not changed in the last two years.
4. *Possible response:* There is no evidence to suggest that he is biased but to be sure the writer should look him up further.

6-6 Comparing Sources: Primary and Secondary Sources

6-6 Reinforcement

1. *Possible Response:* "Water Man Comics" is a primary source. It is written by Pilkey about his own experiences. "Always to Remember" is a secondary source. It is written by Brent Ashabrenner about an event in American history.
2. *Possible Response:* Ashanti could use a book about comics as a secondary source about Water Man. She could use one of the submissions for the design of the Vietnam memorial as a primary source about it.
3. *Answers will vary but should contain a quotation accurately transcribed from the Ashabrenner article.*

6-6 Extension

1. primary
2. It provides background information about Stephen King and includes facts researched by the interviewer.
3. Primary; It gives her opinion.
4. *Answers will vary. Secondary source examples could include Stahl's voiceovers in which she list King's writings and writing habits, identifies where he lives, and describes elements from his films. Primary source examples could include any of King's remarks and comments by Stahl that suggest her personal observations or opinions, such as that "a vicious canine beast" lives with King.*

6-7 Analyzing an Informational Text: Interview Transcript

6-7 Reinforcement

1. *Possible Response:* The ellipses mean that Jamie interrupted Meg before she finished her sentence.
2. *Possible Response:* Yes, Meg talks directly to the audience when she tells how Jamie taught all of the kids on their street to do some circus tricks.
3. *Possible Response:* Jamie is a multi-tasker who likes to play with lots of things at once and expects to enjoy working for the circus. Jamie has taught the kids on the street circus tricks and will be auditioning to join the circus tomorrow. Jamie is nervous only when not practicing, but when practicing, Jamie gets into her/his routine so well that she/he is no longer nervous.

6-7 Extension

1. *Possible response*: King earns more than $30million in a year (shows he is highly successful); King writes at least four hours every day (shows his dedication to his career and craft); questions King on sleeping with a night-light (provides a personal, little-known fact and opens discussion for King's life beyond the books and movies)
2. *Check students' outlines.*

6-8 Language Coach: Run-on Sentences and Sentence Fragments

6-8 Reinforcement A

1. fragment; *Possible response:* When Tanya finally got home, it was very late at night.
2. fragment; *Possible response:* The traffic was bad when she left.

3. run-on; *Possible response:* The flight was badly delayed in Philadelphia because there was bad weather.
4. fragment; *Possible response:* Because she had extra time in Philadelphia, Tanya finished both books.
5. run-on; *Possible response:* The buses had stopped running, so she took a cab.
6. run-on; *Possible response:* Her trip was successful, but she was exhausted.

7–10 *Sentences will vary but students should provide 2 examples of each run-ons and fragments.*

11–14 *Check students' revisions.*

6-8 Language Coach: Revising to Use Quotation Marks and Block Quotes

6-8 Reinforcement B

1. "Hi, Mrs. Tobin," Jamil said.
2. "Good afternoon, Jamil. Have you seen your mother," she asked.
3. "Yeah. She's at Mrs. Papetti's house," he replied.
4. Mrs. Tobin asked, "If you see her, can you please ask her to call me?"
5. Jamil told her, "Sure, no problem."

6-8 Language Coach: Revising Run-on Sentences and Sentence Fragments

6-8 Extension

1. *Sample revision:*
   When the meeting began, Abby believed the problem could be solved. She proposed a new way to organize the recycling program at school. She suggested electing recycling officers for each grade. These officers would come up with at least two ways to get classmates involved in recycling. Abby and the other leaders of the program would then explain all the options to the whole school community. She thought her idea was a good one, but the others voted against it. They wanted to keep the program the way it is.
2. *Sample revision:*
   According to the local Chamber of Commerce, there are very few jobs available this year for teens. "Teens will have to look long and hard this year to find good jobs," predicted Bob Philbrick, head of the chamber. He urged teens to "start looking early" and to be creative. "Young people may want to identify a need in the community and find a way to fill that need," he suggested. Bob gave the example of a young man who noticed that several of his neighbors' homes were empty. He wrote to the owners and offered to water lawns and keep an eye on the houses. "Before long, I had a booming house-sitting business," reported the young man.

6-9 Writers Workshop: Research: Interview Report

6-9 Reinforcement

1. *Questions will vary.*
2. *Questions will vary.*
3. *Interview reports will vary, but should have a logical organization and be free of errors.*
   Possible Response:
   Singer/songwriter Sam Singer was born near Boston about thirty years ago. He credits his mother as his first musical influence. Because our time was limited, I focused on what he's doing these days.
   Which do you like best: writing songs, touring, or performing?
   Performing is really fun, and I like meeting people on tour, but nothing is as satisfying as song-writing at those times when song seems to write itself.
   What are you working on now?
   I'm writing some songs about people I met when I went to New Orleans to help out after the hurricane.
   That was all the time we had, as Sam had to get ready for a performance. It was a thrill to meet someone I've admired for so long.

6-9 Extension

1. *Characters and accomplishments will vary.*
2. *Responses will vary. Background should include some background information on the character as well as research on the character's accomplishment (For example: Accomplishment for Cinderella may have been going to the ball, so students should give some background about attending a ball).*
3. *Questions will vary but should be creative and thought-provoking.*
4. *Students should present a creative interview and do their best to act it out, not just read their questions and answers.*

Unit 6 Mid-Unit Benchmark Test

MULTIPLE CHOICE

1. A	9. B	17. B	25. C
2. H	10. H	18. G	26. G
3. A	11. D	19. A	27. A
4. F	12. G	20. H	28. J
5. C	13. A	21. C	29. C
6. J	14. J	22. J	30. F
7. A	15. C	23. B	21. B
8. J	16. F	24. J	32. J

SHORT ANSWER

33. Skim the text for key words. Then scan the text's organization and features, such as headings, photos, and diagrams.

34. Was my purpose for reading the selection fulfilled?
35. newswatch, net browse, self-interview, and brainstorm (free-write)
36. An interview transcript is a written copy of an interview.

ESSAY

37. Students' topics should be clearly stated. Their questions should relate directly to their topic.
38. Students should write a paragraph explaining why they chose a particular place. Then they should write three questions that would narrow the research topic.
39. Students should provide a list of at least ten questions to ask their historical figure. Students should arrange the questions in a logical order.

Unit 6 Diagnostic Test 2

MULTIPLE CHOICE

1. B	3. C	5. D	7. C
2. J	4. F	6. H	8. F

6-10 Reading Skills: Summarizing

6-10 Reinforcement

1. *Compsognathus* was probably the smallest dinosaur of all time.
2. the first sentence
3. B
4. The dinosaur has been studied by paleontologists; It was a flesh-eating dinosaur that lived during the last part of the Jurassic period.
5. *Check that summaries include only information that is pertinent to the main idea of the passage. Possible response:* Paleontologists believe that *Compsognathus* was the smallest dinosaur. About 2 feet long, it had a maximum weight of only 22 pounds.

6-10 Extension

1. *Possible response:* Bicycles offer a better transportation alternative to the 130 million cars on the road today. Bicycles offer many benefits, such as exercise, relaxation, and kindness to the environment. Problems arise only because cars and bicycles get in each other's way. We should encourage bicycle riding by creating safe ways for cars and bikes to share space.
2. *Letters should cite specific main ideas from the provided letter and either support them or reject them and provide reasons for doing so.*

6-11 The Research Process: Drafting: Thesis Statement

6-11 Reinforcement

1. *Possible response:* It helps to present the topic of the report in a clear and progressively more focused way. It include the student's view of the topic background and answers questions that help narrow the topic.
2. *Possible response:* Readers must know very generally who Alexander is and what he did in order to understand why the discussion of his greatness is meaningful.
3. *Diagrams will vary but should include the components of a topic, at least two questions that focus the topic, the writer's overall view on the topic, identification of any background necessary to state that view, and a 1 or 2 sentence thesis statement.*

6-11 Extension

Answers will vary according to the outline section selected, but should contain the following elements:

- *Roman numeral and section letter*
- *completed sentence outline with one sentence for each entry in the outline paragraph created from the sentence outline*

The sentence outline may combine items within an entry into one sentence. Paragraphs should use transitions and other added words to create a smooth flow.

6-12 The Research Process: Revising Your Research Report

6-12 Reinforcement

1. It belongs as the first sentence.
2. Darius may have been a poor leader, but he was no coward.; Adding *but* shows the contrast between the two statements.
3. It is also believed that Darius called for the assassination of Alexander the Great's father, Philip II, who was trying to free the Greek cities from Achaemendid rule.; Darius was unprepared to defend his empire and was eventually defeated by Alexander the Great.
4. *Possible responses:*
   I would suggest that the student add another sentence at the end so it comes to more of a conclusion or the student could add the word "Eventually" to make it sound more conclusive: "Eventually, Darius headed toward Bactria for safe retreat, but he was dethroned and murdered by the Bactrian satrap Bessus."
   The sentence about Darius not being a coward needs to be backed up with supporting reasons why he's not a coward.

6-12 Extension

1. as shown by his comments after his father had conquered a city
   The transition links the quotation first to the statement that Alexander was very ambitious and also to the paragraph's larger idea that Alexander inherited his military genius and bravery from his father.
2. As the ancient historian Arrian reports
   The transition explains who is speaking in the quote and links the quote first to the statement that Darius was afraid. It also helps the quote support the larger idea that Alexander was a fierce warrior who terrified his opponents.
3. *Answers will vary but should include these elements: a paragraph from the student's report in which a quotation is used; an underlined transition that links the quotation to surrounding text and ideas; and an explanation of the link.*

6-13 The Research Process: Sources and Publishing

6-13 Reinforcement

1. Author's name listed incorrectly; should be Moro, Julio H.
2. The authors' names should go before the title.
3. Should be Philadelphia, PA: Rocket Publishers, 2004.
4. Should be a colon after NY instead of a period.
5. Place the name of the article in quotes, instead of italicizing it.
6. The author is an organization, not a person. It is Jameson Chamber of Commerce.
7. Deane, Jameson, Moro, Roosevelt
8. Start the citation with the title. In this case, the book would still be at the end of the bibliography.

6-13 Extension

1. There is no author's name given.
2. InfoTrac One File
3. Donald Malcarne's article; Malcarne begins with M, which comes before T in Two.
4. *Answers will vary, but citations should be formatted to match one of the styles presented.*

6-14 Listening and Speaking: Evaluating Media Messages

6-14 Reinforcement

1. *Possible responses:*
   Fact: 99% of people surveyed use soap in the shower, but only 20% are happy with their skin.
   Why misleading: The audience doesn't know who did the survey, who participated it it, or what the questions were.
   Fact: no other soap approved by the American Association of Dermatology is proven to give you softer, smoother skin.
   Why misleading: The reader does not know what other soaps are approved by the association. Also, the fact that no other soap is proven to be better does not mean that DermaClean is any better than the rest.
2. *Possible responses:*
   Opinion: "I love new and improved Derma Clean. It makes my skin feel just like an angel's!"
   Supported? The opinion is not supported by any facts or other opinions. It just expresses how one person feels about the soap.
   Opinion: You and your family deserve great skin.
   Supported? The opinion is not supported by anything, except perhaps the reader's own opinion.

6-14 Listening and Speaking: Evaluating Messages

6-14 Extension

1. The author's purpose is to persuade you that school days should not be lengthened.
2. a. None.
   b. Weaker, because it forces the reader to question the credibility of the message.
   c. *Possible response:* Those who favor this plan have not thought through all the consequences.
3. Students might not learn more, and they are already busy.
4. *Possible response:* The message would be stronger if the writer included statistics that show the following: whether or not lengthening the school day leads to more learning; the potential effects on the community and the student; and facts that will counter arguments from the opposing viewpoint.

6-15 Language Coach: Commas, Semicolons, and Colons

6-15 Reinforcement A

1. Carrots, which get soft when cooked, are high in Vitamin A
2. A person holding binoculars told us that the tall, long-legged bird was a heron.
3. I got an A in math last term; you'd never guess it used to be hard for me.
4. To knit a sweater you need these things: yarn, knitting needles, and a pattern.
5. Even though it was raining, we decided to take a walk.

6-15 Language Coach: Capitalization

6-15 Reinforcement B

PS 122 Middle School

American Museum of Natural History

New York City

It

Central Park

Mrs. Beasley

Milstein Hall of Ocean Life

Blue Whale

Leo Johnson

I

Stegosaurus

Mr. Nelson

"Not

6-15 Language Coach: Commas, Semicolons, and Colons

6-15 Extension

1. *Possible response:* Jon, who started painting when he was six, showed his artwork in the city-wide show.
2. *Possible response:* The kinds of books I like to read have the following elements: vivid characters, intricate plots, and streamlined writing.
3. *Possible response:* The speaker, Dr. Ralph Mills, talked for about forty minutes.
4. *Possible response:* After the storm broke and the sun came out, we went swimming.
5. *Possible response:* The fair lasted until sunset; there were fireworks after dark.
6. *Paragraphs will vary. Check that students use incorrect punctuation in their original paragraphs and that the revised paragraphs show correct punctuation.*

6-16 Writers Workshop: Multimedia Report

6-16 Reinforcement

1. It is too broad. Sara can't possibly cover all the animals of Africa in a single report.
2. *Possible response:* Sara could select only one type of animal butterflies, for example.
3. *Possible response:* She could include video of the life cycle of a butterfly and photographs showing various types of butterflies found in Africa. She could obtain and present an entomologist's collection of butterfly specimens.

6-16 Extension

1. *Responses will vary but might include ideas about using video, music, photos, and even hands-on props for a multimedia presentation for a very young audience.*
2. *Responses will vary but should be creative, mentioning a variety of media sources. Students may have the idea to make a video that shows clips from various classes or school activities. Students may also mention taking pictures and using funny captions to appeal to classmates.*
3. *Students should list a topic that is narrow, a clear focus for the main idea, two examples of media, and an explanation of how research will be done. They should also write a brief description of their plans for the multimedia report.*

Unit 6 End-of-Unit Benchmark Test

MULTIPLE CHOICE

1. C	8. G	15. C	22. J
2. F	9. D	16. G	23. D
3. C	10. F	17. C	24. F
4. G	11. C	18. F	25. D
5. B	12. F	19. D	
6. F	13. C	20. J	
7. B	14. H	21. C	

SHORT ANSWER

26. Determine the main idea for each paragraph in the passage; review each idea to determine the main idea of the passage; identify the sequence in which events occur or information is listed; select pertinent information needed to write a strong summary.
27. *Possible responses:* in the film or book section of a newspaper; on the back cover of a book; on the back cover of a DVD case
28. Combine short sentences; replace tired, overused words with precise action verbs and vivid nouns and adjectives; cut unnecessary words.
29. at the end of sentences containing quotations, facts that are not commonly known, or ideas that are not your own

ESSAY

30. Students' summaries should include the main idea of the passage, pertinent details, and the sequence of pertinent details and events. Students should use their own words and sentence structure.
31. Students' summaries should consist of two paragraphs and include the title of the work, the main idea, and any pertinent details about the plot or characters.
32. Students' drafts should include a thesis statement along with a description of their intended audience and how they plan to present their topic to that particular audience. Students should also describe how they will organize their ideas and list the sources they will need to consult in their research.

End-of-Course Assessment

MULTIPLE CHOICE

1. C	10. H	19. A	28. H
2. J	11. C	20. H	29. B
3. D	12. F	21. C	30. J
4. F	13. D	22. G	31. B
5. B	14. G	23. D	32. J
6. G	15. B	24. F	33. C
7. B	16. F	25. D	34. J
8. J	17. C	26. J	35. A
9. A	18. F	27. A	36. G

ESSAY

37. Student should write a business letter to an organization, a business, or a person. Their letters should contain appropriate language for a business letter and should thank this organization, business, or person.

Acknowledgment is made to the following for copyrighted material:

Bancroft Library, University of California, Berkeley
Excerpt from "Tears of Autumn" by Yoshiko Uchida from *The Forbidden Stitch: An Asian American Women's Anthology.* Copyright © 1989 by Yoshiko Uchida.

Curtis Brown, Ltd.
Excerpt from "The Day It Rained Cockroaches" by Paul Zindel from *The Pigman and Me.* Copyright © 1992 by Paul Zindel. First appeared in *The Pigman and Me,* published by HarperCollins.

Dutton Signet, a division of Penguin Group (USA) Inc.
From "The Piano Lesson" by August Wilson from *The Piano Lesson.* Copyright © 1988, 1990 by August Wilson.

HarperCollins Publishers, Inc.
Excerpt from "Let Me Hear You Whisper" by Paul Zindel from *Let Me Hear You Whisper.* Copyright © 1970 by Zindel Productions Incorporated.

Naomi Shihab Nye
"Hamadi" by Naomi Shihab Nye from *America Street.*

Random House, Inc.
Excerpt from "America the Not-so-Beautiful" by Andrew A. Rooney from *Not That You Asked. . . .* Copyright © 1989 by Essay Productions, Inc. Excerpt from "Occupation: Conductorette" by Maya Angelou from *I Know Why The Caged Bird Sings.* Copyright © 1969 by Maya Angelou. Excerpt from *The Diary of Anne Frank* by Frances Goodrich and Albert Hackett. Copyright © 1956 by Albert Hackett, Frances Goodrich Hackett, and Otto Frank. Professionals and amateurs are hereby warned that *The Diary of Anne Frank* by Frances Goodrich and Albert Hackett being fully protected under the copyright Laws of the United States of America, the British Empire, including the Dominion of Canada, and all other countries of the Universal Copyright and Berne Conventions, are subject to royalty. All rights, including professional, amateur, motion picture, recitation, lecturing, public reading, radio and television broadcasting, and the rights of translation into foreign languages, are strictly reserved. Particular emphasis is laid on the question of readings, permission for which must be secured in writing. All inquiries for *The Diary of Anne Frank* should be addressed to Random House, 1745 Broadway, 3rd Floor, New York, N.Y. 10019 and Flora Roberts Inc., 275 Seventh Avenue, New York, N.Y. 10001.

Suhrkamp Verlag
Excerpt from "The Burning of Books" from Selected Poems by Bertolt Brecht, translated by H.R. Hays. Copyright © 1961 Suhrkamp Verlag Frankfurt am Main.

Piri Thomas
Excerpt from "Amigo Brothers" by Piri Thomas from *Stories from El Barrio* by Piri Thomas.

Note: Every effort has been made to locate the copyright owner of material reproduced in this component. Omissions brought to our attention will be corrected in subsequent editions.